THE MORROW
ANTHOLOGY OF
YOUNGER
AMERICAN
POETS

THE MORROW
ANTHOLOGY OF
YOUNGER
AMERICAN
POETS

Edited by
Dave Smith &
David Bottoms

QUILL · NEW YORK

Diane Ackerman: "A Fine, A Private Place," "Space Shuttle," "Spiders," "In the Silks," and "Patrick Ewing Takes a Foul Shot" originally published by William Morrow and Company, Inc.

Ai: "Twenty-Year Marriage" and "29 (A Dream in Two Parts)" from *Cruelty* by Ai. Copyright © 1970, 1973 by Ai. Reprinted by permission of Houghton Mifflin Company. "She Didn't Even Wave," "Almost Grown," and "Guadalajara Hospital" from *Killing Floor* by Ai. Copyright © 1979 by Ai. Reprinted by permission of Houghton Mifflin Company. "Immortality" was originally published in *The Seattle Review.*

Jon Anderson: "Witness," "Rosebud," "American Landscape with Clouds & a Zoo," "Homage to Robert Bresson," "Falling in Love," "The Secret of Poetry," "Refusals," and "The Milky Way" copyright © 1982 by Jon Anderson. From *The Milky Way* by Jon Anderson, published by The Ecco Press in 1983. Reprinted by permission.

David Baker: "Caves" from *Laws of the Land*, Ahsahta Press, 1981. "The Wrecker Driver Foresees Your Death" originally published in *The American Scholar.* "8-Ball at the Twilite" originally appeared in *Memphis State Review.* "Running the River Lines" first published in *The Kenyon Review.*

Peter Balakian: "Jersey Bait Shack" from *New Directions*, #47. "Father Fisheye" and "Homage to Hart Crane" from *Father Fisheye*, published by Sheep Meadow Press. "In the Turkish Ward" from *Sad Days of Light*, published by Sheep Meadow Press.

John Bensko: "Mowing the Lawn" originally appeared in *The Georgia Review.* "Mail Call," "A Veteran of the Great War," and "The Night-Blooming Cactus" from *Green Soldiers*, copyright by John Bensko, published by Yale University Press.

Chana Bloch: "A Life," "Goodbye," "Deer in the Bush," and "The Death of the Bronx" reprinted by permission of Sheep Meadow Press.

Michael Blumenthal: "Mushroom Hunting in Late August: Peterborough, N.H.," "Squid," "Today I Am Envying the Glorious Mexicans," and "In Assisi" from *Days We Would Rather Know* by Michael Blumenthal. Copyright © 1982, 1983, 1984 by Michael Blumenthal. Reprinted by permission of Viking Penguin Inc.

David Bottoms: "In a U-Haul North of Damascus," "Under the Boathouse," "Sign for My Father, Who Stressed the Bunt," "The Copperhead," and "Wrestling Angels" from *In a U-Haul North of Damascus*, copyright © 1983 by David Bottoms. Printed by William Morrow and Company. "The Desk" reprinted by permission of the author.

Sharon Bryan: "Hollandaise," "Big Sheep Knocks You About," and "Corner Lot" from *Salt Air*. Copyright © 1983 by Sharon Bryan. Reprinted by permission of Wesleyan University Press. "Lunch with Girl Scouts" reprinted by permission of the author.

Nicholas Christopher: "John Garfield," "Walt Whitman at the Reburial of Poe," "The Track," and "The Driver in Italy" from *On Tour with Rita*, by Nicholas Christopher. Copyright © 1982 by Nicholas Christopher. Reprinted by permission of Alfred A. Knopf, Inc.

Peter Cooley: "The Other," "Such Comfort as the Night Can Bring to Us," "Frog Hunting," and "To a Wasp Caught in the Storm Sash at the Advent of the Winter Solstice" reprinted by permission of Carnegie-Mellon University Press.

Alfred Corn: "Darkening Hotel Room" and "Fire: The People" from *A Call in the Midst of a Crowd* by Alfred Corn. Copyright © 1975, 1977 by Alfred Corn. Reprinted by permission of Viking Penguin Inc. "Moving: New York–New Haven Line" and "Grass" from *The Various Light* by Alfred Corn. Copyright © 1978, 1979 by Alfred Corn. Reprinted by permission of Viking Penguin Inc. "The Documentary on Brazil" from *All Roads at Once* by Alfred Corn. Copyright © 1974 by Alfred Corn. Reprinted by permission of Viking Penguin Inc.

Gerald Costanzo: "Nobody Lives on Arthur Godfrey Boulevard" and "Introduction of the Shopping Cart" reprinted by permission of Bits Press, Case Western. "Nobody Lives on Arthur Godfrey Boulevard" from *The Georgia Review.* "Introduction of the Shopping Cart" originally appeared in *The Ohio Review.* "Jeane Dixon's America" reprinted by permission of *The North American Review* (September 1981, Vol. 266, No. 3). "The Meeting" from *In the Aviary* by Gerald Costanzo, University of Missouri Press, 1974; first appeared in *Mundus Artium VI (2),* 1973.

W. S. Di Piero: "Second Horn" reprinted by permission of *The Agni Review.* "Four Brothers" reprinted by permission of Elpenor Books. "Fat Tuesday" reprinted by permission of Porch Publications. "Lines to a Friend in Trouble" reprinted by permission of *Triquarterly*.

Stephen Dobyns: "The Window," "Getting Up," "The White Skirt," "The Triangular Field," "Dream," "Girl in White," and "Japanese Girl with Red Table" from *The Balthus Poems*. Copyright © 1981, 1982 by Stephen Dobyns. Reprinted by permission of Atheneum Publishers.

Rita Dove: "Dusting," "Ö," "Champagne," and "Planning the Perfect Evening" reprinted by permission of Carnegie-Mellon.

Norman Dubie: "Elizabeth's War with the Christmas Bear," "Comes Winter, the Sea Hunting," "The Circus Ringmaster's Apology to God," "The Fox Who Watched for the Midnight Sun," "Parish," "At Midsummer," and "Elegy to the Sioux" from *Selected and New Poems* by Norman Dubie, by permission of the author and W. W. Norton & Company, Inc. Copyright © 1983 by Norman Dubie. "The Funeral" reprinted by permission of *The American Poetry Review*.

Gretel Ehrlich: "The Orchard," "Cutting Wood on Shell Creek," "A Sheeprancher Named John," and "A Way of Speaking" reprinted by permission of Ahsahta Press.

Lynn Emanuel: "Berlin Interior with Jews" reprinted from *Hotel Fiesta* by permission of the University of Georgia Press, copyright © 1984 by the University of Georgia Press. "The Sleeping" reprinted by permission of *The Iowa Review*, University of Iowa. "Of Your Father's Indiscretions and the Train to California" reprinted by permission of *The American Poetry Review*, later reprinted in the *Anthology of Magazine Verse and Yearbook of American Poetry*. "Frying Trout While Drunk" first appeared in *Poetry*, copyright © 1983 by The Modern Poetry Association, and is reprinted by permission of the editor of *Poetry*.

Daniel Mark Epstein: "The Follies," "At the Millinery Shop," and "Cash Only, No Refund, No Return," from *The Follies* by Daniel Mark Epstein. Copyright © 1977 by Daniel Mark Epstein. Published by The Overlook Press. "Mannequins" and "Miami" from *The Book of Fortune* by Daniel Mark Epstein. Copyright © 1982 by Daniel Mark Epstein. Published by The Overlook Press.

Calvin Forbes: "Some Pieces," "The Chocolate Soldiers," "The Other Side of This World," and "M.A.P." copyright © 1974 by Calvin Forbes. Reprinted from *Blue Monday* by permission of Wesleyan University Press.

Carolyn Forché: "The Memory of Elena," "For the Stranger," "Reunion," "City Walk-up, Winter 1969," "Selective Service," and "Because One Is Always Forgotten" from *The Country Between Us* by Carolyn Forché. Copyright © 1977, 1978, 1980, 1981 by Carolyn Forché. "For the Stranger" originally appeared in *The New Yorker*. All selections reprinted by permission of Harper & Row, Publishers, Inc.

Tess Gallagher: "Black Silk," "The Shirts," "Crêpes Flambeau," "Each Bird Walking," "Skylights," and "Some Painful Butterflies Pass Through" from *Willingly*, printed by Graywolf Press. "Women's Tug of War at Lough Arrow" and "Under Stars" from *Under Stars*, printed by Graywolf Press.

Reginald Gibbons: "The Ruined Motel," "Luckies," "The Cedar River," and "Breath" from *The Ruined Motel* by Reginald Gibbons. Copyright © 1981 by Reginald Gibbons. Reprinted by permission of Houghton Mifflin Company. "Eating" reprinted by permission of *The New Republic*. "Make Me Hear You" reprinted by permission of *Ploughshares*.

Margaret Gibson: "Catechism Elegy," "Gemini Elegy," "To Speak of Chile," "Burning the Root," and "Long Walks in the Afternoon" from *Long Walks in the Afternoon* by Margaret Gibson, reprinted by permission of Louisiana State University Press.

Christopher Gilbert: "Charge," "Now," "Saturday Morning at the Laundry," and "Touching" reprinted by permission of Graywolf Press.

Louise Glück: "Happiness," "Palais des Arts," "Lamentations," and "The Mirror" copyright © 1980 by Louise Glück, from *Descending Figure* by Louise Glück, published by The Ecco Press in 1980. Reprinted by permission. "Horse" copyright © 1981 by Louise Glück. First published in *Antaeus*, 40/41, Winter/Spring 1981. Reprinted by permission. "Brooding Likeness" and "Night Song" reprinted by permission; copyright © 1981, 1983 Louise Glück; originally appeared in *The New Yorker*. "Mock Orange" reprinted by permission of *The Yale Review*, copyright Yale University.

Albert Goldbarth: "A History of Photography" reprinted by permission of New Rivers Press. "A History of Civilization," "A Theory of Wind," "All-Nite Donuts," and "Before" reprinted by permission of Ontario Review Press. "A Film" first appeared in *Poetry*, copyright © 1982 by The Modern Poetry Association, and is reprinted by permission of the editor of *Poetry*.

It is the policy of William Morrow and Company, Inc., and its imprints and affiliates, recognizing the importance of preserving what has been written, to print the books we publish on acid-free paper, and we exert our best efforts to that end.

Library of Congress Cataloging in Publication Data

Main entry under title:

The Morrow anthology of younger American poets.

1. American poetry—20th century. 2. Poets,
American—20th century—Biography. I. Smith, Dave,
1942-   . II. Bottoms, David. III. Title:
Anthology of younger American poets.
[PS615.M64 1985b]   811'.54'08   84-18044
ISBN 0-688-03450-0 (pbk.)

Printed in the United States of America

11   12   13   14   15

The Anthology in Our Heads

The publication of an anthology of new poets is an opportunity to observe the language discovering its possibilities as if for the first time. It is an occasion of the historic and the temporal, the panoramic and the telescopic, the collective and the individual perspectives. More than anything else it is the moment a reader whose passion is poetry may experience that acute excitement which is partly recognition of the art extended and partly delight in the future becoming visible. For such a reader, the world is poetry, or potentially poetry—the poems that, as the jargon has it, might blow us away with vision as radical as a body scanner or passion as intense as Job's or language as shimmering and indelible as Whitman's. Emerson greeting Whitman at the beginning of a new poetry suggests the hopeless innocence and surge of gladness with which we attend to the next poem, the next book, the next poet. For such a reader, the poem knows more than God and may yet say what has never been completely, locally, and truly said.

During most of our adult lives we have been relentless readers of new poems. Like others, we have found them in journals large and small, in anthologies, in the endless, often almost secretively published books that stream in annually from garage presses and glossy conglomerate houses alike. These have come in review copies or gifts, in trade, or have been purchased at something more than a strain on family budgets. We've read the poems as magazine editors, contest judges, and simply as poets asked for an opinion. We've read them as teachers and as referees for academic promotions. They have been handed to us over fences, in cars, at airports, and we have read them all with the silent hope of arriving in the presence of that emotional thunderclap that poetry can sometimes be. What does it matter this hope is often disappointed? It is often enough fulfilled.

As poets and as teachers of contemporary literature, we are frequently asked who the younger poets are, who should be read. The question is always startling and usually provokes a mumbling of names, along with a feeling that terminal dumbness has ill served the poets and the questioner. Ordinarily, we might add that our practice, common enough among poetry readers, has been to casually walk the stacks of local libraries, browsing through the thin books—poetry being distilled expression—always checking out the new volumes that appear interesting. This practice, indeed all reading, is a kind of anthology making. Anyone who gives himself to poetry so entirely cannot fail to find himself assembling an anthology of favorite contemporaries in his head. Most readers are never asked to see such a collection into print.

But in the spring of 1982, Maria Guarnaschelli approached us about the possibility of editing for William Morrow a new anthology of contemporary American poets. Preliminary discussions showed that it would be impossible to do the kind of book we thought most attractive: a collection beginning with Lowell and Roethke and including those contemporaries, now in their fifth and sixth decades, who had altered the directions of American poetry with their first books in the fifties and sixties. Such a book was prohibited by enormous permission fees. We both agreed, however, that a new collection of younger poets was badly needed. This seemed like an attractive project and an easy enough task.

We soon discovered what ought to have been obvious: no anthology could be assembled that was capacious enough or organized enough to contain all the poems we thought had merit. We would have to establish guidelines for selection, the fewer the better. This, too, appeared simple enough. We would include only the poems we liked best. More than two years of telephone bills, meetings in Georgia, Virginia, New York, and Vermont, and prolonged debates have not allowed us to articulate any better that initial standard: We wanted poems we liked. Those we liked had to be interesting, exert an immediate, dramatic presence, possess a character of language that sustained and renewed our attention, and demonstrate a treatment of subject that moved us beyond the subject to an enlarged and resonant awareness of being alive. They had to be poems with individual authority, formal grace, and final unity. More than anything else, they had to be poems likely to outlive this anthology.

We needed guidelines. We established two of them: The poets chosen must have published one full-length book, preferably recent in appearance, and a book that indicated future work of quality from the poet. We were aware that the proliferation of excellent small presses and university presses in the last two decades meant a constituency we could hardly cover even with this book stipulation. This constituency had not been, on the whole, anthologized. Daniel Halpern's *American Poetry Anthology*, published in 1975, was in print but badly dated. Edward Field's *A Geography of Poets*, 1979, was in our view democratic and eccentric in its selection of poets by regional location. We determined to focus on "younger" poets, by which we meant poets who had mostly not appeared in these or any other national anthologies but who had otherwise begun to establish themselves. We decided we would use only poets born in 1940 or after, a decision that eliminated many fine poets but few who had not been afforded significant public recognition through anthologies, critical reception, prizes, and book publication.

With these two guidelines, and quite independently, we compiled lists of poems and poets to be considered. We read journals, books, and manuscripts. We wrote to poets and editors. We exchanged lists. We re-read and debated and re-made lists. We pruned, then added. Newly published books changed our minds. Into the thousands of poems, we were getting nowhere. We decided to arbitrarily divide the work and, generally, to trust each other's judgment. Each of us would take responsibility for the poets nearer his own age. We could and, of course, we did read and propose for inclusion poets from the other's camp. We began making progress.

Our assumption, it was not quite an intention, was that we would collect fifty to seventy-five poets. We wanted to include a minimum of four poems by each poet, ensuring a healthy sampling, and we expected there would be few poets beyond our prospective number with even four undeniable poems. In fact, the difficulty came in limiting ourselves to the one hundred-plus poets we have collected. Had we not been constrained by Maria Guarnaschelli's gentle admonitions about space and cost, as well as by contract deadlines, there would be more. That person who maintains contemporary American poetry is anything other than vigorous, rich, and diverse speaks from a hidden agenda.

When our final selections had been made, we felt uncomfortable writing an introduction to a book in which we both appeared. Anthony Hecht responded to our invitation with a splendid and generous commentary, and it would be hard to express better how much any anthology is a tissue of compromises. The collection in each of our heads is a manifestation of taste. It is also, as Emerson shows us, an approximation of the unwritten and hoped-for poem that might bear the world as we imagine it. Obviously, we as editors do not share an equal enthusiasm for each of the poets here, nor will any reader find this anthology to be exactly his own. The convention of prefaces and introductions is to note those who might have been chosen and were not, to apologize for errors of omission and sins of commission. Or compromise. Yet we think no apology is warranted. Each of us can name many poets we'd like to have included, a list of friends, of prize winners, of yet-unrecognized talents, and so on. To choose among living poets, especially those just emerging, is to take a sort of snapshot. Necessarily this ignores the context of the past and blinks at the unforeseen moment of the future into which each of these poets has already passed without our viewing. In time, of time, like a snapshot, our collection is finally one moment's judgment and an arranged opinion. Yet we do not regard this opinion as the presentation of an aesthetic statement or as a democratic portrait of the state of the art. We have appended no critical commentary and little assertion of value that would justify our selections. As Baudelaire said, poetry exists to be poetry; we think an anthology exists to be an anthology, a gathering of what we liked in the context of compromise. We have tried to represent the most attractive of the younger poets but we have also tried, through the number of poems included, to indicate the scope and significance of individual accomplishment. This, too, is a signifier of compromise between our tastes and what we think this poetry is, what it does.

Still, a few words about who the younger poet is seem necessary. There will be individual but not collective surprises for our readers. If our poets are any good they are not reducible to an index. Indeed, the assertion of an individuality, discovered and in creation, is a dominant characteristic of their poems.

Who, then, is the younger poet here? He, frequently she, is born between 1940, at the onset of World War II, and 1955, the third of Eisenhower's smiling presidential years. A child of suburban parents, television, and the nuclear nightmare, he is often the first in his family to complete college and escape a life of physical labor, the first to fight in or publicly oppose an unpopular national war, and among the first writers for whom intimate and personal revelation would not result in obscenity prosecution. He is also young enough to think of Vietnam as the war of the older brothers, of Haight-Ashbury as the scene of curious movies, of Martin Luther King, Jr., as a day off from school. He has one or more graduate degrees in literature or writing and teaches both in a college. Yet he is sometimes a lawyer, a psychotherapist, a businessman, a librarian, a filmmaker, a rock musician, or a sheepherder. On the average, he is thirty-seven years old, married with children, has been or is an editor of a literary magazine, has published widely, frequently translates poems from the Spanish, French, Hebrew, Swedish, Polish, and Italian, has been awarded a grant from the National Endowment for the Arts or the Guggenheim Foundation, or both, and rarely lives where he grew up.

In his poems the younger poet tends to be himself, an invented version of himself. He is increasingly interested in traditional forms of verse yet tends to be discontinuous and irregular in his formal practices, manifesting the style of open, personal, and sometimes garrulous poetry that his senior contemporaries evolved in the seventies. Yet he has become cool in demeanor as he is haunted by a life that seems inconsequential or less than fully lived. His knowledge, while eclectic, seems focused on the psychological and mythical resonances in the local surface, event, or subject. He is haunted by time and death yet God seems a minor problem. He is rarely a card-carrying group member, political or aesthetic, rarely an expatriate or veteran or eccentric. He speaks Williams as fluently as he speaks Eliot, Neruda and Milosz as quickly as James Wright or Elizabeth Bishop. He seems to jog more than to write literary criticism, but the poem he writes is more often stern than funny as he discovers again and again, as Louis Simpson has written, "you find yourself standing against the wall."

Of course, none of the poets here is precisely that younger writer. Each is more and less. Seventy of them have published first or second books, tipping the anthology heavily toward the youngest contributors. Sixty-four have not appeared in a national anthology. In the more than two and a half years of our preparation, many of them have completed new collections and have, in truth, become different poets than we present. Doubtless there will be future assignments to literary categories, characteristic themes and forms articulated, names for the species provided. That, we think, is the work of literary critics and we leave it to them. Our work has been to present the younger poets who we believe are saying with imagination and passion and power what has not been so necessarily said. If we are successful, our work will give readers the shock and pleasure of poetry's thunderclap. This is the anthology in our heads.

Just as we discovered an anthology is a compromise, we discovered that the anthology goes from the head to the page only with the labor and assistance of many people. This book exists because of the suggestion and the sustaining energy of our editor, Maria Guarnaschelli. It owes much of its life to her assistant, Kathy Jankowski. We are extremely grateful to Anthony Hecht for his timely and thoughtful introduction. We are more than grateful to our patient wives, Dee Smith and Lynn Bottoms. But there is one additional debt of gratitude to acknowledge. We undertook a project with a budget for permission fees so modest as to make questionable any success. That budget required us to seek the help of each poet in negotiating with nearly fifty publishers. The publishers could easily have refused our offers and killed the book. The publishers and poets were cooperative beyond all expectation. It is therefore with great thanks that we dedicate this anthology to those who made it possible and those who made it.

—DAVE SMITH
—DAVID BOTTOMS

August 1984

Contents

Introduction

This is a lively, intelligent, compelling, and adventurous anthology, selected from the work of American poets born since 1940. I make this claim for the book with conviction, and as one who more than once has been severely tempted into becoming an anthologist and who, in consequence, has become a fairly careful student of anthologies over a period of many years. By now I'm old enough—having passed beyond the fleeting moment of being a sixty-year-old smiling public man—to have witnessed the follies and errors of other anthologists, and to be able to congratulate myself on having avoided similar or greater follies.

Anthologists all too often succumb to occupational hazards of habit, of received taste, and even language. Nothing is so safe as to characterize poet X as "one of the best of her generation," a locution cloudy enough to seem like praise without committing the anthologist to anything firm. And all too often it becomes apparent that anthologists of poetry do not actually read poets so much as they read other anthologies. Even thus are chestnuts born. I've recently received in the mail one of the safest, and consequently dullest, anthologies of English poetry I've ever seen. The key to its conventionality is most evident where the anthologists have decided to let a lesser poet be represented by a single poem. So we are given Raleigh's "The Lie," Nashe's "Adieu, Farewell, Earth's Bliss," King's "The Exequy," Waller's "Go, Lovely Rose," Lovelace's "To Althea, from Prison," and Leigh Hunt's rondeau, "Jenny kissed me . . ." The volume is throughout an undeviating excursion into the totally expected. A sad thing, of course, for the reader. How much sadder, though, for the poets. Every poet must surely go in fear of writing a "standard anthology piece," a chestnut. Because once some poem of his has been singled out as characteristic by an enterprising anthologist, the rest of the tribe, unwilling, in the words of Sheridan, "to undergo the fatigue of judging for themselves," will supinely repeat that choice. There came a time when T. S. Eliot declared he was sorry he had ever written "The Love Song of J. Alfred Prufrock."

If there is the danger of tedium in simply reproducing the choices of others, there is another and more curious peril in at least some attempts at originality. When I was three years old, Edwin Markham, the celebrated author of a "standard anthology piece," a chestnut called "The Man with the Hoe," produced an impressive, six-volume anthology titled, with considerable bravado and a sharp eye for the marketplace, *Anthology of the World's Best Poems*. A few of the editor's partialities were almost immediately detectable. The six volumes were arranged with Americans first and English poets second. This filled up the first five and a half of the six volumes. The other poetries, ancient and modern, were neatly fitted into the last half of the final volume, all of that work appearing, of course, in English translation. So into that modest compass was compressed the best of Greek, Latin, Medieval Latin, Italian, Arabian, Persian, French, German, Spanish, Chinese, Indian, Irish, Welsh, Polish, Cuban, Brazilian, Peruvian, and Nicaraguan poetry. Italy, better represented than most, got a rich fourteen pages. Greece got less.

But some of the greatest innovations came in the English and American sections. Andrew Marvell's fine poem, "The Garden," was smoothly abridged from nine stanzas to five (omitting the first, third, fourth, and seventh) and retitled "Thoughts in a Garden." Also included were selections from "To His Coy Mistress." And the English section exhibited work by a poet with the memorable name of Monk Gibbon. But it was the American section that was at once the most enterprising and inclusive, offering works by, among others, Fitz-Greene Halleck, Joseph Rodman Drake, Isaac McClellan, Nathaniel P. Willis, Thomas Lake Harris, David A. Wasson, Celia Thaxter, Lloyd Mifflin, Anna Hempstead Branch, and Elsa Barker. None of these was allowed to take away more than rightful space from Homer or Dante or Villon.

So the nervous anthologist must make his way between the pitfalls of bland orthodoxy and possibly misguided enthusiasms—unless, as in the present case, the anthology is the work of very careful and judicious poets who not only know their craft but their fellow poets as well. Misguided personal enthusiasm is the more probable pitfall for any anthologist who hopes for independence and originality of choice; and it always seems a little quaint in retrospect, when the taste that governed it has become outdated. Here, for example, is a passage from Martin Seymour-Smith's biography of Robert Graves, in which the Sir Walter Raleigh referred to is the late Oxford don and critic, not the Elizabethan courtier and poet:

Wishing to shake up his Oxford contemporaries, he [Graves] managed to persuade Sir Walter Raleigh to give him permission to invite the Illinois poet Vachel Lindsay, then in England, to read in Oxford. He described Lindsay as "Middle-Western clay with a golden streak," but was hardly himself prepared for the shattering effect this "jazz Blake, St Francis of Assisi playing the saxophone at the Fireman's Ball" would create. Lindsay gave an electrifying performance of his work— in the rhetorical style he had originally based on the poetry readings of Professor S. H. Clark of the University of Chicago. He and his mother were entertained in [T. E.] Lawrence's rooms. Of the reading, which took place in the morning, Graves on 19 October 1920 wrote to a friend:

> *Vachel Lindsay was a most staggering success. I meant to hit Oxford a pretty heavy blow by arranging for his invitation to the University, but I did not expect to inflict a knockout, as occurred. . . . By two minutes, Lindsay had the respectable and intellectual and cynical audience listening. By ten, intensely excited; by twenty elated and losing self-control, by half an hour completely under his influence, by forty minutes roaring like a bonfire. At the end of the hour they lifted off the roof and refused to disperse, and Raleigh in returning thanks said he had never been so moved by a recitation in his life—quite like the pictures.*

Lindsay's is a curious case. He was born in the same year as Wallace Stevens, and was the contemporary of Graves, Yeats, Frost, Robinson, W. C. Williams, D. H. Lawrence, Edwin Muir, Eliot, Pound, Marianne Moore, Wilfred Owen, Hart Crane, and John Crowe Ransom; and he was, I think, the inferior of all of these. While not a contemptible poet, his range was oddly limited, and the *brio* of his work relied more heavily than perhaps it should have on his capacities as a performer and, in the current idiom, "a personality." Richard Ellmann and Robert O'Clair, in their own anthology of modern poetry, say this of him:

> *Lindsay wrote verses which created an instant effect . . . he proposed the "Higher Vaudeville imagination." . . . His poems are a kind of solemn farce with ritualized ecstasy. . . . Every tawdry hero, from the heavyweight champion John L. Sullivan*

> *to P. T. Barnum . . . can be seen on a stage where he is made
> to become a vegetation god like Johnny Appleseed.*

One cannot help feeling, in rereading as much of Lindsay's poetry
as one can bear, that he may consciously have sacrificed something of
the "endurance" of his art for what he regarded as its jazzlike spon-
taneity and improvisational liberty, and that "instant effects" and a de-
fiant mixture of entertainment and evangelism, a startling brew of
popular ingredients, were the means by which he meant to win his
audience. The tribute to him lies in the sorts of successes he enjoyed,
including the unlikely one of his Oxford ovation and Sir Walter
Raleigh's stunned, groupie-eyed response. The cost remains in the keen
sense we have of how dated his work has become and how lifelessly
much of it lies upon the page.

Judging the works of the past is hard enough, but judging among
contemporaries is much harder. The well-known anthologist Louis Un-
termeyer was very early a champion of the works of Robert Frost. But it
seemed to him that to like Frost forbade you at the same time to like T.
S. Eliot, and the condescending remarks made about Eliot's poetry in
some of Untermeyer's early anthologies were once dismissive and are
now silly. They may, of course, have reflected Frost's own embattled
and combative feelings; for the fact is that poets have some trouble being
just to one another. Their instinctive competitiveness may seem child-
ish and misguided in retrospect, since no one now feels that admiration
for and loyalty to the poems of Donne prohibit love for and delectation
in the poems of Marvell. All that is safely behind us. But our contem-
poraries give us pause. As Dr. Johnson said: "While an author is yet
living we estimate his powers by his worst performance, and when he is
dead we rate them by his best."

II.

And therein lies the daring as well as the impressiveness of this
book. Its editors have surveyed a fresh field of new and ripening talent,
and have assembled an anthology of originality, variety, power, and
authority. On the face of it, the book presents a virtual demonstration
that poetry in the United States is in a vigorous state of buoyant good
health, brilliantly practiced in a wide and generous variety of idioms.
Not so long ago, when Swinburne died, Yeats was able to lay claim to

the mantle of reigning poet with the declaration, "Now I'm king of the cats." But the mantle eventually was transferred to our shores, and one can no longer say, given the multiplicity of expertly talented poets, that it belongs to any particular one of them—only that it has become an ample American canopy, sheltering a considerable crowd of excellence. That breadth of view is perhaps the first admirable feature of this volume. It contains the work of some poets I have long admired and whom I have ventured publicly to praise. And there are others whose works were entirely new to me, and afforded me the delight of personal discovery, as I hope will be the case with many readers. There is to this collection very little in the way of uniformity except in regard to a general excellence. The poems range from exacting formality to near brute force, from delicacy of perception to cries of rage, encompassing along the way every tactic and pitch of lyric utterance.

But this is not to say the collection is definitive. There are, alas, poets of excellence and of the proper generation who should have found themselves here. Some that future generations will be puzzled to find absent have been denied their place by freaks of fate. One such poet, for example, was kept out at the whim of her publisher, without a word of explanation. Two others I know of, a young woman and a young man, both of whom, I would wager, will be poetic celebrities within a year, have been scheduled to bring out their first books a mere matter of months after this anthology appears and are thereby disqualified. And there is at least one poet whose name and work I should have added to the roster in this book. Still and all, there is so much talent gathered in these pages that one may feel confident a number of future kings and queens of the cats have here made their first anthology appearances. It would be invidious for me to single out any for special notice, and in any case the business of making new acquaintances, the excitement of discovering new voices, belongs to the reader. The initial triage has been done for him superbly well by the editors, a task that was nothing less than formidable.

III.

It would be difficult to characterize the generation of poets represented in this book, except to say of them that they share at least one notion of poetry as an art: their poems are not offered as the adornments or by-products of colorful or eccentric personal lives, but are meant to stand on their own as verbal constructs. One cannot fail to be struck by how evasive and unassuming are the fragmentary biographical details offered by these poets, when the facts are not withheld outright. "Literary egotism," wrote Paul Valéry, "consists in playing the role of *self*, in making oneself a little more natural than nature, a little more oneself than one was a minute before." There are few "confessors" here. Which is not to say that these poems are not personal, or that no identifiable poet stands behind them. But it is fair to say of this group as a whole that they are not their own impresarios, that performance for them takes place on the page, unaccompanied by rock music or even a modest guitar. They are all seriously in the business of writing poems, which is an imaginative and verbal activity, and whether or not, or just how much, it may bear upon their personal lives is not to them a central issue, as it has been for some poets of an earlier generation. Neither does any of them fancy the use of archaic diction, in the manner of Ezra Pound or Robert Duncan. There are no "thous" or "thees," no quaintnesses or dated usages to be found here. This is emphatically not to say that these poets have no interest in the past, that they are mesmerized by their own immediate situations and sensations. A good deal of searching into the dark backward and abysm of time goes on in these poems, and there is even evidence of a touching nostalgia in some of them. But they have found their own idiom in some variety of native American speech. These are nearly the only common denominators to be found among the poets whose group includes an aviatrix, a psychotherapist, a lawyer, an editor, and a number of moon-lighting novelists. Not a bartender or safe-cracker among them. Indeed, most of them are shockingly well educated, and not a few are college and university teachers.

Not so long ago it was held ruinous to the poetic sensibility, to the very life of the imagination, for a poet to hold a teaching position. Anyone who did so was branded "academic," suspected of being thin-blooded, timid, guilty of all the classic clichés that characterize the absentminded professor. Poets were supposed to go out and "live," the more recklessly the better, and if their lives were thus abbreviated by tragic accidents or overdoses, why that was the just forfeit they were supposed gladly to pay for being geniuses and writing immortal stuff. This debased pastoral sentimentalism was seriously urged upon a young poet in the early 1950s by a certified academic, a professor at Columbia University, an urging which the poet judiciously rejected, and is still with us, having won a Pulitzer Prize and other awards, and having settled into a decent teaching job. That curious attitude has long since disappeared, and poets are no longer thought enfeebled for being better educated. Every so often the public will acclaim an untutored genuis— Joseph Blacket, "the cobbler-poet," John Taylor, "the water poet," James Hogg, "the Ettrick Shepherd"—but these tastes pass quickly, and if such unassailable and maverick talents as Theodore Roethke and James Wright can teach, the practice can't be quite as ossifying as has been claimed. As Randall Jarrell has written: "Kepler said, 'God gives every animal a way to make its living, and He has given the astronomer astrology'; and now, after so many centuries, He has given us poets students. But what He gives with one hand he takes away with the other: He has taken away our readers."

IV.

Some of the poets here assembled are already well launched upon their poetic careers, and have earned praise from the likes of Robert Lowell, Elizabeth Bishop, Robert Penn Warren, Richard Wilbur, James Merrill, Helen Vendler, Irvin Ehrenpreis, Richard Eberhart, James Dickey, and Howard Nemerov. Blurbs, however, are often enough beside the point, and are in any case part of the world of pro- motion and advertising that should be the concern of publishers. But whether widely acclaimed or newly discovered, all are, by the rules of this volume, and by my own measure, young. Young poets are likely to agree with Paul Valéry that "lyric poetry is the development of an ex- clamation." It is, in other words, precise in focus as in emotion, the expression of a single frame of mind or unified experience. That itself, of course, is not an easy thing to do. But it may be said to be the beginning of the lyric range, which, with maturity, grows more complex and more willing to bear and balance contradictions within its own se- vere limits. It is part of the brilliance of lyric poetry that it affords us both those pristine moments of nearly unrecapturable exaltation or sud- den insight and, at what might be called the other end of the spectrum, those piercing visions in which gain and loss are simultaneously real- ized; poems that range from the lyric praise of a psalm or Ben Jonson's lovely "Queene and Huntresse, chaste and faire," to those densely ironic poems of Yeats, like "Easter: 1916," or the following by George Herbert:

BITTER-SWEET

Ah my dear angrie Lord,
Since thou does love, yet strike;
Cast down, yet help afford;
Sure I will do the like.

I will complain, yet praise;
I will bewail, approve:
And all my sowre-sweet days
I will lament and love.

There is perhaps a further point that might be made about these
poets. Lyric poetry in the course of its long history may be said to oscil-
late not only between the impromptu, spontaneous utterance and the
thoughtful, reconsidered meditation, or even to blend the two into
Wordsworth's formulation about "emotion recollected in tranquillity,"
but also to swing back and forth between an impulse to speech, the
normal speech of ordinary men, and, on the other hand, to the for-
malities of song. And between song and speech lie other formalities of
rhetorical strategy and literary convention. Of the poets whose work ap-
pears here, it may be said that by far the greater number are nearer to
speech than to song, though for some that speech is highly formal and
contained within the strictest of measurable limits. They are of a gener-
ation that seems disinclined to sing (for which there are plenty of sound
social and historical reasons) and, though sometimes infuriated, they are
disposed to voice themselves in soft-spoken tones, tones that can turn
icy, but are usually unassuming and touchingly modest. Indeed, the
quietness of some of these voices will challenge the reader's sensibilities.
There are poets here as gentle as Chekhov, as retiring as Dickinson, and
who repay a reader's attention nearly as well.

V.

"This is so much an age of anthologies," wrote Randall Jarrell,

that it is surprising that poets still waste their time on books of
verse, instead of writing anthologies in the first place. If you
are about to print a book of poems, don't; make up a few

names and biographical sketches with which to punctuate your manuscript, change its title to Poems of Democracy, *and you will find yourself transformed from an old pumpkin, always in the red, to a shiny black new coach. For the average reader knows poetry mainly through anthologies, just as he knows philosophy mainly from histories of philosophy or textbooks: the* Complete Someone—*hundreds or thousands of small-type, double column pages of* poetry, *without one informing, repentant sentence of ordinary prose—evokes for him a start of that savage and unreasoning timidity, that* horror vacui, *with which he stares at the lemmas and corollaries of Spinoza's Ethics.*

Jarrell proceeds to have a lot of fun at the expense of anthologists, chiefly of Oscar Williams, who was the anthological entrepreneur of his time, and who doubtless deserved much of what Jarrell did to him. But the sad fact is that Jarrell's premise is still true: most readers would rather encounter poetry in an anthology than in its pure form in a single volume by a single author. Both timidity and a certain prudential canniness tell them that a selection of any size is a hedge against being completely wrong, will save them from being a complete fool who has wasted every cent of his or her investment. But anthologists should not therefore be looked upon as the booking agents of some literary borscht circuit. Theirs, when well performed, is an exceedingly difficult and demanding task, requiring patience, balanced judgment, uncommon taste; and all these gifts must be raised to the seventh power when the anthology is, like this one, made of the work of new poets who are not already part of some anthological canon to be appealed to for authority and comfort. The great service such a volume as this performs lies in its introduction of new poets to new readers, with such a rich variety of poems that almost anyone browsing through these pages will be charmed or electrified by one poet or another, and perhaps by several. If sufficiently charmed or electrified, that reader might even be rash enough to go out and buy a book or two by a poet whose work he or she now admires. And, the distinguished editors apart, I can imagine that there must be very few readers of modern poetry who can claim familiarity with the work of all the poets in this book.

These poets, like their elders, may not feel altogether comfortable in one another's company, but time, with its cold clarity, will eventually sort things out. Poets are lumped together into groups for critical or

editorial convenience only until real scrutiny and familiarity distin-
guishes among them. So that what was once called "the Pylon School,"
or the Auden, Spender, MacNeice, Day-Lewis group, split up into what
it always really was: four very distinct poets, each with his independent
gifts and singular limitations. Robert Frost used to be infuriated at being
mistaken for Carl Sandburg by hazy-minded poetry-lovers with a vague
sense that there was some old rustic American with a thatch of white
hair, who wore galluses and wrote poems. But what anthologists in their
priestly instincts have linked together the wisdom of ages will put
asunder, and each poet, like the blessed in heaven and the damned in
hell, will find his proper place. Meanwhile, if there are marriages of
convenience, there are also elective affinities, shared tastes, methods,
and goals that form real connections and sound friendships between
poets.

The task assigned to me of composing an introduction to *The Mor-
row Anthology of Younger American Poets* has been an agreeable one,
but one that has not failed to make me feel my age. That can be sa-
lubrious in its way, especially if one is tempted to believe one has not
aged of late. That's a dangerous frame of mind for a writer. So I'm
grateful, while being made uncomfortable. And in saluting these many
diverse and gifted poets at somewhere not so very far from the beginning
of their careers, I recall a poem of Thomas Hardy's called "An Ancient
to Ancients." Most of that poem is indeed addressed to those of his own
generation, now well into sere, autumnal days. But the last stanza is
reserved as a greeting to the young who shall take over the reins of
poetry, and of the world:

> And ye, red-lipped and smooth-browed; list,
>   Gentlemen;
> Much is there waits you we have missed;
> Much lore we leave you worth the knowing,
> Much, much has lain outside our ken:
> Nay, rush not: time serves: we are going,
>   Gentlemen.

—ANTHONY HECHT

August 1984

Diane Ackerman

Barbara Ball

Diane Ackerman was born in 1948. She received a B.A. from Pennsylvania State University, and an M.F.A., M.A., and Ph.D. from Cornell University. In addition to her collections of poetry, *The Planets: A Cosmic Pastoral* (1976), *Wife of Light* (1980), and *Lady Faustus* (1983), she has also published a prose memoir, *Twilight of the Tenderfoot*, all from William Morrow and Company, and *On Extended Wings* (nonfiction), from Atheneum (1985). She teaches at Washington University.

A *Fine,* A *Private Place*

He took her one day
under the blue horizon
where long sea fingers
parted like beads
hitched in the doorway
of an opium den,
and canyons mazed the deep
reef with hollows,
cul-de-sacs, and narrow boudoirs,
and had to ask twice
before she understood
his stroking her arm

with a marine feather
slobbery as aloe pulp
was wooing, or saw the octopus
in his swimsuit
stretch one tentacle
and ripple its silky bag.

While bubbles rose
like globs of mercury,
they made love
mask to mask, floating
with oceans of air between them,
she his sea-geisha
in an orange kimono
of belts and vests,
her lacquered hair waving,
as Indigo Hamlets
tattooed the vista,
and sunlight
cut through the water,
twisting its knives
into corridors of light.

His sandy hair
and sea-blue eyes,
his kelp-thin waist
and chest ribbed wider
than a sandbar
where muscles domed
clear and taut as shells
(freckled cowries,
flat, brawny scallops
the color of dawn),
his sea-battered hands
gripping her thighs
like tawny starfish
and drawing her close
as a pirate vessel
to let her board:
who was this she loved?

Overhead, sponges
sweating raw color
jutted from a coral arch,
Clown Wrasses
hovered like fireworks,
and somewhere an abalone opened
its silver wings.
Part of a lusty dream
under aspic, her hips rolled
like a Spanish galleon,
her eyes swam
and chest began to heave.
Gasps melted on the tide.
Knowing she would soon be
breathless as her tank,
he pumped his brine
deep within her,
letting sea water drive it
through petals
delicate as anemone veils
to the dark purpose
of a conch-shaped womb.
An ear to her loins
would have heard the sea roar.

When panting ebbed,
and he signaled *Okay?*
as lovers have asked,
land or waterbound
since time heaved ho,
he led her to safety:
shallower realms,
heading back toward
the boat's even keel,
though ocean still petted her
cell by cell, murmuring
along her legs and neck,
caressing her
with pale, endless arms.

Later, she thought often
of that blue boudoir,
pillow-soft and filled
with cascading light,
where together
they'd made a bell
that dumbly clanged
beneath the waves
and minutes lurched
like mountain goats.
She could still see
the quilted mosaics
that were fish
twitching spangles overhead,
still feel the ocean
inside and out, turning her
evolution around.

She thought of it miles
and fathoms away, often,
at odd moments: watching
the minnow snowflakes
dip against the windowframe,
holding a sponge
idly under tap-gush,
sinking her teeth
into the cleft
of a voluptuous peach.

√ Space Shuttle

By all-star orchestra, they dine in space
in a long steel muscle so fast it floats,
in a light waltz they lie still as amber
watching Earth stir in her sleep beneath them.

They have brought along a plague
of small winged creatures, whose brains are tiny
as computer chips. Flight is the puzzle,
the shortest point between two times.

In zero gravity, their hearts will be light,
not three pounds of blood, dream and gristle.
When they were young, the sky was a tree
whose cool branches they climbed,
sweaty in August, and now they are the sky
children imagine as invisible limbs.

On the console, a light summons them
to the moment, and they must choose
between the open-mouthed delirium in their cells,
the awe ballooning beyond the jetstream,
or husband all that is safe and tried.

They are good providers. Their eyes do not wander.
Their fingers do not pause at the prick
of a switch. Their mouths open for sounds
no words rush into. Answer the question
put at half-garble. Say again
how the cramped world turns, say again.

Spiders

The eight-legged aerialists
of the tented dawn are up and about.
One leaves a pale orchid,
its exoskeleton, on a twig,
while another fly-casts
against the wind, angling for the leaf
where it would sooner be;
the silk hardens, and it crosses,

tiptoe, the tiny span,
eager to turn mummies
from wing crisp to liquid caramel.

They dote on the tang of quarry,
however they nab it,
with trap door, or purse web,
or keen, jagged fangs,
holding out for that bronchial
shudder of the net, when something
angel-faint, ensnared and hairy
begins the tussle in rigged silk
that can start a greedy eye,
make gossamer hum and, at long last,
even their slack jams quiver.

✓ *In the Silks*

The alarm sounds. The starting gates are empty,
there are no crowds, the track is clotted mud,
there is no finish line, there are no jockeys,
and, anyway, the horses are unride-able.

Nonetheless, at the bell all her muscles tense,
she leans to the jagged withers in her chair,
and her hand grips something wand-like and hard,
a man's body, or a memory, either one a whip.

Patrick Ewing Takes a Foul Shot

Ewing sweating,
molding the ball
with spidery hands,
packing it, packing it,
into a snowball's
chance of a goal,
rolling his shoulders
through a silent earthquake,
rocking from one foot
to the other, sweating,
bouncing it, oh, sweet
honey, molding it,
packing it tight,
he fires:

floats it up on one palm
as if surfacing
from the clear green Caribbean
with a shell
whose roar wraps around him,
whose surf breaks
deep into his arena
where light and time
and pupils jump
because he jumps

Ai

Ai was born in 1947. She holds a B.A. in Oriental studies and an M.F.A. in English, and she is the author of three collections of poetry, *Killing Floor* (1979), the Lamont Selection of the Academy of American Poets, and *Cruelty* (1973), both from Houghton Mifflin, and *Sin* (to be published in January 1986). Her awards include fellowships from the National Endowment for the Arts, the Ingram Merrill Foundation, and the Guggenheim Foundation.

Brad Franckum

√ Twenty-Year Marriage

You keep me waiting in a truck
with its one good wheel stuck in the ditch,
while you piss against the south side of a tree.
Hurry. I've got nothing on under my skirt tonight.
That still excites you, but this pickup has no windows
and the seat, one fake leather thigh,
pressed close to mine is cold.
I'm the same size, shape, make as twenty years ago,
but get inside me, start the engine;
you'll have the strength, the will to move.
I'll pull, you push, we'll tear each other in half.

Come on, baby, lay me down on my back.
Pretend you don't owe me a thing
and maybe we'll roll out of here,
leaving the past stacked up behind us;
old newspapers nobody's ever got to read again.

✓ 29 (A Dream in Two Parts)

1.

Night, that old woman, jabs the sun
with a pitchfork,
and dyes the cheesecloth sky blue-violet,
as I sit at the kitchen table,
bending small pieces of wire in hoops.
You come in naked.
No. Do it yourself.

2.

I'm a nine-year-old girl,
skipping beside a single hoop of daylight.
I hear your voice.
I start running. You lift me in your arms.
I holler. The little girl turns.
Her hoop rolls out of sight.
Something warm seeps through my gown onto my belly.
She never looks back.

She Didn't Even Wave

For Marilyn Monroe

I buried Mama in her wedding dress
and put gloves on her hands,
but I couldn't do much about her face,
blue-black and swollen,
so I covered it with a silk scarf.
I hike my dress up to my thighs
and rub them,
watching you tip the mortuary fan back and forth.
Hey. Come on over. Cover me all up
like I was never here. Just never.
Come on. I don't know why I talk like that.
It was a real nice funeral. Mama's.
I touch the rhinestone heart pinned to my blouse.
Honey, let's look at it again.
See. It's bright like the lightning that struck her.

I walk outside
and face the empty house.
You put your arms around me. Don't.
Let me wave goodbye.
Mama never got a chance to do it.
She was walking toward the barn
when it struck her. I didn't move;
I just stood at the screen door.
Her whole body was light.
I'd never seen anything so beautiful.

I remember how she cried in the kitchen
a few minutes before.
She said, *God. Married.*
I don't believe it, Jean, I won't.
He takes and takes and you just give.
At the door, she held out her arms
and I ran to her.
She squeezed me so tight:

I was all short of breath.
And she said, *don't do it.*
In ten years, your heart will be eaten out
and you'll forgive him, or some other man, even that
and it will kill you.
Then she walked outside.
And I kept saying, I've got to, Mama,
hug me again. Please don't go.

✓ *Guadalajara Hospital*

I watch the orderly stack the day's dead:
men on one cart, women on the other.
You sit two feet away, sketching
and drinking tequila.
I raise my taffeta skirt above the red garter,
take out the pesos
and lay them beside you.
I don't hold out on you.
I shove my hand under my skirt,
find the damp ten-dollar bill.
You're on top. You call the shots.
You said we'd make it here and we have.
I make them pay for it.

Later, we walk close,
smoking from one cigarette
until it's gone. I take your arm.
Next stop *end of the line.* You pull me to you
and push your tongue deep in my mouth.
I bite it. We struggle. You slap me.
I lean over the hood of the car.
You clamp a handkerchief between your teeth,
take the pesos and ten-dollar bill from your pocket

and tear them up.
Then you get in the car
and I slide in beside you.

When we finally cross the border,
I stare out the back window.
The Virgin Mary's back there
in her husband Mendoza's workroom.
She's sitting on a tall stool,
her black lace dress rolled up above her knees,
the red pumps dangling from her feet,
while he puts the adz to a small coffin;
a psalm of hammer and emptiness
only the two of them understand.
You say, *sister, breathe with me.*
We're home, now, home.
But I reach back, back through the window.
Virgin Mary, help me. Save me.
Tear me apart with your holy, invisible hands.

Almost Grown

I swing up on the sideboard of the old car. I'm wearing
the smell of hay better than I do these starched coveralls,
my dead father's shirt, patched under each arm, and the
underwear I bought especially for today. Mother says nothing,
just watches me and sucks on her unlit pipe. My sister,
still too young to get away, wipes a few tears with the end
of her blue apron. The red bitch runs behind yapping, then
veers into the charred field, where she chases her tail
and, building speed, makes wider and wider circles, until
she is just a streak of fire, finally burning herself to a quick stop.

I get off at the feed store. The old men playing cards ignore me.
It's Saturday afternoon. I carry the cardboard box that holds my

things under one arm, swinging the other. I see Jake the Bootlegger's
car, parked in front of the café. When I'm close, the sun
strikes its gray steel with a hammer and I have to shade my eyes
from the glare. I grope for the door, then stagger inside. The
cooler rattles a welcome. Mae, the waitress, hollers from the
kitchen, but I can't make out what she says. I sit on a stool with
the box propped up beside me.

Suddenly, Jake comes out and Mae follows him. He winks at me.
I stare through Mae's sheer nylon blouse at her lace bra. She
takes my order and I watch her as she walks to the far end of the
counter, where Jake sits, waiting, twisting the long gold chain
of his watch. I grunt with satisfaction. Good I moved, left the
farm to finish dying without me. I take out my ten-dollar bill,
rub it, feeling all the things I can buy with it: a striped tie,
one more box of cigars, a room for a week at the hotel. Hell!
It's great. Two more days and I start work at the gas station.
I take a big bite out of the hamburger Mae has set on the counter.

Jake gets up, Mae reaches for him. He shakes his head and
walks outside. She goes into the kitchen, and soon I hear her crying.
I hesitate, then follow her. She's lying on a cot, jammed against
the wall. I bend over her and she lifts her hand and touches me
the way no one ever has. I'm clumsy, but it gets done, same as
anything, I guess. She shoves me, cursing. Money, she wants
money. I'm nervous, I clutch the ten, then throw it at her. I run,
grabbing my box. In the street again, the heat, my empty pockets
heavy, as if filled with coins. At the gas station, I slip into the
Men's room and bolt the door. I sit on the dusty toilet and lean
back against the tank. Shit! I'm not through yet. I heard this
somewhere and it's true, it's got to be: you can't tell a shotgun
or a man what to do.

✓ *Immortality*

I dreamed I was digging a grave
that kept filling with water.
The next day, you died.
I dressed you in a wool skirt
and jacket,
because you were always cold
and I had promised to do that much for you.
Then I took a potato to eat, went outside
and started to dig.

I thought of the Great War;
the day we met.
You, thin as a spade handle,
wearing cotton in Winter.
The sunset, a clot of dull-red
floating in a bowl of cobalt blue,
as we lay on our backs in the mud,
my hand on your mons
and yours pushing at it,
pushing it away,
just like that.
And just like that, we parted.
Then one day, you found me hoeing potatoes.
Let me help, you said,
and handed me a child
with bright red hair like yours.
I married you. We fought.
Blood sanctifies and blesses;
it binds.
Anna, where are you now?—
waltzing down a long mirrored corridor,
wrapped in glory that is red, bitter?

I toss a shovelful of dirt on your coffin.
It isn't that I hate you for giving it all up
with your poison.
But I wanted to do it.

To finally ease this hunger,
to be holy in my devotion to you
and have you acknowledge it
the moment before I brought
the mallet down and set you free.
Life to you was yellow
like the Vicar's daughter's braids,
it was morning glories,
All Hallow's Eve,
your dead sister's baby teeth
for good luck.
But I wanted us to go on
day and night, without terror or hope.
I can't forgive your going.
I take the potato from my pocket.
One bite, then another.
If only this were all it took
to live forever.

Jon Anderson

Jon Anderson was born on Independence Day, 1940. He is the author of six books of poetry, the most recent of which is *The Milky Way: Poems 1967–82* (The Ecco Press, 1983). He received a fellowship from the Guggenheim Foundation in 1976 and from the National Endowment for the Arts in 1981. He has taught at Ohio University, the University of Pittsburgh, the University of Iowa, and currently teaches at the University of Arizona.

Lois Shelton

Witness

Now "you," if you are still yourself,
Remembered, remembering,
An homage to the passage of days floating—
Pale jets of water on a millionaire's lawn
You pass some moments
In a car—

"You" must extend yourself
As, perhaps, a hand might apply light pigment
On a stucco wall, meaning
To fill in, not contour, but color,
A tint which will reveal the texture

Of an otherwise sallow face:
It is the face of Dürer! Wrapped, below, in furs
A single seemingly arthritic hand
At once clutches to him & makes the gesture
We must not mistake the meaning of:

He *is* himself,
As we are not, having come to this
Self-witnessing through so many days
Of informed, almost public, conjecture;
So, if you are not yourself, neither

Are you any other. That passing car,
Funereal in its steady pace,
Can only be ominous, so you pull the drapes
Only to lean back, weary, in your chair:
Another day, & all that money can buy—

The immense house glutted with memorabilia—
The lawn now darkening,
The strict spokes of a few trees
Will not buy back, though
It is night & already there are stars.

Rosebud

There is a place in Montana where the grass stands up
        two feet,
Yellow grass, white grass, the wind
On it like locust wings & the same shine.
Facing what I think was south, I could see a broad valley
& river, miles into the valley, that looked black & then
        trees.
To the west was more prairie, darker
Than where we stood, because the clouds

Covered it; a long shadow, like the edge of rain, racing
    toward us.
We had been driving all day, & the day before through
    South Dakota
Along the Rosebud, where the Sioux
Are now farmers, & go to school, & look like everyone.
In the reservation town there was a Sioux museum
& "trading post," some implements inside: a longbow
Of shined wood that lay in its glass case, reflecting light.
The walls were covered with framed photographs,
The Oglala posed in fine dress in front of a few huts,
Some horses nearby: a feeling, even in those photographs,
The size of a book, of spaciousness.
I wanted to ask about a Sioux holy man, whose life
I had recently read, & whose vision had gone on
    hopelessly
Past its time: I believed then that only a great loss
Could make us feel small enough to begin again.
The woman behind the counter
Talked endlessly on; there was no difference I could see
Between us, so I never asked.

                              The place in Montana
Was the *Greasy Grass* where Custer & the Seventh
    Cavalry fell,
A last important victory for the tribes. We had been
    driving
All day, hypnotized, & when we got out to enter
The small, flat American tourist center we began to
    argue,
And later, walking between the dry grass & reading
    plaques,
My wife made an ironic comment: I believe it hurt the land, not
Intentionally; it was only meant to hold us apart.
Later I read of Benteen & Ross & those who escaped,
But what I felt then was final: lying down, face
Against the warm side of a horse, & feeling the lulls
    endlessly,
The silences just before death. The place might stand for
    death,

Every loss rejoined in a wide place;
Or it is rest, as it was after the long drive,
Nothing for miles but grass, a long valley to the south
& living in history. Or it is just a way of living
Gone, like our own, every moment.
Because what I have to do daily & what is done to me
Are a number of small indignities, I have to trust that
Many things we all say to each other are not intentional,
That every indirect word will accumulate
Over the earth, & now, when we may be approaching
Something final, it seems important not to hurt the land.

American Landscape with Clouds & a Zoo

You can be walking along the beach
Of a quaint Northwestern coastal town
On the one hand the great Pacific Ocean
Held placid, restless, in the Sound
When it comes over: like those immense,
Woollen-gray clouds layer upon layer,
That pour from their Pacific composure
Suddenly troubled, moving, troubling,
Roaring easterly overhead for the inland.
America is in trouble & you're too
Fucked-up to even understand, buy it.
Is America fucked-up because it understands
Itself only too well as you do you?
Every time your girlfriend chucks you
A lusciously coy smile, you're beside
Yourself like a sailboat & every time
You think happiness is just like this,
Forever, you're fooled, like a kid.

America, I'm glad I'm hardly you,
I've got myself to think about.
In my zone is a fairly large zoo,
Plenty of room to walk around; shade,
& the shade that is increasingly, bitterly,
Called shadow. Of animals there are but 2,
Arranged in unpredictable cadence & sequence.
One is the renowned leopard of the snow:
Lazy, humorous, speckled pepper a bit—
Like the wren that flies from shadow to cage
To shade to shadow. When I mistakenly
Awaken at night, I dread both the darkness
& the inevitable increasingly querulous
Birdsong of the inevitable increasingly
Wide stun of light. Everything
Is too brief, eternal, stable, unpredictable.
Everything always says, I'm all there is
Forever, chum, just see it my way, & I do.

Homage to Robert Bresson

    Spaces await their people.
An alabaster row of public urinals.
    An empty theater. A table,
Chairs, an oak door, heavily grained,
    Brass knob turning & who
Shall enter, already lost forever

    In their lives? Now
Will a soul reveal its human face,
    Secret luminous flesh,
& because the soul is speechless
    There will be little talk,
Better revealed in this single plate

Set like a day-moon or
Lidless eye before its chair.
    Who sits shall eat, because
It is important to stay alive, to
    Bear the soul's countenance
Down into the streets, their traffic,

    Its endless movement. Here
A young priest, shaken, prays to give
    False solace to the dying;
A girl, too young, casually prepares
    To drown. Why are these
Forsaken, too long in anguish?

    Why does the tree bear leaves,
The water bear downward into the earth?
    This is the law, the rest
A commentary. She takes off her clothes,
    Folding them. He enters
A room. Though nothing can be done,

    They are not resigned.

Falling in Love

1.

The bird on the wire was an accident.
October, a kingdom. Then rains came

&, attendant, your short, thick hair,
A recent harvest, like oranges, pungent.

Singular the zoo, its late collection of wonders:
Discreet plumage, rounded shoulders:

& how do you like my valentine derrière?
I have always enjoyed the movies.

Dodging traffic, hand-in-hand,
Like woolly Parisian lapdogs or lovers,

Gaze: *imbecile lunaire.*

2.

Abrupt & charming mover,
Look how the swallows dart, loop, twine

& intertwine, a passing
Glance in the broad blue sky.

Hilarious sparrows. Cricket & music & faucet:
Our nightly counterpoint.

Vivaldi's viola, Fauré's flute,
A laughing fit,

Warm glove of your vagina,
I, the aggressor—pointed & slightly confused—

Abrupt & charming mover.

3.

Yet even as you now beside me lie breathing,
How well I do not remember what brought us here,

It is not given: the bird on the wire,
Late leafy breath of October—

Not with enough precision.
The dusky gourdlike eggplant

We will batter & fry come morning
Adorns the kitchen table,

A little shade of vegetable contemplation.
I think it is lonely.

I think it would like you to awaken.

The Secret of Poetry

When I was lonely, I thought of death.
When I thought of death I was lonely.

I suppose this error will continue.
I shall enter each gray morning

Delighted by frost, which is death,
& the trees that stand alone in mist.

When I met my wife I was lonely.
Our child in her body is lonely.

I suppose this error will go on & on.
Mornings I kiss my wife's cold lips,

Nights her body, dripping with mist.
This is the error that fascinates.

I suppose you are secretly lonely,
Thinking of death, thinking of love.

I'd like, please, to leave on your sill
Just one cold flower, whose beauty

Would leave you inconsolable all day.
The secret of poetry is cruelty.

Refusals

Sometimes we get down to loneliness
& poetry is just talking about things.
In the wake of those graceful verses,
Those boats loaded with spiced meat & jewels,
Is a silence meant to kill.

                    So you talk
About death; you expel it,
The sweets of dioxide, into the air.
And driving all night, in silence,
You see it flying by.

Is it sweet, that you love it so? You're not
A poor bastard yet; you give some affection . . .
Like alms, or smooth as cheese.

And you still love the loneliness in marriage:
Refusals of sex & shared meals, frustrated
Appetites, for which you slam a door.
For sex should retain its adolescent shyness,
Shouldn't it?
                Or better to meet at sea,
Two dark gunboats that thump & shoot fire
All night, trying hard not to win.

These refusals begin to look like courage.
You're trying hard not to give in.

But you can't come down from yourself;
You wouldn't if you could.

So you end up speechless, writing it down:
That tapping all night is yourself.
    Mornings you wake up listless;
How could you choose this life, & how
Among friends, deny kindness? You keep your eye
At death—or death's abyss;
You never choose to drop.

Sometimes you refuse to put up with yourself
But you go on talking,
Thinking, maneuvering
Over the dark & chartless waters
& under mysterious orders not to come in.

The Milky Way

When I was a boy, the Milky Way
    Floated just over the City
Of Boston, so I was lucky to live
    In that place, that
House where my father lathered
    His face & like the moon
Went out, came back, walking
    Winter nights beneath
The Milky Way. Few thoughts,
    Few fears, a way of
Sleeping through the night.

    When my son lay sewn
To the sheets, adrift in his
    Diabetic coma among
The blown, seductive stars,
    I could not think of
Anything to say, for he was
    Not anywhere nearby.

He said *Papa* & came back.
   Tonight, in his play
He captains a sleek starship
   Toward the Milky Way.

When I was a boy, the City of
   Boston lay miles away
Within our sight. Evenings we
   Set our chairs upon
The lawn & talked. Few thoughts,
   A way of watching until
Dark. Then as our small wickers
   Floated through the night
I wished I might be taken away
   To live forever in that
Distant City made wholly of light.

David Baker

David Baker was born in 1954 in Bangor, Maine. He received a Ph.D. from the University of Utah, where from 1980 to 1983 he served as poetry editor and editor-in-chief of *Quarterly West*. His first book of poems, *Laws of the Land*, was published by Ahsahta Press in 1981; *Summer Sleep*, a chapbook, appeared in 1984, and his second book, *Haunts*, was published in 1985 by Cleveland State. He has served as Bridgman Scholar of Poetry at Bread Loaf, has taught at Kenyon College, and presently teaches at Denison University.

Eugene Dwyer

Caves

Deep in these Ozark hills, dark-limbed
    trees thinning with each toss
  of wind, the brush dying
brown and stiff, the caves become visible, even
    frequent, appearing
  like sunken mushrooms in the hillside.
But it is not spring here, and nothing's growing
    where the frost has already
  bitten the ground dry: I feel, climbing
this slope, the tentative shift of shale
    beneath my feet—feel,
  pulling myself up by vine and trunk,
these very roots ready to tear loose, give way.

Standing at the entrance to one, finally,
    is no different. The ground
  going in is bare, clawed with prints
of coon, patted flat as rock, slick with seepage,

and leads uncertainly
into darkness, a passage too narrow
and low for myself. So I bow back out and move
    laterally along the hill-face
  where I can see as many as
half a dozen more of those same dim openings.
    Who knows, perhaps
  this whole hill, its sides pocked
with tiny caves, is hollow, one huge cavern,

and I am standing on it. There could be
    beneath my feet, in fact,
  another kind of world, darker,
not warmed by this sun, but by a timeless seeping
    of heat from the heart
  of the earth. Its wind would have to be
slight, stirred only by a bat, the silent song
    of its wings swooping up
  some even more sightless insect
in that fine membrane of tail, or dropping
    to the level of black
  water: a still pool, fish with eyes
grown skin-covered, the echo of oceans, faint.

A fine stream of pebbles plunges away now
    at my step. It falls
  in a rush of dust down the hillside,
then is gone. A woodpecker knocks at a tree, far away,
    though insistent as some vague
  pulse. The world here remakes itself
slowly. It must be the same down there: the persistent
    molding of rock, the young
  bats nosing the breasts of their mothers.
Or those blind salamanders I've heard about—larva-
    white and eyeless, their heads as
  blunt as hammers—stumbling,
falling, no less, yet surely no more, than I.

Running the River Lines

For Tim Gaines

Tonight, on a bank line strung
for catfish, a crawdad hooked through the tail
and dangled scarcely an inch
in the murky water, we catch a loon.

It must have seen our bait, scouting
overhead for something to eat, a school of minnows
or a washed-up mussel to pick apart,
and somehow snagged itself. No wonder

we haven't caught any fish,
the way it flaps there splashing and crying
its hideous cry, hurt
by the small hook at the corner of its beak

but more utterly amazed
that its wings will not bear it away from the bank.
It shrieks and splashes as we draw close,
straining against the willow pole

until it finally rips itself loose, beats its way
low over the water,
lifting at last, disappearing
into the depth of the river evening,

its cry still strung between us like a fine line.

The Wrecker Driver Foresees
Your Death

I DON'T DRIVE FOR PLEASURE ANYMORE

If you walked past the lot on any good Sunday,
stopped to stare, and jays were
flying any way you turned
like blue flowers
tossed up to the wind and rolled over,
so light they never fell,
and the air was fruity with fresh-mown grass,

you could never know the horror of it.
Looking at the rows of cars wrinkled
like wads of paper,
windshields webbed with cracks,
oil still oozing from the fresh ones
hauled in the night before, you still could
not believe the pain. You would try to

hear them collide, perhaps, and might even
convince yourself you could.
You might see the black well of night
crossed with lights flashing
in your mind, or imagine yourself pushing
a stuck door to help the dying
woman crying for you, holding up her damp stub,

the smell of singed hair thick
as honeysuckle, and far sweeter.
For that moment you would stand there
blackhearted, scared of your own mind,
the distant bells and slow
Sunday wind barely discernible,
the birds descending with their shadows,

and you would turn to go, scuffing
through the cut grass, your shoes slick with it.

You would go on like that
swearing to be more careful in your life—
swearing never to drive again,
or never to be so close to people they might die
weeping in your arms, or you in theirs,

each of these a promise you could never keep.

8-Ball at the Twilite

For Ed Byrne

The team of Budweiser horses
circling the clock above the bar
must have run a thousand miles already tonight.
What a great place they must want to go,
to work so hard in the smoky air. They've kept on running
though our game fell apart, though the music turned
bad, even though the cowboys at the corner booth
slugged it out over a halter-
topped waitress and had to leave.

It's late now and we should go too.
But we've got one more quarter on the table-edge,
pressing our luck, and half a pitcher
still cool enough to drink.
Connie Francis may say she loves us, if we stay.
So we pass the nub of chalk between us again,
rubbing the last of it over our tips
as a new rack of balls explodes,
running hard for the far green corners.

Peter Balakian

John Hubbard

Peter Balakian was born in 1951 in Teaneck, New Jersey. He received his B.A. from Bucknell University and his Ph.D. from Brown University. He is the author of two books of poetry, *Father Fisheye* (1979) and *Sad Days of Light* (1983), both from Sheep Meadow Press. He teaches at Colgate University.

Father Fisheye

The sun is gray and without a rim,
what light there is the water catches and keeps.
Fishmongers bear the crossed keys of the saint
on their arms. St. Christopher lived on the gulf
and sang for the kingfish when the winds left,
let his arms out from their joints when the old men
left in the dark with their trawl.

Father Fisheye, I come here to the rocks where the fires
are all ash, where the dockmen have disappeared
for the day of Gennaro and the boys with straw hats
have left with their fathers' empty creel and sandworms
in their pockets, where old men still sit staring
at the short ripples that go white at their feet.

I come to this inlet for eels and crabs
for gangs of minnows that move like a long tail
and turn silver in the gray sun.
Father Fisheye, the air is still, trees motionless
the sky touches my chest.
The sun is lost in the gray dusk water, gone into gullets
of fishes that wander slowly out to the far waves.

Jersey Bait Shack

If I can find this place near-abandoned
in early fall with its weather-bitten shingles
still the grainy color of ash and its roof
warping from the etching spray,
the only window boarded up—

but still there is a secret side door
that now in September unswells,
and if I work the latch just right
I'll find the dark calm inner air
growing toward my face.

Into a room where barrels—once
filled with clams, chubs, crab-ends,
grassy flags of minnow, night crawlers,
sand worms, squid-bits purple and brown—
are now dark holes reeking of the deep,
I come and search on hands and knees—

the overwhelming stink of aftermath:
all these creatures from the slime,
which in my arms, on my line could
lure and sniff and find the simple swimming
fish—the ghostly gaze of its eyes
gliding in the adoring tide.

Now in the dark salty air of the shack
the seaweed, dry and black in piles,
is stinking sweet and telling me
how long it waits to soak beneath the bait.

Homage to Hart Crane

This morning kelp is drying on the dockside,
women leave the laundromat early.
I walk the low bank
in the low air
and feel the long bones in the river's belly
hiss in the warming water.
How many warmings of current wound through
your eyes Hart Crane?
This morning your dry rib
passes this juncture of ocean and calm.
Here where there's no bridge
and gulls roost on tied barges
and skim the black harbor for carp,
your marrow goes the way of slow mollusks.

The sun moves
in a steady progression upwards
to a point
for a fraction of light
before it starts to fall
and here, Hart Crane

even the falling warehouses
look like cathedrals for a moment.

This morning a drunken fisherman
wakes on cinder with dead bait in his hand,
not knowing the day of week
the month or year,
not knowing anything
but the spot he sees the sun in,
the noon wind riveting his ribs.

It's a good thing, Hart Crane
that I'm baitless and hookless
that I leave the bay without a fish,
my net shredded and hanging on the old post at the South Dock.
It's a good thing my girl took the first train south
and that this noon I unwrap my sandwich alone
under the empty elm, with three birds singing in my ears
and the cats meowing over empty clam shells and shrimp husks.

What luck Hart Crane
that I came this morning to feel your one bone
dragging along the bottom
just as the sun was climbing to the top
and the fisherman was waking,
just as the tugs were disappearing
and the barges were settling in
to the winter lapping of the harbor,
just as the cod heads were softening around the eye
so the gulls could snap them up.

In the Turkish Ward

(in memoriam: my grandfather
Diran Balakian, 1877–1939)

1.

Over my head the fan moves slowly.
Ceiling lights flicker and dizz.
The corridor door opens and closes,
stirs the medicinal vapors which hang
all night over these damp bodies;
the air settles on everything. All week
I've wrapped heads, arms, numb legs,
the ointment on my hands is red.
I smell the Turkish boots in the hall,
piles of brown canvas pants.

2.

They give me nothing—not bread, tea.
The guards leer at me when I come and go.
"When they're asleep and you're waiting
for the day, you'll want some sweet—
small plums and figs." I should listen
to my wife. They stare at me,
these wounded, swelling in their sleep.
An Armenian doctor conscripted in
the Turkish army, "our only way to stay
alive," my wife reminds me in my sleep.

3.

For three days the sirocco slows
over the channel, the iridescent dirty water.
Boats unload. All day I wandered market
to square, the smell of carbolic trailing me.

Fruit gone to sear: strawberries dead-ripe,
slit currants, the sodden heads of melons
I could bandage with my hands. The cores,
rind, pits along the wharf . . . a man's eyes,
a dead man's eyes. If I could find some
fine dyed silk for my daughter . . .

4.

East and West, the great circle propped
on two half-hemispheres, Sophia.
Hagia Sophia. The water might well leak
into what used to be the apse and rise
along the whitewashed tiles—disclose
the robes translucent, mute eyes,
glittering acanthus. O unhealthy tide,
grout the cherubim lost in the dome.
This sea should rise into the basilica
of light pouring each day from the open eye
upon the backs of the groaning in prayer.

5.

Yesterday, bloody news from my friend,
the poet, Siamanto. I must know what I believe.
"The Ottoman sticks deeper in the heartland:
all night; screaming infants lit like candles,
the wheat full of body parts and clothes.
The riverside is Armenia wafted by a soundless
desert air. This firmament is blind . . .
shrieking in the dawn, Mother, one fell swoop,
the herds become debris, hills a heap of flesh.
What leaks from the midnight air of Anatolia,
my good friend, I'm too weak to say."

6.

I'm hemmed here. The Allies like sump
in the harbor. If I could shake one British
Admiral, he'd not believe this tale—
a hundred miles from his bow. Here, a poet's
words, "Armenia is a scarlet herb, a walking
shadow." Each letter he says, "look upon your
surgeon's skill and your conscription
as a blessing, we need you in the city
to help us with night passage out."

7.

Another day of waste. Even at this dull night-
hour I smell the sun inland. These cots,
pillows, sheets of phlegm, sallow heads.
"Father, what are you, your hands; each night
in the Sultan's den . . . men whose teeth
fall apart with our flesh. Tonight
who knows, have I a cousin left?" Each night
dear daughter, I write this letter in my head

in the brown dawn, the poet's voice—a cat's
out on the steppe . . . I need a cistern
for my yellow bile. "Stay close to the docks . . .
three men, a family, to Athens, Marseilles."

Sweet one, what's fate—to hold arms
by healing, force my blood to pitch
because to face each night here
is not to know whose blood is whose.

8.

There are sacred secrets, Hippocrates,
you could not dream of. What is Law in
my Art; my speculum, stethoscope, the mirror

banded to my head; if these instruments
vanished, would I let the dying go?
Would my hands dissolve?

Good Moor, Christian Moor, unhappy Moor,
what course led you to this chidden sea.
What dog set your heart upon itself;
in this room your wife's tears are mere water.

If my daughter knew how my hands tremor,
how a scant tendon keeps my heart from
dropping through my bottom . . . in this hour

the heavy air settles on the wharf and windows,
close to my head, I hear the whole town . . .
nothing—plashing water, wind in the moorings.

Siamanto, Armenian poet (1878–1915), was among the Armenian intellectuals killed
by Turkish security agents at the beginning of the genocide committed by the Turkish
government against the Armenians in which almost two million Armenians perished.
His last book of poems, *Bloody News from My Friend*, was based on his correspondence
with my grandfather.

John Bensko

Rosemary Bensko

John Bensko was born in Birmingham, Alabama, in 1949. He holds degrees in mathematics and creative writing from the University of Alabama, and he has taught at the University of Alabama and at Old Dominion University. His first book of poetry, *Green Soldiers* (1981), was awarded the 1980 Yale Series of Younger Poets Award. He is currently a university Fellow at Florida State University.

Mowing the Lawn

Saturday morning,
lying on my couch, I think:
a boy like an angel will save me.

He comes up the hill on a ten-speed bike,
dragging his mower. He parks them
and comes up the walk to the door.
Looking through the peephole
I see the small, freckled face . . .

if it were that easy. If the boy,
the angel that he could be,
weren't just like us, worrying

about the time, the wear and tear, the cost,
we could negotiate our dreams:
one lying on the couch;
the other following a new,
self-propelled mower
into an even greater machine.
A Honda? A Corvette? God knows . . .

Our ways part. From his bright,
perfect lawn my neighbor scowls
at the boy's leavings, at the shaggy
threat of windblown seeds.

But we're all just alike.
On the couch we lie secure
in the knowledge. We imagine
the well-manicured lawn
spreads in all directions.

Mail Call

He expects the old names to return
in the haze of rain through the garden trees
interrupted by his wife setting down coffee
with the morning mail. Even when rain
smears their letters to purple and green, he knows

who they are. The rain stops. The sun is bright.
He is walking down the trench to collect the mail.
All is well. The smells of food and coffee are
nearly enough to cover the rot. The boys
mark their postcards. "I am fine" means

I am at the front. Those at home never understand.
He wants to take the cards and erase them.

A shout, a machine gun, the sounds of feet
across the wire almost on him.
He jumps to the light and scans the shattered trees.

The trees are blasted. The brick wall of the garden
is an enemy plan, a confusion, a reminder of home.
Then it's years later and he is looking beyond it
into the sun. For a moment the pain and blindness
bring together the two codes: the one

his wife sees, the other in which all life
is point blank, the enemy guns,
the bright sun on the day of battle
and postcards home for the dead,
the instinct of their hands to block out pain.

A Veteran of the Great War

It all seems like today: he returns
in the same uniform, on the same trolley,
to the house where his aunt
stepping out into the hallway, her blouse
open to the navel, is the woman he once
had dreams about. Your father is dead
she tells him. He watches her red lips harden
and drops his bag. He listens to himself
wheezing on the steps, past the figures
his father carved into the banister,
past the old photographs,
and into the bedroom. The green walls
remind him first of his father; then
a green cloud drifts around him,
loosing the insides of his body, the chlorine
and the trenches and the men scrambling for their masks.

He wakes screaming and finds a hand
pressed over his face. It is not the sergeant's hand.

His aunt gives him some water. He wants
to hold her, to hold someone
who feels warm and can make him believe
the six months he has are six months to live.
She kisses him. In the Twenties
and the Thirties, and the Sixties
when he has made his six months
into a lifetime, he remembers
her shade of red. He watches her
move through the green room
and out. A day later her bags are packed.
So this is how it ends, he says.

Later, he confuses his story. Two friends
from the Great War were found in the Fifties,
the two skeletons huddled in the buried trench,
masks in place, their hands over their ears.
One, one of them, he says, is her.
I had an aunt in the Great War, he says.

Each night at dusk if the air is cooler and wet
he comes wheezing dry as a cicada
down the steps and past where she stood
when he dropped his bag: earlier in the day, he thinks,
before his father lighted the porch lamps.
He stares into the warm glow.
His lungs are taking in the wet air.
Yellow drops he coughs into his hand.
He calls together the neighborhood children
and tells them stories in which every day
is today. The portraits on the stairs, the soldiers,
are real people; they are children who believe
like he does, in today, and today, and today.

The Night-Blooming Cactus

This has little to do with the flower
except for a man on the far side of the room
who has been watching it all night.
To concentrate on it from a distance
helps him understand the dark-haired girl
asleep on the far side of town.

In his meditation he has been
the plant which blooms in the night desert.
He is the survivor in a house
of dead relatives. The victim
of friends and lovers. *They* knew
he would always be there. The flower
is motionless. It will always be

a flower and nothing else, except for the man
who draws it in:
a part of himself which cares
for nothing. The girl might be on the verge
of unfolding a new face
and she would still mean nothing.
He tries to believe what he sees in her.

So the love and the meditation
go on, turning a white sheet and a girl
into a night-blooming cactus.
The cactus unfolds to explain something:
he sees it take on colors,
not of meaning, real colors which mean absolutely
nothing. And that, he understands, is what she feels.

Chana Bloch

Chana Bloch was born in the Bronx, New York, in 1940. She holds a B.A. from Cornell, an M.A. from Brandeis, and a Ph.D. from the University of California. Her first book of poetry, *The Secrets of the Tribe* (1981), was published by Sheep Meadow Press. She is also the author of *Spelling the Word: George Herbert and the Bible* (1985) and the translator of *A Dress of Fire: Selected Poems of Dahlia Ravikovitch* (1978). She has won awards for both her poetry and her translations. She teaches at Mills College.

Layle Silbert

A Life

She sinks
into the tub of herself
up to the neck,
an available warmth.

With one hand I can start her.
It's my pain.
Don't tell me what to do.
I was young too.

Once I stood on the table
to be her size.

She brushed my hair with her fingers,
stroking it like fur.

Damp, crumpled,
now she is mine.
I can stuff her into my pocket
and carry her home.

So this is America, she says
to the closet, a life
in camphor
with no one to talk to.

And in that darkness the fox-heads,
sharp-nosed,
amber-eyed,
dreaming her dreams.

Goodbye

For Martin Fincke

The repairman in the doorway,
yellow hard-hat, scrub-jacket: *Goodbye.*
Name flashed on a plastic card.
He slips back into his life with
a fence around it.
Draped windows. Not mine.

Lately I am so hard
people slide off me forever.

This emptiness sharpens me.
Light prints itself on the plate of memory,
acid on metal.

It's twenty years since we invented, you and I,
a ritual for leaving.
Back to back in the city street at noon
we walked five paces apart, and were swallowed up
by our lives.

When they said, If you eat this fruit
you will die,
they didn't mean right away.

Deer in the Bush

They come down
in the mornings, sniff
the green edges of our lives,
munch the hydrangeas.

Shadows let them.
They step
in a pool of shade,
their legs spindly as twigs,

inquisitively
nosing our flowers,
nudging us out on the porch
to watch them

watch us for a sign.
They do not blink.
They measure our moving towards them
and won't be fooled,

letting their pleasure wilt on the bush
till they can be sure of us.
Nothing between us now but
wood and air. Wait,

I can see a buck
up on his hind legs, wrestling a
branch down, his velvet mouth
dripping berries.

He's at home in our patch of seasons
like an old uncle
who comes when he pleases, and keeps
the secrets of the tribe.

The Death of the Bronx

Summer hangs
between the gray buildings.
The old ladies are out
rocking the heat away.
The bad boys are throwing stones.
Time to go home for supper.

The sidewalk flashed
when I jumped over the cracks
for luck.
All the time thinking
the mothers
forget what it's like.

Startled, my mother waits
under the hump she's growing.
Why me? she asks.
The love letters
stiffen in her hands.
Look how I was loved, she says.

When I approach she holds me
up to the light
to count my fingers and toes.

Again she sees I am perfect.
Her shame says
You are not my child.

They have come for the furniture,
the sofa with its blue leaves
and the coffin
wheeled through the double doors.
The bald man keeps asking
How old was he.

At sundown we recite
God of mercy
Renew our youth like the eagle's
and we eat
the last of the honeycake
behind the drapes.

Michael Blumenthal

Cynthia Curtner

Michael Blumenthal was born in 1949. He holds a B.A. in philosophy from S.U.N.Y. at Binghamton and a J.D. from Cornell University Law School. His first book, *Sympathetic Magic*, was the winner of the 1980 Water Mark Poets of North America First Book Award. *Days We Would Rather Know* (1984) was published by The Viking Press, and *Laps* (1984) was published by the University of Massachusetts Press and awarded the Juniper Prize. Among his other awards is a fellowship from the National Endowment for the Arts. He is currently Briggs-Copeland lecturer in poetry at Harvard University.

Mushroom Hunting in Late August, Peterborough, N.H.

The drosophila wing of the morning moon
is still in the heavens
when, looking for the lesson in nature
we are always looking for, I walk,
basket in hand, through the damp woods,
parting the secretive ferns, twisting
my thin body among the asters and loosestrife,
checking beneath the stones and stumps
as I plunder the pine-needled floor
for the chanterelles and puffballs.

It is so much like life, which is why
I love it: the delectable and the deadly
so resembling each other, the sexual rise
of the false morel a mere flirtation,
and the sweet viscosity we'd like to swim in
an elegy to movement. Holding a knife
in my right hand, I work from the base,
cutting beneath the stipe, recording
in my small book the particulars
that separate delicacy from demise, hallucination
from the smaller contentments of mere vision.

Finally, placing each in its own small bag
and into my basket, I wend my way back
through the mossy woods to my soft chair,
to the embering fire where, with my book
and my magnifying glass, I start to separate,
because separating is, in the end, what this
is about: the doubtful from the certain,
the brief scintillations of beauty
from the urge for survival. Some, in fact,
are so beautiful I would like, this very moment,
to taste them: to feel the pale, red flesh
and feathery gills take on their sexual softness
beneath my tongue, but I am thinking again
of what a friend's psychiatrist said about women:
*"Just because they're beautiful and you're hungry,
doesn't mean you have to eat all of them."*

Until at last, what began as a large harvest
is merely a small bundle of certainty and safety.
And I sit there with my three piles of caps
and stems, of torn gills and the bruised flesh
of holiness and nature. Loving what little
I know for certain, I gather
the smallest pile toward me. *Oh life,*
I say to myself, *so this is what you are.*
I stumble out into the sunlight.
I pucker my lips at the morning moon.

And I eat.

Squid

So this is love:

How you grimace at the sight
of these fish; how I pull
(forefinger, then thumb)
the fins and tails from the heads,
slice the tentacles from the accusing eyes.

And then how I pile the silvery ink sacs
into the sieve like old fillings, heap
the entrails and eyes on a towel in the corner;
and how you sauté the onions and garlic,
how they turn soft and transparent, lovely
in their own way, and how you turn to me
and say, simply, *isn't this fun, isn't it?*

And something tells me this all has to do
with love, perhaps even more than lust
or happiness have to do with love:
How the fins slip easily from the tails,
how I peel the membranes from the fins
and cones like a man peeling his body
from a woman after love, how these
ugly squid diminish in grotesqueness
and all nausea reduces, finally, to a hunger
for what is naked and approachable,

tangible and delicious.

Today I Am Envying
the Glorious Mexicans

Today I am envying the glorious Mexicans,
who are not afraid to sit by the highway
in the late afternoons, sipping tequila
and napping beneath their wide sombreros
beside the unambitious cactus. Today
I am envying the sweet *chaparita* who waits
for her lover's banjo in the drunken moonlight
and practices her fingers against the soft tortilla.
Today I am envying the green whiskers of God
that protrude through the ground and we call:
grass. Why, today is so lovely I even envy
the singing dead with their proximity to earth
and genitals of flowers. O Lord, I don't
want to die yet, I just want to emulate
the beautiful purposelessness of the flowers
and Mexicans! I want to be the perfect madman,
without remorse or metaphor, without reflection.
I want to sit here babbling to myself about lust
and disobedience until it kills me, so I can join
the chorus of the singing dead and the sleeping
Mexicans beside the wild chrysanthemums—
beside the rose, the sangría and the happy earth.

In Assisi

This morning, in Assisi, I woke
and looked into my wife's face
and thought of Saint Francis:
how he explained to Brother Leo
that Perfect Joy is only on the Cross,
how he told him that, if they should come

to the Convent of Saint Mary of the Angels,
soaked with rain and frozen by the cold
and soiled with mud and suffering
from hunger, and if they should knock
on the gates and a porter should come out
and beat them over the head with a knotty club
and throw them down into the mud and snow
and cover their bodies with wounds, only then
might they know Perfect Joy. And I thought
of how Saint Anthony converted the heretics
by talking to the fishes, and of how blood flowed
from a picture of Saint Francis's stigmata,
and of the beautiful death of Brother Bernard.
And I looked again into my wife's lovely eyes,
both green and grey at once in the Umbrian light,
and swore to myself, rolling over beside her,
that I would never be a man who flings his body
like dirt against the thorns, that I would never
lie down to sleep on a bed of stone; that,
if I were ever fit to preach to the birds,
I would sing to them in praise of their wings,
I would urge them to fly off in all directions
at once, over the trees and the hills and
the lustful bodies of small animals. And this
is how it was this morning, when—after
making love in the large bed—we walked
through the Porta dei Cappuccini toward the
Eremo delle Carceri, where Saint Francis
is said to have blessed the birds, and past
the thousand-year-old oak, now supported
by steel bars, and watched the white doves
kiss atop the stone balustrade. And I looked
at my wife, and praised her body and my body
and all the bodies of this earth for what pleasure
they can give. And I bathed my eyes in salt,
as Saint Francis did, for the little love we find
and how we cling to it and how, once we find it,
we live constantly in dread of losing it, as
the Buddhists say. And I blessed this life
once more for what it has given me, and

for what it has failed to give me, and will
fail again tomorrow. And I held my wife
in these dust-driven arms and spoke to her
in this one language I know so well: the old oak
creaking in the blessed air, the pious fishes
singing in the stream, this all I know of Perfect Joy,
and all the white doves kissing in its name.

David Bottoms

David Bottoms was born in Canton, Georgia, in 1949. He holds a B.A. from Mercer University, an M.A. from West Georgia College, and a Ph.D. from Florida State University. His first book, *Shooting Rats at the Bibb County Dump*, was chosen by Robert Penn Warren as winner of the 1979 Walt Whitman Award of the Academy of American Poets, and was published by William Morrow and Company in 1980. His second book, *In a U-Haul North of Damascus*, was published by William Morrow in 1983. He teaches at Georgia State University.

Jon Coppelman

Under the Boathouse

Out of my clothes, I ran past the boathouse
to the edge of the dock
and stood before the naked silence of the lake,
on the drive behind me, my wife
rattling keys, calling for help with the grill,
the groceries wedged into the trunk.
Near the tail end of her voice, I sprang
from the homemade board, bent body
like a hinge, and speared the surface,
cut through water I would not open my eyes in,
to hear the junked depth pop in both ears
as my right hand dug into silt and mud,
my left clawed around a pain.

In a fog of rust I opened my eyes to see
what had me, and couldn't, but knew
the fire in my hand and the weight of the thing
holding me under, knew the shock of all
things caught by the unknown
as I kicked off the bottom like a frog,
my limbs doing fearfully strange strokes,
lungs collapsed in a confusion of bubbles,
all air rising back to its element.
I flailed after it, rose toward the bubbles
breaking on light, then felt down my arm
a tug running from a taut line.
Halfway between the bottom of the lake
and the bottom of the sky, I hung like a buoy
on a short rope, an effigy
flown in an underwater parade,
and imagined myself hanging there forever,
a curiosity among fishes, a bait hanging up
instead of down. In the lung-ache,
in the loud pulsing of the temples, what gave first
was something in my head, a burst
of colors like the blind see, and I saw
against the surface a shadow like an angel
quivering in a dead-man's float,
then a shower of plastic knives and forks
spilling past me in the lightened water, a can
of barbequed beans, a bottle of A.1., napkins
drifting down like white leaves,
heavenly litter from the world I struggled toward.
What gave then was something on the other end,
and my hand rose on its own and touched my face.
Into the splintered light under the boathouse,
the loved, suffocating air hovering over the lake,
the cry of my wife leaning dangerously
over the dock, empty grocery bags at her feet,
I bobbed with a hook through the palm of my hand.

Sign for My Father,
Who Stressed the Bunt

On the rough diamond,
the hand-cut field below the dog lot and barn,
we rehearsed the strict technique
of bunting. I watched from the infield,
the mound, the backstop
as your left hand climbed the bat, your legs
and shoulders squared toward the pitcher.
You could drop it like a seed
down either base line. I admired your style,
but not enough to take my eyes off the bank
that served as our center-field fence.

Years passed, three leagues of organized ball,
no few lives. I could homer
into the garden beyond the bank,
into the left-field lot of Carmichael Motors,
and still you stressed the same technique,
the crouch and spring, the lead arm absorbing
just enough impact. That whole tiresome pitch
about basics never changing,
and I never learned what you were laying down.

Like a hand brushed across the bill of a cap,
let this be the sign
I'm getting a grip on the sacrifice.

The Copperhead

A dwarfed limb
or a fist-thick vine, he lay stretched
across a dead oak fallen into the water.

I saw him when I cast my lure
toward a cluster of stumps near the half-buried trunk,
then pulled the boat to the edge of the limbs.
One ripple ran up his back like the tail
of a wake,
and he lay still again, dark and patterned,
large on years of frogs and rats.

I worked the lure around the brush,
oak and poplar stumps rising out of the water
like the ruins of an old pier,
and watched his spade head shift on the dry bark.
But no bass struck
so I laid the rod across the floor of the boat,
sat for a long time watching the shadows
make him a part of the tree,
and wanted more than once to drift into the shaded water,
pull myself down a fallen branch toward the trunk
where he lay quiet and dangerous and unafraid,
all spine and nerve.

Wrestling Angels

For J. and Diana Stege

With crowbars and drag chains
we walk tonight through a valley of tombs
where the only sounds are frogs in the reeds
and the river whispering at the foot of Rose Hill
that we have come to salvage from the dead.

Only the ironwork will bring us money,
ornamental sofas overlooking graves,
black-flowered fences planted in marble,
occasionally an urn or a bronze star.

But if there is time
we shatter the hourglasses,
slaughter lambs asleep on children's graves,
break the blades off stone scythes,
the marble strings on silent lyres.
Only the angels are here to stop us, and they have grown
too weak to wrestle.
We break their arms and leave them wingless
leaning over graves like old men lamenting their age.

In a U-Haul North of Damascus

1.

Lord, what are the sins
I have tried to leave behind me? The bad checks,
the workless days, the scotch bottles thrown across the fence
and into the woods, the cruelty of silence,
the cruelty of lies, the jealousy,
the indifference?

What are these on the scale of sin
or failure
that they should follow me through the streets of Columbus,
the moon-streaked fields between Benevolence
and Cuthbert where dwarfed cotton sparkles like pearls
on the shoulders of the road. What are these
that they should find me half-lost,
sick and sleepless
behind the wheel of this U-Haul truck parked in a field
    on Georgia 45
a few miles north of Damascus,
some makeshift rest stop for eighteen wheelers

where the long white arms of oaks slap across trailers
and headlights glare all night through a wall of pines?

2.

What was I thinking, Lord?
That for once I'd be in the driver's seat, a firm grip
on direction?

So the jon boat muscled up the ramp,
the Johnson outboard, the bent frame of the wrecked Harley
chained for so long to the back fence,
the scarred desk, the bookcases and books,
the mattress and box springs,
a broken turntable, a Pioneer amp, a pair
of three-way speakers, everything mine
I intended to keep. Everything else abandon.

But on the road from one state
to another, what is left behind nags back through the distance,
a last word rising to a scream, a salad bowl
shattering against a kitchen cabinet, china barbs
spiking my heel, blood trailed across the cream linoleum
like the bedsheet that morning long ago
just before I watched the future miscarried.

Jesus, could the irony be
that suffering forms a stronger bond than love?

3.

Now the sun
streaks the windshield with yellow and orange, heavy beads
of light drawing highways in the dew-cover.
I roll down the window and breathe the pine-air,
the after-scent of rain, and the far-off smell
of asphalt and diesel fumes.

But mostly pine and rain
as though the world really could be clean again.

Somewhere behind me,
miles behind me on a two-lane that streaks across
west Georgia, light is falling
through the windows of my half-empty house.
Lord, why am I thinking about this? And why should I care
so long after everything has fallen
to pain that the woman sleeping there should be sleeping alone?
Could I be just another sinner who needs to be blinded
before he can see? Lord, is it possible to fall
toward grace? Could I be moved
to believe in new beginnings? Could I be moved?

The Desk

Under the fire escape, crouched, one knee in cinders,
I pulled the ball-peen hammer from my belt,
cracked a square of window pane,
the gummed latch, and swung the window,
crawled through that stone hole into the boiler room
of Canton Elementary School, once Canton High,
where my father served three extra years
as star halfback and sprinter.
                              Behind a flashlight's
cane of light, I climbed a staircase almost a ladder
and found a door. On the second nudge of my shoulder,
it broke into a hallway dark as history,
at whose end lay the classroom I had studied
over and over in the deep obsession of memory.

I swept that room with my light—an empty blackboard,
a metal table, a half-globe lying on the floor
like a punctured basketball—then followed

that beam across the rows of desks,
the various catalogs of lovers, the lists
of all those who would and would not do what,
until it stopped on the corner desk of the back row,
and I saw again, after many years, the name
of my father, my name, carved deep into the oak top.

To gauge the depth I ran my finger across that scar,
and wondered at the dreams he must have lived
as his eyes ran back and forth
from the cinder yard below the window
to the empty practice field
to the blade of his pocket knife etching carefully
the long, angular lines of his name,
the dreams he must have laid out one behind another
like yard lines, in the dull, pre-practice afternoons
of geography and civics, before he ever dreamed
of Savo Sound or Guadalcanal.
                                        In honor of dreams
I sank to my knees on the smooth, oiled floor,
and stood my flashlight on its end.
Half the yellow circle lit the underedge of the desk,
the other threw a half-moon on the ceiling,
and in that split light I tapped the hammer
easy up the overhang of the desk top. Nothing gave
but the wall's sharp echo, so I swung again,
and again harder, and harder still in half anger
rising to anger at the stubborn joint, losing all fear
of my first crime against the city, the county,
the state, whatever government claimed dominion,
until I had hammered up in the ringing dark
a salvo of crossfire, and on a frantic recoil glanced
the flashlight, the classroom spinning black
as a coma.
                    I've often pictured the face of the teacher
whose student first pointed to that topless desk,
the shock of a slow hand rising from the back row,
their eyes meeting over the question of absence.
I've wondered, too, if some low authority of the system
discovered that shattered window,

and finding no typewriters, no business machines,
no audio-visual gear missing, failed to account for it,
so let it pass as minor vandalism.
                                    I've heard nothing.
And rarely do I fret when I see that oak scar leaning
against my basement wall, though I wonder what it means
to own my father's name.

Sharon Bryan

Sharon Bryan was born in 1943. She received a B.A. from the University of Utah, an M.A. from Cornell University, and an M.F.A. from the University of Iowa. Her first book of poetry, *Salt Air* (1983), was published by Wesleyan University Press. Among her awards is a "Discovery"/*The Nation* award. She teaches at the University of Washington.

Carmen Matthews

Hollandaise

The sauce thickens. I add more butter,
slowly. Sometimes we drank the best wine
while we cooked for friends,
knowing nothing could go wrong,
the soufflé would rise, the custard set,
the cheese be ripe. We imagined
we were reckless but we were just happy,
and good at our work. The cookbook is firm:
It is safer not to go over two ounces
of butter for each egg yolk. I try to describe
to myself how we could have been safer,

what we exceeded. If the sauce "turns"
there are things to be done, steps
to be taken that are not miraculous,
that assume the failed ingredients,
that assume a willing suspension of despair.

Big Sheep Knocks You About

*I've shorn over two hunn'ert in a day, but big sheep
knocks you about. I used to go mad at it, twisting
and turning all night. Couldn't sleep after a rough
day with the sheep.*

1.

In town, in the foodshop, men are making sandwiches,
cutting bread, cutting meat, cutting onions. The essence of
all these mixes with grease on their aprons, and blood from
cut thumbs. When they wipe their faces at night it is to
remember the day. They are good at what they do, and
beautiful to watch: silver, flesh, silver, flesh.

2.

In the foodshop a boy with thick 15-year-old hands is trying
to help, but the bread breaks and mixes with the bits of meat
and sauce, though his hands move after theirs the way a
poem is said to be after the Greek. They laugh, knowing
they can teach him, and his hands go on rising and falling
like lungs.

The boy's hands on himself at night are surer, though
hurrying makes them clumsy, and shame that they should be

graceful at what they're doing. When his hands move over a
girl's body they are lost to him, so he dreams of sea skates
brushing coral. Of killing someone without meaning to. His
mother settling over his face like a pillow. Home he makes
himself come twice before he can sleep.

3.

And the boy's father dreams of England and Nettie leaning
fat against the wall with nothing on but her stockings, saying
Roll me 'round again, dearie. You know how I like it.

4.

One stinks of blood and grease, flinty dead cells of hooves.
Two always face each other in profile, in the Greek curls of
	their horns and snouts and lips.
Three form a wedge that comes to a point just out of sight
	behind you.
Four run earnestly bunched in the same direction.
Five are not a team. They are dumb, they jostle and bump.
Six keep to themselves, just, in the crowd, avoiding each
	other with the grace of passivity.
Seven is used only by people.
Eight is not the seeds of dissent, these are sheep.
Nine is not the beginnings of mathematics.
Ten is a congregation with no preacher.
So is eleven.
Twelve has an unbreachable shape of its own, like a fertilized
	egg,
but at thirteen the edges begin to buckle and scallop,
at fourteen the sheep mill and mutter, and the dust rises
	to their ankles.
Beyond this the only shape comes from fences and short
	grass, humans circling, sheep circling.

5.

In all the jokes it's the men who fuck sheep, drawn to the
puckery assholes, and it's perfectly natural that Black Bart's
girl is the wooliest. But when a woman dreams of sheep, it's
of the weight and thickness, its penis stiff along the sheep's
belly, steamy in the cold, its horns spiraling invisibly in the
    dark.

The story of Leda was begun by a woman: . . . settling over
me, like the sky, and making my tongue swell in my mouth
. . . And ended by a man: . . . . a bird, with air in its bones.
With eyes that see two things instead of one.

Corner Lot

My parents couldn't know, in 1950,
how little they cared for coaxing roses
and patchy lawns from baked clay,
so they asked that their first yard
be a corner lot. As they gingerly

paced the stakes and string
supposed to distinguish street from curb from
erstwhile lawn (as if the net
of latitude and longitude
had sagged to actual earth), they decided

the dowager box elder should be left
to shade the yard. When the houses
had risen their single stories
from the ground, in the bright colors
of separate countries, the tree tilted instead

at the edge of the curb, roots exposed
by workmen reluctant to slow down
for idiosyncrasy. The wind blew
each willow my mother planted
out of the ground, so that the lilac

and honeysuckle along the backyard fence
look like furniture drawn back
before a dance. Of two identical
juniper bushes, the one by the leaky tap
grew twice as high. At the side,

under my window (two parents, two
brothers; in that tiny house
I was the only one with a room to myself),
pale green pods of night-blooming lilies
spread thick as weeds until my mother

hated them and my father chopped and dug
them, but deep in summer I would wake
to their heavy scent and tiptoe outside
to kneel in the glare of the phosphorescent
white throats that could only last the night.

Lunch with Girl Scouts

*. . . the spirit intercedes . . . most eloquently on our
behalf . . .*

These ten-year-olds all want other names
than their own. I'm Heather, but call me
Laura, says the one who should have played
Lolita in the movie. Her lips are damp
and unbitten. My mother still has a bracelet
she made in camp, with her fantasy name,

Louise, in orange beads. Names can break
our hearts. I've been invited to lunch
with Girl Scouts, to talk to them about
poetry. They're braver than I am, to have gotten
this far. Longing for a uniform,
I spent three weeks as a Brownie. The leader
talked about fly-ups. Soon we would all
fly-up. This meant a plane ride,
or becoming an angel. Either way,
we might die. I quit, with nothing
to show for my torment but a cryptic
pin. The others flew-up—they were
promoted. Once more I'd misfigured
the language I loved. *Round John virgin,*
we sang at Christmas. And I believed
that if I rode my thick Schwinn down
the right alley in springtime, I'd be,
as the song promised, *out at the old
ball game.* There, in the stands, gulping
popcorn, cheering for the Bees. Today
I followed a map into the suburbs,
suddenly shy as I was as a child
but old as the teachers we considered
foreign countries. I begin to take hold
of their various names, but by lunchtime
I haven't said anything useful. My hostess
and I eat quiche, the girls spaghetti.
Pasghetti. They giggle. One says
a two-line poem, and another answers
with four. They're quoting a recent book
they've all read. Each recites
her favorite while the others bounce
on their hands. None of this
is for me. Somehow they've found
a long one they all know and are almost
shouting it in unison. They pull up
their socks without missing a beat,
spill out of the room like marbles.
I stare into my coffee. When was I last
so full of love? So innocent of error?

Nicholas Christopher

Nicholas Christopher was born in New York City in 1951. He was educated at Harvard College, and his first book of poems, *On Tour with Rita*, was published by Knopf in 1982. His second collection, *A Short History of the Island of Butterflies*, will be published by Knopf in 1986. He was awarded the Amy Lowell Travelling Scholarship for 1983.

John Garfield

The heat's on, dead wind shoots up
9th Avenue, flutters the T-shirt
On the convertible's antenna, lulls
The stragglers into Billy's Pool Parlour.
The city's last tough guy
Sidles down 44th Street,
Bumming a smoke, feinting a punch—
Used to show a good left, they say . . .
Later, hat doffed, fingers drumming,
He watches East River tugs
Link the bridges with foam;
Whatever left Brooklyn Harbor
In the last war died, or
Maybe is still out at sea.
After Hollywood, the big money,

The girls with the roulette eyes,
He's blacklisted out of pictures
When he won't give names—
"A matinee socialist," McCarthy calls him.
His voice a rattle,
Health gone to hell,
The good looks rumpled into anonymity,
He holes up in West Side hotels
With ex-society girls and B-actresses,
In the end drinks
For nine months straight,
Blacks out regularly at dawn,
Dead at 39, journalists delighted
To report an English girl,
Under-aged and on junk,
In bed with him at the time.

Uptown in a Bronx trainyard
Three kids play blackjack
Under a bridge, blow dope
And belt cough medicine,
Tend a low fire—the fastest one,
In black, keeps losing,
Can't pay up, leans back
And watches rain come down
On a southbound express.

Walt Whitman at the Reburial of Poe

". . . of the poets invited only Walt Whitman
    attended."
                              —Julian Symons

They got him in the end, of course.
In a polling booth, dead-drunk.

Vagrant, ballot-stuffer . . .
Four Baltimore coppers to carry that meager frame.
Our first detective of the broken heart,
he picked through its rubble
with his frenzied calculations,
his delirium of over-clarity,
until he found too many clues . . .
Once I dreamt of a man on a schooner,
compact and handsome, alone on the Sound,
thrilling to a violent storm,
threaded to this world by the silver
of a dying spider:
that man was Edgar.
He loved the moon, and the night-torch,
the notion of blood sea-temperatured,
of the cold rush impelling him . . .
In life, in poetry, my antithesis—
detached from the true life,
of rivers and birds and swaying trees,
of soil red with tubers and pregnant clay,
detached from the wondrous release of sex,
his spleen beating heavier than his heart—
two or three men (at least)
packed in among a dozen demons.
He never much cared for my work.
I admired only a fraction of his.
But I happened to be in Washington
last night . . . and I'm old now, half-wise,
too old not to have a sixth sense—
for the genuine article, anyway . . .
I marvel at all he accomplished
in such a hatcheted life,
electrifying his losses,
celebrating the deer park, the potter's field,
as I celebrated forest and plain . . .
But then to finish here,
another half-forgotten city,
wearing another man's rags—
a scene he might have written:
streets snaking around him,

steaming and sulphurous,
rain dirty as it left the sky—
one last maze before the foothills of hell . . .
And that polling booth . . .
the drinking pals who dumped him there,
frightened perhaps by that dying wolf's voice;
it strikes me now, the eulogies concluded
(I wouldn't give one and I wouldn't say why),
how appropriate he should go that way,
how perversely American in the end—
a man who had consumed himself with exotica,
green as the Republic itself,
poet of our bloodied ankles and ashen
bones, our cankers and lurid dreams:
I wonder who he voted for.
I wonder if he won.

The Track

At the track the horses run
counterclockwise—against time.
In the fields they scatter

around some central idea
which we impose on them.
The thunder breaks differently

on the plateau than on the mountain;
the mice disappear in odd ways,
the owls make contrary moves,

the trees disclose small variations,
but the rain comes in at the same angle
and the wild horses react in the same way—

rearing, white-eyed, under bolts of lightning . . .
Of course all of these horses run
with the clock when they're relaxed.

They connect us to the horizon
with a chain of dust, but too soon
the chain dissolves, the dust settles,

and the wind flies past us, like fire,
into a field which is always empty,
where all the winners go.

The Driver in Italy

For David Fichter

Driving, driven,
The driven sun, the sun-
Slicked autostrada, glare
More slippery than ice . . .
Genova to L'Aquila in ten hours,
The day's work a joke
Of wet leather, dusty glass,
Gears caressed with a finesse
Reserved for women
And not a woman in sight . . .
Tunnel after tunnel,
Gutted mountains, dark mileage,
Mussolini's gallerias;
The only art here is the art
Of the foot to the floor,
A crooked arm browning
Out the window,
Chrome of oncoming cars
Flashing bits of the sea . . .
Landmarks never cease:

Here Shelley drowned,
Here Dante strolled,
Here Boccaccio—meanwhile
The scenery flickers
Into a single image
And our bleared eye
Focuses a mile ahead,
Waiting for the driver's
Epiphany, his golden equation—
That moment when he overtakes
An identical sedan and sees,
Behind the wheel,
The back of his own head.

Peter Cooley

Peter Cooley was born in Detroit, Michigan, in 1940. He was educated at Shimer College, the University of Chicago, and the University of Iowa. He is the author of three collections of poetry: *The Company of Strangers* (1975), published by University of Missouri Press, and *The Room Where Summer Ends* (1979) and *Nightseasons* (1983), both from Carnegie-Mellon University Press. He has been a Robert Frost Fellow at Bread Loaf and is poetry editor for the *North American Review*. He teaches at Tulane University.

Peggy Stewart

The Other

When you come to the other side
of lust the body lays itself
down in others as itself
no longer and the fields till now
fallow, bloom, vermilion.

When you cross to the other side
of pride the heart withers
into tinder, the wind blesses it.
Your body flares, white sticks
this side of anger.

Arriving at the other side
of terror the voice is a dark flame
walking evenings in the garden,

your name unknown to it
if the last light calls you.

And when you have passed the other side
of hope the shore will blaze
finally. We are all light here.
Do not look for me or ask.
You will never have known me.

Such Comfort as the Night
Can Bring to Us

A man and a woman walk out into the summer night.
All evening they have been fighting
and now, arms intertwined, their bodies
wrung with sweat, they ache
numb, to be speechless,
delivered of each other.

Let the night speak then.
First to the woman that she turn to him
here, by the river lifting already to them
the face of its black depths. Then to the man
that he draw her down beneath the willows
where they trade shadows, trade them back
as in the falling light they bartered words,
swapping the coinage weightless.

Let the night sing then.
Let it ring dumb the chorus
of that other life, echoless
in root and vein, rock sucking at the wave
or in midair a note struck warbling.

As in that other time the night played, mute,
walking the garden noons—
where it strolled later in the cool—
before men, before women,
language, their shadows known to them
in parting only, and all flesh ravaging.

To a Wasp Caught in the Storm Sash
at the Advent of the Winter Solstice

Terrorless, I awake.
This is the darkest night
the year can turn to
and I, at the middle of my life,
float up in it, twilight,
from sleep deeper than drifts
canceling rockwall, fence and hill,
all neighbors beyond the window.
Soon gifts will come,
and then good wine and talk
pour through the adjoining rooms
while fires bank and fall.
But now, inside this moment,
between the cerulean panes,
your wizened, tiny, moronic
St. Vitus' wiggle
draws the night sky down around it.
What brings your rasping to this edge
between one blue world and the next?
My face warping the glass?
My soul against your song?

Frog Hunting

Almost always ahead of us,
hippety, in the night,
their sixth sense
radar to pick us up
and give them, hippety,
one jump on us,
the frogs dot the sidewalk
of summer after rain.
They are pursued, hop,
by two little girls,
barefoot, hair loose
in their faces, their hands
hippety, clasped in mine,
tugging this tired father.
Through sidestreets, the puddles
like black marshes, the concrete
buckled and split, hip-
pety, I'm pulled, hop.
But should a tired frog,
hippety, a lazy one,
a dreamer, one fat
with too many flies
or a frogleg-watching stud,
hippety, happen to pause
and feet of a demoiselle or two
land on his clamminess,
then, hippety, hippety, up
the father's legs they jump
to be carried, shrieking,
one in each arm, wriggling,
home to their mother, hop.

Alfred Corn

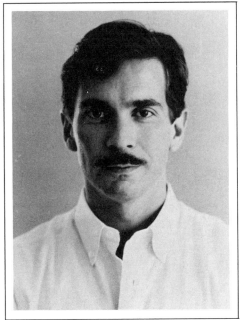

Alfred Corn was born in 1943 in Georgia. He holds a B.A. from Emory University and an M.A. in French literature from Columbia. He is the author of *All Roads at Once* (1976), *A Call in the Midst of the Crowd* (1978), *The Various Light* (1980), and *Notes from a Child of Paradise* (1984), all from Viking Penguin. He has won a number of awards for his poems, including an Ingram Merrill Award, a Fulbright Fellowship, a fellowship from the National Endowment for the Arts, and an award from the American Academy and Institute of Arts and Letters. He lives in New York and Vermont.

The Documentary on Brazil

For David Kalstone

This window frames an alien climate,
Fern-border of frostwork arranged
Around my reflection, whose faint tan
Winter light dilutes to transparence.
The snowscape out there looks drowsy, what
With those temperatures, night coming on;
And doesn't notice the thundertones
At my back, the loud television
Blizzarding indifferently. I hear

But don't see its Brazilian Eden,
Choosing instead my black-and-white still:
Lessons in geometry, scattered
Houses, rapt trees mere line drawings
Of themselves. . . .

                       Photograph and movie—
The real's unlifelike, and snow never
Figured in Adam's coldest dreams. Still
Acquired tastes are strongest, and sages
May see it as fortunate, this fall
Into an unfriendly habitat.
Curiosity and stubbornness
Laid down the fireplace, wove this wool—or
Civilization, its discontents.
We thought ourselves into winter then,
And now thought is most often the frozen
Lace that screens us from the major drawbacks
Of the enterprise. Thought and art,
The pure blind seasons.

                     Not much light left,
And scrim has hardened into mirror,
In which a thousand pewter orchids,
Soot-black toucans, fluorescent monkeys,
Develop ever sharper contrast
In the glimmering tube-window just
To the left of my ear. Light splinters
Among the ice-fronds, shivering off
In every direction from the bright
Collision of three disparate worlds.
Which subsumes which, it's hard to resolve.
The eye adjusts to those darkened panes,
Preferring a mirror to the rest:
Self's the long exile we appear to choose.

Fire: The People

Toplight hammered down by shadowless noon,
A palindrome of midnight, retrograde
From last month's solstice in smoke and flame,
In molten glares from chrome or glass. I feel
Fever from the cars I pass, delirium
Trembling out from the radiators.
The dog-day romance seems to be physical,
As young free lances come into their own,
Sunbrowned, imperial in few clothes,
Heat-struck adulthood a subject to youth
And fitful as traffic, the mind pure jumble
But for that secret overriding voice
Advising and persuading at each crossroads;
The struggle toward freedom to forge a day.

Smoke; flame; oiled, gray-brown air.
Jackhammers and first gear on the avenues;
Stuntmen driving taxicabs; patient, blue,
Hippo aggressiveness of a bus, nudging
Aside the sedans. And the peculiar
Fascination of a row of workshops—
The dark interiors with skylight sunstripes;
A figure walking in slow motion among
Pistons; rough justice of a die cutter;
A helmeted diver, wielding acetylene,
Crouched over some work of sunken treasure
That sparkles gold at a probe from his torch. . . .
Seismic shocks interrupt this dream—a stampede
Of transports flat out to make the light,
Mack truck, Diamond Reo, a nameless tanker,
IH International, a Seatrain destined
For the Port Authority docks—one more
Corrugated block to pile on the rest,
Red, green, gray, and blue, waiting for a ship
In the Grancolombiana line. . . .
The seagoing city radiates invisibly
Over the world, a documentary sublime.

Lunch hour, even the foods are fast, potluck
In the melting pot: the Italian girl
With a carton of chicken; Puerto Rican folding
A pizza; the black woman with an egg roll;
A crop-headed secretary in round,
Metal spectacles eats plain yogurt (she's
Already mantis thin) and devours glamour
Mags. . . . Our crowd scene, a moving fresco:
But is it really there? The adversary
Today is named Random. How capture all this
Without being taken captive in turn,
Install it as something more than backdrop,
As a necessity, not a sundry?
Suppose just an awareness of the way
Living details might be felt as vision
Is vision, full, all there ever was—this
Instant palindromic noon, the joined hands
Of the clock, end and beginning. . . . Surely
The first to consider imagining stars
Constellations had already done as much,
Just by making some brilliant connections;
Mind crowned itself in a round of leaps from point
To point across the empty stage of night. . . .

*   *   *

Now as a pigeon banks, descends, hovers,
And drops on asphalt with back-thrust wings,
Comes a desire to be lifted in the balance,
Rise to some highest point and then be met
By a fierce new light haloing lashes shatter
Into spears of aurora, naked eye become
Prismatic at last and given to see in kind
All the transformed inhabitants forever go
About their errands, on a new scale: the rainbow
Is the emblem for this moment filtering through
The body's meshwork nerves, and a heartbeat impulse
All around puts troops of feet in step with music,
Persistent, availing, that disregards the frayed
Years, vagaries, downfall among trash, accident,

Loss; or because it knows these rushes upward
On something like heartbreak into the only sky,
Air aspirant with fractioned voices, feverfew
Of the sensed illusion, higher ground, progressions
Sounded in the spheres—so each step takes them further,
Sceptered, into daytime, saluting the outcome.
There is a fire that surpasses the known burning,
Its phoenix center a couple that must be there,
Blast furnace, dynamo, engendering a city,
Phosphor spines that bend and meet to weld, to fuse
As a divining rod—sluicings, spillway, braid,
Chorded basses that set myriad threads afire,
Newborn limbs and reach of the proven tendon now
Let go into empowered brilliance, rayed showers,
The garden regained. In this light the place appears:
Hands that rise or fall, muted gestures of welcome
And good-bye, face that turns and comes forward to claim
A smile latent in the afternoon air, vague crowds
Falling down streets without character toward
An offered covenant—love that gives them each a name.

Moving:
New York–New Haven Line

Taut on the leash, at last I have my way:
The train jolts off, just for a split-second
Immobilizing a porter I catch sight of
Through my window, pushing his cart. The platform's
A treadmill or a backward rack; for, his feet
Notwithstanding, he grinds into reverse,
Left behind in underground darkness. . . .
That forward-backward prank gets cruelly played
On every car or truck that races with us
Along the paralleling highway; try
As they might, our motion slowly brakes them,

It sends them backsliding faster and faster
Behind; a feeling I recall from nightmares
(Nightmares, and, to tell the truth, from "real life"
As well). Another stunt of overtaking
(Like my own sharp about-face two months back)
Is the fateful rotation a car makes:
Trunk to grill we see it, a slow, pivotal
Display—practiced, in fact, on every near
Item in the window, especially trees,
Their radially branching form flung into perfect
Umbrella turns (clockwise, because I see them
From the train's left side). Indian file they run
And pirouette together, the closest rank
So much quicker than others farther out,
Which fall behind at a desultory pace.
(This constant shuttle between two points has made
At least some aspects of the pattern clearer.)
Passengers riding backwards, though, see things
Otherwise—and must feel guilty about it;
When I turn and catch them looking, their eyes
Drop, and they assume a preoccupied
Air meant to mime some private train of thought.
Impatience? Funk? A half-wish for derailment?
(They don't have *you* waiting for them, smiling. . . .)
Our steady, legato impetus is barred
At regular intervals by metal poles
That fly by in a soon predictable
Tempo, echoed also by the sag and soar
Of highstrung staff lines hanging down between.
I keep looking for groups of eighth-note starlings
To give the gallop a tune, but none are there,
Nor ever even a rest, just a continuing
Inaudible rush, variably elastic
According to our speed, which hums the landscape
Into a final tableau of motion itself—
A thing so strangely still at its utmost—
The factories, ashheaps, stations, transports caught
In a fastness that wants to hold my eyes
In thrall and lock me up in sleepless dreams.
(Your voice is putting accents in the transit,

Pulling me toward you on a silken line—
And dreams   that ran   on time   were Vehicles-
For-Something-Else. . . ?)

My mind winks on again—yes, there's that river
We cross here now, the same and always different.
A breeze intangible to me suddenly
Wakes the trees and blows on the gray water,
Shriveling the surface into a kind of
Elephant skin. A chevron of migrant geese
Flies into it—bull's eye straight to the heart
Of twenty concentric spreading circles. Water,
Birds, trees, swerve: how is it possible
To be moved in so many ways at once?

Our conductor shouts the listened-for station.
Though I've kept to one spot, the place has changed.
That, along with the name, which, red letter by
Reverse red letter, rolls toward me. Our shared
News—and the rest is neither here nor there,
Is anywhere we both shelter, still moving
Toward deeper welcomes, reunions. This racing
Panic will stop, once it's reminded we are
The only place I really want to go.

Grass

At this range, it's really monumental—
Tall spears and tilted spears, most
Blunted by the last mowing.
A few cloverleafs (leaves?)
And infant plantains fight
For their little plot of ground.
Wing-nuts or boomerangs, the maple seeds
Try to and really can't take root.

There's always more going on
Than anyone has the wit to notice:
Look at those black ants, huge,
In their glistening exoskeletons.
Algebraically efficient,
They're dismembering a dragonfly—
Goggle-eyed at being dead
And having its blue-plated chassis,
Its isinglass delicately
Leaded wings put in pieces.
When you get right down to it,
The earth's a jungle.
The tough grass grows over and around it all,
A billion green blades, each one
Sharply creased down the spine.
Now that I've gotten up to go,
It's nothing but a green background
With a body-shaped dent left behind.
As the grass stretches and rises,
That will go, too.

Darkening Hotel Room

I.

The glass on the picture from the Bible
Has gone pale and reflective, the mirror dull.
A room of rectangles, dark door moldings.

Gray windows; mind itself turning corners
From sleep to awareness to attention
To notions. Up and down the hallway doors

Open to boom shut. And always less light.
The porcelain lamp exists in silver
Outline, drawn something like those solemn curls

On the pillar capital silhouetted
Outside. Ninety winters this room has housed
Other selves—young women in long dresses,

Men like walruses bearded. Bibles, crochet,
Ointment. They would be gathering for warmth
Around the fireplace that now stands empty,

Dark, cold. Others fell asleep in this hour,
That ornate pillar the last image formed
In closing eyes, the curtain descending.

II.

Something between dream and not-dream that goes
Back thirty years and a thousand miles
Away: I almost see her standing
At the sink, wearing . . . a cotton blouse, slacks;
A little thin, what with rationing,
A husband in the Pacific, three children.
She glances at the turk's-caps and lantana
Outside—no, that was a later house.

Afternoon light models her face into
Fatigue, kindness, a worry wrinkle
Between dark brows. Curly hair,
Short and not well arranged. In another
Room someone misses a note of the scale;
And she bends down to me, a mound
Of not much more than self. She smiles,
Her head turning this way, that way. . . .

This is possible, but of course not
Real; unless every picture held in
Thought silently is real. An uncommon radiance

Attaches itself, like the candle's,
To the strain and flicker of recall,
Small incandescence, halo at night.
It appears as a gift, second sight
With the power to transport in safe conduct
To lost houses, forbidden rooms,
To when she still—. But it can't be
Memory. I remember nothing. Absence.

Which came grotesquely, with toys
And birthday cake, they told me later.
To reach in confidence for efficient,
Bony arms and only find—.
Puzzling; and it still is, how
A bereavement, immaterially, goes on,
An asceticism, for a lifetime.
As you might choose caution, and, what,
Thoughtfulness—in order to survive.
Survive! The blunt desire to endure,
Imagining what might be restored.
I don't remember, nonetheless see
Light, afternoon, as she bends down
In large outline, like a cloud approaching.

III.

The man wrapped in darkness is free to dream:
All those I invite may inform this space,
My company until the darkened room
Rises to the surface—coming back like
Someone's biography, summoned up whole,
To be relived and almost understood.

The bearded man may have done as much—
Suddenly reaching out for the young woman
Banked next to him in the loose braid of sleep.
At night's lowest point he divides and numbers
His consolations. She stirs, yawns, neither
Understanding nor minding his rough hug.

But I won't wake you. Sleep, love, rooms that
Shelter us, for how long? The speed of night,
Of thought. Older than my grandparents. . . .
Worlds later, gray light restores a picture
Of the Master teaching his disciples,
Indifferent to, unaware of us.

Gerald Costanzo

Lizabeth Costanzo

Gerald Costanzo was born in 1945 in Portland, Oregon. He is a graduate of Harvard College and holds advanced degrees from Johns Hopkins University. His first book, *In the Aviary* (1975), won the Devins Award and was published by the University of Missouri Press. Bits Press published *Wage the Improbable Happiness*, a second collection, in 1982. Among his awards are fellowships from the National Endowment for the Arts and the Coordinating Council of Literary Magazines. He teaches at Carnegie-Mellon University, where he edits *Three Rivers Poetry Journal* and the Carnegie-Mellon University Press Poetry Series.

Nobody Lives
on
Arthur Godfrey Boulevard

When I first heard about America
it was already too late. When I learned
that its holiest city is Dallas,
Texas, there was nothing I could do
but bear witness to the deckled edge

of Manifest Destiny, California
well on its way to becoming
an island, or some foreign country

where one of the many forms
of English is still spoken.

I had missed the arduous construction
of democracy, though I lived among
its numbered days. What I saw
was the Reconstruction of Fifth Avenue,
and the Army Corps of Engineers

dredging sand from the sea
and piling it back where the beaches
belong. I heard wry assemblages
of Rotarians, Shriners, and Optimists,
Elks and Moose committing business

over lunch. I listened as
my friends wondered at the poverty
which affluence breeds,
not quite believing in the life
lived on Frank Sinatra Drive,

nor in the one where nobody lives
on Arthur Godfrey Boulevard. I watched
brotherhood practiced among corporations,
and freedom in the emporiums
of fast food. The separation of church

and religion. I saw all of us
becoming stranded everywhere
in our land, the new Pilgrims arrived
at last on the shore of a great
desert, mouthing our own sad psalms.

Introduction of the Shopping Cart
OKLAHOMA CITY, 1937

There was a man
who collected facts.

After work he rode twenty stories,
let himself in
to cartons filled with index cards
and his crucial lists.

Facts reveal useful lives.
He got things right.

The shopping cart invented
by Sylvan Goldman,
Oklahoma City, 1937.

When the man passed on
his relatives came.

P. T. Barnum had four daughters.

They searched through his cartons
for ten-dollar bills.

The sky, which on cloudless
days appears to be azure,
has no true color.

He wasn't eccentric.
When they found nothing,
they threw everything
out.

His final fact:
you live and you die.

The shopping cart. P. T. Barnum.

The sky.

Jeane Dixon's America

For Jim Crumley

San Francisco remains in grave personal
danger. Dubuque continues to be a source
of consternation for the entire Hawkeye
state. Tensions could diminish, though only
through an act of subterfuge.

New Jersey will be named in a paternity
suit, but will wage battle in open
court to preserve its good name.
Look for Minneapolis and St. Paul
to split, this time for good. Each
will agree they were never meant
to be together.

New York City will embark on a religious
pilgrimage, either to Rome or Jerusalem.
But there can be no forgiveness.
Overnight stardom is putting a great deal
of pressure on Missoula, Montana, which will
have to choose its roles carefully
in the coming months or risk
being a ghost town by the end of the decade.

Peoria must keep itself from overexposure
once again this year. If it succeeds, its
many problems will continue to go unnoticed.
Honolulu, weary of the long commute,

longs to be part of the mainland,
especially of southern California.
But with things the way they are now,
don't look for this to happen any time soon.

The Meeting

Somewhere along the road
you meet up with yourself.
Recognition is immediate.
If it happens at the proper
time and place, you propose
a toast:

May you remain as my shadow
when I lie down.
May I live on as your ghost.

Then you pass, knowing you'll
never see yourself that way
again: the fires which burn
before you are your penance,
the ashes you leave behind are
your name.

W. S. Di Piero

W. S. Di Piero was born in 1945. He is the author of two collections of poetry, *The First Hour* (Abattoir Editions, 1982) and *The Only Dangerous Thing* (Elpenor Books, 1984). He has also published three volumes of translation from the Italian. He teaches at Stanford.

Lines to a Friend in Trouble

I send your own words back
bent by temperamental need,
mine, too cautious of that
whipped heat, all yours,
of sorrow and uncertainty.
"Great walls of bamboo,
killed back severely in
untimely frost, looked
like the soul of desolation,
bare and gray in the dimlight
before the sun." Don't you see

how that fullness drives out
sympathy? How can I wish
to be closer? It's easier
to touch that language
than come near your grief,
which turns more dreadful,
but more clear, in its saying.
Forgive me. I'm glad you're far,
remote in the purity of speech,
coherent, singular. That much
I can take. It's all I want.

Second Horn

(VENICE, 1975: SCUOLA DI SAN GIORGIO
DEGLI SCHIAVONI)

The sparks showering off the paint
kindle in her gray head, while on the wall,
rampant in his sullen outrage, St. George presses
the lance until it shatters in the scrawny teeth.
Her hand goes up to hold
the point bursting behind the roaring skull:
the dragon's second horn, a warrior's gift
to nature. To kill exaggerated life
is surely goodness, the world's good design
must not be smeared. There's no good reason.

A crooked sense in her bones,
she walks the tangled shade of washlines
and antennae. In the café, with friends,
she tells again what they have heard a hundred times
and she as often forgets.
That once, in Rome, she saw the Duce,
close as that chair, and if she'd had a gun

she would have shot him, because in him she saw
that other Devil, God's worst part,
O kill the Devil where you find him!

The others listen as if this were news.
The mason tells her not to worry, the worst
is yet to come—and they all laugh together.
He says his ancestors said that theirs
had carted the chapel stone. Yet what did they eat
but miserable onions and old bread?
Then there was the time
a soldier, a kid, put a gun to his head
and barked, expecting him to speak a language
he could not possibly have known.

To all this she answers if they've heard
that once she could have shot her Devil, then turns
out the door. Back at her dear place,
under the pitched equilibrium of man and beast,
the chewed limbs of boys and girls rest on the ground.
Still her mind sketches the pure triangulation
of waste, appetite, grace.
Serene, she burns it on the anger in her brain
and lets the sparks, all secular and good,
formlessly rain down.

Four Brothers

1.

Pino the Lizard in his patent leather shoes
wears cologne none of us ever heard of,
though he must have told us a dozen times
Pinaud, you dopes. It's French. Who cares?

Everything we know is hearsay, and what we see
depends on what we know. Pino's the one
who made it big, the only brother of three.
There would have been a fourth, but for something
Mrs. Pino did one night to the lastborn
because she felt too old, too tired. Nobody
talks about it. That was years ago. Now Pino
works outdoors, selling nickel bags to blacks,
writing numbers, lending money to men
outside the neighborhood. He doesn't know
how short his life is going to be, how one day
he'll blink and won't be there anymore to see
himself the way we see ourselves in how we act.
The first time men in good suits came
and took him to jail, in a big honest afternoon
while everybody stood outside watching, Mrs. Pino
stayed in her doorway, silent, and the cardoor closed
as if a stranger's hand had touched a pillow pressed
on an infant's face, then held it, held it there.

2.

Out of respect, maybe out of danger, people refuse
to talk about Frankie, the oldest, as if he were
religion. I don't understand his story, but it
loiters in its mystery the way most stories do.
The morning after the youngest died, Frankie
locked himself inside his upstairs room.
He's lived there ever since. His mother
delivers papers, cigarets, food,
while Frankie listens to the radio
and draws those faces, all big names,
Carole Lombard, Rita Hayworth, Marilyn Monroe,
sending sketches out with half-eaten meals.
All gifts to his mother, a vengeance,
to punish her with images of ladies
who love wild light, real stars who never
have to remember anything. Frankie
isn't crazy, but he needs certain things.

Sometimes I catch myself waiting for him to die
as if I knew he'd leave me his charcoal
or ruffled pads or picture of himself. The worst
would be to find he left nothing, cared nothing
about remembering or being remembered.
If he needs to draw, he must need memory too.

3.

Sally may be trucking through pine barrens
or selling taffy to Camden Puerto Ricans.
Hating both his brothers, snorting what's left of love
while he drinks with the Strongman in Toms River
or buys thread with the Blockhead in Wilmington.
He watched Frankie go upstairs, saw skinny Pino
driven off to prison, and he knew even more.
So he signed on with the carnival. I saw the ad
in a Jersey paper: SEE STRANGE SALVATORE EAT WILD FIRE!
I try to see the strange places he must love
passing through, his mouth his only real house,
every night those knots of fire, big fists between
his lips, past his teeth, down the tunnel to his belly,
all fire in the center of him, then to save it all
at the last minute. *Pull out the fire. Pull it out!*
Later, closing the show in mud and fog, he hauls
canvas with a midget and runaway murderer.
Everybody knows the carnival always brings rain.
Sally remembers everything, so he doesn't need
memory, only his mouth deep in a pillow, breath
trapped in a fire deep inside his throat
while he sleeps with two women, or a man,
owing himself only the need to go and go.

Fat Tuesday

I'll lick these screwfaced torches all night long
and chew the beads and blue doubloons that sail
from iron balconies mossy in the dark,
I'll walk down Royal Street dressed as a sweetgum tree
pretending my back is front, big whiskeybreath for all
who love this season of preparing. I'll be ready
for denial, to put away all fat things, all spoils,
the meat and bulky jewels of wanting
anything, even the wish to want.
The King salutes us from his golden dragon.
He is our food today. Eat his bones, his furs,
his crown and sceptre. Eat his fat throne and flesh,
his voice that laughs us into easy forgiveness.
I'll eat the King and break his will inside me
and toward tomorrow mix him with my swallowed
pearls and coins and whiskey and days.

Stephen Dobyns

Isabel Bize

Stephen Dobyns was born in Orange, New Jersey, in 1941. His first book of poems, *Concurring Beasts* (1972), was the Lamont Selection of the Academy of American Poets and was published by Atheneum. Since then he has published four books of poems, most recently *Black Dog, Red Dog* (Holt, Rinehart, and Winston, 1984). He is also the author of four novels, the latest of which is *Dancer with One Leg* (E. P. Dutton, 1983). Among his awards are two fellowships from the National Endowment for the Arts and a fellowship from the Guggenheim Foundation. He teaches in the M.F.A. Program at Warren Wilson College. The following work is taken exclusively from *The Balthus Poems* (Atheneum, 1982).

The Window

The woman who is waiting for the evening draws
a black line over one eyebrow, then rises from
her dressing table, walks to the gramophone.

Immediately, the tremulous voice of Ada Falcon
singing "Garden of Desire" fills the room
like a perfume whose smell slides over the walls,

over the table by the window and into the autumn
afternoon, crosses the street and drifts through
the top story window of a retired clerk who sits

in his slippers at a table shuffling cards. His
wife is making cabbage soup and all day that smell
has filled his life. Now the tango draws him toward

the window where in the street he sees two children,
perhaps six or seven, poised cheek to cheek, their
joined hands thrust forward like the prow of a ship,

who remain motionless as the woman on the record
sings about loss. As he listens, the clerk recalls
dances he attended as a young man, thinks of a dance

at the seashore where he had gone with his parents.
The dance floor was a pier over the water and pines
along the shore swayed in a summer wind. Standing

at the window, the man begins to see strings of
colored lights, the band in white shirts with blue
ruffles on the sleeves. He tries to picture the faces

of the girls, but sees only a style of hair, a ribbon;
smells the mixture of perfume and sweat; sees the ocean
with white caps emerging like messages from the dark.

He assumed he would someday cross that ocean,
win for himself a life of wealth and excitement—
all the things that never happened, for his life

took other unexpected turnings: a job in an office,
illness, a childless marriage, days falling around him
like scattered cards, bringing him at last to this

small apartment on a small street where his life
seems wrapped in the smell of cabbage soup.
Looking down at the boy and girl poised motionless

in the street, the man wants to call to them.
But what could he say? Instead, he turns aside as
the children take one step, then another, hearing

only the music as their feet stumble forward,
gripping each other tightly as they spin and dip.
Look, they say, see how gracefully we are dancing.

Getting Up

The cat with yellow eyes doesn't yet realize
the bird is made from paper and wood. Hesitating
at the edge of its basket on the bed, the cat
stares at the toy bluebird in the girl's hand.
The girl wants to know what it's like to kill,
wants to see the cat embarrass itself, then start
washing itself. She leans back on white pillows,
white sheets, one foot just touching the floor.
She is naked and holds the bird in her right hand;
with her left she coaxes the cat, encouraging it
to leap as she watches intently with narrowed eyes.

Around her, she hears the house stirring with
morning activity: a smell of coffee from the kitchen,
a door slamming and her father's feet on the stairs.
Soon she must get up, dress for school in her
blue skirt, white blouse. Her father will drive her
on his way to work, while she finishes a report
on Argentina and its exports. Once at school,
she will join her friends, all dressed as she is,
and together they will proceed through the civilized
unwinding of their day. But now, naked with her cat,
she is learning about death and the desire
to kill; she is learning about humiliation and
the manipulation of power; and it's as if
the entire day ahead were a great inverted
pyramid resting on its tip upon these few seconds,
as the girl waits, her lips parted in a half smile,
and the cat takes a half-step, preparing to leap.

The White Skirt

For an hour he wonders what the girl could be thinking
as she sits in the green armchair with her head
slightly lowered, her thick red hair slightly
falling forward. She has unbuttoned her white blouse
and her breasts hang loosely in the halter of her slip.

The man watches from the balcony of an apartment next door.
Strings of Christmas lights dangle between palm trees.
Through the open French windows, the man considers how
the girl stares at some spot on the floor to the right
of her red slippers, the elaborate folds of her white skirt.

Next to him, a neighbor complains that his wife and children
don't love him, while inside the man watches his own wife
dancing with their host: one fat hand massaging
the small of her back. The man would like to go home,
but senses the emptiness of his house waiting for him.

Now he notices how the girl's bare arms hang loosely
over the arms of her chair, that her whole body is limp
as if she'd been dancing all night; as if her lover
had just left her to move to another city; as if
in the knowledge of her beauty, she bears the knowledge

of her own mortality which will at last fall across
whatever she may be doing in the way a curtain can
fall across a sunlit window. The man again considers
how silent his own house must be, like the silence
inside an empty suitcase or empty suit of clothing.

Abruptly, he stands up, leaves the apartment without
speaking to his wife. He feels his life evading him,
slipping past like a puff of air between open fingers.
Once outside he seeks out the lights of the girl's window,
sees the lights of the party he has left. Down the street,

he sees the darkness of his own house. He wants to knock
at the girl's door, find the words to change their lives.

Then he pauses. For every action he can imagine taking,
he imagines reasons for not taking it; for every gain,
he imagines all the losses. He takes a few steps toward

the girl's building, then a few steps back. It's the dance
he's become best at. Gnawing and arguing at himself,
he remains standing as lights blink out in the windows
around him, until his wife finds him and without speaking
grips his arm, draws him down to his own dark home.

The Triangular Field

In bright morning sunlight, the horse appears pink,
and the man is so pleased to see it that he waves
as he walks toward it across the triangular field.
The horse glances up from between two apple trees
and waits. The man was awakened early by dreams of
winter and self-doubt, dreams of no money in the bank;
and now he wants to clear his head by galloping bareback
through summer lanes with dust billowing around him,
light flickering around him in a hundred shades of green.
And he decides to gallop so fast that all the impediments
and small debts of his life will be lost in a swirl
of debris, that even his own death which he thinks
must be as gnarled as the trunks of surrounding trees
will be left deserted and despairing in the middle
of some sun-choked lane.   As he walks toward the horse,
he anticipates the swell of its body beneath him,
pushing out his thighs as he lies with heels pressed
against its belly, urging it to gallop even faster.
And he's sorry he can't take this back to the city:
simply, the flickering light and smell of summer grasses.
Then, in winter, when he and the world fought one another
and he gnawed at himself, was cruel to people around him,

he would think of the morning he galloped the pink horse
between apple trees, and the world fitted together
without angry words and extra pieces, and across
the lurching sky he saw his own name hastily scrawled
as if on an IOU from somebody notoriously disreputable,
someone who has never been known to tell the truth,
but who for the brief moment he has chosen to believe.

Dream

She dreams her girl lover steals toward her
with one red poppy: red the color of her single
exposed nipple, color of her two red slippers.
She lies back on the blue couch, one slipper
just touching the carpet, head on the red cushion
behind her, green blouse open to the waist.
She dreams her lover approaches with one poppy
raised above her sleeping figure. In a moment,
the girl will bend and brush the petals
over her exposed breast, brush the flower
over her cheek until she wakes, startled;
until she sees the blond hair, the angular
tender face above her. Slowly, she will stand and
cup her lover's breasts in her hands, lower
her own red mouth to the girl's neck and bite,
fastening her teeth in the soft white flesh,
feeling the girl arch her back as the pain
cuts through her. Then she will release her,
drawing her mouth free of the delicate flesh,
resting her forehead on the flower-shaped mark.
The two will stand with their arms loosely
supporting each other in the golden room, swaying
like poplars in the first breeze of morning;
while from the room, from the whole house comes
no sound; from the world around them: no sound.

Girl in White

The girl in white sits with her hands in her lap.
Her white dress is pulled down past her shoulders
to a few inches below her breasts. She is perhaps
fourteen. The afternoon sun enters from the right,
lighting her bare shoulder, right side of her face.
She sees nothing in the room, and one by one she
is pushing away the sounds that press down upon her:
sound of parents arguing in the kitchen,
her brothers quarreling; pushing away the violent
sounds of the street: cars honking, buses heaving
themselves through January cold. In her eyes, it is
late spring, and from her bedroom window she watches
the farmer's son leading one white cow out across
the pasture with a tall pine at its center.
The wind brings her the smell of manure and freshly
turned earth. The boy wears a brown coat. Looking back,
he raises his arm as if in greeting. Although she knows
he can't see her, the girl steps away from the window.
It is early morning and she feels her life beginning.

Now, this winter afternoon, sitting with hands folded,
she imagines a man laying one hand against her cheek.
She imagines rising to embrace him, softly at first,
then harder as the buttons of his brown coat dig
into her bare skin. Standing, she presses her wrists
against her breasts, trying to imitate the rough feel
of his hands moving across her body. From the street,
she again begins to hear cars rushing at each other,
people calling and shouting; from the kitchen, she hears
someone crying, then her father's voice raised in anger.

Japanese Girl with Red Table

The Japanese girl thinks she will die today.
In her mirror, she sees she is already dying
and she tries to compose her face into how
it will appear in death: forgiving, forgetful.
Between her white breasts, she already sees
the red mark of the knife—red as the red table
on the floor behind her, red as the red border
of the purple robe falling open around her
as she kneels before her mirror. Yes, she thinks,
she will destroy herself today; and her lover,
who has not come, will hear of it from people
crying to each other as he passes on the street
with his destination a solid object in his mind,
as real as the red table or the black and white
vase upon the table. He will hear that a girl
has been found with a knife in her breast,
but he won't believe it's she as he continues
toward the red table in his mind. Then at last
some friend will bring him the news, tell him
while he sits with his wife in the early evening,
eating sweets and drinking tea as he describes
the small business of his day. He will be holding
a porcelain cup with a picture of a single gull,
and he will listen to how a girl has been found
lying naked in her own blood on the golden rug
he gave her, while within him the words will be
eating his body as fire eats paper, as he tries
hopelessly to hold his cup steady and make no face.

Rita Dove

Rita Dove was born in 1952 in Akron, Ohio. She holds a B.A. from Miami University and an M.F.A. from the University of Iowa. She is the author of two books of poetry, *The Yellow House on the Corner* (1980) and *Museum* (1983), both from Carnegie-Mellon University Press, and she has received a Fulbright/Hays Fellowship, as well as fellowships from the National Endowment for the Arts and the Guggenheim Foundation. She teaches at Arizona State University.

Fred Viebahn

Dusting

Every day a wilderness—no
shade in sight. Beulah
patient among knickknacks,
the solarium a rage
of light, a grainstorm
as her gray cloth brings
dark wood to life.

Under her hand scrolls
and crests gleam
darker still. What

was his name, that
silly boy at the fair with
the rifle booth? And his kiss and
the clear bowl with one bright
fish, rippling
wound!

Not Michael—
something finer. Each dust
stroke a deep breath and
the canary in bloom.
Wavery memory: home
from a dance, the front door
blown open and the parlor
in snow, she rushed
the bowl to the stove, watched
as the locket of ice
dissolved and he
swam free.

That was years before
Father gave her up
with her name, years before
her name grew to mean
Promise, then
Desert-in-Peace.
Long before the shadow and
sun's accomplice, the tree.

Maurice.

Ö

Shape the lips to an *o*, say *a*.
That's *island*.

One word of Swedish has changed the whole neighborhood.
When I look up, the yellow house on the corner
is a galleon stranded in flowers. Around it

the wind. Even the high roar of a leaf-mulcher
could be the horn-blast from a ship
as it skirts the misted shoals.

We don't need much more to keep things going.
Families complete themselves
and refuse to budge from the present,
the present extends its glass forehead to sea
(backyard breezes, scattered cardinals)

and if, one evening, the house on the corner
took off over the marshland,
neither I nor my neighbor
would be amazed. Sometimes

a word is found so right it trembles
at the slightest explanation.
You start out with one thing, end
up with another, and nothing's
like it used to be, not even the future.

Champagne

The natives here have given up their backyards
and are happy living where we cannot see them.
No shade! The sky insists upon its blueness,
the baskets their roped ovals.
Gravel blinds us, blurring the road's shoulders.
Figures moving against the corduroyed hills
are not an industry to speak of, just
an alchemy whose yield is pleasure.

Come quickly—a whiff of yeast
means bubbles are forming, trapped
by sugar and air. The specialist who turns
30,000 bottles a day 10° to the right
lines up in a vaulted cellar
for an Italian red at the end of the day.
On either side for as far as we can see,
racks of unmarked bottles lying in cool fever.

Three centuries before in this dim corridor
a monk paused to sip, said it pricked
the tongue like stars. When we emerge
it is as difficult to remember the monk
as it is to see things as they are:
houses waver in the heat, stone walls
blaze. The hurt we feel is delicate—
all for ourselves and all for nothing.

Planning the Perfect Evening

I keep him waiting, tuck in the curtains,
buff my nails (such small pink eggshells).
As if for the last time, I descend the stair.

He stands penguin-stiff in a room
that's so quiet we forget it is there.
Now nothing, not even breath, can come

between us, not even the aroma of punch
and sneakers as we dance the length
of the gymnasium and crepe paper streams

down like cartoon lightning. Ah,
Augustus, where did you learn to samba?
And what is that lump below your cummerbund?

Stardust. The band folds up
resolutely, with plum-dark faces.
The night still chirps. Sixteen cars

caravan to Georgia for a terrace,
beer and tacos. Even this far south
a thin blue ice shackles the moon,

and I'm happy my glass sizzles with stars.
How far away the world! And how hulking
you are, my dear, my sweet black bear!

Norman Dubie

Peter Schlueter

Norman Dubie was born in Barre, Vermont, in 1945. He is the author of twelve collections of poems, his most recent books are *The Illustrations* (Braziller, 1977), *The City of the Olesha Fruit* (Doubleday, 1979), *The Everlastings* (Doubleday, 1980), and *Selected and New Poems* (W.W. Norton and Company, 1983). Among his many awards is a fellowship from the Guggenheim Foundation. He is professor of English at Arizona State University.

The Funeral

It felt like the zero in brook ice.
She was my youngest aunt, the summer before
We had stood naked
While she stiffened and giggled, letting the minnows
Nibble at her toes. I was almost four—
That evening she took me
To the springhouse where on the scoured planks
There were rows of butter in small bricks, a mold
Like ermine on the cheese,
And cut onions to rinse the air
Of the black, sickly-sweet meats of rotting pecans.

She said butter was colored with marigolds
Plucked down by the marsh
With its tall grass and miner's-candles.
We once carried the offal's pail beyond the barn
To where the fox could be caught in meditation.
Her bed linen smelled of camphor. We went

In late March for her burial. I heard the men talk.
I saw the minnows nibble at her toe.
And Uncle Peter, in a low voice, said
The cancer ate her like horse piss eats deep snow.

Comes Winter, the Sea Hunting

For my daughter

This was your very first wall, your crib against
The wall that was papered in a soft
Fawn color, the powdered wings of a moth
Slowing in the cobwebs of the window—

The moth, poor like us, died
In her paper dress on stilts. The spider
Is a monarch, fat in
Winter chambers, the articles of her
Wealth are also
The articles of the kill: a little narcotic with silk!

We had two rooms in a blue, collapsing roadhouse
At the very lip of a valley
With a deep river and woods. The house
Had been settling for a century.
Those dizzying, tin
Trapezoid rooms . . .
A house built on rock, a rock built on sand,

And while I slept, your mother, who was
Big with you, hammered from silver—

A knife! A spoon! You,
On a crescent of bone, sleep
A sleep of plums: moisture on the plum forms a window

And inside everything reclines tasting meat and wine
From mid-day
Until evening. *That winter came in terms of you* . . .

The wet pods on sticks, mimes playing
Dice in a blizzard! Out of fields of rice come women
From the North, dark pajamas full of explosives . . .

Your mother now is
Naked and dreaming in the corner,
Is the Elder Breughel's inverted, golden doe
On a green pole, being
Shouldered back to the winter village.

Inside a box by the stairs there's an egg
Halved by a hair,
A box filled with sleep and even the retired ferryman,
George Sharon, leaving
Us two bottles of milk in the morning,
Would not look into it!
The cedar balcony in the back took its weight

In ice, first, just three large icicles, then five,
And finally a webbing in between of thin ice.
The balcony was sealed
In a wall of crystals. With your new spoon
I carved into this blue-green wall

Dürer's *Sky-map*
Of the Northern Hemisphere: the silver, ancestral
Figures of crab, spectacle bear,
And *Boötes* with his long pink muscles and spear:

On clear nights the opaque stars above Montpelier
Appeared through this Sky-chart.

Up in the corner, where
'the fish with spilled pitcher' should be,
There was instead
A bat, snow had
Brought the roof in on him and he was
Caught in ice, hanging by a claw in the eaves.

I called him
Pipistrelle, old and dead flittermouse, he was
A reach of bone and a square of fur like a squirrel
Nailed out on a red barn in October. Pipistrelle,
At the corners of his wings, had blackened stars. Valiant

Dürer's Sky-map
Was now different with these triangular ears—
The dead pipistrelle carries a sound picture
That is like our memory of the dark trees, or the spaces
Between the old ferryman's teeth.
The bat would use its wings
Like oars; rowing in the blackish cataracts
Of a winter porch: star room! Lamp room . . .

The winter comes,

A *sea hunting*, and your father after sleeping
Put his fist into the star wall, making a hole;
The wind entered

Moving at the height of the unborn,
This wind erased the lights of hemispheres!
That night, a breaking of ice, and the next morning
The bag-of-waters begins seeping as your
Mother tries a flight of stairs—
An old woman puts a horn to her stomach, and
Listens for you,

You have formed from seawater:
A deep luminous eye, digits, a bridge for a nose—
Abstract, monstrous—you have two oars!
You can only hear the ferryman in the cove,
Walking with his ladder, he somehow hangs his lamp
On the tall pole.

In an earlier season,

You were conceived, touched by *two* sounds of water
In a gulf; you formed your pulse, little patch over nothing,

Drawn in and drawn out—this is the meaning as,
Sadly and much later, a feather
Or candle is put to our mouths!

There were
Agates on the windowsill and a vase of dry pussywillows;

The out-larged map-maker's instruments boiling
Before labor, the towels and basins:
A hatching
In the ruby rhomboidal rooms where

A spider on her lucent thread
Swings into sunlight, then leaves us climbing up
A silken helix to eaves and

Pigeon gloom, but

You have washed up in the surf, and look out over
A new light like water showing,
Another mother,

A first attempt for someone loved, as
Out of her dress dropped in a circle—this nude,
The steady spectre at your birth,
Steps near to kiss you, circle of goldsmith's blue;
The pipistrelles fan the air . . .
This world would deceive us

So live in it as two! This was the very first wall
                    that you had to have passed through . . .

The Circus Ringmaster's
Apology to God

It is what we both knew in the sunlight of a restaurant's garden
As we drank too much and touched
While waiting for the lemon wedges and rainbow trout.
If it's about that door? I'm not sorry.
You smiled through tears. The night clerk said that I was
Crazy like a bear. Laughing, you spilled your beer.

Over the hedge a farmer paints a horse's cankers
With a heavy tincture of violet . . .

Later, in a dark room, both of us speckled, middle-aged, and soft.
I dragged my mouth like a snail's foot up your leg and body
To your mouth. We both shivered.
You ran naked before a window. Shyness increases your importance!

I don't know what you think when we are no one for a moment
Hay-ropes, hands at ankles, gone beyond
Even the dripping faucet and its sink spilling onto the floor . . .

There's no strongbox hidden in the closet.

It's often like laughter, "You go pee for me and I'll boil the water."
Sipping hot coffee, you told me a story about the old ringmaster
On the Baltic shore:
                    he's inside his little house on wheels, and
The goldfinch jumps from its silver platform to the cage's floor that's
Littered with straw and shredded handbills. The ringmaster daydreams
About ponies circling in a white path of ashes . . .

On the table before him there's an ounce of tobacco
And in his plate: blue and gray parsnips, beef and the open letter

That he knows better than the loose floorboard! The two of us
Enjoy our solitude:
                      folded over chairs are the clothes
We never wore. If you die first, I'll sway in the hallway like a bear.
        I'll whisper, "I'm sorry." And you'll
Not unlock the door.
I'll break through with my hip and shoulder . . .
Remember? You were glad that I did it once before!

Parish

I.

God only knows what he'd been doing. Painting or sewing?
All I can say is that from my window
In the old yellow-and-black parsonage
I had been looking across falling snow
To the brick mortuary on the other side of the road.
It had one lamp burning; the mortician
Had thrown off his white gown, washed
His hands above the forearms, was exhausted,
And sat down. The water still running.

II.

I had a little friend once
Who fixed her own dolls: the walleyed, the lame,
And the gutted. She lived in a small town like this one.
She grew up to be odd.

All day I'd waited for a visitor
Who wasn't coming, all highways
Now closed by bad weather.

III.

He'd left the water running cold over porcelain.
He'd thrown down his gown. Looked out at the road.
Hypnotized by the snow and running water,
He gazed off to the body of hills.

IV.

The wind grew for some hours, then it was dawn.
The storm over. I could see footprints
That had shallowed with the drifting snow, that had
Come to our door in the dark.
Perhaps some transient
Looking for an early breakfast after a night
Of journeying and enchantment. I smelled
Dahlias—thoughts of Saint Jerome's lion
    Carrying a burden of wood in for the stove.
    I glanced
    To the footprints,
    Which had circled, waited; circled some more,
    And left our door, leaping the fence

    Or passing through it, all signs
    Of them vanishing into the hills.

At Midsummer

For Jeannine

We had been in the tall grass for hours—
Sleep coming on some barrier of bells
Waking you—you stretched, the moon lost
In clouds, the gravestones below us
To the north had moved
West to a hill, the white rounded stones,
All at cruel angles to the ground,
Had been white and black heifers resting
Beside the stream with its ledges of quartz marl.

Earlier you had thought the stream
Moved like clear muscle and sinew
With their hooks
In the narrow runners of limestone.
You stretched, your breasts uncovered—
You had hurt your back lifting seed basins
Out in the shed; eased,
Touching me, you think of Kabir, saying:

Worlds are being told like beads.
The day began with the famous airs of a catbird,
A white unstruck music, you were downstairs
Sweeping mouse dirt out of the cupboards.
Now, down in the grass I am awake. I look over
To the north. And say: *It's gone? The gravestones?*
You smile and cross over me like a welcome storm.

Elegy to the Sioux

The vase was made of clay
With spines of straw
For strength. The sun-baked vase
Soaked in a deep blue dye for days. The events in this wilderness,
Portrayed in the round of the vase,

Depend on shades of indigo against
The masked areas of the clay, a flat pearl color
To detail the big sky and snow . . .

This Montana field in winter is not sorrowful:
A bugle skips through notes:

We view it all somehow from the center of the field
And there are scattered groups of cavalry. Some of these
Men were seasoned by civil war. Their caps are blue.
Their canteens are frozen. The horses shake their heads
Bothered by the beads of ice, the needles of ice
Forming at both sides of their great anvil heads.

The long, blue cloaks of the officers fall over the haunches
Of the horses. The ammunition wagons
Beside the woods are blurred by the snowy weather . . .

Beyond the wagons, further even, into the woods
There is a sloping stream bed. This is
The dark side of the vase, which is often misunderstood.
From here through the bare trees there's
A strange sight to be seen at the very middle of the field:

A valet is holding a bowl of cherries—archetype and rubric,
A general with white hair eats the fruit while introducing its color,
Which will flow through the woods in early December.
An Indian woman came under dark clouds to give birth, unattended

In the deep wash inside the woods. She knew the weather
Could turn and staked the tips of two rooted spruce trees
To the earth to make a roof.

The deerskin of her robe is in her mouth. Her legs spread,
Her feet are tied up in the roof of darkening spruce. *No stars
Show through!* But on the vase that belonged to a President
There are countless stars above the soldier's campfires . . .

With rawhide her feet are tied high in the spruce
And her right hand is left loose as if she were about
To ride a wild stallion
                 to its conclusion in a box canyon.

President Grant drinks bourbon from his boot. The Sioux
Cough in their blankets . . .

It snowed an hour more, and then the moon appeared. The unborn
    infant,
Almost out on the forest floor, buckled and lodged. It died.
Its mother died. Just before she closed her eyes
She rubbed snow up and down the inside of her bare thighs.

In the near field an idle, stylish horse raised one leg
To make a perfect right angle. Just then a ghost of snow formed
Over the tents of the soldiers,

It blows past the stylish, gray horse,
Unstopped it moves through woods, up the stream bed
And passes into the crude spruce shelter, into the raw open
Woman, her legs raised into sky—
Naked house of snow and ice! This gust of wind

Spent the night within the woman. At sunrise, it left her mouth
Tearing out trees, keeping the owls from sleep; it was angry now
And into the field it spilled, into the bivouac of pony soldiers

Who turned to the south, who turned back to the woods, who became

Still. Blue all over! If there is snow
still unspooling in the mountains
Then there is time yet for the President to get his Indian vase
And to fill it with bourbon from his boot and to put flowers into it:

The flowers die in a window that looks out on a cherry tree
Which heavy with fruit drops a branch:

         torn to its very heartwood
By the red clusters of fruit, the branch fell
Like her leg and foot
Out of the big sky into Montana . . .

The Fox Who Watched
for the Midnight Sun

Across the snowy pastures of the estate
Open snares drift like paw prints under rain, everywhere
There is the conjured rabbit being dragged
Up into blowing snow: it struggles
Upside down by a leg, its belly
Is the slaked white of cottages along the North Sea.

Inside the parlor Ibsen writes of a summer garden, of a
Butterfly sunken inside the blossoming tulip.
He describes the snapdragon with its little sconce of dew.
He moves from the desk to a window. Remembers his studies
In medicine, picturing the sticky
Overlapping eyelids of drowned children. On the corner
Of the sofa wrapped in Empress-silks there's a box
Of fresh chocolates. He mimics the deceptively distant,
Chittering birdsong within the cat's throat.
How it attracts finches to her open window.
He turns toward the fire, now thinking of late sessions in Storting.
Ibsen had written earlier of an emotional girl
With sunburnt shoulders,

Her surprise when the heavy dipper came up
From the well with frogs' eggs bobbing in her water.
He smiles.

Crosses the room like the fox walking away
From the woodpile.
He picks up his lamp and takes it
To the soft chair beneath the window. Brandy is poured.
Weary, he closes his eyes and dreams
Of his mother at a loom, how she would dip, dressing
The warp with a handful of coarse wool.

Henrik reaches for tobacco—tomorrow, he'll write
Of summer some more, he'll begin with a fragrance . . .
Now, though, he wonders about the long
Devotion of his muscles to his bones, he's worried by
The wind which hurries the pages in this drafty room.
He looks out
Into the March storm for an illustration: under a tree
A large frozen hare swings at the end of a snare string.
The fox sits beneath it, his upturned head swinging with it,
The jaws are locked in concentration,

As if the dead hare were soon to awaken.

Elizabeth's War with the Christmas Bear

The bears are kept by hundreds within fences, are fed cracked
Eggs; the weakest are
Slaughtered and fed to the others after being scented
With the blood of deer brought to the pastures by Elizabeth's
Men—the blood spills from deep pails with bottoms of slate.

The balding Queen had bear gardens in London and in the country.
The bear is baited: the nostrils
Are blown full with pepper, the Irish wolf dogs
Are starved, then, emptied, made crazy with fermented barley:

And the bear's hind leg is chained to a stake, the bear
Is blinded and whipped, kneeling in his own blood and slaver, he is
Almost instantly worried by the dogs. At the very moment that
Elizabeth took Essex's head, a giant brown bear
Stood in the gardens with dogs hanging from his fur . . .
He took away the sun, took
A wolfhound in his mouth, and tossed it into
The white lap of Elizabeth I—arrows and staves rained

On his chest, and standing, he, then, stood even taller, seeing
Into the Queen's private boxes—he grinned
into her battered eggshell face.
Another volley of arrows and poles, and opening his mouth he
      showered
Blood all over Elizabeth and her Privy Council.

The very next evening, a cool evening, the Queen demanded
13 bears and the justice of 113 dogs: She slept

All that Sunday night and much of the next morning.
Some said she was guilty of *this* and *that*.
The Protestant Queen gave the defeated bear
A grave in a Catholic cemetery. The marker said:
Peter, a Solstice Bear, a gift of the Tsarevitch to Elizabeth.

After a long winter she had the grave opened. The bear's skeleton
Was cleared with lye, she placed it at her bedside,
Put a candle inside behind the sockets of the eyes, and, then
She spoke to it:

You were a Christmas bear—behind your eyes
I see the walls of a snow cave where you are a cub still smelling
Of your mother's blood which has dried in your hair; you have
Troubled a Queen who was afraid when seated in *shade* which,
      standing,

You had created! A Queen who often wakes with a dream of you at
    night—
Now, you'll stand by my bed in your long white bones; alone, you
Will frighten away at night all visions of bear, and all day
You will be in this cold room—your constant grin,
You'll stand in the long, white prodigy of your bones, and you are,

Every inch of you, a terrible vision, not bear, but virgin!

Gretel Ehrlich

Everett Dunklee

Gretel Ehrlich was born in Santa Barbara, California, in 1946. She was educated at Bennington College and U.C.L.A. She is the author of two books of poetry, *To Touch the Water* (Ahsahta Press, 1981), and *Geode/ Rock Body* (Capra Press, 1970). Among her awards for poetry and film are fellowships from the National Endowment for the Arts and the Corporation for Public Broadcasting. She lives in Shell, Wyoming.

The Orchard

We go into it at night.
In Wyoming an orchard is the
only city around—so many blossoms going up
into trees like lights
and windfall apples like lives
coming down.

In the pickup, heads on the tailgate,
we lie on last year's hay and wait
for the orchard to bloom.

A great horned owl sweeps between
trees as if to cropdust the rising
sap with white for the flowers.

"The first blossom to come," you say,
"I'll give the apple that grows there to you."

Another owl lands
on a bare branch and drops
a plug of micebones to the roots.
Under him, the tree does not think of
the sap's struggle.
I listen to your heart. Divided by
beats and rests, it says yes, then no, then yes.

Above us the Milky Way seams the sky and is
stirred by a hand too big to see.
We watch the stars.

Tonight so many of them fall.

Cutting Wood on Shell Creek

We cut into dead bodies for heat.
Cottonwoods that stood up for
the first cattlemen in this valley
and pointed to water,
now firewood.
Dead too are your
grandfathers who bathed
and made children on this river,
then closed their eyes to
its surging brightness until
it spread forward to you.

When we use water in
Wyoming, we're using time.
Nine hours on a mountain
are melted out by simple
ablutions after love—
spring water, holy,
cupped over cockhead and face.

Even though I want to marry
you, be your sister-father-brother,
we can't adjust the river's
heretic clock of births, break-
ups and marriages to fit
who we are or learn
what water knows, that letting go
is real time, actual
passion whose
natural velocity mends
what is separate in the world.

Fourteen months gone by.
A skull's slow-moving
season of being "just friends"
hammered open. Inside:
your mind like a bee
stung by another bee—
fast, brooding, fiesty.
And in front of those
accordioned workings,
your eyes—trout-spotted,
sagging at far corners as if
pulled by some ancient
understanding of gravity—
that we are simply here.

Tonight Northern lights
shimmy up black poles and
shine, Kirilian, against
the Big Horn's false
scaffolding of permanence.

I've been flung to the dark
side of this planet and rise
as those black moons in your eyes,
swimming upstream in iris
towards the private
blue tenderness pulsing
there.

A Sheeprancher Named John

A swarming.
Orange as bees into hair, a face.
In a long overcoat of them he moves swiftly
by stings and grace across Big Horn Mountains
against an upstream current of sheep.
When he speaks it is brutally to the point.
His fingers taper. A diamond ring orbits one of them
and is glazed by the silkdust of oats.
Orange, not direct light but
slanted, helplessly elegant, a color of
minor disrepute—faded chiffon draped
on the high, startled bones of his face.
Skin crisscrossed, uncertain tracks of aging,
irregular hems sewn, the threads pulled out.
His whole body, orange and burnt orange.
The abalone shell of his back with rich meat
under it, perfectly plumbed and moving sideways in
the sign of Cancer.
On his arms, sunspots like birdseed melted and
scraped smooth—burns on powdery skin.
How could it be so soft in a climate that weathers?
Mouth, a loose tear across the face, rarely
moved by shapes of words, but a listening apparatus—
lips slide apart, mark feelings awash and received.

Eyes are steady-state. Burnt all the way brown.
Shy penis, mostly
swirled white.

A Way of Speaking

Tonight is the one
that neither bosoms nor
spits us out, that cannot hatch
its eggs of desire or even
the ones that come after,
of nothingness.
Your hand does not go
around my breast to find
the milk there.
It was on this range we met,
moving your father's cattle.
We rode in dust. We laced our
strangers' lives behind the herd.
We did not know what kind of knot
we would make.
Standing in the stirrups at a dead run,
you showed me how to throw a loop and dally up
without losing fingers.
During the day our legs
touched, moved apart, touched again.
To live with cattle as we did
was to enter the inward blousing of grass
and drift there.
Once you showed me
what time was by leaving me;
when I forgot, you showed me again
by coming back.
That fall, on the Greybull River,
I saw how cowboys fish:

mounting a moss-slick rock
with high-heeled leaps, you hulked
over water.
You faced the current.
You dared trout to collide
with your too-big hook tied to bailing string
and when nothing bit you said,
"See, even fish think it's boring."
Once we entered that river.
It slit its neck so we
might use its voice.
Even so, I do not know if there is
a way of speaking that ever
takes one person to another,
or forward to what they might become.

Lynn Emanuel

Mark Chin

Lynn Emanuel was born in 1949 in New York City. Her first book of poems, *Hotel Fiesta*, was published by The University of Georgia Press in 1984. She has been awarded fellowships from the Pennsylvania Council on the Arts and the National Endowment for the Arts. She teaches at the University of Pittsburgh.

Berlin Interior with Jews, 1939

This is the year Europe looks up in sublime disregard
From the margin between two wars' classic accessories.
I am tired of the standard pictures of the Jews.
Even the Black Forest reminds me of my grandfather
Whose watch hands were tiny as pine needles.
I am tired of the fire twisting on the hearth where the maid
Brews hot mint tea in the middle of summer,
Tired of the sweet lip of the glass she lifts
To her mouth, tired of the reading of the *Aeneid*
And Dido lying down on the burning pyre—
Goodbye, goodbye the fire whispers to her flesh

Although no one listens. I am tired of my grandmother
Having to stand at the window to watch a train
That trickle of darkness at the horizon, slow, slightly crooked.
This is the year only the lamplight sleeps
Against her breast, the year she will wear her husband's
Gloves to bed because the buttons at the wrist,
Small, shiney as the eyes of her parakeet,
Stare as though they know her and this is the year
The maid in her red shawl bending to the kettle
On the hearth resembles a flame blown down by wind
And is about to be snuffed back to the wick of her black shoes.

Frying Trout While Drunk

Mother is drinking to forget a man
Who could fill the woods with invitations:
Come with me he whispered and she went
In his Nash Rambler, its dash
Where her knees turned green
In the radium dials of the '50s.
When I drink it is always 1953,
Bacon wilting in the pan on Cook Street
And mother, wrist deep in red water,
Laying a trail from the sink
To a glass of gin and back.
She is a beautiful, unlucky woman
In love with a man of lechery so solid
You could build a table on it
And when you did the blues would come to visit.
I remember all of us awkwardly at dinner,
The dark slung across the porch,
And then mother's dress falling to the floor,
Buttons ticking like seeds spit on a plate.
When I drink I am too much like her—
The knife in one hand and in the other

The trout with a belly white as my wrist.
I have loved you all my life
She told him and it was true
In the same way that all her life
She drank, dedicated to the act itself,
She stood at this stove
And with the care of the very drunk
Handed him the plate.

Of Your Father's Indiscretions and the Train to California

One summer he stole the jade buttons
Sewn like peas down aunt Ora's dress
And you, who loved that trail of noise and darkness
Hauling itself across the horizon,
Moths spiraling in the big lamps,
Loved the oily couplings and the women's round hats
Haunting all the windows
And the way he held you on his knee like a ventriloquist
Discussing the lush push of grass against the tree's roots
Or a certain crookedness in the trunk.
Now everything is clearer.
Now when the train pulls away from the station
And the landscape begins to come around, distant and yet familiar,
That odd crease of yellow light
Or the woods' vague sweep framed in the window forever
Remind you of the year you were locked up at the Hotel Fiesta
While father went out with fast black minks.
And how wonderful it was
When he was narrow as a hat pin in his tux
And to have come all that way on his good looks.
How wonderful to have discovered lust
And know that one day you would be on its agenda
Like the woman who drank and walked naked through the house

In her black hat, the one you used to watch
Through a stammer in the drapes.
In that small town of cold hotels, you were the girl in the dress
Red as a house burning down.

The Sleeping

I have imagined all this:
In 1940 my parents were in love
And living in the loft on West 10th
Above Mark Rothko who painted cabbage roses
On their bedroom walls the night they got married.

I can guess why he did it.
My mother's hair was the color of yellow apples
And she wore a black velvet hat with her pajamas.

I was not born yet. I was remote as starlight.
It is hard for me to imagine that
My parents made love in a roomful of roses
And I wasn't there.

But now I am. My mother is blushing.
This is the wonderful thing about art.
It can bring back the dead. It can wake the sleeping
As it might have late that night
When my father and mother made love above Rothko
Who lay in the dark thinking *Roses, Roses, Roses*.

Daniel Mark Epstein

Daniel Mark Epstein was born in 1948. He holds a B.A. from Kenyon College and an M.F.A. from Vermont College. *No Vacancies in Hell* was published by Liveright in 1973. His other books of poems, *The Follies* (1977), *Young Men's Gold* (1978), and *The Book of Fortune* (1982), are all from Overlook/Viking Press. He is the recipient of the Prix de Rome and fellowships from the National Endowment for the Arts and the Guggenheim Foundation. He is writer-in-residence at Towson State University.

June Chaplin

Miami

After years of stock-car racing, running
rifles to Cuba, money from Rio, high
diving from helicopters into the Gulf;
after a life at gunpoint, on a dare,
my father can't make the flight out of Miami.

Turbojets roar and sing, the ground crew
scatters out of the shadow of the plane.
My father undoes his seat belt, makes his way
up the aisle, dead-white and sweating,
ducks out the hatchway, mumbling
luggage was left at the dock, his watch
in the diner. Head down
he lurches through the accordion boarding tube,
strides the shining wing of the airport, past
windows full of planes and sky, past bars,

candy machines and posters for Broadway shows.
Gasping in the stratosphere of terror, he
bursts through the glass doors and runs
to a little garden near the rental cars.
He sits among the oleanders and palms.

It started with the Bay Bridge.
He couldn't take that steel vault into the blue
above the blue, so much horizon!
Then it was the road itself, the rise and fall,
the continual blind curve.
He hired a chauffeur, he took the train.
Then it was hotels, so many rooms
the same, he had to sleep with the light on.
His courage has shrunk to the size of a windowbox.

Father who scared the witches and vampires
from my childhood closets, father
who walked before me like a hero's shield
through neighborhoods where hoodlums honed their knives
on concrete, where nerve was law,
who will drive you home from Miami?
You're broke and I'm a thousand miles away
with frightened children of my own.
Who will rescue you from the garden
where jets flash like swords above your head?

Mannequins

This indecent procession of the undead
    invades the Avenue windows, dressed to kill,
sporting tomorrow's clothes and yesterday's faces.

One struts in a velvet shaft of midnight blue,
    slashed down the back in a diamond heat of lust,

gold crown at the wrist and throat, a garnet ring.
Here Lucie Anne side-slits a terry dress
      trimmed in Venetian lace
and petal edging on the camisole. There a lady
      most unladylike, lounges
in silk of liquidly drapable muscadine,
      grinning the wine-red of wickedness. Another
borrows the schoolgirl's kiss, the cupie bow,
eyes round and empty as pots, and the apple cheek.
For we also yearn to join the innocent in their clothes:
      Jill in her jumper, Johnnie in his jeans,
sheep in their fleece, the pig in his narrow poke.

But I prefer them naked, the posturing frauds,
free from any trace of shame, and without nipples
      or the fur that friction-proofs our parts for love.
I like them headless, oh Marie Antoinette,
      what beauty knocked in the executioner's bucket!
I like them wigless, as a rack of bullets.
I like when a leg is kicked out of its socket
or an arm flings back in some preposterous gesture
as if to say
"So happy to have missed the agony of meeting you,"
or
"We who are early salute you from the backs of our heads."
I love when the feet swivel for a fast retreat,
and the head jerks in wonder defying the neck.

But when they are assembled and decked out,
they turn vicious, whispering through the glass:
"How have you achieved your shabbiness?
Where is your glamour, the youth you were born with?
Where, if you have one eye, is the other,
and if you have three limbs, where is the fourth?
Where is your hair, marcelled or carefully windblown,
your eyebrows, the artfully painted lips?
Put your face to the glass, you wretched snail,
kiss me, you desecration of a man."

The Follies

Blind Mr. Klugel loves the baritone of Mr. Cantini.

Mr. Klugel rocks on the back porch, listening
while his wife begins her nightly striptease
      in the bright showcase of her bedroom window:
a benefit for the ragged voyeurs of the South City
    who can look but cannot touch.

Time for all good children to be in bed.

From the tar roof of a row house over the wharves
      pours the wide baritone of the moderately drunk Mr. Cantini
singing the sun into a new country, singing
the boats to sleep in their slips, taming the oil rainbows
      to a flat shimmer in the harbor lights,
calling the stevedores to battle in dockside bars and blank alleys,
tuning up the full moon chorus of neighborhood dogs,
      summoning the sluggard moon,
waking up everybody's children.

At the Millinery Shop

She wants what no clerk in the city can bring her,
    a hat that will make up her mind.
White satin speaks to the red in her cheeks,
    red satin to the white.
Blue crepe shades the clear well of her eye.

She wants a hat to fit her head like an idea
    so perfect only she could have dreamed it up,
a hat that draws attention to itself by disappearing
    and to the head by building on it
a profusion of silent worlds in incomparable colors.

She wants a hat that can think for itself,
        that will select the proper head for its household.
She turns her back on the round table-mirror
    and a garden of hats on spindles,
admiring the beige lid with a feathery band.

Holding it at arm's length,
        her eyes half-closed,
she leans back
under a straw bonnet crowned with flowers
    that casually tries itself on her.

Cash Only, No Refund, No Return

Earl stood on two legs when he had one to spare,
    then on one leg when the cancer got him,
a short leg and a wicked crutch.
By his own count Earl was accomplice to thirty-four
        murders, ninety-two muggings and five suicides.
His finger followed the headlines in the paper
    spread out on a glass case that bristled with knives:
Florentine daggers, Arkansas toothpicks,
black bone and pearl-handled stilettos with blades
that kick loose and lock fast with a flick of the wrist,
Turkish daggers with serpentine blades
        to snake the guts from the meanest vendetta.

He stood there in the back end of the arcade
        and they came to him
from bars, the precinct lock-up, from flop-houses,
whore houses, foreclosed houses, faithless wives,
good friends gone bad, betrayals, threats, divorces.
Earl had the voice and nose of Jimmie Durante
        and knew how to sell knives.
He just stood there behind the display case.

Calvin Forbes

Calvin Forbes was born in 1945. He is the author of two collections of poetry, *Blue Monday* (Wesleyan University Press, 1974) and *From the Book of Shine* (Burning Deck Press, 1979). Among his awards is a fellowship from the National Endowment for the Arts. He teaches at Howard University.

Bryan Studios

Some Pieces

When two elephants fight
It's only the grass that suffers

In the land of nod
Coke is king and scag god

I'm going I'm gone
Baby look what you've done
Left me and now day has come

The statues of some people never smile
Buddha does like a senile grandmother

Between us the bread was always stale

Should I lay my head on railroad tracks
Or should I lay my head on your wide lap

They can't plow the river
Snow lies on everything except
The road and it's black black

If I were a catfish swimming
In the deep blue sea
I'd start all you women
Jumping in after me

Somebody's in my bed
And they got my long johns on
I don't mind you taking my woman
But you better take my long johns off

And the white hand
Which bought me here
Which I learnt to hold
Now pushes me off the cliff

You can go home now

Your fingers are negroes
They do all the work for your fat arms

The Chocolate Soldiers

Where's the winning without chocolate
I asked the General when the white bombs

Landed on Venus beach and the natives
Shot their tongues into our ears. Once

Chocolate was in front, and strangers
Bit what our hands extended, not laying

Us but we laying them in the dungy hay.
Brown candy melted in colonial mouths

When chocolate was sweet politics; white
Sons wrote home about Guam and bodies

With nude ankles. Now natives lay waste.
The brown will dominate even on Venus beach

Though I want to admit to taking my mirror
To insure courageous chocolate dwells there.

The Other Side of This World

Put my glad rags in a cardboard box—
This old jiggerboo never grew mature.
Is everything in its place except me?
Don't be surprised; I called all day

And the only person I could reach was
The operator; and it's a sorry day when
Nothing is coming down but your foot.
And how deep is your stomach cause

That's how far your heart will fall!
When I'm gone I might come back cause
I'm always forgetting something special.
A crease in my overalls, my collar stiff,

I cried as many tears as I have teeth.
And I only got two in my mouth. Son of the

Sun look out: as you get black you burn.
Is everything in its place except me?

M.A.P.

For Marcia

They can have your thighs,
Your ripe behind;
And even your Ibo eyes.
Or trade your breast on Wall Street.

But give me your mouth.
Save that for me
So I might hear you singing.

Even your tasty labia,
Delicate as the petals of a flower,
Can't speak as well

As the mouth
Below the plateau of your nose.
Send me your lips C.O.D.

And I will crown you Dancing Mouth
For your lips
Mambo across my face.

You may die,
But will me your bright mouth.
You may visit your Mother
At the basin of the Nile—

But surely you are kind enough
To leave my source
With me?

Or should I get a prescription
For a chastity belt
For your lips?

Or insure them under Lloyds of London?
Or form an organization
With the good acronym M.A.P.

her Mouth Always Pleases—
And claim we're charitable
And tax-exempt?

Carolyn Forché

Carolyn Forché was born in Detroit, Michigan, in 1950. Her first book of poems, *Gathering the Tribes* (1975), received the Yale Series of Younger Poets Award. Her second book, *The Country Between Us* (1982), was the Lamont Poetry Selection of the Academy of American Poets and was published by Harper & Row. A volume of translations of the poetry of Claribel Alegria, *Flowers from the Volcano* (1982), was published by the University of Pittsburgh Press. Among her awards are fellowships from the National Endowment for the Arts and the Guggenheim Foundation. She teaches at Columbia University.

For the Stranger

Although you mention Venice
keeping it on your tongue like a fruit pit
and I say yes, perhaps Bucharest, neither of us
really knows. There is only this train
slipping through pastures of snow,
a sleigh reaching down
to touch its buried runners.
We meet on the shaking platform,
the wind's broken teeth sinking into us.
You unwrap your dark bread
and share with me the coffee
sloshing into your gloves.
Telegraph posts chop the winter fields

into white blocks, in each window
the crude painting of a small farm.
We listen to mothers scolding
children in English as if
we do not understand a word of it—
sit still, sit still.

There are few clues as to where
we are: the baled wheat scattered
everywhere like missing coffins.
The distant yellow kitchen lights
wiped with oil.
Everywhere the black dipping wires
stretching messages from one side
of a country to the other.
The men who stand on every border
waving to us.

Wiping ovals of breath from the windows
in order to see ourselves, you touch
the glass tenderly wherever it holds my face.
Days later, you are showing me
photographs of a woman and children
smiling from the windows of your wallet.

Each time the train slows, a man
with our faces in the gold buttons
of his coat passes through the cars
muttering the name of a city. Each time
we lose people. Each time I find you
again between the cars, holding out
a scrap of bread for me, something
hot to drink, until there are
no more cities and you pull me
toward you, sliding your hands
into my coat, telling me
your name over and over, hurrying
your mouth into mine.
We have, each of us, nothing.
We will give it to each other.

The Memory of Elena

We spend our morning
in the flower stalls counting
the dark tongues of bells
that hang from ropes waiting
for the silence of an hour.
We find a table, ask for *paella*,
cold soup and wine, where a calm
light trembles years behind us.

In Buenos Aires only three
years ago, it was the last time his hand
slipped into her dress, with pearls
cooling her throat and bells like
these, chipping at the night—

As she talks, the hollow
clopping of a horse, the sound
of bones touched together.
The *paella* comes, a bed of rice
and *camarones*, fingers and shells,
the lips of those whose lips
have been removed, mussels
the soft blue of a leg socket.

This is not *paella*, this is what
has become of those who remained
in Buenos Aires. This is the ring
of a rifle report on the stones,
her hand over her mouth,
her husband falling against her.

These are the flowers we bought
this morning, the dahlias tossed
on his grave and bells
waiting with their tongues cut out
for this particular silence.

Because One Is Always Forgotten

IN MEMORIAM, JOSÉ RUDOLFO VIERA
1939–1981: EL SALVADOR

When Viera was buried we knew it had come to an end,
his coffin rocking into the ground like a boat or a cradle.

I could take my heart, he said, and give it to a *campesino*
and he would cut it up and give it back:

you can't eat heart in those four dark
chambers where a man can be kept years.

A boy soldier in the bone-hot sun works his knife
to peel the face from a dead man

and hang it from the branch of a tree
flowering with such faces.

The heart is the toughest part of the body.
Tenderness is in the hands.

Selective Service

We rise from the snow where we've
lain on our backs and flown like children,
from the imprint of perfect wings and cold gowns,
and we stagger together wine-breathed into town
where our people are building
their armies again, short years after
body bags, after burnings. There is a man
I've come to love after thirty, and we have
our rituals of coffee, of airports, regret.
After love we smoke and sleep

with magazines, two shot glasses
and the black and white collapse of hours.
In what time do we live that it is too late
to have children? In what place
that we consider the various ways to leave?
There is no list long enough
for a selective service card shriveling
under a match, the prison that comes of it,
a flag in the wind eaten from its pole
and boys sent back in trash bags.
We'll tell you. You were at that time
learning fractions. We'll tell you
about fractions. Half of us are dead or quiet
or lost. Let them speak for themselves.
We lie down in the fields and leave behind
the corpses of angels.

Reunion

*"Just as he changes himself, in the end eternity
    changes him."*
                                        —MALLARMÉ

On the phonograph, the voice
of a woman already dead for three
decades, singing of a man
who could make her do anything.
On the table, two fragile
glasses of black wine,
a bottle wrapped in its towel.
It is that room, the one
we took in every city, it is
as I remember: the bed, a block
of moonlight and pillows.
My fingernails, peeks of light

on your thighs.
The stink of the fire escape.
The wet butts of cigarettes
you crushed one after another.
How I watched the morning come
as you slept, more my son
than a man ten years older.
How my breasts feel, years
later, the tongues swishing
in my dress, some yours, some
left by other men.
Since then, I have always
wakened first, I have learned
to leave a bed without being
seen and have stood
at the washbasins, wiping oil
and salt from my skin,
staring at the cupped water
in my two hands.
I have kept everything
you whispered to me then.
I can remember it now as I see you
again, how much tenderness we could
wedge between a stairwell
and a police lock, or as it was,
as it still is, in the voice
of a woman singing of a man
who could make her do anything.

City Walk-up, Winter 1969

There is the morning shuffle of traffic confined
to a window, the blue five p.m. of a street
light, a yellow supper left untouched.

A previous month is pinned to the wall where
days are numbered differently and described by
the photograph of a dead season. If I could
move from the bed I would clear the window
and cold-palmed watch myself at twenty, walking
in frozen socks with sacks of clothes and letters,
wearing three winter coats from Goodwill,
keeping a footing on the slick silence
of the hysterical deaf. When I tell of my life
now it is not this version.

I would see her climb three flights
of a condemned house with her bags
because she is still awakened
by a wrecking ball swung to the attic ribs
and the shelled daylight that followed her
everywhere after that: a silent implosion
of rooms, the xylophone bells as a fire
escape plummeted toward the ice.
Even now the house itself is etched
on the hard black air where it had been.
No one knew about it then: meals
of raw egg and snow, rolls of insulation
in which she wrapped herself, a blanket
of brown paper and spun glass.
From Kosinski she took the idea of a tin
can, its white lard given to birds, small
holes of punched light on her face.
She wrote names on walls and was aware
of her hands, chewing the skin into small
white scraps around each nail. She still
eats her hands and steals bread: street
screamer, housewife, supermarket thief.

We do not rid ourselves of these things
even when we are cured of personal silence
when for no reason one morning
we begin to hear the noise of the world again.

Tess Gallagher

Maureen Hurley

Tess Gallagher was born in 1943. Her books of poetry are *Instructions to the Double* (1976), *Under Stars* (1978), and *Willingly* (1985), all from Graywolf Press. She has received two fellowships from the National Endowment for the Arts and a fellowship from the Guggenheim Foundation. She is currently teaching at Syracuse University.

Women's Tug of War at Lough Arrow

In a borrowed field they dig in their feet
and clasp the rope. Balanced
against neighboring women, they hold
the ground by the little gained
and leaning like boatmen rowing into
the damp earth, they pull
to themselves the invisible waves, waters
overcalmed by desertion
or the narrow look trained to a brow.

The steady rain has made girls of them,
their hair in ringlets. Now they haul
the live weight to the cries
of husbands and children, until the rope
runs slack, runs free
and all are bound again by the arms
of those who held them, not until, but so
they gave.

Under Stars

The sleep of this night deepens
because I have walked coatless from the house
carrying the white envelope.
All night it will say one name
in its little tin house by the roadside.

I have raised the metal flag
so its shadow under the roadlamp
leaves an imprint on the rain-heavy bushes.
Now I will walk back
thinking of the few lights still on
in the town a mile away.

In the yellowed light of a kitchen
the millworker has finished his coffee,
his wife has laid out the white slices of bread
on the counter. Now while the bed they have left
is still warm, I will think of you, you
who are so far away
you have caused me to look up at the stars.

Tonight they have not moved
from childhood, those games played after dark.
Again I walk into the wet grass

toward the starry voices. Again, I
am the found one, intimate, returned
by all I touch on the way.

Black Silk

She was cleaning—there is always
that to do—when she found,
at the top of the closet, his old
silk vest. She called me
to look at it, unrolling it carefully
like something live
might fall out. Then we spread it
on the kitchen table and smoothed
the wrinkles down, making our hands
heavy until its shape against Formica
came back and the little tips
that would have pointed to his pockets
lay flat. The buttons were all there.
I held my arms out and she
looped the wide armholes over
them. "That's one thing I never
wanted to be," she said, "a man."
I went into the bathroom to see
how I looked in the sheen and
sadness. Wind chimes
off-key in the alcove. Then her
crying so I stood back in the sink-light
where the porcelain had been staring. Time
to go to her, I thought, with that
other mind, and stood still.

The Shirts

They would be shamed to see back at us,
themselves among the others.
I have done this, have hung them
side by side. Did I ask this
or did they come to me? And what
can it mean that I keep their shapes
without them?

They are all colors and one
has thin stripes with lavender. My hands
from the sleeves are another's, reminding,
and the small, exact musculature
of his arms takes on my body.
When I left he said, "Take this. Until
I see you next." Much later
he would tell her name, the woman
who bought it. Its changed face
where my breasts force out
and the one thought: our size, the same.

The green one like the moss-light
of lovers on the forest floor, its
shoulders too broad, the collar sharp
with intention. Flannel, the fur
of winter, fires that light up the forehead
and cast the eyes in shadow. In it,
I am the young girl whose protector
fills her with dread and does not
return. Its caution: "Don't
wear this when you meet her."

This one is blue and the man of it
had eyes like that. "Blue," I said,
"send me some good books. I
want to know how you think."
He had a lot of shirts like this one.
When I took it, he could not
miss it as the special one.

Only this have I given back.
The red one. The one with the blotch
of pitch that would not wash out.
Fire-shirt of the question: will it end?
Man with the passion to burn his love out
in me, nightly, daily, the white-hot
tongs of love. He wears it to breakfast.
Wants pure maple syrup. He likes the pitcher
full. He can stand the sweetness.

Crêpes Flambeau

We are three women eating out
in a place that could be California
or New Jersey but is Texas and our waiter
says his name is Jerry. He is pink
and young, dressed in soft denim
with an embroidered vest and, my friend says,
a nice butt. It's hard not to be intimate
in America where your waiter wants
you to call him Jerry. So why
do you feel sorry for him
standing over the flames
of this dessert?

The little fans of the crêpes are
folding into the juice. The brandy
is aflare in a low blue hush and golden
now and red where he spills
the brown sugar saved
to make our faces wear the sudden burst. We
are all good-looking and older and he
has to please us or try
to. What could go wrong? Too much

brandy? Too little sugar? Fire
falling into our laps, fire
like laughter behind his back, even
when he has done it just right. "Jerry,"
we say, "that was wonderful," for now
he is blushing at us
like a russet young girl. Our lips

are red with fire and juice.
He knows we could go on
eating long into the night until the flames
run down our throats. "Thank you,"
he says, handing us our check, knowing,
among the ferns and napkins, that he has
pleased us, briefly, like all
good things, dying away
at the only moment, before
we are too happy, too
glad in the pioneer decor: rough boards,
spotted horses in the frame.

Each Bird Walking

Not while, but long after he had told me,
I thought of him, washing his mother, his
bending over the bed and taking back
the covers. There was a basin of water
and he dipped a washrag in and
out of the basin, the rag
dripping a little onto the sheet as he
turned from the bedside to the nightstand
and back, there being no place

on her body he shouldn't touch because
he had to and she helped him, moving
the little she could, lifting so he could
wipe under her arms, a dipping motion
in the hollow. Then working up from
the feet, around the ankles, over the
knees. And this last, opening
her thighs and running the rag firmly
and with the cleaning thought
up through her crotch, between the lips,
over the V of thin hairs—

as though he were a mother
who had the excuse of cleaning to touch
with love and indifference
the secret parts of her child, to graze
the sleepy sexlessness in its waiting
to find out what to do for the sake
of the body, for the sake of what only
the body can do for itself.

So his hand, softly at the place
of his birth-light. And she, eyes deepened
and closed in the dim room.
And because he told me her death as
important to his being with her,
I could love him another way. Not
of the body alone, or of its making,
but carried in the white spires of trembling
until what spirit, what breath we were
was shaken from us. Small then,
the word *holy*.

He turned her on her stomach
and washed the blades of her shoulders, the
small of her back. "That's good," she said,
"that's enough."

On our lips that morning, the tart juice
of the mothers, so strong in remembrance, no
asking, no giving, and what you said, this
being the end of our loving, so as not to hurt
the closer one to you, made me look
to see what was left of us
with our sex taken away. "Tell me," I said,
"something I can't forget." Then the story of
your mother, and when you finished
I said, "That's good, that's enough."

Skylights

In the night I get up and walk
between the slices of deep blue sky.
After a time, I lie down on the floor
and stare up like a child on a roof. Stars
tug at my face. The rooms commune
like hillsides. I think of antelope, of
the talons of owls, of a tiger
that has not eaten for days.
"Come to bed," the man calls to me. "What
are you doing?" The moon
has floated into my coffin.
In a cool, white light I rise
and go downstairs to the kitchen table.
A little starlight clings
to the tablecloth, the clock face, the rim
of a water glass. "Is anything
the matter?" he calls. It is then
the wild sound comes to my throat and
for a moment my house hurtles through space
like the word *hungry*
uttered by an army of tigers
advancing on a column of children.

207 / TESS GALLAGHER

Stillness. The moon
caresses the carcasses of tigers
and children. I alone am spared.
Softly then, his footsteps.

Some Painful Butterflies Pass Through

I saw the old Chinese men standing
in Nanjing under the trees where
they had hung their caged birds
in the early morning as though a cage
were only another branch that travels
with us. The bird revolves and settles,
moving its mind up and down the tree
with leaves and light. It sings
with the free birds—what else
can it do? They sit on the rungs
and preen or jit back and down and
back. But they are busy
and a day in the sky makes wings
of them. Then some painful butterflies
pass through.

The old men talk and smoke, examine
each other's cages. They feel restored,
as if they'd given themselves a tree, a sky
full of companions, song
that can travel. They depend
on their birds, and if their love stories
swing from their arms as they walk
homeward, it may be they are chosen
after all like one tree
with one bird that is faithful,
an injured voice traveling high into silence

with one accustomed listener
who smiles and walks slowly with
his face in the distance so
the pleasure spreads, and the treasured
singing, and the little bursts
of flying.

Shanghai / June 11, 1983

Reginald Gibbons

Elaine Miller

Reginald Gibbons was born in 1947 in Houston, Texas. He holds an A.B. from Princeton University, and an M.A. and a Ph.D. from Stanford University. His books of poetry are *Roofs, Voices, Roads* (The Quarterly Review of Literature, 1979) and *The Ruined Motel* (Houghton Mifflin, 1981). He is the editor of *The Poet's Work* (Houghton Mifflin, 1979) and the translator of *Selected Poems of Luis Cernuda* (University of California Press, 1977) and *Guillén on Guillén* (with A. L. Geist, Princeton University Press, 1979). He is the recipient of a Fulbright Fellowship and fellowships from the National Endowment for the Arts and the Guggenheim Foundation. He teaches at Northwestern University, where he edits *TriQuarterly*.

The Ruined Motel

Give the mourning doves any sun
at all and they will begin to grieve.
Their song, riding the steam that poured up
from the snow on the window-ledge,
came in to us as we scanned
the damp wreck of a seaside room,
all the things no one inherited:
the sour pink and beige paint,
a throng of water-stain shapes
on the walls—splotchy heads

and moldy animal herds—and behind us
brown vines leaning in at the door
to greet the webs and frost-burnt
mushrooms in the closet.

We sheltered there while our car
held alone the whole weedy expanse
of asphalt fronting the ocean,
and we listened to the cold wind
spill through the sea-grove and splash
against the line of downed carports
and the crowd of pines in the pool.

Looming ahead of us
at the end of the empty road, the shell
of the place had made us think
that it must have been ugly
even when new. Maybe ruined
it suits the small outposts of worshippers
nearby at Immanuel Baptist Church
(Fundamental and Independent)
who grasp their tradition with such force
they tear it apart, their fierce
conviction shredding the creeds
while doves coo and with a useless hiss
the sea bites into the beach-snow
and falls back across the crescent sands.

I was thinking, This was where we had brought
the nation, to neighboring new tries
either abandoned or shuddering inward with extremes—
till you said to me, The ghosts in this place
are unhappy. Then I too could hear them—
couples revenging the hours they had
together under ceilings
that never fell on them, the too-loud talk
at dinner and the hedging, hopeful
postcards in the morning.
We stepped away from them, from the boards

and slats of their collapsed beds,
from their fatigue, from musty air and dead wires,
we went back into the salt wind
and the noisy swaying pines, out
of that heap of winter-storm
tide-wrack. We didn't want to make
any mistakes but those we could say were ours.

But in that time we stayed there
we took the loss into ourselves,
obsessed with it—not stones
but rotting beaverboard and cold snake-nests,
not columns but dark hallways half-floored with sand.
And if the light that fell on us
as we walked toward the water,
that warmed our bones and stirred the doves,
made the scene seem a lesson-book—
the angles of human spaces, the path
upward—what did we read?
Under light-shafts from broken clouds,
an immense illumination
of breached walls, frail trees,
a narrow road, snow on the dunes,
dry weed-wisps and bright bits of plastic . . .
and rolling in the waves
like heads that strove
against their own deformity
the great whelks
dashed and battered till hope
was the hollowness in their cold clean skulls.

"Luckies"

The loop of rusty cable incises
its shadow on the stucco wall.
My father smiles shyly and takes
one of my cigarettes, holding it

awkwardly at first, as if it were
a dart, while the yard slowly
swings across the wide sill of daylight.
Then it is a young man's quick hand

that rises to his lips, he leans against the wall,
his white shirt open at the throat,
where the skin is weathered, and he chats
and daydreams, something he never does.

Smoking his cigarette, he is even
younger than I am, a brother who
begins to guess, amazed, that what
he will do will turn out to be this.

He recalls the house he had
when I was born, leaning against it
now after work, the pale stucco
of memory, 1947.

Baby bottles stand near the sink inside.
The new wire of the telephone, dozing
in a coil, waits for the first call.
The years are smoke.

The Cedar River

For Mark Haverland

You bring the Dardevle back fast,
left wrist whirling in a circle
as the line fills the reel—
back from the water near reeds
where at the end of a long arc
it hit with a pop and leapt toward you.
It zags, jerks, darts, describes
a progress so quick
no nerves could catch it. Then
a tail-swirl riffles the surface . . .
and another pass, so high
the fins break through.
The marauding head—
eyes as low as the long jaw
that will snap sideways out of what
seems pure spite—rushes up
but the shape of the canoe
clouds its heaven and it panics.
The big splash of the escape
comes over the gunwale
and the lure hangs in its wake,
teasing the delicate tip of the rod
that nods like an innocent stalk of wild rice.

Breath

I remember coming up,
pushing off from the bottom
through dull ringing silence
toward the undersurface of the water

where light sparkled—or patterns
fanned across the roof-fabric:
that deep comfort, long ago, of
being carried to the house
in the dark, half-asleep, only
half-interrupting the dreams
that had made the car a craft
among stars. But the air—
and the house—held
depths too, where someone else,
someone larger, locked the doors,
did late-night chores and turned out
the lights, too tired now
to stop the inevitable
fight, rising to it . . .

Underwater, you hear bodies
burble over you, smashing the sunlight—
and voices in other rooms begin
to swell, drawers shutting, bags
slammed down from closet shelves,
footsteps . . . Till a child's fear,
held under, shudders free, floating up
to explode with a gasp, and splashes
out of sleep, and sucks air,
and discovers that nothing
consoles, there is no air,
there is no waking, not anywhere.

Make Me Hear You

When my Aunt Lera—tiny now,
slow moving and slow talking—
wanted to tell me about
her life, she began by saying,

"Curtis and me had just one . . .
year . . . together." Curdiss
(the way she says it) was
a genial great man by all
remembrances of him, and the two
of them, just married, would go
fishing in the evening from
the banks of the Pearl,
the green stream in Mt. Olive,
Mississippi. A year of that—
quiet aloneness together
after supper, things each showed
the other, the bed turned down—
and then Curtis's father
came to live with them
in their tiny house and while
Curtis was away at work
in the mill the old man would
find his way out to the yard
and have fits, twirling around,
falling, so she'd have to
pick him up and carry him
back inside, and that was
how they lived till
Curtis died, and then his father.
The pain that Lera wouldn't
cry of now is like what I'm
now the cause of: the things
gone in time that you and I
held only as sweet memories
of towns, walks, rivers,
beds, kingdoms, I took away
a second time when I killed
your hopes—*and mine,
and mine*—for more sweet days
to come, and I left that
best time locked in the past.
Dead Curdiss is Lera's
old ghost who's flown with her
into every day, the lost chance

to live alone with him as he was
and could have been, and you're
the ghost who'll fly alongside
me into the ruins and rooms
I decided we would never
share again—hovering up just
when you see the thing you want
to show me, and unable to
make me hear you, unable to hear
me say back to you, *Oh, love, I would
never have seen that without you.*

Eating

As if it's been waiting until he can't have it,
some moment they lived, that he didn't want
when it was his, begins to raise a craving in him—
good dinner that she used to hear him
bring thoughtfully upstairs to where
she was waiting, reading or watching TV.
They'd spend a half-hour eating it,
their familiar life was a comfort, then from
the next room where he'd be brooding
over books or just hoarding himself
he'd listen for her quiet movement,
sometimes laughter as she watched TV or read.
Did she want him to think she was happy?
But he'd sit still and ponder what
was expected of him, or hoped.
Later they'd snack, or one of them would.

Remorse now makes him remember her saying
one time when they were crying in her new
living room filled with familiar things

that were just hers, not his any more,
"I wish I'd stayed to have breakfast with you."
She meant all those mornings she had
hurried away to work, him still in bed
debating with himself whether to get up,
whether to have an egg or skip to lunch.

(Once at a dinner when they were admiring
all the work their hosts had finished together
on floors and walls, but famished, she had
told him how she liked something he had done
and he'd bitten at her, red with his own
unsuspected anger, then sick at her tears.)

It wasn't her fault he'd lain in bed.
His too-wistful asking her to stay those mornings
only showed he thought it would be easier
if she went, though there were days
he did get up to walk to the diner
with her at that special pace they hit
together, that came to life from them
like a child, but was broken
when after breakfast he watched her go on
alone to work and he walked the other way
full of coffee and bread—
as it would break if they were tired
after those dinners with friends
where they'd eaten too much. And even if
he'd done nothing cruel, walking home
side by side late and out of step,
each could silently take back—
and *he* often would—what had seemed
affectionately given in the company of others.
A brief safe walk to the bed—the distance
sometimes growing, the closer they got to home.

And in bed, whether they did or they didn't;
snugged against each other or not;
with the silence denying all hurts

or tears from either or both;
with him refusing to answer
or her taking a sharp
quick breath to say *yes*;
good food and too much wine
or bad and none—
                              they were hungry
lying awake, and hungry they fell asleep,
and sleeping, all night long, they were hungry.

Margaret Gibson

James Holzworth

Margaret Gibson was born in 1944. She is the author of *Signs* (1979) and *Long Walks in the Afternoon*, the 1982 Lamont Selection of the Academy of American Poets, both from the L.S.U. Press. She teaches at the University of Connecticut.

Catechism Elegy

All night the long rain encloses the house
and I wake in quick confusion, as if the slow
winter wasp I'd seen inside the window last week
had stung my throat. I'm held in a dark hive,
struggling to speak.

As deeply as years, around me you curve your parenthesis,
mother and father. Never far from you, or near,
even in dreams I listen for questions that gather

unnoticed. *Where are you? Where's your sister?*
Who are you? What have you done?

You taught me to love these questions like milk.
Daily I was to sound them, echo, and compel an inner life
so rich I'd pour through a hole in the cosmos,
a white river spilled from a source
still and invisible.

But they aren't the questions curved by your intimate
own pain, not the ones that curled their small
fists and knocked, asking in vain for breath
to unlock them.

These I heard at night when I'd stand
at the door of my room, listening.
I wasn't afraid of the dark,

only the sound of your breathing across the hall—
ragged, as if you struggled with an exacting
angel, a wrestling out of the ground
dark roots, or a sowing of stone.

I held back my longing to wake you.
What would you say?
                   And now, as the long rain circles
the house I hear—as in sleep I hear dreams blow
against me like gusts of rain—your voices
wake me.

Whether they unfurl from the narrow solitude of death
or from the wider one of love, I cannot tell.
You ask me

What can you give? What have you abandoned?
For whom are you poor enough?

and I want to answer *death* to all three, to let the long
sigh of it smooth and diminish
your discontent.
                  Isn't this what you want?

For the sting of death hummed in our daily bread,
it sweetened the coffee, it hemmed in the moment,
it sharpened the rude intent of our silence.

It was there, like a lemon held invisibly in your hands,
the only answer no one questioned,
a radiance that ripened.

Gemini Elegy

You are not here, I cannot touch you, or be still.

I walk out of the house to watch the stars, and stay
hours after the last plume of smoke from the chimney.
Wind in his ribs, the Bear tips his nose to the east,
keen for the dawn.

I walk these ridges on a tilted light. I look for the orchid
whose blossom floats from its slender stalk, the one
the Greeks knew resembled the scrotum, wildflower
delicate between your thighs.

Through hemlocks and oaks I hear an owl cry,
low. Breath only, but it startles—like that first
forlorn gasp of hunger, pretext enough
for a lifetime's headlong desire.
                              And the stars—
every one of them speeds out of breath towards the rim, apart.
Even Polaris, even the Twins, our Gemini lovers, their hands
joined in a single star, distant
so distant their feet, on fire, walk
calmly into the River of Milk.

Even ordinary lovers suspect
they must rid themselves of desire. But to take
expectation by the taproot and keep tugging on the line
coiling it, that takes inhuman effort.
And to hang the coiled root on a nail in the sunroom like garlic,
not as a trophy but as seasoning for soup, that takes a wisdom
we require only of mothers, old women, saints.

Yesterday I planted wild iris in the morning's low mist and woodsearth
by a shelf of rock near the brook. I felt as though I were tending
your body—it is such gentle work—and the roots,
dark threads, brushed wetly over my hands
like nerves, quickening.

To Speak of Chile

Sometimes, what is most real shimmers, a dark
geography of dream—a film off its reel, tangled
on the cutting room floor. Someone edits
what we know.
              Take Chile, where the songs
of Victor Jara swelled like a harvest—now a film script
of sunflowers spotted with blood, silent banners of smoke.
In the market, a car black as a tornado stops for you,
and you disappear. Chile, a mass grave in a mine,
workers like sacks of potatoes thrown down cellar.

And these are facts. If I am silent, I consent to them.
In such a silence, I could not take my own life into my hands,
rubbing its skin like an apple's. I could not touch it
with the reverence I hold for the newborn, or for the dead
bodies of those I love enough to wash and dress for burial.

Things your hands know, you respect, my exiled friend
Ulises said, up to his elbows in flour, making bread.

And if dignity becomes a habit, as I believe in labor it does,
and in the courage to resist even those who cut off hands—
a man in prison can whisper songs. Ulises Torres did.

Burning the Root

Cedar at first, then a splay of staghorn put to the torch,
it burns, a relic of Georgia O'Keeffe's, in the fireplace.
We distance ourselves from the cedar's simple wood,

shape-changers, making love on the floor.
When smoke curls up one protruding sharp antler
and puffs in the room, you get up, poke the fire,

shift the root. In front of the fire, you turn suddenly,
close-up, a blue movie in my brain. You burn there,
fire licking your horn, your fine fur.

Then we finish and sleep, who knows what secrets
smoking, banked down deep. Though we fit together
simply, like spoons,

the room is a saracen plain, cedar root turned
sacrificial ram on the spit, seen from the underside,
hind legs out stiff.

And it keeps burning, the smoke a curl of contempt
in the wind, not unlike the smoke of a cigarette
held to a bound woman's nipple.

Long Walks in the Afternoon

Last night the first light frost, and now sycamore
and sumac edge yellow and red in low sun
and indian afternoons. One after another

roads thicken with leaves and the wind
sweeps them fresh as the start of a year.
A friend writes she is tired of being one

on whom nothing is lost, but what choice
is there, how can she close her eyes?
I walk for hours—either

with hands behind my back like a prisoner,
neck craning up to the sky where chain gang
birds in tight nets

fly south—or with hands swinging free at my sides
to the brook, the water so cold it stings
going down. Either way, I whisper

to dogwood, fern, stone walls, and the last
mosquito honing in, *we're in this together.*
Here is the road. Honest dirt

and stone. Some afternoon, heading home before dark,
if I walk by mistake, lost in thought, far beyond
the steep trees, the satellites and stars,

up over the rim to a pitfall, past any memory of words—
even then I can give my body its lead,
still find my way back.

Christopher Gilbert

Karen L. Durlach

Christopher Gilbert was born in 1949. He was educated at the University of Michigan and Clark University. His first book, *Across the Mutual Landscape*, was chosen by Michael Harper as winner of the 1983 Walt Whitman Award of the Academy of American Poets and was published by Graywolf Press in 1984. Trained in clinical and cognitive psychology, he works as a psychotherapist, and is a psychologist with Worcester Youth Guidance Center and Cambridge Family and Children's Service in the Boston area.

Saturday Morning at the Laundry

Things the way they are
and things the way they strive to be:
the yellow perfect, even goldgleaming
on the Sunoco Sign out the window
is not dead plastic and not
some piece flaked from a more perfect place
somewhere else, and not
the yellowness because I say
IT'S EARLY MARCH AND THE SLANT OF THE SUN
AT 9:18 IS RIGHT
as I'm sitting in the laudramat
drinking orange spice tea

while my couple of washers is going,
but a chance, a blessing, a beginning—
as a thing of this world is, is the use
it will put me to;

so I say YELLOW SIGN, YELLOW SIGN,
obliging this moment with prayer—
kissing the little laughing sun on my lips—
while my voice is falling on things
as yet wordless inside my self
already golden with the black force
some good god has given to show what is.

*

You are Lionel, if
when you're twelve
and the dollar changer swipes the bill
you have to do the family wash with,
and the owner of the joint
like it's none of his business
drives off in his Caddie
leaving you yelling at the air
loud enough to make someone hear,
and it is somehow only the messenger
who lives deeper inside your self
who had planned to go through the world today
clear headed and wearing sparkling clothes
who hears, goes to a chair and sits confused
knowing what he had to say
but knowing it can't be loud enough.

*

More vision than dream, wearing green
and her hair in corn row fashion,
when the girl walks to him, a bloom
as the bright red beads in her braids
was the ripeness of the world he had waited for, he needed
to recognize her. A young kid, he wonders
trying to make her a memory of a friend—

someone he knew when he was younger, he thinks,
trying to get on top of the feeling she astonishes with.
So he cannot stop the sudden clouding over
between them, when they talk the gap
where he is exiled from her and the summer
stuff in her eyes his speech cannot reach,
where the failed part of him refuses to go forward to
her particulars. Her particulars? When he recognizes the region
opened in him by her life, he will get to them.
First, she has her own voice and he must learn to sing
to talk to her: making the usual speech is nonsense—
broken phrases while the washers work, abstract
accidentals they each must will to keep outside their heads.
She knows a carrying forth, confidently telling she goes
back down to touch the hand of her mother
who has awakened calling her name.
How full of sense the click while they jointly
fold their winged moment of fresh wash—
pants, towels, blouses, sheets, t-shirts,
and her mother's bright Puerto Rican *party dress*. Each item
hanging on its keen label in the mind, so deep
the connection granted, worked for
despite the washers arguing. Imagine that.

Now

I park the car because I'm happy,
because if everyone parked we'd have a street party,
because the moon is full—
it is orange, the sky is closer
and it would be wrong to drive into it.
This is the first day of summer—
everyone is hanging out,
women walk by in their bodies so mellow
I feel I'm near a friend's house.

The small white flakes of the headlights
sweat for a second on the storefronts.
In the windows, darkened afterhours,
a reflection stares back
looking more like me than me.
I reach to touch
and the reflection touches me.
Everything is perfect—
even my skin fits.

Hanging out,
the taillights of the turning cars
are fires, going out—
are the spaces of roses flowered
deeper in themselves. I close my eyes
and am flowered deeper in myself.
Further up the street a walking figure
I can't make out, a face
behind a bag of groceries, free arm swinging
in the air the wave of a deep red
fluid shifting to and fro.

At the vegetarian restaurant
I see it's Michael the Conga Drummer—
been looking for him 2 months.
He asks me, "what's happening?"
I love his fingers.
When we shake hands I mix his grip
with the curve of my fathers'
toting cantelope in the house from the market.
We are two griots at an intersection.
I answer him in parable:
the orange that I've been carrying
is some luminous memory, bursting,
bigger than my hand can hold,
so I hand him half.

Charge

Gimme the ball, Willie is saying
throughout this 2-on-2 pick-up game.
Winners are the ones who play, being
at the sidelines is ridiculous.
So what happens here is a history
won not by the measure of points,
but by simply getting into it.
Willie plays like it could all be gone
at once, like his being is at stake.
Gimme the ball, he cusses.
Gwen Brooks' player from the streets.
The game is wherever there's a chance.
It is nothing easy he's after,
but the rapture gained with presence.
His catalogue of moves represents
his life. Recognize its stance.
So alive to be the steps
in whose mind the symbol forms,
miraculous to be the feeling
which threads these steps to dance.
The other side is very serious—
they want to play him 2-on-1.
Messrs. Death and Uniformity.
He's got a move to make them smile.
Gimme the ball, Willie says again
and again, "*Gimme the goddamn ball.*"

Touching

Light is a distant world
though at 5 a.m. in the bedroom
window where the spider plant hovers

shining, there is a silken presence
where it traces, leaves a constellation.
I roll over and the room moves
a little closer, it is light-
like when Karen sleeps beside me
turned away but warm rubbing back
and I curve myself like hers
to hold her body for seeing
whatever is far in her.
Now I'm almost dreaming.
Words run transparent from my mouth
and almost find the edge of things.
Across the street in the park
a big hawk sails, gently flapping,
its outspread arms hugging the air
just as the sun kisses upward
to find its way through the sky.
Back here off the edge of the bed
my fingers, blind at both ends,
dangle in a void like starlight
travelled so far its source burned out.
Now a light goes off in my head as
I hold this hand that seems so far away.
I think of the monster fullback
in highschool, after running over me
he dropped the ball to see was I hurt.
Where is he now, or the woman
who put the message in the bottle
I found splashing in the fouled waters
off Point Pelee.
What was on her mind
writing, *"kindness anywhere is still kindness,*
I'm in Cleveland, cold, alone—
wherever you are you hold this part of me."
I roll over in the glow
where sunrise goes across the bed,
knowing our age thinks light is wavelike
bundles spreading outward like ships
floating home in measured gaps toward each shore.

So part of the world waits distant.
For all I know as a man it might happen
like kelp bits drifting to no shore.
Still if there's a moment somewhere
equal to this light filling my skin,
then there is a constant I can count on
and I'll go forth and live with that.

Louise Glück

James Baker Hall

Louise Glück was born in New York City in 1943. Her books are *First-born* (1963), *The House on the Marshland* (1975), and *Descending Figure* (1980), all from The Ecco Press. Her awards include fellowships from the National Endowment for the Arts, the Rockefeller Foundation, and the Guggenheim Foundation, as well as an award from the American Academy and Institute of Arts and Letters. She teaches at Williams College.

Happiness

A man and woman lie on a white bed.
It is morning. I think
Soon they will waken.
On the bedside table is a vase
of lilies; sunlight
pools in their throats.
I watch him turn to her
as though to speak her name
but silently, deep in her mouth—
At the window ledge,
once, twice,
a bird calls.

And then she stirs; her body
fills with his breath.

I open my eyes; you are watching me.
Almost over this room
the sun is gliding.
Look at your face, you say,
holding your own close to me
to make a mirror.
How calm you are. And the burning wheel
passes gently over us.

Palais des Arts

Love long dormant showing itself:
the large expected gods
caged really, the columns
sitting on the lawn, as though perfection
were not timeless but stationary—that
is the comedy, she thinks,
that they are paralyzed. Or like the matching swans,
insular, circling the pond: restraint so passionate
implies possession. They hardly speak.
On the other bank, a small boy throws bits of bread
into the water. The reflected monument
is stirred, briefly, stricken with light—
She can't touch his arm in innocence again.
They have to give that up and begin
as male and female, thrust and ache.

Lamentations

1. The Logos

They were both still,
the woman mournful, the man
branching into her body.

But god was watching.
They felt his gold eye
projecting flowers on the landscape.

Who knew what he wanted?
He was god, and a monster.
So they waited. And the world
filled with his radiance,
as though he wanted to be understood.

Far away, in the void that he had shaped,
he turned to his angels.

2. Nocturne

A forest rose from the earth.
O pitiful, so needing
God's furious love—

Together they were beasts.
They lay in the fixed
dusk of his negligence;
from the hills, wolves came, mechanically
drawn to their human warmth,
their panic.

Then the angels saw
how He divided them:
the man, the woman, and the woman's body.

Above the churned reeds, the leaves let go
a slow moan of silver.

3. The Covenant

Out of fear, they built a dwelling place.
But a child grew between them
as they slept, as they tried
to feed themselves.

They set it on a pile of leaves,
the small discarded body
wrapped in the clean skin
of an animal. Against the black sky
they saw the massive argument of light.

Sometimes it woke. As it reached its hands
they understood they were the mother and father,
there was no authority above them.

4. The Clearing

Gradually, over many years,
the fur disappeared from their bodies
until they stood in the bright light
strange to one another.
Nothing was as before.
Their hands trembled, seeking
the familiar.

Nor could they keep their eyes
from the white flesh
on which wounds would show clearly
like words on a page.

And from the meaningless browns and greens
at last God arose, His great shadow

darkening the sleeping bodies of His children,
and leapt into heaven.

How beautiful it must have been,
the earth, that first time
seen from the air.

The Mirror

Watching you in the mirror I wonder
what it is like to be so beautiful
and why you do not love
but cut yourself, shaving
like a blind man. I think you let me stare
so you can turn against yourself
with greater violence,
needing to show me how you scrape the flesh away
scornfully and without hesitation
until I see you correctly,
as a man bleeding, not
the reflection I desire.

Night Song

Look up into the light of the lantern.
Don't you see? The calm of darkness
is the horror of heaven.

We've been apart too long, too painfully separated.
How can you bear to dream,
to give up watching? I think you must be dreaming,
your face is full of mild expectancy.

I need to wake you, to remind you that there isn't a future.
That's why we're free. And now some weakness in me
has been cured forever, so I'm not compelled
to close my eyes, to go back, to rectify—

The beach is still; the sea, cleansed of its superfluous life,
opaque, rocklike. In mounds, in vegetal clusters,
seabirds sleep on the jetty. Terns, assassins—

You're tired; I can see that.
We're both tired, we have acted a great drama.
Even our hands are cold, that were like kindling.
Our clothes are scattered on the sand; strangely enough,
they never turned to ashes.

I have to tell you what I've learned, that I know now
what happens to the dreamers.
They don't feel it when they change. One day
they wake, they dress, they are old.

Tonight I'm not afraid
to feel the revolutions. How can you want to sleep
when passion gives you that peace?
You're like me tonight, one of the lucky ones.
You'll get what you want. You'll get your oblivion.

Brooding Likeness

I was born in the month of the bull,
the month of heaviness,

or of the lowered, the destructive head,
or of purposeful blindness. So I know, beyond the shadowed
patch of grass, the stubborn one, the one who doesn't look up,
still senses the rejected world. It is
a stadium, a well of dust. And you who watch him
looking down in the face of death, what do you know
of commitment? If the bull lives
one controlled act of revenge, be satisfied
that in the sky, like you, he is always moving,
not of his own accord but through the black field
like grit caught on a wheel, like shining freight.

Horse

What does the horse give you
that I cannot give you?

I watch you when you are alone,
when you ride into the field behind the dairy,
your hands buried in the mare's
dark mane.

Then I know what lies behind your silence:
scorn, hatred of me, of marriage. Still,
you want me to touch you; you cry out
as brides cry, but when I look at you I see
there are no children in your body.
Then what is there?

Nothing, I think. Only haste
to die before I die.

In a dream, I watched you ride the horse
over the dry fields and then

dismount; you two walked together;
in the dark, you had no shadows.
But I felt them coming toward me
since at night they go anywhere,
they are their own masters.

Look at me. You think I don't understand?
What is the animal
if not passage out of this life?

Mock Orange

It is not the moon, I tell you.
It is these flowers
lighting the yard.

I hate them.
I hate them as I hate sex,
the man's mouth
sealing my mouth, the man's
paralyzing body—

And the cry that always escapes,
the low, humiliating
premise of union—

In my mind tonight
I hear the question and pursuing answer
fused in one sound
that mounts and mounts and then
is split into the old selves,
the tired antagonisms. Do you see?
We were made fools of.
And the scent of mock orange
drifts through the window.

How can I rest?
How can I be content
when there is still
that odor in the world?

Albert Goldbarth

Betty Gottlieb

Albert Goldbarth was born in Chicago in 1948. He is the author of a dozen books of poems, including *JAN 31* (Doubleday, 1974), which was nominated for the National Book Award, and the book-length poem *Different Fleshes* (Hobart and William Smith Colleges Press, 1979), which was awarded the Texas Institute of Letters Prize. His most recent book, *Original Light: New & Selected Poems 1973–1983*, was published by Ontario Review Press. Among his awards are two fellowships from the National Endowment for the Arts and a fellowship from the Guggenheim Foundation. He teaches at the University of Texas.

A History of Civilization

In the dating bar, the potted ferns lean down
conspiratorially, little spore-studded
elopement ladders. The two top buttons
of every silk blouse have already half-undone all
introduction. Slices of smile, slices of sweet brie,
dark and its many white wedges. In back

of the bar, the last one-family grocer's is necklaced
over and over: strings of leeks, greek olives, sardines.
The scoops stand at attention in the millet barrel,
the cordovan sheen of the coffee barrel, the kidney beans.
And a woman whose pride is a clean linen apron polishes
a register as intricate as a Sicilian shrine. In back

of the grocery, dozing and waking in fitful starts
by the guttering hearth, a ring of somber-gabardined grandpas
plays dominoes. Their stubble picks up the flicker like filaments
still waiting for the bulb or the phone to be invented. Even their
coughs, their phlegms, are in an older language. They move the simple
pieces of matching numbers. In back

of the back room, in the unlit lengths of storage, it's
that season: a cat eyes a cat. The sacks and baskets
are sprayed with the sign of a cat's having eyed a cat, and
everything to do with rut and estrus comes down to a few
sure moves. The dust motes drift, the continents.
In the fern bar a hand tries a knee, as if unplanned.

A *Film*

1.

It's strangely like a man
and a display of toy cars. It is,
in a sense. Collected by the hundred
at the base of the drive-in

movie screen, we're toyed
before the larger life—its anguishes
and joys—that's our life
given grandiosity

of size to match our feelings.
And we come down from the mountains,
down from the keeping of stars,
to watch: a single beam of light

become a world—the oldest story.
Now a woman's joined the man. The second
oldest story is going to start now,
jumbo, with butter, with salt.

2.

The story's thin: some little
aspiration, flawed and baubled.
The dialogue's thin: "I never
thought . . ." "Why, you . . ." A house

is a sheet of cannily painted plywood,
propped by rods. "Inside,"
our days and nights
are taking place on a kind of scale

so enormous, their height and width
must be a function of flattenings like
the cats and dogs receive,
in cartoons, from steamrollers. Maybe

these actors' real lives are convoluted
and fecund . . . All I know is everything,
people, house, a background extending to outer
space, is a coating of white paint.

3.

Out in the mountains around us
tonight, if the paper's correct, a couple
of dozen believers have come to wait
for the end of the world, and their

select ascension—"the Rapture,"
they call it—to some new world.
They have candles. They sing. Their knees
are naked on rock. The date has been

ordained for a decade . . . any minute now,
"the Testament of Fire." And when tomorrow
comes, is snoozy, is crumpled
popcorn boxes like always? Won't their

disappointment be blinding, be the fierce sun
as it rises and covers the lake, covers
it completely, a film
over water that's deep and abiding.

A *Theory of Wind*

This is how the page must feel: it doesn't
understand God. Whatever the language
on that page, an Eastern script as fine
as dendrite, or the harsh Germanic squatting
of black retrievers at obedience school, or
even the floating eye and spiked sun
of pictographs, that language
has a saying for God's inscrutable ways.
I mean a woman is wailing and there's
nothing the shaman can do. I mean

it's night. The wind at my body is wild
animals licking for salt. I've set a
sheet of galleys down and come outside for these
rough tongues! The wind in the monstrous condor
flappings of my banana tree leaves,
the wind in the twiddling back grasses.
No ant egg is free.
Everywhere, objective and efficient:
its assessment. No wonder tribal life thought
God behind such touch. It deepens,

mnemonic, my own taking stock
of the night: a slippery siamese-conjoining
where two cars' oil drippings braid at the curb;
these separate orange lips
of fungus making the rotten log a portraitist's
day's doodling; every follicle in catflesh, and its
millipartite contributing toward a perfect arch . . .
It *is* perfect, all of it, each burr an asterisk
calling attention to limitless exactitude. Even the
word *burr*, how it—click!—fits. But

the wind is indifferent to this. Out of a window
a long cry, *why*, and again, *why*, *why*, whatever
the reason, is saying something of how an oak
goes down in gale force, a marble column is
found in pieces, breezes lick another inch of forest
fire along the green floor . . . it was *burn*, not
burr. Just when we write it: perfectly wrought,
the typesetter reads it: perfectly wrong. And then
the long hours, correcting. If it's true for this
level it's true for that level, but anyway no shaman

or oncologist explains it. *Why?* The wind
is come chill through her room tonight. *Why?* And what
was my page supposed to say? Our lively lust,
list?, last?, our lovely dust . . . it's so hard
to remember. It's always night, somewhere.
Some tree is always unsafe. And all we can do
is pray for ours, in our backyard, that we thought
so pure of form, its bark moire like Persian lamb . . .
but what do we know? The wind is going over
everything tonight, proofing for error.

A *History of Photography*

Everything was bleak then, and
the photographs too—their gray—date
from before the invention of color. Here,
my Grandma over a loaf of bread with
all the command and wonder of a magician
over a girl's rising body. The bread
gray. The ghetto gray. The decade gray.

The fish, and the ice that kept the fish,
and the whole idea of keeping:
gray. And every night she'd come
home to Louie, their 3rd-story flat, the
stink of kipper wouldn't wash
off her hands, and its workscent mixed
with their lovescent, like oil and water.

Here, later, a little gill-and-tail
fishface in her—Mommy,
forming. There's no photo of the birth but
I know how happy it made them, how
once when I was little Mommy tilted a
gray glug of oil into a pan of
gray water and taught me rainbow.

Here, my Mommy round with my
sister Livia forming—a girl's
rising body. By now there's tint, some
rouge in the lips, some powder blue in eyes.
Not that it was easy yet, this coloring
of keeping. Like the house itself, like the
day's wage, like the night's first small excitements,

they did it by hand.

Before

The class was History, that's
what I wanted—the bridge
the bent Yid ragman took reluctantly
between steamship and sweatshop, or
older than that: the landbridge
something almost a horse was
grazing its way to Alaska
across on something almost hooves,
or older: something almost a leg
that was the grayveined print of a leg
in a web, before a bridge could be anything
more than a body's own
furthest extension. I was
seventeen. It was sunny. I'd come
from History, and before that
from a lineage of ragpickers,
songpluckers, kettlemenders, renderers
of humpfat for the candles, masters of
disputation over a nuance of scripture,
debtors, diddlers, elegiasts and jewelers
—history too, though the textbook
didn't say it. The page said Presidents
and paper. I wanted something from
before paper—wasps,
the fluted home of their making.
I wanted the first bone
of my bones. I wanted the word
before the alphabet, the word like a suckstone
working up spit. And then I stopped,
near Washtenaw and Ainslie, on the bridge
above the sewerage ditch, and sun
as if meeting a challenge made the stars
of a constellation-story burn
that urban rut's otherwise lustreless
flow. It was the sign of The Cart,
and there too, in the story, sun
bedazzled dull surfaces: all those heaps

of garment district scraps he peddled,
a few abused tin pots, and who knows
how or why but some wholeskinned Spanish onions,
wool socks, and a single tired rose. I
still remember this: his humming something
tuneless, as if from before the idea of song
took full root in American soil—but
like the rose, though it drooped, though maybe
the worm ate in it, his song was handsome,
a lady would accept it and understand. And
this: my face was reflected, wavery
but ascertainably wide-eyed, on his pots.
Or in the sewerage currents—and then the
stars shifted, light was
sun again, and I was something almost
a man, on its way home,
humming its wanting. I was a boy
with a book. And this was long before
I'd learn to have words for what I wanted,
but what I wanted was something
like a bottle with a notepage in it,
thrown to sea—the clarity of glass,
but from before glass; and the urgency
of that written note, before writing.
—Maybe the water itself,
the message its salt.

All-Nite Donuts

A customer's blowing
smoke rings almost

heavy as the dough o's rising
out of the vat of grease.

Outside, the whores are whistling
their one note, lips thick

donuts strawberry-glazed.
Inside, the register will open its drawer

for a quarter and make its single cheep.
At midnight I thought it

ugly, all these lime and lavender
stools along the counter like a used

car salesman's breath mints.
Maybe it is. But somehow now, by

three, the special bloodshot view
of overdue eyes finds special beauty

in this neon and its attendant fly,
both fitfully buzzing.—Not a classic beauty,

no, the whores don't swivel slightly
toward a passing trick like flowers

toward the sun, it isn't a bit like that.
But all of our zeroes are here

made sweet. I dunk one in a mug,
I raise decaffeinated instant in a toast

to what's available, when we need it,
all night. Some guy drives by. The whores

curve slightly, like plastic spoons
being worked in a hardening cheese dip.

Jorie Graham

Jorie Graham was born in 1951. She was educated at New York University, Columbia University, and the University of Iowa. Her first book, *Hybrids of Plants and of Ghosts,* (Princeton University Press, 1980) received the Great Lakes Colleges Association Award. *Erosion* was published by Princeton in 1983. She has received fellowships from the Ingram Merrill Foundation, the Bunting Institute, and the Guggenheim Foundation. She teaches at the University of Iowa.

Bill Pepper

Wanting a Child

How hard it is for the river here to re-enter
the sea, though it's most beautiful, of course, in the waste
of time where it's almost
turned back. Then
it's yoked,
trussed. . . . The river
has been everywhere, imagine, dividing, discerning,
cutting deep into the parent rock,
scouring and scouring
its own bed.
Nothing is whole
where it has been. Nothing
remains unsaid.
Sometimes I'll come this far from home

merely to dip my fingers in this glittering, archaic
sea that renders everything
identical, flesh
where mind and body
blur. The seagulls squeak, ill-fitting
hinges, the beach is thick
with shells. The tide
is always pushing upward, inland, into the river's rapid
argument, pushing
with its insistent tragic waves—the living echo,
says my book, of some great storm far out at sea, too far
to be recalled by us
but transferred
whole onto this shore by waves, so that erosion
is its very face.

Reading Plato

This is the story
    of a beautiful
lie, what slips
    through my fingers,
your fingers. It's winter,
    it's far

in the lifespan
    of man.
Bareheaded, in a soiled
    shirt,
speechless, my friend
    is making

lures, his hobby. Flies
    so small

he works with tweezers and
      a magnifying glass.
They must be
      so believable

they're true—feelers,
      antennae,
quick and frantic
      as something
drowning. His heart
      beats wildly

in his hands. It is
      blinding
and who will forgive him
      in his tiny
garden? He makes them
      out of hair,

deer hair, because it's hollow
      and floats.
Past death, past sight,
      this is
his good idea, what drives
      the silly days

together. Better than memory. Better
      than love.
Then they are done, a hook
      under each pair
of wings, and it's Spring,
      and the men

wade out into the riverbed
      at dawn. Above,
the stars still connect-up
      their hungry animals.
Soon they'll be satisfied
      and go. Meanwhile

upriver, downriver, imagine, quick
　　in the air,
in flesh, in a blue
　　swarm of
flies, our knowledge of
　　the graceful

deer skips easily across
　　the surface.
Dismembered, remembered,
　　it's finally
alive. Imagine
　　the body

they were all once
　　a part of,
these men along the lush
　　green banks
trying to slip in
　　and pass

for the natural world.

Kimono

The woman on the other side
　　of the evergreens
a small boy is hidden in,
　　I'm wearing
valleys, clear skies,
　　thawing banks

narcissus and hollow reeds
　　break through.

It means the world to him, this flat
        archaic fabric
no weather worries.
        Each time I bend,

brushing my hair, a bird
        has just dipped
through its sky out of
        sight. He thinks
I don't see him, my little man
        no more than seven

catching his lost stitch of breath.
        What he sees,
in my garden, is the style
        of the world
as she brushes her hair
        eternally beyond

the casual crumbling forms
        of boughs. I bend
and reeds are suddenly
        ravines . . . How soothing
it is, this enchanted gap, this tiny
        eternal

delay which is our knowing,
        our flesh.
How late it is, I think,
        bending,
in this world we have mis-
        taken, late

for the green scrim to be
        such an open
door. And yet, even now, a small
        spirit accurate
as new ice is climbing
        into the gentle limbs

of an evergreen, the scent rubbing off
    on his elbows
and knees, his eyes a sacred store
    of dares,
to watch, as on the other side,
    just past

the abstract branches, something
    most whole
loosens her stays
    pretending she's alone.

Salmon

I watched them once, at dusk, on television, run,
in our motel room half-way through
Nebraska, quick, glittering, past beauty, past
the importance of beauty,
archaic,
not even hungry, not even endangered, driving deeper and deeper
into less. They leapt up falls, ladders
and rock, tearing and leaping, a gold river
and a blue river travelling
in opposite directions.
They would not stop, resolution of will
and helplessness, as the eye
is helpless
when the image forms itself, upside-down, backwards,
driving up into
the mind, and the world
unfastens itself
from the deep ocean of the given . . . Justice, aspen
leaves, mother attempting
suicide, the white night-flying moth

the ants dismantled bit by bit and carried in
right through the crack
in my wall . . . How helpless
the still pool is,
upstream,
awaiting the gold blade
of their hurry. Once, indoors, a child,
I watched, at noon, through slatted wooden blinds,
a man and woman, naked, eyes closed,
climb onto each other,
on the terrace floor,
and ride—two gold currents
wrapping round and round each other, fastening,
unfastening. I hardly knew
what I saw. Whatever shadow there was in that world
it was the one each cast
onto the other,
the thin black seam
they seemed to be trying to work away
between them. I held my breath.
As far as I could tell, the work they did
with sweat and light
was good. I'd say
they travelled far in opposite
directions. What is the light
at the end of the day, deep, reddish-gold, bathing the walls,
the corridors, light that is no longer light, no longer clarifies,
illuminates, antique, freed from the body of
the air that carries it. What is it
for the space of time
where it is useless, merely
beautiful? When they were done, they made a distance
one from the other
and slept, outstretched,
on the warm tile
of the terrace floor,
smiling, faces pressed against the stone.

My Garden, My Daylight

My neighbor brings me bottom fish—
    tomcod, rockcod—
a fist of ocean. He comes out
    from the appletrees between us
holding his gift like a tight
    spool of thread.

Once a week he brings me fresh-catch,
    boned and skinned
and rolled up like a tongue. I freeze them,
    speechless, angelic
instruments. I have a choir of them.
    Alive, they feed

driving their bodies through the mud,
    mud through their flesh.
See how white they become. High above,
    the water thins
to blue, then air, then less . . .
    These aren't as sweet

as those that shine up there,
    quick schools
forever trying to slur over, become water.
    But these belong to us
who cannot fall out of this world
    but only deeper

into it, driving it into the white
    of our eyes. Muddy
daylight, we utter it, we drown in it.
    You can stay dry
if you can step between the raindrops
    mother's mother

said. She's words now you can't hear.
    I try to wind my way

between what's here: chalk, lily, milk,
      titanium, snow—
as far as I can say
      these appleblossoms house

five shades of white, and yet
      I know there's more.
Between my held breath and its small hot
      death, a garden,
Whiteness, grows. Its icy fruit
      seems true,

it glows. *For free* he says
      so that I can't refuse.

Erosion

I would not want, I think, a higher intelligence, one
simultaneous, cut clean
of sequence. No,
it is our slowness I love, growing slower,
tapping the paintbrush against the visible,
tapping the mind.
We are, ourselves, a mannerism now,
having fallen
out of the chain
of evolution.
So we grow fat with unqualified life.
Today, on this beach
I am history to these fine
pebbles. I run them
through my fingers. Each time
some molecules rub off
evolving into

the invisible. Always
I am trying to feel
the erosion—my grandfather, stiffening
on his bed, learning
to float on time, his mind like bait presented
to the stream ongoing, or you, by my side,
sleep rinsing you always a little less
clean, or daily
the erosion
of the right word, what it shuts,
or the plants coming forth as planned out my window, row
after row, sealed
into here. . . .
I've lined all our wineglasses up on the sill,
a keyboard, a garden. Flowers of the poles.
I'm gifting each with a little less water.
You can tap them
for music.
Outside the window it's starting to snow.
It's going to get colder.
The less full the glass, the truer
the sound.
This is my song
for the North
coming toward us.

Debora Greger

Lillian Magow

Debora Greger was born in 1949. She holds a B.A. from the University of Washington and an M.F.A. from the University of Iowa. She is the author of *Movable Islands* (Princeton University Press, 1980), *Cartography* (Penumbra Press, 1980), *Normal Street* (Sea Pen Press, 1983), *Blank Country* (Meadow Press, 1984), and *Aud* (Princeton University Press, 1985). Among her many awards are a Bunting Fellowship, a National Endowment for the Arts Fellowship, and an Ingram Merrill Foundation grant.

The Armorer's Daughter

My father is a hard man.
When my mother couldn't give him a son,
he made the best of it, that is
he made me into what was missing.
So I polish a breastplate until
my smudged face is reflected blue-black
and my arm is stiff as a gauntlet.

I have my father's stubborn jaw
they tell me, those boys from the village
who tease, envious of my lot.
The roughened men who come for a mending,
who bring their smooth sons to be measured,
say I have his hands, too wide for a woman.
Then I think of the beetle on the stoop
whose shell shamed the finest armor.

It scuttled away when I reached down.
With his hand.
                        I am and am not him.
Give me the dusty wings of the moths
that dared spend the night on his workbench
and I would fly—where?
Out to the hill with the shepherd?
To the mill where the miller's son
is clouded in the finest-ground flour?

This wool-gathering angers my father.
He pounds music from metal,
a chorus of glow and chill, bend and stay.
I drop a helmet with a carelessness
I barely recognize and run into the yard,
into the road, tripping on my skirts.
Late afternoon, after a rain, already
the sun's low flame lights the edges
of everything. This world shines,
rings and shines, like his dream of heaven.

The Light Passages

A day later than he said in the letter,
still humming, half-whistling
the theme of the piece he stayed on to practice,
he leaves the car at the last road sign
and climbs the fence, taking the old shortcut
through the orchard at sunrise.
He stumbles through weeds,
sending up sleepy birds,
the only sounds their stiff wings
and ice cracking on the branches
from which they have risen,

thinking not of them but of how
Beethoven, playing a new sonata for friends,
hardly touched the keys
in the *pianissimo,*
imagining a light passage
that the others, not deaf, could not hear.

From the porch he looks back—
the orchard, still again,
is another world, a trick of the eye,
as the house in silhouette was before.
The house, still dark inside,
is still home.
Careful not to wake his family
after all the years,
he slips through the door
and surefooted as if he had never left
goes to the piano
and begins to play.

The Man on the Bed

*In late September 1958, I visited his South Truro
studio and saw on the easel not an unfinished
painting, nor even a stretched canvas, but a large
empty stretcher. "He's been looking at that all
summer," Jo Hopper said.*
        —Lloyd Goodrich, of Edward Hopper

He lay on the bed, thinking
of what he could see from the window
as a little landscape of failure,
glittering after the rain,
the roses within reach but rusted,
a red bird lost in the thick

wet leaves of the oak,
the tree, caught in mirrors, shaking.
He lay on the bed,
his shirt turning blue with evening,
thinking, in the dark a red bird
might as well be black.

He slept then
and dreamt of a man
who slept with his glasses on,
the easier to find them when he woke.
The room seemed smaller,
the wind against the corner
of the house stronger.
If the heart is a house, he thought,
it is rented to strangers
who leave it empty.
If the heart is a house,
it is also the darkness around it
through which a black bird flies, unseen,
and unseeing, into the window,
beating and beating its wings
against the glass.

Patches of Sky

Like a map blanketing a bed,
the flat fields slope enough so
under snow at sunrise some are coral,
some cornflower—cartographer's tints
taken from an old quilt.

Four hawks revolve over the square
where the wind has hollowed out a house,

and the next one, where it fills a tree
with feathered leaves, beaked cries.
Or so I say. Expansive for once,

I want to show you a countryside,
not a bed. Look—low hills folding
over centuries and at their base
someone's ragged crocuses
in what must have been a garden,

a civilizing introduction of the frivolous
to dirt that supports not much but itself.
Think of the first tenants of this house,
two schoolteacher spinsters.
Did they wear red,

the intensity missing in the view?
What held them, sisters, together?
They slept, one on each side
of the double fireplace, under these quilts.
Look—the dark side of each square

is patched from a man's old suits,
the light from flowered dresses.
Did one of them ever feel like this,
asking who she belonged to,
the other answering, "Whom?"

Linda Gregg

Jean McLean

Linda Gregg was born in 1942 in Suffern, New York. She received a B.A. and M.A. from San Francisco State University. Her first book of poems, *Too Bright to See* (1981) was published by Graywolf Press. She is the recipient of a fellowship from the Guggenheim Foundation.

Goethe's Death Mask

The face is quite smooth
everywhere except the eyes,
which are bulges
like ant hills someone tried to draw
eyes on. It is normal, of course,
that the mouth is shut
like a perfect sentence.
But there is nothing of Italy
or the rooms. As though it were
all a lie. As if he had not fed there
at all. I suppose there was never a choice.

If the happiness lasts,
it is the smoothness. The part
we do not notice. The language he made
was from the bruises. What lasted
are the eyes. Something ugly
and eaten into. What a mess his eyes are.

The Small Lizard

My lizard just beyond the lamp's shine
is a gentle lizard.
Is the color of an old peach.
Has lived with me all summer
and kept his tail.

(I am a little better, but love is leaving.
I who never loved birds am growing wings.)

When I move, my lizard does not.
But watches and makes himself ready.
The moon has gone above my window now,
and will go over the roof top.

(Now, when I could help, I hold back.
My heart is sad, not wanting to fly.
Who moves from grace by choice?)

We are three stages. The lizard,
more than I or the moon, is the soul
developed. The moon will dim
and I will change;
but this immortal lizard will stay
breathing in this stone room,
without evidence.

Whole and Without Blessing

What is beautiful alters, has undertow.
Otherwise I have no tactics to begin with.
Femininity is a sickness. I open my eyes
out of this fever and see the meaning
of my life clearly. A thing like a hill.
I proclaim myself whole and without blessing,
or need to be blessed. A fish of my own
spirit. I belong to no one. I do not move.
Am not required to move. I lie naked on a sheet
and the indifferent sun warms me.
I was bred for slaughter, like the other
animals. To suffer exactly at the center,
where there are no clues except pleasure.

Summer in a Small Town

When the men leave me,
they leave me in a beautiful place.
It is always late summer.
When I think of them now
I think of the place.
And being happy alone afterwards.
This time it's Clinton, New York.
I swim in the public pool
at six when the other people
have gone home.
The sky is grey, the air hot.
I walk back across the mown lawn
loving the smell and the houses
so completely it leaves my heart empty.

Marilyn Hacker

Marilyn Hacker was born in 1942 in New York City. *Presentation Piece* (Viking, 1974) was the Lamont Selection of the Academy of American Poets and the winner of the National Book Award in 1975. Since then she has published three other collections, *Separations* (1976), *Taking Notice* (1980), and *Assumptions* (1985), all from Knopf. Among her other awards are fellowships from the Ingram Merrill Foundation and the Guggenheim Foundation.

The Hang-Glider's Daughter

For Catherine Logan

My forty-year-old father learned to fly.
Bat-winged, with a magic marble fear
keeping his toast down, he walks off a sheer
shaved cliff into the morning. On Sunday
mornings he comes for us. Liane and I
feed the baby and Mario, wash up, clear
the kitchen mess. Maman is never there;
that is the morning she and Joseph try
to tell the other pickers how the Word

can save them. Liane gets me good and mad
changing her outfit sixteen times, while I
have to change the baby. All the way
up the hill road she practices on him, flirt-
ing like she does at school. My back teeth hurt

from chewing Pepper Gum on the bad side.
She's three years younger. I'm three years behind.
Did he *mean* it? Shift the gum. Did I remind
Mario, if the baby cries, he needs
burping? I can stretch out on the back seat.
The olive terraces stacked in the sunshine
are shallow stairs a giant child could climb.
My hiking shoes look giant on my feet.
Maman says "a missed boy." What do I miss?
I wonder what the word in English is
for that. Funny, that we should have been born
somewhere we wouldn't even understand
the language now. I was already three
when we left. If someone hypnotized me

would I talk English like a three-year-old?
The bright road twists up; bumpily we shift
gears, breathe deep. In the front pouch of my sweat-
shirt, I've still got my two best marbles. Rolled
in thumb and finger, they click, points gained, told
beads. Not for Joseph's church. If I forgot
French, too, who would I be inside my head?
My hands remember better: how to hold
my penknife to strip branches, where to crack
eggs on a bowl rim, how to pile a block
tower—when I was little—high as my nose.
Could I, still? The box of blocks is Mario's
now. My knee's cramped. I wish that I could walk
to Dad's house, or that I was up front, talk-

ing to him. How does he feel, suddenly slung
from brilliant nylon, levering onto air
currents like a thinking hawk? I'd be scared.

I'd be so scared I can't think it. Maybe a long
slope on my skateboard's like that. Climbing
isn't scary: no time. The air's fizzy, you're care-
ful what rock you hang your weight from, and where
your toes wedge. My calves ache, after, ribs sting,
but I'm good for something. What I like high
is mountains. I'll go up the hill behind
Dad's house this afternoon. I'll pick Liane
flowers. Nahh, we'll be leafing magazines
for school clothes on the sun porch after lunch.
I like those purple bell-spikes. My cleats crunch

the crumble; I stretch to the ledge and pull
out the whole rooted stalk. Sometimes there's twelve
bells, purple as—purple as nothing else
except a flower, ugly and beautiful
at once. Across my face come the two smells:
grandmother's linen-chest spice-sweet petals
and wet dirt clinging, half meat, half metal,
all raw. Between them I smell myself,
sweaty from climbing, but it's a woman's
sweat. I had one of the moon dreams again.
I stood on the flyover facing purple
sea, head up, while a house-huge full moon hurtled
toward me; then it was me flying, feet still
on the road. We're here, on top of the hill.

Elektra on Third Avenue

For Link

At six, when April chills our hands and feet
walking downtown, we stop at Clancy's Bar
or Bickford's, where the part-time hustlers are,

scoffing between the mailroom and the street.
Old pensioners appraise them while they eat,
and so do we, debating half in jest
which piece of hasty pudding we'd like best.
I know you know I think your mouth is sweet
as anything exhibited for sale,
fresh coffee cake or boys fresh out of jail,
which tender hint of incest brings me near
to ordering more coffee or more beer.
The homebound crowd provides more youth to cruise.
We nurse our cups, nudge knees, and pick and choose.

Sonnet Ending with a Film Subtitle

For Judith Landry

Life has its nauseating ironies:
The good die young, as often has been shown;
Chaste spouses catch Venereal Disease;
And feminists sit by the telephone.
Last night was rather bleak, tonight is starker.
I may stare at the wall till half-past-one.
My friends are all convinced Dorothy Parker
Lives, but is not well, in Marylebone.
I wish that I could imitate my betters
And fortify my rhetoric with guns.
Some day we women all will break our fetters
And raise our daughters to be Lesbians.
(I wonder if the bastard kept my letters?)
Here follow untranslatable French puns.

Lines Declining a Transatlantic Dinner Invitation

For Charlie and Tom

Regretfully, I proffer my excuses.
Number not less than Graces, more than Muses:
Auden's casting call for a dinner party.
He was a genius who was often smart. He
did not think hosts should count their guests in pairs,
unless they had loveseats and no hard chairs.
He was benignly daft for Small Odd Numbers:
a table choked with elbows soon encumbers
wit. I'm sure you'll all be very witty.
I'll miss it, snowed in here in New York City.
But, being *d'un certain age*, we come to know:
better to be discussed than be *de trop*.
The unexpected often is disaster.
If one arrives a month or an hour faster
than looked for, something that one cannot like
might happen: cab drivers would be on strike;
one's friends would be that morning reconciled
with lover, spouse, or adolescent child,
whose tears, A-Levels, or Social Disease
will call them home before the fruit and cheese;
the woman-poet-hating editor
looms ominously near the kitchen door
where a zinc bucket slops up the cold rain
that's sluiced down since the roof fell in again;
one host is wrapped in blankets in the attic: a
damp-inspired episode of his sciatica;
the other, peeling sprouts in a clogged sink,
scowls through a fourth compensatory drink;
somebody else has brought along a new
chum who was scathing in *The New Review*;
there'd be the flight to Amsterdam at nine;
simply, there might be insufficient wine.
As passports take two weeks to put in shape,
this all may have a flavor of sour grape.
Speaking of grapes—I hope you bought *Biscuit*—
pour one more brandy, as it were, on me.

Daniel Halpern

Jeannette Wieser

Daniel Halpern was born in 1945. He is the author of four collections of poetry, *Traveling on Credit* (1972), *Street Fire* (1975), *Life Among Others* (1978), and *Seasonal Rights* (1982), all from Viking/Penguin. Among his many awards are the "Discovery"/*The Nation* award, a fellowship from the National Endowment for the Arts, the Great Lakes Colleges National Book Award, and a New York State CAPS Grant. In 1975 he edited *The American Poetry Anthology* for Avon Press, and he is the editor of The Ecco Press and *Antaeus*. He teaches at Columbia University.

The Dance

No one's dancing here tonight.
Wouldn't you know it.
The cat in profile smiles at the light,
the rain is just a little sound on the metal
of the roof—out of season.

The cat doesn't dance and I wouldn't watch
if she did. Her little soul though
dances tonight, she is so pleased we are alone.
She smells the roast in the kitchen
and for my sake appreciates its progress.

There is a little fire burning: sawdust pressed
into a log and sold for a dollar keeps the light
the right tone and the heat up, although
it isn't really cold. No one is dancing,
the candles have been punched out,

and the amber has worn off the hardwood box.
Even the music, if it were playing, would make it
no different. Not even the rain or the food.
It doesn't matter little friend.
No one's dancing here tonight—wouldn't you know it.

How to Eat Alone

While it's still light out
set the table for one:
a red linen tablecloth,
one white plate, a bowl
for the salad
and the proper silverware.
Take out a three-pound leg of lamb,
rub it with salt, pepper and cumin,
then push in two cloves
of garlic splinters.
Place it in a 325-degree oven
and set the timer for an hour.
Put freshly cut vegetables
into a pot with some herbs
and the crudest olive oil
you can find.
Heat on a low flame.
Clean the salad.
Be sure the dressing is made
with fresh dill, mustard
and the juice of hard lemons.

Open a bottle of good late harvest zinfandel
and let it breathe on the table.
Pour yourself a glass
of cold California chardonnay
and go to your study and read.
As the story unfolds
you will smell the lamb
and the vegetables.
This is the best part of the evening:
the food cooking, the armchair,
the book and bright flavor
of the chilled wine.
When the timer goes off
toss the salad
and prepare the vegetables
and the lamb. Bring them out
to the table. Light the candles
and pour the red wine
into your glass.
Before you begin to eat,
raise your glass in honor
of yourself.
The company is the best you'll ever have.

Snapshot of Hue

For Robert Stone

They are riding bicycles on the other side
of the Perfume River.

A few months ago the bridges were down
and there was no one on the streets.

There were the telling piles on corners,
debris that contained a little of everything.

There was nothing not under cover—
even the sky remained impenetrable

day after day. And if you were seen
on the riverbank you were knocked down.

It is clear today. The litter in the streets
has been swept away. It couldn't have been

that bad, one of us said, the river barely moving,
the bicycles barely moving, the sun posted above.

Nude

In one of Watteau's pencil sketches
there's a woman sleeping on her side,
partly covered, the space behind her
darkly penciled in, her right arm
reaching out, probably around someone
who has left.
What makes me think her arm
is not merely cast out
is the way Watteau sketched dampness into her hair,
the way he remembered to pencil in
the good-time cloth-bracelet on that wrist,
and the space next to her,
which he left without a mark.

277 / DANIEL HALPERN

Portoncini dei Morti

In the *Analects* Confucius says,
The way out is via the door. How is it
that nobody recognizes this method?

In Gubbio, an Umbrian city
the most purely medieval in Italy, the buildings
have what the Italians call *portoncini dei morti,*
the little doorways of the dead.
When the dead of the family went through the door
for the last time they plastered it up.

It wasn't for the dead they did this,
but for themselves—they knew
death was the last farewell,
plastered or not, remembered or not.

Confucius was wrong, wasn't he? A door
is not the simplest solution.
I'm thinking about history and the departure
of the loved, about fathers
or men who raised sons they couldn't know.

I'm talking to those who have no ghost doorway
to mark their leaving us, who were carried
to the place that takes care of lost love—
in our country people die away from home,
it's part of the economy,
and the economy of loving.

The medieval Italians knew something
about dying and about love,
they closed the door for the dead.
What do the dead open for us
but the door that opens onto what there was?
What do we do for the dead but lower them
into the earth, shovel earth over

their eyes, and this, like the plaster
of the Italians, keeps the living out of
the way of those dead we have lost.

Intelligence is not needed to find a door
after death in the presence of love,
nor are doors answers to anything
that hides some part of ourselves.
The question is how to turn back—
the Italians were right: let the dead
leave us unattended and unencumbered.
Let us build new doors that the family
may leave together. This is the solution
and Confucius too was right,
that we will find new ways of being together
among the living.

Epithalamium

In the streets the crowds go about their business
like they always do here, in the rain, or in the clear,
cold mornings before the shops close for the midday.

It is possible to do nothing but participate outside
along with everyone else, to look through the glass
and imagine unwrapping what is perfectly displayed.

They have lit small oil lamps the entire length
of the Via di Ripetta, where our rooms are ready for you.
The only information you need now is to know

that the walls are salmon-colored and there are carpets
to make the mornings easier to negotiate. The kitchen
is serviceable—enough for coffee and good toast.

We'll walk through the city that is so familiar to us:
the Piazza di Spagna with Keats' window at one o'clock,
the Caravaggios in San Luigi and the Piazza del Popolo,
and the *trattoria* sprinkled like parmigiano over the city.

I have alerted the notaries and the witnesses,
the officials at the Campidoglio and the embassy,
and the offices that will ask if there is anything

that speaks against what we're about to do. Even
the gold bands have been located in Via della Croce—
the time has come. I am waiting for you.

The Summer Rentals

For my father

Today we went to see the summer rentals
that belong to Mrs. Marian Forster.
Her house, up the road from the Camden marina,
was off to the left, placed on the bay
across from the Curtis Island lighthouse.

She was a talker, with a quick, momentary smile—
you would have likened it to a jab,
but would have liked her handsome good looks.
I thought of you because she had just married
a man she knew in Los Angeles thirty years ago

who was built like you, tall and thin, elegant
in his dark suit and tie. A European with your face,
had you lived long enough, and your good humor
that lived in the eyes. His name was Harry.
Over proper drinks we talked summer rentals

with Mrs. Forster, or Mrs. Someone Else now—
we weren't given Harry's last name.
It was clear from the way he watched her
he was in love for the first time,
or still in love with his first love.

Talking to him was like talking to you.
Although I don't think we spoke of anything
in particular, it was like the talk we had
tossing a ball back and forth outside our house,
or walking down Van Nuys Boulevard.

Mrs. Forster liked us—we were "an interesting couple."
She took Jeanne's face in her hands
and asked me, "Is this a summer thing?"
Mrs. Forster, working the world of possibility,
never lost the spirit of romance.

She showed us, with delicate speed, "the small house,"
in which we could hear the sounds of the bay—
but not as well as in her house, she explained.
The stove in our kitchen had only four burners
and used electric heat, on which she refused to cook,

hers being a Garland with six gas burners
and a salamander, suitable for her style of living.
She told us the guests who lived on her property
had keys to every door, but as we grew silent,
followed with a confirmation that she of all people

believed in the importance of privacy.
I wonder what you would have thought.
Certainly you would have voted against renting,
in spite of being charmed by Mrs. Forster
and her property's flawless situation on the water.

We returned to her house and the women wandered off
to look at other rooms, pieces of furniture,
photographs of the second wedding and of her first husband,

who remained one rarely referred to in that house.
Harry and I talked a bit about his work in California,

his new life with Mrs. Forster, and he even explained
that when Mr. Forster died he had arrived to take her
"out of the woods." I knew he was Swedish
by the quick intake of breath that occurred when I said
something he agreed with. His sidelong glance and smile

presented the one context we could share.
It seemed to me, as we talked, that he knew
I was talking to you.
It was his eyes that allowed me to imagine asking
the two or three things I've wanted to ask you.

For some reason, as we left, knowing it would be impossible to return,
I remembered the first room I rented, against your better judgment,
as well as the room where I last saw you. I shook Harry's hand.
It was large and dry and surprisingly strong. As strong,
I returned the handshake you taught me as a boy.

Return, Starting Out

There it is, the jagged sprawl of the familiar
landscape gripping the bay, urging itself
forward into the warming water of the straits
and the lean winter fish that are picking up speed.

How much the same it is! Only I turned slightly, just now,
against it—this familiar! I touch it now and everything
is slightly less known and unknown—myself,
and others, houses the same color, repainted, or not here.

Now if I reach out into the air there is no sadness
in the empty space I receive, no sadness in the wood
of the oars when I take a rented boat into the bay
and let it drift, not driven but enchanted by current and wind.

Sitting in this boat, I look back at the rooms of houses.
What irritable knots of light they seem from here in half-light,
what irresistible nests of only a little warmth, smells
of whatever meats are over the braziers.

I am not fishing in this boat, it is becalmed.
I am not thinking deeply out here, no meditation.
I am floating, moving where the wood of the boat
moves, merely floating, looking back.

Robert Hass

Robert Hass was born in 1941. He attended St. Mary's College and Stanford University. His first book, *Field Guide*, won the Yale Series of Younger Poets Award. His second book of poetry, *Praise* (1979), and a book of criticism, *Twentieth Century Pleasures* (1984), were published by The Ecco Press. He is also the co-translator (with Robert Pinsky) of *The Separate Notebooks* by Czeslaw Milosz (Ecco, 1984). He has been the recipient of fellowships from the Guggenheim and MacArthur foundations.

Robert Selden Smith

Weed

 Horse is Lorca's word, fierce as wind,
or melancholy, gorgeous, Andalusian:
  white horse grazing near the river dust;
and parsnip is hopeless,
  second cousin to the rhubarb
which is already second cousin
  to an apple pie. Marrying the words
to the coarse white umbels sprouting
  on the first of May is history
but conveys nothing; it is not the veined
  body of Queen Anne's lace
I found, bored, in a spring classroom
  from which I walked hands tingling

for the breasts that are meadows in New Jersey
	in 1933; it is thick, shaggier, and the name
is absurd. It speaks of durable
	unimaginative pleasures: reading Balzac,
fixing the window sash, rising
	to a clean kitchen, the fact
that the car starts & driving to work
	through hills where the roadside thickens
with the green ungainly stalks,
	the bracts and bright white flowerets
		of horse-parsnips.

Meditation at Lagunitas

All the new thinking is about loss.
In this it resembles all the old thinking.
The idea, for example, that each particular erases
the luminous clarity of a general idea. That the clown-
faced woodpecker probing the dead sculpted trunk
of that black birch is, by his presence,
some tragic falling off from a first world
of undivided light. Or the other notion that,
because there is in this world no one thing
to which the bramble of *blackberry* corresponds,
a word is elegy to what it signifies.
We talked about it late last night and in the voice
of my friend, there was a thin wire of grief, a tone
almost querulous. After a while I understood that,
talking this way, everything dissolves: *justice,
pine, hair, woman, you* and *I*. There was a woman
I made love to and I remembered how, holding
her small shoulders in my hands sometimes,
I felt a violent wonder at her presence
like a thirst for salt, for my childhood river

with its island willows, silly music from the pleasure boat,
muddy places where we caught the little orange-silver fish
called *pumpkinseed*. It hardly had to do with her.
Longing, we say, because desire is full
of endless distances. I must have been the same to her.
But I remember so much, the way her hands dismantled bread,
the thing her father said that hurt her, what
she dreamed. There are moments when the body is as numinous
as words, days that are the good flesh continuing.
Such tenderness, those afternoons and evenings,
saying *blackberry, blackberry, blackberry.*

Old Dominion

The shadows of late afternoon and the odors
of honeysuckle are a congruent sadness.
Everything is easy but wrong. I am walking
across thick lawns under maples in borrowed tennis whites.
It is like the photographs of Randall Jarrell
I stared at on the backs of books in college.
He looked so sad and relaxed in the pictures.
He was translating Chekhov and wore tennis whites.
It puzzled me that in his art, like Chekhov's,
everyone was lost, that the main chance was never seized
because it is only there as a thing to be dreamed of
or because someone somewhere had set the old words
to the old tune: we live by habit and it doesn't hurt.
Now the *thwack . . . thwack* of tennis balls being hit
reaches me and it is the first sound of an ax
in the cherry orchard or the sound of machine guns
where the young terrorists are exploding
among poor people on the streets of Los Angeles.
I begin making resolutions: to take risks, not to stay
in the south, to somehow do honor to Randall Jarrell,

never to kill myself. Through the oaks I see the courts,
the nets, the painted boundaries, and the people in tennis
whites who look so graceful from this distance.

Child Naming Flowers

When old crones wandered in the woods,
I was the hero on the hill
in clear sunlight.

Death's hounds feared me.

Smell of wild fennel,
high loft of sweet fruit high in the branches
of the flowering plum.

Then I am cast down
into the terror of childhood,
into the mirror and the greasy knives,
the dark
woodpile under the fig trees
in the dark.
        It is only
the malice of voices, the old horror
that is nothing, parents
quarreling, somebody
drunk.

I don't know how we survive it.
On this sunny morning
in my life as an adult, I am looking
at one clear pure peach
in a painting by Georgia O'Keeffe.
It is all the fullness that there is

in light. A towhee scratches in the leaves
outside my open door.
He always does.

A moment ago I felt so sick
and so cold
I could hardly move.

Late Spring

And then in mid-May the first morning of steady heat,

the morning, Leif says, when you wake up, put on shorts and that's it
for the day,

when you pour coffee and walk outside, blinking in the sun.

Strawberries have appeared in the markets, and peaches will soon;

squid is so cheap in the fish stores you begin to consult Japanese and
Italian cookbooks for the various and ingenious ways of preparing *ika*
and *calamari*;

and because the light will enlarge your days, your dreams at night will
be as strange as the jars of octopus Basho saw under the summer moon;

and after swimming white wine, and the sharing of stories before dinner
is prolonged because the relations of the children in the neighborhood
have acquired village intensity and the stories take longer telling;

and there are nights when the fog rolls in that nobody likes—hey fog,
the Miwoks sang, who lived here first, you better go home, pelican is
beating your wife—

and after dark, in the first cool hour, your children sleep so heavily in their beds, exhausted from play, it is a pleasure to watch them,

Leif does not move a muscle as he lies there; no, wait; it is Luke who lies there in his eight-year-old body,

Leif is taller than you are and he isn't home; when he is, his feet will extend past the end of the mattress, and Kristin is at the corner in the dark, talking with the neighborhood boys;

things change; there is no need for this dream-compelled narration; the rhythm will keep me awake, changing.

Rusia en 1931

The bishop of El Salvador is dead, murdered by no one knows who. The left says the right, the right says the provocateurs.

But the families in the barrios sleep with their children beside them and a pitchfork, or a rifle if they have one.

And posterity is grubbing in the footnotes to find out who the bishop is,

or waiting for the poet to get back to his business. Well, there's this:

her breasts are the color of brown stones in moonlight, and paler in moonlight.

And that should hold them for a while. The bishop is dead. Poetry proposes no solutions: it says justice is the well water of the city of Novgorod, black and sweet.

César Vallejo died on a Thursday. It might have been malaria, no one is sure; it burned through the small town of Santiago de Chuco in an

Andean valley in his childhood, it may have flared in his veins in Paris on a rainy day;

and nine months later Osip Mandelstam was seen feeding off the garbage heap of a transit camp near Vladivostok.

They might have met in Leningrad in 1931, on a corner; two men about forty; they could have compared gray hair at the temple, or compared reviews of *Trilce* and *Tristia* in 1922.

What French they would have spoken! And what the one thought would save Spain killed the other.

"I am no wolf by blood," Mandelstam wrote that year. "Only an equal could break me."

And Vallejo: "Think of the unemployed. Think of the forty million families of the hungry. . . ."

Spring Drawing II

A man says lilacs against white houses, two sparrows, one streaked, in a thinning birch, and can't find his way to a sentence.

In order to be respectable, Thorstein Veblen said, desperate in Palo Alto, a thing must be wasteful, i.e., "a selective adaptation of forms to the end of conspicuous waste."

So we try to throw nothing away, as Keith, making dinner for us as his grandmother had done in Jamaica, left nothing: the kitchen was as clean at the end as when he started; even the shrimp shells and carrot fronds were part of the process, and he said, when we tried to admire him, "Listen, I should send you into the chickenyard to look for a rusty nail to add to the soup for iron."

The first temptation of Shakyamuni was desire, but he saw that it led to fulfillment and then to desire, so that one was easy.

Because I have pruned it badly in successive years, the climbing rose has sent out, among the pale pink floribunda, a few wild white roses from the rootstalk.

Suppose, before they said *silver* or *moonlight* or *wet grass*, each poet had to agree to be responsible for the innocence of all the suffering on earth;

because they learned in arithmetic, during the long school days, that if there was anything left over,

you had to carry it. The wild rose looks weightless, the floribunda are heavy with the richness and sadness of Europe

as they imitate the dying, petal by petal, of the people who bred them.

You hear pain singing in the nerves of things; it is not a song.

The gazelle's head turned: three jaguars are eating his entrails and he is watching.

William Heyen

William Heyen was born in Brooklyn, New York, in 1940. He was educated at S.U.N.Y. at Brockport, and Ohio University. He is the author of seven books of poems, most recently, *Erika: Poems of the Holocaust* (Vanguard Press, 1984). He is also the editor of A *Profile of Theodore Roethke* (1971), from the Charles Merrill Company, and *American Poets in 1976*, from Bobbs-Merrill. Among his many awards are the Witter Bynner Prize of the American Academy and Institute of Arts and Letters, and fellowships from the National Endowment for the Arts and the Guggenheim Foundation. He teaches at S.U.N.Y. at Brockport.

Dark in the Reich of the Blond

I had my papers, but I was running.
I had my proof, but I was running.
I had my trees of Aryan descent,
but I was running,

but I'd been dreaming,
and woke beneath a pile of corpses.
I was happy, hidden,
and I had my papers.

The moon shone down, but I was hiding.
The stars winked down, but I was hiding.

The sky had eyes, and they were open,
but I was hiding.

I am here now, where you are, too.
I live here now, where you will, too.
We two will wait here, quiet, still,
while the night forgets. . . .

Do you have your papers? Lie here quiet.
Let the eyes run down like rain, let
the bodies turn to grass above us
as we wait here with our papers. Lie here quiet.

Mantle

Mantle ran so hard, they said,
he tore his legs to pieces.
What is this but spirit?

52 homers in '56, the triple crown.
I was a high school junior, batting
fourth behind him in a dream.

I prayed for him to quit, before
his lifetime dropped below .300.
But he didn't, and it did.

He makes Brylcreem commercials now,
models with open mouths draped around him
as they never were in Commerce, Oklahoma,

where the sandy-haired, wide-shouldered boy
stood up against his barn,
lefty for an hour (Ruth, Gehrig),

then righty (DiMaggio),
as his father winged them in,
and the future blew toward him,

now a fastball, now a slow
curve hanging
like a model's smile.

Fires

*"The prairies burning form some of the most
beautiful scenes that are to be witnessed in the
country, and also some of the most sublime."*
                                        —George Catlin

I.

Where, on prairie elevations,
grass clings thin, sparse, as low
as in what Easterners would call a meadow, no
animal fears the gentle fire it smells

from far away. Sometimes invisible,
the burn's feeble flame
travels to the eyes as only its black line,
and when they must, as they must each autumn

when lightning seems to strike off
yellow sections of itself
lateral cross this land,
the wild bodies who know fire

will wait for it to tongue their lairs,
will step over it or walk through it

across the warm cinders
to another year. At night, the flame's

luminous blue wavery liquid edge
   pours over the sides and tops
      of bluffs in chains, "hanging suspended,"
as George Catlin put it in 1830,

"in graceful festoons from the skies."
   With him, we could watch this nightfire
      for a long time: even the stars appear
to rise from ground that the sinuous

soft flame blackens behind it.
   With him, we could watch this nightfire
      for a long time, bed down
on the still-warm ground behind it,

and sleep, the waving
   flames receding
      in grasshead sparkles
like Andromeda, or a dream.

II.

But Catlin knew that the place came
   for us to stand erect
      in our mounts' stirrups, to stare for fire
over the tall cover of flatland grass,

in other country, along the Missouri,
   the Platte, the Arkansas.
      To be caught here is to die:
pea-vines tangle the eight-foot grasses,

fire drives smoke before it, booms
   terror into the horses rearing up in circles:
      the leaping flames soon surround
to take all horsehair and flesh

in screams and thunderous noise. We
would not be the first. Whole
parties of Indians, herds
of buffalo and deer have burned into a charred meal

only ants are left alive to eat, and the roots
of next spring's prairie. These scenes
roll with black smoke and streaks of red,
both beautiful and sublime, as the painter said.

III.

Those galaxies, each at least one hundred
billion bodies falling away from us,
one hundred billion, ten to the eleventh power,
billions dead and invisible already—

that is the far darkness. Planets
burn out, turn, for all we know,
into ice, or cold moons, if anything only an unseen
trace of fern or beings in fossil to prove perished fire,

but here, for now, on this earth,
even for those creatures whose marrow
boiled within their bones
and through whose ribs the prairie wind

tuned itself to its own truth,
even for these the fires sear
something else. Just now, within this revery of him,
not knowing, as in all of Catlin's paintings,

how to end this, or where, of its own discord, it does,
I looked up again out
of my twentieth-century window
over my left shoulder:

Catlin's West is dead, yes, in its own way,
　　but the same sun's unimaginable power drives suburban
　　　　and miraculous through flowers banked
against these houses, flames the black-flecked, slashed vivid

undiminished orange heads of tiger lily, and even the most
　　domestic geranium along a front border
　　　　bursts with spots of fire red
as the open mouths of horses trapped in that other world.

IV.

If much of this is sad, this
　　necessary "civilized
　　　　wilderness"
our minds have made for us,

still the fires kindle and begin,
　　somewhere beneath the breastbone,
　　　　somehow under the lungs,
radiate from rooftops,

the sunlit concrete,
　　brick, even the black
　　　　macadam to abdomen and groin, begin,
in their last stages, to leap up

into the city, into the brain's
　　nerves and grasses, out
　　　　into the fingers' touch, even
into love. Catlin's West is lost, except

we still feel these fires, by night
　　a necklace blue as a glass snake in the heavens,
　　　　by day as flickering sun
tongues its way along a walk, the flash of steel

smokestacks, or in lightning, or the rains'
　　rolling fog, at sunset

in the burnished clouds rising
over lines of trees rising

over lines of buildings still
   burning, outside, within,
      with wild and elemental meanings
from our living sun.

The Berries

My wife already there to comfort,
I walked over icy roads
to our neighbor who had lost her father.
The hard winter starlight glittered, my breath
formed ascending souls that disappeared,
as he had, the eighty-year-old man
who died of cancer.

In my left coat pocket, a jar
of raspberry jam. . . . I remembered
stepping into the drooping canes, the ripe
raspberry odor. I remembered bending over,
or kneeling, to get down under the leaves
to hidden clusters. . . .

Then, and on my walk, and now, the summer berries
made / make a redness in my mind. The jar
presses light against my hip, weight
to hand to the grieving woman. This gift
to her, to me—being able to bear
the summer's berry light like that, like this,
over the ice . . .

When I was a boy, the Lord I talked to
know me. Where is He now? I seem to have

lost Him, except for something
in that winter air, something insisting on being
there, and here—that summer's berries, that mind's
light against my hip, myself kneeling again
under the raspberry canes.

The Elm's Home

I.

A dark sky blowing over
our backyard maples,
the air already cool,
Brockport begins its autumn.
My mower's drone and power
drift past the first leaves fallen
curled into red and yellow fists.
In a corner of lawn against
an old wire fence against the older woods,
a grove of mushrooms the kids
already hacked umbrellaless with golfclubs
rots into a mush of lumped columns,
pleats and fans.

These are the suburbs
where I loved that tree, our one elm.
Now, an inch under the loam,
its stump is a candle
of slow decay, lighting, above it,
thousands of perfect pearls
tiered like ant-eggs,
and these, by nature, growing so low
my mower's blades will never touch them.

II.

My precious secrets come
to this, then? Yes.
Stay away from them,
you careless bastards.

But listen: sometimes,
at night, kneeling
within a dream within
the elm's oval shadow,

I can look down
into my leg-bones,
into my own marrow
clustered with eggs,

small and perfect pearl
mushrooms
living for all my life.
I can look up

into the elm and hear each leaf
whisper in my own breath, *welcome*
home, this is your home,
welcome home.

III.

Sun, shine through me,
    for I have lost my body,
        my old elm gone home
    to its earthly city, O
sun, shine through me.

IV.

Downward leader flash track
driving: 1,000 miles per second;
inconceivable return track:
87,000 miles per second.

But if we could stop it with our eyes:
its central core, hotter and brighter
than the surface of the sun,
only a half-inch to an inch diameter;

its corona envelope, or glow discharge,
ten to twenty feet. Lightning:
our eyeballs' branched after-image. Lightning:
smell of ozone in the air,

pure stroke and electric numen.

V.

Last night, heat
lightning branching
the blue-black sky,
alone on our back lawn,
when I closed my eyes for the right time,
when I knelt within the nimbus
where the elm I loved
lived for a hundred years,

when I touched the loam fill over the elm's stump,
its clusters of tiny noctilucent mushrooms,
I saw through them
into the ground, into the elm's dead
luminous roots, the branches of heaven
under the earth, this island home,
my lightning lord,
my home.

Auction

Late, I was in the back circle.
　　Just out of beginning rain,
　　　　the auctioneer stood on a wagon

pulled to the central doors of a sagging barn,
　　and sold—rolls of barbed wire, tools, feed,
　　　　furniture, depression glassware, a mirror,

linens, a shotgun, Christmas decorations—
　　all held up by his young helpers.
　　　　Then, a box of books. I bid a dollar,

and they were mine, passed back
　　by a dozen hands. I knelt to sort them,
　　　　knowing what they'd be, as they were—

those same popular weeping novels
　　of the century before: a woman, of course,
　　　　who stands in her doorway wondering whether

to wed her city or her country suitor; a priest,
　　of course, who loves the village's spinster teacher
　　　　for sixty years of heartbreak without a word. . . .

You know what I mean—the language-cloying
　　conventional sublime
　　　　that dazes and bores us. But there, too,

in the bottom of the box, a scrapbook,
　　and pasted on its first yellowed and chipped page,
　　　　a photograph of the girl who'd kept it

seventy years before, who'd pressed into it
　　and labeled leaves she'd known,
　　　　oak and maple, apple, linden,

black birch, catalpa, and then, still green
    in folds of waxed paper, "American Chestnut,"
        these leaves bought at auction

in arrogance in the gentle rain, but now down
    on my knees, eyes blurred in the light of dead
        trees and the face of a girl who gathers

the farm's beauty in fallen leaves,
    who needed to touch, touched, still
        touches these pages of the chestnut rain.

The Snapper

He is the pond's old father, its brain
and dark, permanent presence.

He is the snapper, and smells
rich and sick as a mat of weeds; and wears

a beard of leeches that suck frog, fish,
and snake blood from his neck; and drags

a tail ridged as though hacked out
with an ax. He rises: mud swirls

and blooms, lilies bob, water washes
his moss-humped back where, buried

deep in his sweet flesh, the pond ebbs
and flows its sure, slow heart.

This Night

Which is our star this night?
Belsen is bathed in blue,
every footworn lane, every
strand of wire, pale blue.
The guards' bodies,
the prisoners' bodies—all
black and invisible. Only
their pale blue eyes
float above the lanes
or between the wires.
Or they are all dead,
and these are the blue eyes of those
haunted by what happened here.
Which eyes are yours,
which mine? Even
blue-eyed crows
drift the darkness overhead. Even
blue-eyed worms
sip dew from the weeping leaves
of the black Erika
over the graves. . . .
But now, at once, every
eye, every blue light
closes. As we do.
For rest. For now.
Which was our star this night?

Edward Hirsch

Edward Hirsch was born in Chicago in 1950. He was educated at Grinnell College and the University of Pennsylvania. His first book of poems, *For the Sleepwalkers* (Knopf, 1981) was nominated for a National Book Critics Circle Award. He has received awards and fellowships from The Academy of American Poets, the Ingram Merrill Foundation, and the National Endowment for the Arts. He teaches at Wayne State University.

Janet Landay

For the Sleepwalkers

Tonight I want to say something wonderful
for the sleepwalkers who have so much faith
in their legs, so much faith in the invisible

arrow carved into the carpet, the worn path
that leads to the stairs instead of the window,
the gaping doorway instead of the seamless mirror.

I love the way that sleepwalkers are willing
to step out of their bodies into the night,
to raise their arms and welcome the darkness,

palming the blank spaces, touching everything.
Always they return home safely, like blind men
who know it is morning by feeling shadows.

And always they wake up as themselves again.
That's why I want to say something astonishing
like: *Our hearts are leaving our bodies.*

Our hearts are thirsty black handkerchiefs
flying through the trees at night, soaking up
the darkest beams of moonlight, the music

of owls, the motion of wind-torn branches.
And now our hearts are thick black fists
flying back to the glove of our chests.

We have to learn to trust our hearts like that.
We have to learn the desperate faith of sleep-
walkers who rise out of their calm beds

and walk through the skin of another life.
We have to drink the stupefying cup of darkness
and wake up to ourselves, nourished and surprised.

Dawn Walk

Some nights when you're asleep
Deep under the covers, far away,
Slowly curling yourself back
Into a childhood no one
Living will ever remember
Now that your parents touch hands
Under the ground
As they always did upstairs
In the master bedroom, only more
Distant now, deaf to the nightmares,
The small cries that no longer
Startle you awake but still
Terrify me so that

I do get up, some nights, restless
And anxious to walk through
The first trembling blue light
Of dawn in a calm snowfall.
It's soothing to see the houses
Asleep in their own large bodies,
The dreamless fences, the courtyards
Unscarred by human footprints,
The huge clock folding its hands
In the forehead of the skyscraper
Looming downtown. In the park
The benches are layered in
White, the statue out of history
Is an outline of blue snow. Cars,
Too, are rimmed and motionless
Under a thin blanket smoothed down
By the smooth maternal palm
Of the wind. So thanks to the
Blue morning, to the blue spirit
Of winter, to the soothing blue gift
Of powdered snow! And soon
A few scattered lights come on
In the houses, a motor coughs
And starts up in the distance, smoke
Raises its arms over the chimneys.
Soon the trees suck in the darkness
And breathe out the light
While black drapes open in silence.
And as I turn home where
I know you are already awake,
Wandering slowly through the house
Searching for me, I can suddenly
Hear my own footsteps crunching
The simple astonishing news
That we are here,
Yes, we are still here.

Dino Campana and the Bear

Here, in the night, I'm staring
At the photograph of a stranger faking
A brave heel and toe, a lyrical
Dance with the gypsy's favorite bear
Stumbling in front of the dying
Campfire light
In a small clearing of birches
On the outskirts of Odessa. Tambourines
Flash like swords in the spoked
Shadows, and you can almost
Feel the drunken bear stagger
And weave with exhaustion
From too many cities, too many
Ringing triangles and suspicious eyes,
Too many bored adults, pawing children.
All the bear wants is to
Collapse in his own poor cage
Under stars scattered
Like red kerchiefs through the trees;
All he wants is to sleep. But
The stranger whispers something
Indecipherable, something convincing
In a strange tongue, and so
The four thick arms continue to
Grip and lock and hug,
The four heavy legs stagger on.
Fur and skin. Dino Campana
And the bear. 1911. Russia.
In three long years the bear
Will have left his body forever
To travel easily, in another forest,
While the stranger will still
Be selling flowers and stoking
Furnaces, peddling songs in cafes
Out of hard need. But tonight
All he knows is that wherever
He is going is going

To be better than wherever
He is, wherever he was.
And so he tilts the bear's grim
Forehead to the sky
And keeps on dancing and dancing.
He wants to feel the moon's
Wild eye staring
Into their dark faces. He wants
To vanish into its hard, cold light.

In the Middle of August

The dead heat rises for weeks,
Unwanted, unasked for, but suddenly,
Like the answer to a question,
A real summer shower breaks loose
In the middle of August. So think
Of trumpets and cymbals, a young girl
In a sparkling tinsel suit leading
A parade up Fifth Avenue, all
The high school drummers in the city
Banging away at once. Think of
Bottles shattering against a warehouse,
Or a bowl of apricots spilling
From a tenth-floor window: the bright
Rat-a-tat-tat on the hot pavement,
The squeal of adults scurrying
For cover like happy children.
Down the bar, someone says it's like
The night she fell asleep standing
In the bathroom of a dank tavern
And woke up shivering in an orchard
Of lemon trees at dawn, surprised
By the sudden omnipotence of yellows.

Someone else says it's like spinning
A huge wheel and winning at roulette,
Or drawing four aces and thinking:
"It's true, it's finally happening."
Look, I'm not saying that the pretty
Girl in the fairy tale really does
Let down her golden hair for all
The poor kids in the neighborhood—
Though maybe she does. But still
I am saying that a simple cloud
Bursts over the city in mid-August
And suddenly, in your lifetime,
Everyone believes in his own luck.

Poor Angels

   At this hour the soul floats weightlessly
through the city streets, speechless and invisible,
astonished by the smoky blend of grays and golds
seeping out of the air, the dark half-tones

of dusk suddenly filling the urban sky
while the body sits listlessly by the window
sullen and heavy, too exhausted to move,
too weary to stand up or to lie down.

At this hour the soul is like a yellow wing
slipping through the treetops, a little ecstatic
cloud hovering over the sidewalks, calling out
to the approaching night, "Amaze me, amaze me,"

while the body sits glumly by the window
listening to the clear summons of the dead
transparent as glass, clairvoyant as crystal . . .
Some nights it is almost ready to join them.

Oh, this is a strange, unlikely tethering,
a furious grafting of the quick and the slow:
when the soul flies up, the body sinks down
and all night—locked in the same cramped room—

they go on quarrelling, stubbornly threatening
to leave each other, wordlessly filling the air
with the sound of a low internal burning.
How long can this bewildering marriage last?

At midnight the soul dreams of a small fire
of stars flaming on the other side of the sky,
but the body stares into an empty night sheen,
a hollow-eyed darkness. Poor luckless angels,

    feverish old loves: don't separate yet.
Let what rises live with what descends.

Jonathan Holden

Steve Briggs

Jonathan Holden was born in 1941. He was educated at Oberlin College, San Francisco State University, and the University of Colorado. His first book, *Design for a House* (1972), won the Devins award and was published by the University of Missouri Press. *Leverage* (1982) won the AWP Award Series for Poetry and was published by the University Press of Virginia, and *Falling from Stardom* (1984) was published by Carnegie-Mellon University Press. He has also published a critical study of William Stafford and a book of essays, *Rhetoric of the Contemporary Lyric*. He teaches at Kansas State University.

A Poem for Ed "Whitey" Ford

I wanted my name
curt: Ed
Ford: a name that gave away
nothing. I wanted
a cute cocky face. To be
a low-ball specialist
but sneaky fast, tough
in the clutch. Not
to retire the side with power
but with finesse.
I never wanted to go

soft, to fall in love fall
through it and keep
falling like this,
letting the light and air
pick my pockets at will.
Or dwell in this gray
area, this interval
where we search out by feel
the seams in the day,
homesick for the warm
map of a hand.
I planned to be
immune as Ford
on the throne of the mound,
my position defined
by both taut foul-lines,
the fence against my back.
To sight on the vanishing point
in the core of the mitt.
My delivery strict,
classic.
Not to sit thinking like this
how I drive the blunt wedge
of my breath before me
one space at a time,
watching words
I thought were well meant
miss. I wanted
what we all wanted then:
To be ice.
To throw uncontradicted
strikes. To be
like Ed Ford at work—
empty, cruel, accurate.
Our beauty pure expertise.

Losers

*"The best part of NFL playoff games is those shots of
the losing bench."*

—*overheard in a bar*

Without their helmets,
their faces betray everything:
defeat, an open political
scandal. Some are
crying. I want to thank
them: They admit. I'd like to shake
their homely, trustworthy hands.
But they just sit there,
each of them going
over his own private score
again, checking the bland words
of his rejection

like a man sorting slowly
through all of the flattering
hackneyed constructions
his lover had once placed
on his eyes, on his mere
hands—*I'll do anything
for you*—each word a smooth
flat stone, a *tabula
rasa* he still strokes absently
under his thumb, remembering
when the act of simply
unbuckling his belt
was cruel,
a command that could crush
her parts of speech to a single
vowel, the same
stark question begging
his answer—a short
hard retort he'd thought only he
could give her again
and again—what he'd always

suspected of his true
worth, the secret he'd scarcely dared
whisper even to her—

Not like these
men, slumped on the losing
bench, staring ahead, trying
to comprehend the rudiments
of some old standard system of
weights and measures
they'd once learned they had
to go by—
these men who, out of
power now, relieved
of their secrets, are as honestly
miserable as they look.

Liberace

It took generations to mature
this figure. Every day it
had to be caught sneaking off
to its piano lesson and beaten up.
Every day it came back
for more. It would have been
trampled underground, but
like a drop of mercury, it was
too slippery. Stamped on,
it would divide, squirt away
and gather somewhere else, it was
insoluble, it had nowhere to go.
All it could do was gather again,
a puddle in the desert, festering
until the water had gone punk, it
was no good for anything anymore.

315 / JONATHAN HOLDEN

It wears rubies on its fingers now.
Between its dimples, its leer is
fixed. Its cheeks are
chocked, its eyes twinkle. It
knows. Thank you, it breathes
with ointment in its voice,
Thank you very much.

Why We Bombed Haiphong

When I bought bubble gum
to get new baseball cards
the B-52 was everywhere you looked.
In my high school yearbook
the B-52 was voted "Most Popular"
and "Most Likely to Succeed."

The B-52 would give you the finger
from hot cars. It laid rubber,
it spit, it went around in gangs,
it got its finger wet and sneered
about it. It beat the shit
out of fairies.

I remember it used to chase
Derek Remsen around at recess
every day. Caught, he'd scream
like a girl. Then the rest
of us pitched in and hit.

The Swimming Pool

Long after he'd wearied of the work
I recall my father sloshing in hip boots,
ignoring the mosquitoes on his back
to lay by hand, around the stone
swimming pool he'd built, this tile
drain to divert the brook when it
turned brown in thunderstorms, how
he grunted as he pried up each sucking
shovelful of muck, his face
a shiny little mask of wrinkled sweat,
hating every minute of it.
And I remember how, later, in July,
when the wet heat would make you
claustrophobic and despair
he'd step up to that pool—
shy almost—gingerly dip in a toe,
exclaim wryly, then begin the ritual,
first rinse the arms,
then wash the chest,
his legs meanwhile feeling their way
on tiptoe as he waded forward, becoming
shorter and shorter, the cold lip
of the water crawling up his stomach
until, ready to receive the cold,
he'd lie back on his back and sigh,
then close his eyes as though
that pool could never give him back
enough or fast enough or long enough
all that he'd put into it.

Garrett Kaoru Hongo

Garrett Kaoru Hongo was born in
Hawaii in 1951. He received a B.A.
from Pomona College and an
M.F.A. from the University of Cal-
ifornia at Irvine. He is the co-author
of *The Buddha Bandits Down High-
way 99* (1978), from Buddahead
Press. *Yellow Light* (1982) was pub-
lished by Wesleyan University Press.
Among his awards are the "Discov-
ery"/*The Nation* award and an
N.E.A. fellowship. He teaches at the
University of Missouri–Columbia.

Cynthia Thiessen

Yellow Light

One arm hooked around the frayed strap
of a tar-black, patent-leather purse,
the other cradling something for dinner:
fresh bunches of spinach from a J-Town *yaoya*,
sides of split Spanish mackerel from Alviso's,
maybe a loaf of Langendorf; she steps
off the hissing bus at Olympic and Fig,
begins the three-block climb up the hill,
passing gangs of schoolboys playing war,
Japs against Japs, Chicanas chalking sidewalks
with the holy double-yoked crosses of hopscotch,
and the Korean grocer's wife out for a stroll
around this neighborhood of Hawaiian apartments

just starting to steam with cooking
and the anger of young couples coming home
from work, yelling at kids, flicking on
TV sets for the Wednesday Night Fights.

If it were May, hydrangeas and jacaranda
flowers in the streetside trees would be
blooming through the smog of late spring.
Wisteria in Masuda's front yard would be
shaking out the long tresses of its purple hair.
Maybe mosquitoes, moths, a few orange butterflies
settling on the lattice of monkey flowers
tangled in chain-link fences by the trash.

But this is October, and Los Angeles
seethes like a billboard under twilight.
From used-car lots and the movie houses uptown,
long silver sticks of light probe the sky.
From the Miracle Mile, whole freeways away,
a brilliant fluorescence breaks out
and makes war with the dim squares
of yellow kitchen light winking on
in all the side streets of the Barrio.

She climbs up the two flights of flagstone
stairs to 201-B, the spikes of her high heels
clicking like kitchen knives on a cutting board,
props the groceries against the door,
fishes through memo pads, a compact,
empty packs of chewing gum, and finds her keys.

The moon then, cruising from behind
a screen of eucalyptus across the street,
covers everything, everything in sight,
in a heavy light like yellow onions.

What For

At six I lived for spells:
how a few Hawaiian words could call
up the rain, could hymn like the sea
in the long swirl of chambers
curling in the nautilus of a shell,
how Amida's ballads of the Buddhaland
in the drone of the priest's liturgy
could conjure money from the poor
and give them nothing but mantras,
the strange syllables that healed desire.

I lived for stories about the war
my grandfather told over *hana* cards,
slapping them down on the mats
with a sharp Japanese *kiai.*

I lived for songs my grandmother sang
stirring curry into a thick stew,
weaving a calligraphy of Kannon's love
into grass mats and straw sandals.

I lived for the red volcano dirt
staining my toes, the salt residue
of surf and sea wind in my hair,
the arc of a flat stone skipping
in the hollow trough of a wave.

I lived a child's world, waited
for my father to drag himself home,
dusted with blasts of sand, powdered rock,
and the strange ash of raw cement,
his deafness made worse by the clang
of pneumatic drills, sore in his bones
from the buckings of a jackhammer.

He'd hand me a scarred lunchpail,
let me unlace the hightop G.I. boots,

call him the new name I'd invented
that day in school, write it for him
on his newspaper. He'd rub my face
with hands that felt like gravel roads,
tell me to move, go play, and then he'd
walk to the laundry sink to scrub,
rinse the dirt of his long day
from a face brown and grained as koa wood.

I wanted to take away the pain
in his legs, the swelling in his joints,
give him back his hearing,
clear and rare as crystal chimes,
the fins of glass that wrinkled
and sparked the air with their sound.

I wanted to heal the sores that work
and war had sent to him,
let him play catch in the backyard
with me, tossing a tennis ball
past papaya trees without the shoulders
of pain shrugging back his arms.

I wanted to become a doctor of pure magic,
to string a necklace of sweet words
fragrant as pine needles and plumeria,
fragrant as the bread my mother baked,
place it like a lei of cowrie shells
and *pikake* flowers around my father's neck,
and chant him a blessing, a sutra.

Off from Swing Shift

Late, just past midnight,
freeway noise from the Harbor
and San Diego leaking in
from the vent over the stove,
and he's off from swing shift at Lear's.
Eight hours of twisting circuitry,
charting ohms and maximum gains
while transformers hum
and helicopters swirl
on the roofs above the small factory.
He hails me with a head-fake,
then the bob and weave
of a weekend middleweight
learned at the Y on Kapiolani
ten years before I was born.

The shoes and gold London Fogger
come off first, then the easy grin
saying he's lucky as they come.
He gets into the slippers
my brother gives him every Christmas,
carries his Thermos over to the sink,
and slides into the one chair at the table
that's made of wood and not yellow plastic.
He pushes aside stacks
of *Sporting News* and *Outdoor Life*,
big round tins of Holland butter cookies,
and clears a space for his elbows, his pens,
and the *Racing Form*'s Late Evening Final.
His left hand reaches out,
flicks on the Sony transistor
we bought for his birthday
when I was fifteen.
The right ferries in the earphone,
a small, flesh-colored star,
like a tiny miracle of hearing,
and fits it into place.

I see him plot black constellations
of figures and calculations
on the magazine's margins,
alternately squint and frown
as he fingers the knob of the tuner
searching for the one band
that will call out today's results.

There are whole cosmologies
in a single handicap,
a lifetime of two-dollar losing
in one pick of the Daily Double.

Maybe tonight is his night
for winning, his night
for beating the odds
of going deaf from a shell
at Anzio still echoing
in the cave of his inner ear,
his night for cashing in
the blue chips of shrapnel still grinding
at the thickening joints of his legs.

But no one calls
the horse's name, no one
says Shackles, Rebate, or Pouring Rain.
No one speaks a word.

The Hongo Store
29 Miles Volcano
Hilo, Hawaii
FROM A PHOTOGRAPH

My parents felt those rumblings
Coming deep from the earth's belly,
Thudding like the bell of the Buddhist Church.
Tremors in the ground swayed the bathinette
Where I lay squalling in soapy water.

My mother carried me around the house,
Back through the orchids, ferns, and plumeria
Of that greenhouse world behind the store,
And jumped between gas pumps into the car.

My father gave it the gun
And said, "Be quiet," as he searched
The frequencies, flipping for the right station
(The radio squealing more loudly than I could cry).

And then even the echoes stopped—
The only sound the Edsel's grinding
And the bark and crackle of radio news
Saying stay home or go to church.

"Dees time she no blow!"
My father said, driving back
Over the red ash covering the road.
"I worried she went go for broke already!"

So in this print the size of a matchbook,
The dark skinny man, shirtless and grinning,
A toothpick in the corner of his smile,
Lifts a naked baby above his head—
Behind him the plate glass of the store only cracked.

T. R. Hummer

T. R. Hummer was born in Macon, Mississippi, in 1950. He received his B.A. and M.A. from the University of Southern Mississippi and his Ph.D. from the University of Utah. He is the author of three collections of poetry, *Translation of Light* (Cedar Creek Press, 1976), *The Angelic Orders* (L.S.U. Press, 1982), and *The Passion of the Right-Angled Man* (University of Illinois Press, 1984). He is also the co-editor, with Bruce Weigl, of *The Imagination as Glory: Essays on the Poetry of James Dickey* (University of Illinois Press, 1984). He was a Bread Loaf Fellow in 1983 and currently teaches at Kenyon College.

Marion Hummer

Where You Go When She Sleeps

What is it when a woman sleeps, her head bright
In your lap, in your hands, her breath easy now as though it had never
   been
Anything else, and you know she is dreaming, her eyelids
Jerk, but she is not troubled, it is a dream
That does not include you, but you are not troubled either,
It is too good to hold her while she sleeps, her hair falling
Richly on your hands, shining like metal, a color
That when you think of it you cannot name, as though it has just
Come into existence, dragging you into the world in the wake
Of its creation, out of whatever vacuum you were in before,

And you are like the boy you heard of once who fell
Into a silo full of oats, the silo emptying from below, oats
At the top swirling in a gold whirlpool, a bright eddy of grain, the boy,
You imagine, leaning over the edge to see it, the noon sun breaking
Into the center of the circle he watches, hot on his back, burning
And he forgets his father's warning, stands on the edge, looks down,
The grain spinning, dizzy, and when he falls his arms go out, too thin
For wings, and he hears his father's cry somewhere, but is gone
Already, down in a gold sea, spun deep in the heart of the silo,
And when they find him, his mouth, his throat, his lungs
Full of the gold that took him, he lies still, not seeing the world
Through his body but through the deep rush of the grain
Where he has gone and can never come back, though they drag him
Out, his father's tears bright on both their faces, the farmhands
Standing by blank and amazed—you touch that unnamable
Color in her hair and you are gone into what is not fear or joy
But a whirling of sunlight and water and air full of shining dust
That takes you, a dream that is not of you but will let you
Into itself if you love enough, and will not, will never let you go.

What Shines in Winter Burns

December sun sits low over hedgerows, glitter
Of morning bright on cottonfield frost, on the dead
Stalks left brittle in rows to crumble
Under rain and cold-snap ice. The sun, silver
Over silver trees, is surely a star, scarcely

Too brilliant to look on through the window
Of the school bus bounding over washboard gravel
Roads, noisy as a tin can tied to the tail
Of a bird dog—bird dog weather,
This cold morning, when the smell

Of bob white hangs close to the ground, keen
To a dog's nose as alum—the scent of passion
A boy cannot know himself, but has to follow

Watching the quivering nose of the dog freeze
In a perfect point. Alone in the bus

With the driver, in the front seat, the first
Stop on the route, I am wanting so hard
To be walking those fields and hedgerows
With a dog, gunmetal cold in my hand,
That the thought of the gun speaking death

Into cold air is love, the covey breaking
Loud in the still morning, one bird black
Against that dim silver sun, the dark gun-barrel
Rising. In that dream I am a man
With power no boy ever learned

Anywhere a school bus might take him. I aim
My notebook out the windshield, sighting down
The spine of it, firing my desire
Over and over into the stiff dead stalks
The bus rattles through, not wondering whether love

Outlives the deaths we make for it:
I look for something, I pull the trigger, the gun
In my hand explodes, and I am a man about to say
Look, I am alive, I have touched the world
The way a man touches the body of the one

Woman he can never live without again.
But I do not say it, for suddenly I see
What I am aiming at: over the back of the notebook,
I am squinting at the body
Of a man half lost in dead silver cottonstalks,

Half in the road, a black man, frozen, silver,
Glinting with sunlight and frost. I shout,
But the driver knows, the bus squeals, stopping,
Quivering, hood pointing, tires
Not a foot from that shining head,

The driver saying *Stay here, stay here, don't look,*
As he goes out the door, but too late, I have seen already
The man's right hand frozen to the whiskey bottle,
The left hand clutching together the patched denim coat,
And his eyes, his dead eyes frozen open

Staring up at me, answering *Boy, you will never*
Understand love until you lay your hand
Where mine is. Touch me. This is the body. I know.

The Beating

Everybody knew Clifton Cockerell was not half bright,
But nobody knew his passion
Till we found him on the playground back of the junior high
Carving names on a tree. His poor secret
Stood no more chance of staying one

Once we had it, than Clifton did of knowing
Why we cared—but we couldn't let it rest
Till everybody heard it, especially the girl, who was pretty
And thought he was some brand of animal. We'd sing
Their names together every chance we got, impressed

With her way of changing color, like some
Exotic lizard trying to disappear,
And forgot about Clifton pretty much till he came on us
Sudden one afternoon, wrathful and dumb
And swinging a length of cable. It wasn't fear

That defeated us. It was surprise
That it mattered so much what we'd done.
How could we know? He'd been one of us all our lives,
So close it was hard to see how he'd beat us
This once: he was already man enough to think he loved a woman.

So he came down on us sudden, boys,
All of us, and he gave us a taste of the hurt

We'd live to know another way: how love
Can be wrong and still be the only joy
That's real—how, when we come to it,

We stand amazed but take the blow, transfigured, idiot.

Cruelty

It was a dare that made us break
Into the locked storeroom where the sweet
Dust we raised coming shone
In the door's shaft of light.
My brother took me deep
In the dark of heaped junk
My grandfather left there knowing
It was good and someone would want it,
Someone would need to touch it,
Find something there he could name:
Gloves. Beeveil. Smoker.

My brother brought them out
Of those shadows, put them on me,
And I stood there strange to myself
Holding the lamp of the smoker
As he filled it with pinestraw, struck it
With fire, fitted the lid.
Then the smell of pinesmoke rose
Out of my hands, and he led me
Into the grove, the ruined
Beeyard. My brother
Held my arm and we heard

The hum in the air, saw the quick
Gold bodies flash

Through swaths of shadow and sun.
You know what you said you'd do
He told me. *I dare you.*
That morning I was not half
As tall as a man, had never torn
Anything open, never touched
What sweetness a man might find,
But when my brother pushed me
I could only stumble

To the nearest hive, lay my hand
On the lid, feel
Its pure presence, white
As the body of the woman I would not
Come to for years: I stood there afraid
Of what I could not stop
From doing, afraid my heart
Would choke on its own
Thick blood: and I knelt
To touch the slit
Where the bees came, bodies

Dusted with pollen, glowing.
Smoke, my brother yelled, *smoke!*
I raised all the heat I could hold
All the fire he had given me, knowing
The power of that one
Word, *dare:* not the bitter
Incense of passion, not the gold
Stunned clustering of bodies
In the dark my grandfather put there:
Needing to know, but not knowing
The pain, what flesh would come to

When I ripped off the lid.

Love Poem: The Dispossessed

In March, the small river,
Gray in the heart
Of your small gray city,
Thaws. I am cold
In this northern wind.
The part of the world
I come from would not know
What to call this gray

Stone wall I walk on.
There, they would name it
Levee. Snow
Banks in the deep
Shadow below me. Sun
Will get to it
Weeks from now, I guess,
But there are many things here

I would not try to predict:
When these strict silver
Trees will put their names
On with their leaves:
Gray, they are all
One tree to me,
Winter, the cold
Scum-white roil

Of river-water,
The high sweet call
Of a bird I cannot see,
Have never thought of.
I have walked
A long way in your cold
City where I should not be,
Thinking *cold*, thinking *love*,

Following the margin,
Skirting broken stones

In the wall that holds back
This river no one knows
I am walking beside alone,
Your river I cannot write down
The name of, can never
Say I was here beside

In this life, this time
Of year. I move
Slowly with the wind
From left to right, a small
Figure in an old
Photograph on the back
Of a postcard, black and white,
Mailed years ago:

Years lost
In the small post office
Of an obscure Southern town,
A gray thing come to light
Unsigned in your mailbox:
A dim winter
Scene of how this city
Looked a life ago.

The river has broken out
Of its winter ice a block
From the nameless motel
I have let myself in for,
A place it is hard to live
The good love that will not let me
Write down the things we know, the words
We call each other by:

Above me, high in the silver
Light, you can just make out
The dark shape of an unknown
Bird that hangs on the wind.
God knows who sent it.

God knows why
Anyone would bother
To forward such a thing.

Any Time, What May Hit You

The foreman whacks him hard
In the back of the head and calls him
Dumbass because he is lost
In the dream of the woman he touched
Last night and lets the milk-can slip.
It goes over in a sudden
Explosion of white,
The Holsteins jerk in their stalls,
And the foreman swings
Before the clatter has time to stop.

He lies there a long time after
The foreman stomps out cursing,
Lies flat on his belly
In a puddle of milk, watching one
White rivulet vanish
In the concrete dung-trough.
The cattle stop their bucking
And the barn goes still:
The milk, udder-warm, soaks through
His shirt and he shakes
His head to stop the spinning, feeling
The hand on him sudden
Out of the dark, the wordless
Breath, the lurch
The world took at her touch:
The letting go, the spilling.

Denis Johnson

Denis Johnson was born in Munich, Germany, in 1949. He received his B.A. and M.F.A. from the University of Iowa. He is the author of a book of poems, *The Incognito Lounge* (Random House, 1983), and a novel, *Angels* (Knopf, 1983), which won the Sue Kauffman Prize for First Fiction of the Academy and Institute of Arts and Letters. Among his other awards are fellowships from the National Endowment for the Arts and the Book-of-the-Month Club. He is a freelance writer and lives in Wellfleet, Massachusetts.

Lucinda Johnson

The Boarding

One of these days under the white
clouds onto the white
lines of the goddamn PED
X-ING I shall be flattened,
and I shall spill my bag of discount
medicines upon the avenue,
and an abruptly materializing bouquet
of bums, retirees, and Mexican
street-gangers will see all what
kinds of diseases are enjoying me
and what kind of underwear and my little
old lady's legs spidery with veins.
So Mr. Young and Lovely Negro Bus
Driver I care exactly this: zero,

that you see these things
now as I fling my shopping
up by your seat, putting
this left-hand foot way up
on the step so this dress rides up,
grabbing this metal pole like
a beam of silver falling down
from Heaven to my aid, thank-you,
hollering, "Watch det my medicine
one second for me will you dolling,
I'm four feet and det's a tall bus
you got and it's hot and I got
every disease they are making
these days, my God, Jesus Christ,
I'm telling you out of my soul."

A Woman

There's nobody here
but you, sitting under
the window at the corner
table as if waiting
for somebody to speak,
over your left shoulder the moon,
behind your head a vagina,
in pencil, emblazoned
above a telephone number.
For two hours you've been
looking across the street,
quite hard, at the grand store,
the Shopper's Holiday felled
across the sunset.
It grows dark in this climate
swiftly: the night

as sudden and vacuous
as the paper sack the attendant
balloons open with a shake
of his scarred wrist,
and in the orange parking
lot's blaze of sulphur
lamps, each fist
of tissue paper is distinct,
all cellophane edged
with a fiery light that seems
the white heat of permanence
and worth; of reality;
at this hour, and in this
climate where how swiftly
the dark grows, and the time comes.

Minutes

You and I—we agitate
to say things, to dress every gash
with a street address or a relative.
We are found in the places of transport at an hour
when only the criminals are expected to depart.

We are blind and we don't know that our mouths
are moving as we place a hand to stay
the janitor's mop—*I'll tell you the story
of my life, you'll make a million*—
blind and we don't know that our parents are dead

as we enter the photo-booths.
In there is the quiet like the kernel of a word:
in there everything we were going to say
is taken from us and we are given
four images of ourselves. What are we going

to do with these pictures? They hold
no fascination for the abandoned,
but only for us, who have
relinquished them to the undertow
that held us, too, but let us go,

so that the hospitals opened like great vaults
for us and we stepped from bed to bed
on the faces of the diseased, the beloved,
moving like light over a necklace
of excruciations—*I'll tell you*

the story of my life,
you'll make a million . . .
this is what it means to be human,
to witness the heart of a moment like a photograph,
the present standing up through itself relentlessly like a fountain,

the clock showering the intersection with minutes
even as it gathers them to its face
in the so often alluded
to Kingdom of Heaven—
to watch one of those minutes open

like a locket and brandish a picture
of everyone we ever loved who drowned,
while the unendurable generosity of everything
sells everything out. Would you like
to dance? Then here, dance with the terror

that now is forever,
my feet are stumps. The band is just
outbreaking now with one that goes
all the evidence / the naughty evidence / persuades
the lovers endearing by the ponds /

the truants growing older in the sleazy arcades /
there's no banishing / of anything /
only con- / quering within /
make it enough / make it enough / or eat
suffering without end

337   /   DENIS JOHNSON

Passengers

The world will burst like an intestine in the sun,
the dark turn to granite and the granite to a name,
but there will always be somebody riding the bus
through these intersections strewn with broken glass
among speechless women beating their little ones,
always a slow alphabet of rain
speaking of drifting and perishing to the air,
always these definite jails of light in the sky
at the wedding of this clarity and this storm
and a woman's turning—her languid flight of hair
traveling through frame after frame of memory
where the past turns, its face sparking like emery,
to open its grace and incredible harm
over my life, and I will never die.

Don Johnson

George Murphy

Don Johnson was born in 1942. He received his undergraduate degree and his M.A. from the University of Hawaii and his Ph.D. from the University of Wisconsin. His first book of poems, *The Importance of Visible Scars* (1984), was published by the Wampeter Press. He teaches at East Tennessee State University.

The Sergeant

When others mustered out in '46, you soldiered
on, commanding a squad that buried box
after narrow box the Army sent home from abroad.

For a year the wind off the Kasserine,
peasants mudded to their knees on Mindanao
and oceans being oceans all over the world
kept turning up dead West Virginians.

You brought all the known soldiers home,
to Coal Fork, Seth, Clendinin,

to the smudged daguerreotypes of company shacks
that lay beyond slick rivers without bridges.

Your honor guard traveled the state that year
making heroes.
                     You and your men were heroes—
the War ceremonially perfect—
in hills the newsreels never reached.

Sometimes twice a day you stiffened
against the world's first standing order:
assigning remains to the last slit trenches
they would hold, awarding the widows flags
they would bundle away under cedar
or hang on the wall of the child
conceived a month before Pearl Harbor.

                     *   *   *

You were occupied with death
                     and mother ironed
ten uniforms a week to keep you creased
and properly rigid. Starch drifted
like dry snow in parlor corners where I etched
stick figures in the dust—
                     my own command.
And I learned to fold the flags
into tight blue parcels of stars, to execute
the manual of arms with the snap
of a garrison corporal.
                     But you never said
"Death" or took me along to the hills.

Coming in to the warm laundry smells of your room,
I'd find you silently polishing brass or trying to coax
from your boots the last bright sheen the leather
remembered. And I knew I would rise the next morning
in darkness, roused by the small-bore crack

of your clothes—your limbs forcing open shined khaki—
to watch you go quietly off to your men.

*   *   *

One summer night you had the neighbors in the yard
for home-made peach ice cream and army films
projected on the flaking wall of the hen-house.

G.I.'s bridged the Rhine at Remagen; Jap bodies
spilled like sun-struck worms from a pill box,
their faces scaled like snakes in the old wall's
peeling paint.
        And I wondered who buried them
but lay in the sweet summer grass unafraid
until the black-and-white war was done. Barrages
stopped. Helmeted winners of medals marched home.

Still the film reeled on, to Buchenwald, Dachau,
where bulldozers shoved gray bones into pits
without ritual, where the living were mute
fluoroscopic ghosts you called D.P.'s, real stick people
crushed into huts like our mildewed sheds.

Out of your sight, in the dark, I cried
for them all, and for the man with a child
thinner than any mountain stray. His face,
framed in a single paint chip, leaned into the yard
and, with eyes like the half-blind bank mules'
at the mines, he seemed to stare at the light
from my bedroom window.

                After the films
had run out, while your friends were gathering plates
or whispering good-night, I sat by your polished
brown shoes, wanting to say,
                "The man . . . ,"

that he held that child in his coat-hanger arms
then shoved him through the warp in the lapped boards

covering our coop. That the boy was in there
huddled in the dung and feathers, waiting.

But you never knew how he clung
to those humid walls with the hens
or how the flung door's slicing trapezoid of light
cornered him in shadow.

                    You were occupied with death,
while every day I trooped the darkened rows of nests,
gathering the still-warm eggs with held breath.

Above the Falls at Waimea

In these ohias light depends
upon the soft wind off the mountain
where this stream begins in steady rain.
With the breeze, torch ginger flares
like embers in the bending ferns
and you whisper, shadow-bound,
"I don't know how to be here."

And while we occupy this stone
the river pools around us
and descends. To ease you here
I dream you home:

                    shake the cold
from your hair; hold me there
in the quiet light from one small lamp;
touch the eyelids of my sleeping child.

Showers drift down the valley.
As you stare at the backs of my hands

over yours I search the veined stones
for words. Then you turn,
your eyes like the light side of leaves,
to lie with me here at mid-stream,
tight in the lap of the rain.

Tick Picking in the Quetico

In that dark world the only light
for sixteen miles played slowly over
each of us standing stripped, shivering
in the middle of the tent. Four times
six eyes examined armpits, crotches,
cracks, for ticks, swelling in those spots
that even lovers never see. Clinging
there by our life's blood, they'd
disregard the light,
but with the match's application
squirm, kick,
let go.

I recall long strips of largemouths
caught on poppers just past dawn,
the full-grown bream still whole
inside the northern's gut; there are snapshots.
But in my mind the nights remain
most vivid: inspections done,
I lay there, hearing the loons on Lake Aroo,
waiting for the beaver slaps to start,
waiting for night to crawl
into folds and crevices,
haired cracks,
to stay.

Night Dive

For Harry Bjornson

No moon. Night water shapes all light
to a cone that tows me like a lure
over coral. Breath makes the only sound.

Movements sharpen to fish in my beam,
fade, then hover somewhere on the edge
of brightness,
                  real again when I shift
the track of my sweep. But that leaves
other fish shadows, the volume of darkness
unchanged,

          till I dive
                  and the circle
of light tightens, grows elliptical on slopes
or disappears in holes where hump-backed cowries
mantle themselves in gold and the spines
of the sea urchins heel in the surge
like beach grass in a summer storm.

Alone, deep in the dark
I can scrutinize small things,
scribe broad, momentary arcs
across blackness

or switch off the light

and hang like a drowned child in the waves
where heat would seep from my veins,
my dilating eyes create whales,
dolphins to dandle my body in swells.

Before dawn
I would take up the breathing of ocean.

Rodney Jones

Gloria Jones

Rodney Jones was born in 1950 in Hartselle, Alabama, and educated at the University of Alabama and the University of North Carolina at Greensboro. His first book, *The Story They Told Us of Light*, was selected by Elizabeth Bishop for the Associated Writing Programs Award Series and subsequently published by the University of Alabama Press in 1980. His second book, *The Unborn*, will be published in April 1985 by The Atlantic Monthly Press. His poems have appeared in many magazines, including *The Atlantic, Poetry, Poetry Northwest, New England Review,* and *Virginia Quarterly Review*. He has been awarded the Academy of American Poets Prize, the Theodore Roethke Prize from *Poetry Northwest*, and a Pushcart prize, and he has received creative writing grants from the Tennessee Arts Commission and the National Endowment for the Arts. He teaches at Southern Illinois University at Carbondale.

Remembering Fire

Almost as though the eggs run and leap back into their shells
And the shells seal behind them, and the willows call back their
    driftwood,
And the oceans move predictably into deltas, into the hidden
    oubliettes in the sides of mountains,

And all the emptied bottles are filled, and, flake by flake, the snow
    rises out of the coal piles,
And the mothers cry out terribly as the children enter their bodies,
And the freeway to Birmingham is peeled off the scar-tissue of fields,

The way it occurs to me, the last thing first, never as in life,
The unexpected rush, but this time I stand on the cold hill and
    watch
Fire ripen from the seedbed of ashes, from the maze of tortured glass,

Molten nails and hinges, the flames lift each plank into place
And the walls resume their high standing, the many walls, and the
    rafters
Float upward, the ceiling and roof, smoke ribbons into the wet
    cushions,

And my father hurries back through the front door with the box
Of important papers, carrying as much as he can save,
All of his deeds and policies, the clock, the few pieces of silver,

He places me in the shape of my own body in the feather mattress,
And I go down into the soft wings, the mute and impalpable country
Of sleep, holding all of this back, drifting toward the unborn.

Thoreau

It is when I work on the old Volvo,
lying on my back among the sockets,
wrenches, nuts, and bolts,
with the asphalt grinding the skin
over my shoulderblades, and with the cold grease
dripping onto my eyeglasses,
that I think of Thoreau
on his morning walks around the pond

dreaming of self-sufficiency.
I think of the odometer that shows
eight circuits of the planet.
I drop the transmission and loosen
the bolts around the bellhousing.
I take it in both hands, jerk,
and it pops like a sliced melon.
Carefully, so I won't damage
the diaphragm, I remove the clutch
and place it on a clean cloth
beside the jackstand. I look
at the illustrations in the manual,
and I think of the lists that Thoreau made.
By the time I get to the flywheel,
grease is clotted in my hair,
my knuckles are raw and bleeding
against the crankcase, and I am thinking
of civil disobedience. I am looking
up into the dark heaven of machinery,
the constellations of flaking gaskets,
and I am thinking of Thoreau's dry cow,
of his cornstalks splintered by hail.

The Mosquito

I see the mosquito kneeling on the soft underside of my arm,
        kneeling
Like a fruitpicker, kneeling like an old woman
With the proboscis of her prayer buried in the idea of God,
And I know we shall not speak with the aliens
And that peace will not happen in my life,
        not unless
It is in the burnt oil spreading across the surfaces of ponds,
        in the dark

Egg-rafts clotting and the wiggletails expiring like batteries..
Bring a little alcohol and a little balm
For these poppies planted by the Queen of Neptune.
In her photographs, she is bearded and spurred, embellished
        five hundred times,
Her modular legs crouching, her insufferable head unlocking
To lower the razor-edge of its tubes, and she is there
        in the afternoon
When the wind gives up the spirit of cleanliness
And there rises from the sound the brackish oyster and squid smell
        of creation.
I lie down in the sleeping bag sodden with rain.
Nights with her, I am loved for myself, for the succulent
Flange of my upper lip, the twin bellies of my eyelids.
She adores the easy, the soft. She picks the tenderest blossoms
        of insomnia.
Mornings while the jackhammer rips the pavement outside my window,
While the sanitation workers bang the cans against the big truck
        and shout to each other over the motor,
I watch her strut like an udder with my blood,
Imagining the luminous pick descending into Trotsky's skull
        and the eleven days
I waited for the cold chill, nightmare, and nightsweat of malaria;
Imagining the mating call in the vibrations of her wings,
And imagining, in the simple knot of her ganglia,
How she thrills to my life, how she sings for the harvest.

The First Birth

I had not been there before where the vagina opens,
the petals of liver, each vein a delicate bush,
and where something clutches its way into the light
like a mummy tearing and fumbling from his shroud.
The heifer was too small, too young in the hips,

short-bodied with outrigger distending her sides,
and back in the house, in the blue *Giants of Science*
still open on my bed, Ptolemy was hurtling toward Einstein.
Marconi was inventing the wireless without me.
Da Vinci was secretly etching the forbidden anatomy
of the dark ages. I was trying to remember
Galen, his pen drawing, his inscrutable genius,
not the milk in the refrigerator, sour with bitterweed.
It came, cream-capped and hay-flecked, in silver pails.
At nights we licked onions to sweeten the taste.
All my life I had been around cows named after friends
and fated for slaughterhouses. I wanted to bring
Mendel and Rutherford into that pasture,
and bulb-headed Hippocrates, who would know what to do.
The green branch nearby reeked of crawfish.
The heavy horseflies orbited. A compass, telescope,
and protractor darted behind my eyes. When the sac
broke, the water soaked one thigh. The heifer lowed.
Enrico Fermi, how much time it takes, the spotted legs,
the wet black head and white blaze. The shoulders
lodged. The heifer walked with the calf wedged
in her pelvis, the head swaying behind her like a cut blossom.
Did I ever go back to science, or eat a hamburger
without that paralysis, that hour of the stuck calf
and the unconscionable bawling that must have been a prayer?
Now that I know a little, it helps, except for birth
or dying, those slow pains, like the rigorous observation
of Darwin. Anyway, I had to take the thing, any way
I could, as my hands kept slipping, wherever it was,
under the chin, by tendony, china-delicate knees,
my foot against the hindquarters of the muley heifer,
to bring into this world, black
and enourmous, wobbling to his feet, the dumb bull, Copernicus.

For the Eating of Swine

I have learned sloppiness from an old sow
wallowing her ennui in the stinking lot,
a slow vessel filled with a thousand candles,
her whiskers matted with creek mud,
her body helpless to sweat the dull spirit.
I have wrestled the hindquarters of a young boar
while my father clipped each testicle
with a sharpened Barlow knife, returning him,
good fish, to his wastery, changed life.
And I have learned pleasure from a gilt
as she lay on her back, offering her soft belly
like a dog, the loose bowel of her throat
opening to warble the consonants of her joy.
I have learned lassitude, pride, stubbornness,
and greed from my many neighbors, the pigs.
I have gone with low head and slanted blue eyes
through the filthy streets, wary of the blade,
my whole life, a toilet or a kitchen,
the rotting rinds, the wreaths of flies.
For the chicken, the cow, forgetfulness. Mindlessness
blesses their meat. Only the pigs are holy,
the rings in their snouts, their fierce, motherly indignation,
and their need always to fill themselves.
I remember a photograph. A sheriff had demolished
a still, spilling a hundred gallons of moonshine.
Nine pigs passed out in the shade of a mulberry tree.
We know pigs will accommodate demons,
run into rivers, drowning of madness.
They will devour drunks who fall in their ways.
Like Christ, they will befriend their destroyers.
In the middle of winter I have cupped my hands
and held the large and pliable brain of a pig.
As the fires were heating the black kettles,
I have scrupulously placed my rifle between pigs' eyes
and with one clean shot, loosened the slabs
of side-meat, the sausages that begin
with the last spasms of the trotters.

O dolphins of the barnyard, frolickers
in the gray and eternal muck, in all your parts
useful, because I have known you, this is the sage,
and salt, the sacrificial markers of pepper.
What pity should I feel, or gratitude, raising you
on my fork as all the dead shall be risen?

Erica Jong

Thomas Victor

Erica Jong was born in 1942. She received a B.A. from Barnard College and an M.A. from Columbia University in eighteenth-century English literature. Her awards include a fellowship from the National Endowment for the Arts and the Alice Faye di Castagnola Award. Her novels are *Fear of Flying* (1973), *How to Save Your Own Life* (1977), both from Holt, Rinehart, and Winston, *Fanny: Being the True History of the Adventures of Fanny Hackabout-Jones* (New American Library, 1980), and *Parachutes & Kisses* (New American Library, 1984). She has also written a children's book, *Megan's Book of Divorce* (New American Library, 1984). Her books of poetry are *Fruits & Vegetables* (1971), *Half-lives* (1973), *Loveroot* (1975), and *At the Edge of the Body* (1979), all from Holt, Rinehart, and Winston, and *Ordinary Miracles* (New American Library, 1983). *Witches* (1980), a book of poetry and non-fiction, was published by Abrams (and New American Library-Plume). Her novels and poems have been translated into more than fifteen languages.

Becoming a Nun

For Jennifer Josephy

On cold days
it is easy to be reasonable,
to button the mouth against kisses,
dust the breasts
with talcum powder
& forget
the red pulp meat
of the heart.

On those days
it beats
like a digital clock—
not a beat at all
but a steady whirring
chilly as green neon,
luminous as numerals in the dark,
cool as electricity.

& I think:
I can live without it all—
love with its blood pump,
sex with its messy hungers,
men with their peacock strutting,
their silly sexual baggage,
their wet tongues in my ear
& their words like little sugar suckers
with sour centers.

On such days
I am zipped in my body suit,
I am wearing seven league red suede boots,
I am marching over the cobblestones
as if they were the heads of men,

& I am happy
as a seven-year-old virgin
holding Daddy's hand.

Don't touch.
Don't try to tempt me with your ripe persimmons.
Don't threaten me with your volcano.
The sky is clearer when I'm not in heat,
& the poems
are colder.

In Praise of Clothes

If it is only for the taking off—
    the velvet cloak,
    the ostrich feather boa,
    the dress which slithers to the floor
    with the sound of strange men sighing
    on imagined street corners . . .

If it is only for the taking off—
    the red lace bra
    (with rosewindows of breasts),
    the red lace pants
    (with dark suggestion
    of Venus' first name),
    the black net stockings
    cobwebby as fate,
    the black net stockings
    crisscrossed like our lives,
    the silver sandals
    glimmering as rain—

clothes are necessary.

Oh bulky barrier between soul & soul,
soul & self—
how it comforts us
to take you down!
How it heartens us to strip you off!

    & this is no matter of fashion.

Jubilate Canis

(With apologies to Christopher Smart)

For I will consider my dog Poochkin
(& his long-lost brothers, Chekarf & Dogstoyevsky).
For he is the reincarnation of a great canine poet.
For he barks in meter, & when I leave him alone
his yelps at the door are epic.
For he is white, furry, & resembles a bathmat.
For he sleeps at my feet as I write
& therefore is my greatest critic.
For he follows me into the bathroom
& faithfully pees on paper.
For he is *almost* housebroken.
For he eats the dogfood I give him
but also loves Jarlsburg and Swiss cheese.
For he disdains nothing that reeks—
whether feet or roses.
For to him, all smells are created equal by God—
both turds and perfumes.
For he loves toilet bowls no less than soup bowls.
For by watching him, I have understood democracy.
For by stroking him, I have understood joy.
For he turns his belly toward God
& raises his paws & penis in supplication.
For he hangs his pink tongue out of his mouth
like a festival banner for God.
For though he is male, he has pink nipples on his belly
like the female.
For though he is canine, he is more humane
than most humans.
For when he dreams he mutters in his sleep
like any poet.
For when he wakes he yawns & stretches
& stands on his hind legs to greet me.
For, after he shits, he romps and frolics
with supreme abandon.
For, after he eats, he is more contented

than any human.
For in every room he will find the coolest corner,
& having found it, he has the sense to stay there.
For when I show him my poems,
he eats them.
For an old shoe makes him happier than a Rolls-Royce
makes a rock star.
For he has convinced me of the infinite wisdom
of dog-consciousness.
For, thanks to Poochkin, I praise the Lord
& no longer fear death.
For when my spirit flees my body through my nostrils,
may it sail into the pregnant belly
of a furry bitch,
& may I praise God always
as a dog.

The Buddha in the Womb

Bobbing in the waters of the womb,
little godhead, ten toes, ten fingers
& infinite hope,
sails upside down through the world.

My bones, I know, are only a cage
for death.
Meditating, I can see my skull,
a death's head,
lit from within
by candles
which are possibly the suns
of other galaxies.

I know that death
is a movement toward light,
a happy dream
from which you are loath to awaken,
a lover left
in a country
to which you have no visa,
& I know that the horses of the spirit
are galloping, galloping, galloping
out of time
& into the moment called NOW.

Why then do I care
for this upside-down Buddha
bobbling through the world,
his toes, his fingers
alive with blood
that will only sing & die?

There is a light in my skull
& a light in his.
We meditate on our bones only
to let them blow away
with fewer regrets.

Flesh is merely a lesson.
We learn it
& pass on.

Yusef Komunyakaa

Yusef Komunyakaa was born in Bogalusa, Louisiana, in 1947. He received an M.F.A. from the University of California and is the author of *Copacetic* (Wesleyan University Press, 1984). Among his awards is a fellowship from the National Endowment for the Arts.

Somewhere Near Phu Bai

The moon cuts through
night trees like a circular saw
white hot. In the guardshack
I lean on the sandbags,
taking aim at whatever.
Hundreds of bluesteel stars
cut a path, fanning out
silver for a second. If anyone's
there, don't blame me.

I count the shapes ten meters
out front, over & over, making sure
they're always there.
I don't dare blink an eye.
The white-painted backs
of the Claymore mines

like quarter moons.
They say Victor Charlie will
paint the other sides & turn
the blast toward you.

If I hear a noise
will I push the button
& blow myself away?
The moon grazes treetops.
I count the Claymores again.
Thinking about buckshot
kneaded in the plastic C-4
of the brain, counting
sheep before I know it.

Starlight Scope Myopia

Gray-blue shadows lift
shadows onto an ox cart.

Making night work for us,
the starlight scope brings
men into killing range.

The river under Vi Bridge
takes the heart away

like the Water God
riding his dragon.
Smoke-colored

Viet Cong
move under our eyelids,

lords over loneliness
winding like coralvine through
sandalwood & lotus,

inside our skulls years
after this scene ends.

The brain closes down.
What looks like
one step into the trees,

they're lifting crates of ammo
and sacks of rice, swaying

under their shared weight.
Caught in the infrared,
what are they saying?

Are they talking about women
or calling the Americans

beaucoup dien cai dau?
One of them is laughing.
You want to place a finger

to his lips & say "shhhh."
You try reading ghost-talk

on their lips. They say
"up-up we go," lifting as one.
This one, old, bowlegged,

you feel you could reach out
& take him into your arms. You

peer down the sights of your M-16,
seeing the full moon
loaded on an ox cart.

April Fools' Day

They had me laid out in a white
satin casket. What the hell
went wrong, I wanted to ask.
Whose midnight-blue sedan
mowed me down, what unnameable fever
bloomed amber & colchicum
in my brain, which doctor's scalpel
slipped? Did it happen
on a rainy Saturday, blue
Monday, Vallejo's Thursday?
I think I was on a balcony
overlooking the whole thing.
My soul sat in a black chair
near the door, sullen
& no-mouthed. I was fifteen
in a star-riddled box,
in heaven up to my eyelids.
My skin shone like damp light,
my face was the gray of something
gone. They were all there.
My mother behind an opaque veil,
so young. My brothers huddled like stones,
my sister rocked her Shirley Temple
doll to sleep. Three fat ushers fanned
my grandmamas, used smelling salts.
All my best friends—Cowlick,
Sneaky Pete, Happy Jack, Pie Joe,
& Comedown Jones.
I could smell lavender,
a tinge of dust. Their mouths,
palms of their hands
stained with mulberries.
Daddy posed in his navy-blue suit
as doubting Thomas: some twisted
soft need in his eyes, wondering if
I was just another loss
he'd divided his days into.

Copacetic Mingus

"'Mingus One, Two and Three.
Which is the image you want the world to see?'"
　　　　—Charles Mingus, Beneath the Underdog

Heartstring. Blessed wood
& every moment the thing's made of:
ball of fatback
licked by fingers of fire.
Hard love, it's hard love.
Running big hands down
the upright's wide hips,
rocking his moon-eyed mistress
with gold in her teeth.
Art & life bleed
into each other
as he works the bow.
But tonight we're both a long ways
from the Mile High City,
1973. Here in New Orleans
years below sea level,
I listen to *Pithecanthropus
Erectus:* Up & down, under
& over, every which way—
thump, thump, dada—ah, yes.
Wood heavy with tenderness,
Mingus fingers the loom
gone on Segovia,
dogging the raw strings
unwaxed with rosin.
Hyperbolic bass line. Oh, no!
Hard love, it's hard love.

Sydney Lea

Hathorne-Olsen Studios

Sydney Lea was born in Pennsylvania in 1942. He received his B.A. and Ph.D. from Yale University. He is the founder and editor of *New England Review* and the author of two poetry collections, *Searching the Drowned Man* (1980) and *The Floating Candles* (1982), both published by the University of Illinois Press. He is also the author of a book of criticism, *Gothic to Fantastic* (1981). He teaches at Middlebury College.

The Train Out

Fluff from his lap robe hangs in a rift
in the curtains, as his eyes un-gum.
Nebraska yawns. Mergansers shift
in their mudholes. Morning: aluminum
track sheds begin to flare.

Blood ticks in his temples. Where
did he toss his coat, his keys?
As well in Topeka. Inanities
from a dream of her linger—a china jug,
hot liquor, a room

he cannot place. A tinsel bug
revives against the kindling panes.
Stiff old porters in the corridor
swear to a time when "a train was a train,"
mutter against the diesel's roar.

A green dead dawn. . . .
All borders are ends. . . .
He conjures a cove; a bed; a song;
rings and a necklace; a barbered lawn.

A catalogue past. Old words, thick as wax.
Exhaust expires in a feint of wind,
and the sun glows dull on the tracks.

Night Trip Across the Chesapeake and After

Mind a clutter: sick with love for another
woman, and set on murder (wildfowl would dive
next day to our brush-built blind). The diesel smeared
air with its fumes. Its wake roiled clumps of phosphor.
The hunters' "paradise" was a spit of land to the north
of Tangier Island. Dragged up from a barge, tin trailers
shuddered to windward amid knife-thin headstones
with jackets of slime. The marsh to the south was rank
with ages of feather-strewn nests and tangled lines
for crab, fish, otter. It weltered in weather,
sighing resignation.   The cooking station
reeked coal oil and antimacassars drenched
in sweat and the cheap pomade of insular men
and women. One saw one's life. A clotted flock
of newsy letters, cozy ancestral bones
that leaned from too many mantelpieces, squalid

crowd to be joined, babies' playthings, spattered
food, old grease in a covey of rusted spiders.

Come dawn, they swarmed: inedible shags and scoters.
They croaked black warning against desire.
Barnacles crept observably over the wharf-posts,
thickened with ruin. The rain was steady, soaking.
Thoughts were kin to the wrack of lowest tide.
The mudflats smelled, o God, like hell.　　The front
came suddenly on, from an antithetical quarter:
a cobalt-colored sky advanced against
the obvious wind. The boats of oyster dredgers
weighed their anchors, scudding free as stallions.
"Don't know what's in that rim," said Don our guide,
a different hue in his eyes. Rafts of coots
and trash-ducks rose, headed for weedy bayou,
moss-choked brake.　　Only the trumpeting hosts
of swans flew pure and wonderful into the weather.
Don, the guide, spat his cud of Red Man away,
declaring, "I'd just as soon shoot down an angel."
A cold breath swept the bay.

Bernie's Quick-Shave (1968)

For Roland Mochary

At dawn three shearsmen
dress in white, exact
non-shade of the blank
prospect that they'll encounter
but—out of their courage—
they refuse to acknowledge.
Or is it their impotence?
Out on the Green,

which in this February
is more in fact
a White, long-haired
students from the college.
return to their monuments of ice:
the carnival theme
this winter is *Life*
in the Future. Machines
in this fantastic tableau
are conceived to replace
all dulling labor.
The students in arrogance
consider *themselves* the Future.
Sad, the way
that Frank, Ed, Mike
—pale monoliths,
three plinths
behind the pane—all day
will regard these children in beards
and tattered pants
as the Future, too:
a season gone away
before its own arrival.
The chair keeps yawning like
a dead man's abandoned
recliner. The lather won't rise
to match the drifts
and windrows by their trailers.
It remains the latent billow
within their minds,
as fog and whitecap waves
become mere thought in sailors
grounded—vague things
to fill the void they prophesy
as yet another night
falls on the village
shops, forlorn and white
as those few unconsoling early stars.

At length, berobed,
they struggle to their cars,
whose windshields seem at first
to cloud with steam.
Their radios often bear them
news of former
clients now, last regulars
turned in this decade hairless
or thinly crowned with slow-
grown locks that shiver
in the frigid estate to which
their whiteness is witness. . . .
The radios announce
old shavers gone,
like figures one has met
within a dream
or landscapes that will never
be replenished.
Snow drifts down like talcum.
But tomorrow dawn
they'll stand again,
tragic as winter gravestones,
those for whom some central thing has vanished.

Coon Hunt, Sixth Month (1955)

By late in spring the cottonmouths and rattlers
began to move. You didn't dare use dogs.
Sam Spurley eased the flatbed truck along
the red-dirt lanes, and Purdy sang out loud:
"Hey FROG! Hey CRIP! Hey Billy-BEAN!"
And true to every witless white cliché
the black men loped from their cabins, every stop,
visible only by teeth and eyes. And I

and my two brothers would blush, embarrassed, shamed,
when Purdy, playing his light among the cypress,
hooted "Thar one!" And we three couldn't
see him for our lives, and all the blacks
would shake with laughter: "What? You white boys *blind?*"
And we would have to hand our shotgun over
to one of them, who would tumble the coon to ground.

There came a night when we heard the bawl of hounds
in spite of snakes, just as we saw the cruiser
—GEORGIA STATE POLICE in black along
the front-door panels—and a light switched on.
A fat cop pulled a gun and bellowed, "What
the fuck you niggers doin' here?" Then saw
us three, as pale as possum kits. And one
of us spoke up, "We're just out hunting coons."
And laughing, he: "Hot damn, son! So are we. . . ."
And told us all we'd best be headed now,
because the handlers, cussing through the swamp,
might hear our shots and think they had their man.
"Not if you wasn't plannin' to shoot him they won't,"
sang Purdy, bolder than hell, if only we knew it.
The cracker trained the light on his eyes, so blinding

bright that even Purdy couldn't see through it.

Old Dog, New Dog

With the stylish young brood bitch, the old dog showed
the way sex still explodes
like a double barrel into the blanking winter

of a life. His ears were blanks, his eyes—
those snowy bays of cataracts. His nose
remained, and the gleaming pinkish member.
They locked, the high-blood nervous white-and-liver
dam and he. He couldn't hear his howls
that shook the kennel roof and shocked her
there beneath him. Ground, rain-soaked
with spring, gave to my spade and in I rolled
his carcass, quick, still loose in body, loose
again as when he ranged this ground a puppy,
stiffened. Whirr. A shot. Dead bird. The first.
I winced as the clots fell in on him.
Pain. And nerves when the shovel clanked on rock.
The new-age farmer neighbor wouldn't
understand this rite. He bought the farm
and on the trunk of every tree he hung
his signs: NO HUNTING-FISHING-TRESPASSING.
Face wet with weather, sweat, and another thing,
I shouldered my tool, but swung it once across
the almost casual path in air of a woodcock
unalarmed in June.
              The pup I saved
is in the old dog's run. He squalls. I chose him
by his chest and length of leg, proportion
of white to orange markings (so I could see
him locked on point in brush or choking alder),
by the brightness in his eye. By superstition.
Released, he flushes hosts of starlings, grackles
from the meadow into hardhack whips and popple.
They spend their music rashly, shrill and apt.
Slow as dream, bright moths spin through the haze.
There is the sound of waters everywhere.
A grouse chick rises bee-like, barely airborne.
The dog for a moment stiffens. Then he bolts
as all the brood erupts. I let him go
for now, for birds will be his business. The hen
sits longer than the rest, then clatters out
the other way. And fooled, he chases, nose erect,
ears cocked, eyes wide, while I

—out of shape with summer, heart a hammer—
pursue downhill, half blind with my own laughter.

The Floating Candles

For my brother Mahlon (1944–1980)

You lit a firebrand:
old pine was best.
It lasted, the black
pitch fume cast odors
that, kindling a campfire
or such, today
can bring tears. You held
the torch to one dwarf
candle stub then another
and others till each
greased cup filled up
and the stiff wicks stood.
Ten minutes a candle,
but we were young
and minutes seemed long
as the whole vacation.
We chafed and quarreled.
The colors bled
like hues in jewels.
At last we carried
a tub of the things
down the path to the Swamp
Creek pond through seed-
heavy meadows where katydids
whined like wires
in mid-August air's
dense atmosphere.
An hour before bedtime.
Reluctant grownups
would trail behind,
bearing downhill
the same dull patter

and cups brimful
of rye, which they balanced
with the same rapt care
that balanced our load.
The bullfrogs twanged
till you touched a wick
with the stick, still flaming,
then quieted. We heard them
plop in the shallows,
deferring to fire,
and heard in the muck
turtles coasting in flight.
The night brought on
a small breeze to clear
the day that all day
had oppressed us, to dry
the sweat that our purposeful
hour had made,
to spread the glims
like dreamboats of glory
in invisible current.
That slow tug drew
the glowing flotilla
south to the dam.
The bank brush—hung
with gemmy bugs—shone
and made great shadows
as the candles slipped by,
erasing the banal
fat stars from the surface.
This was, you could say,
an early glimpse
of a later aesthetic.
Nonsense. We know
it was cruder than that
and profounder, far.
It showed us the way
the splendid can flare
despite the flow

of the common. Now,
despite the persistence
of heat and quarrel,
the thickness of wives
and children and time,
such shinings on water
are fact. Or sublime.

Brad Leithauser

Brad Leithauser was born in 1953, and educated at Harvard College and Harvard Law School. His first book, *Hundreds of Fireflies*, was published by Knopf in 1982. Among his awards are a MacArthur Award and fellowships from the Ingram Merrill Foundation and the Guggenheim Foundation. He teaches at Amherst College.

Mary Jo Salter

The Ghost of a Ghost

I.

The pleasures I took from life
were simple things—to play catch
in the evenings with my son,
or tease my daughter (whom I addressed
as Princess Pea), or to watch
television, curled on the floor.
Sometimes I liked to drink too much,
but not too often. Perhaps best

of all was the delight I found
waking to a drowse at one
or two at night and my wife
huffing (soft, not quite a snore)
beside me, a comforting sound.

We had our problems of course,
Emily and I, occasions when
things got out of hand.—Once she threw
a juice glass at me that broke
on the wall (that night I drew
a face there, a clownish man
catching it square on the nose,
and Emily laughed till she cried).
It's true I threatened divorce
a few times (she did too), but those
were ploys, harmless because love ran
through every word we spoke—
and then, an accident, I died.

II.

Afterwards, my kids began
having nightmares—when they slept
at all; Emily moved in a haze,
looking older, ruined now, and wept
often and without warning.
The rooms had changed, become mere
photographs in which my face
was oddly missing . . . That first year
without me: summer twilight, and those
long leaf-raking Saturdays
without me, and Christmas morning—
the following August a new man,
a stranger, moved in and took my place.

You could scarcely start to comprehend
how queer it is, to have your touch

go unfelt, your cries unheard
by your family. Princess!—I called—
Don't let that stranger take your hand!
And—*Em, dear, love, he has no right
to you.*
        Where did they think I'd gone?
who walked the house all day, all night,
all night. It was far too much
for anyone to endure, and,
hammered by grief one ugly dawn,
I broke. I am still here!—I bawled
from the den—Still here! And no one stirred.

But in time I learned a vicious trick,
a way of gently positing
a breath upon a person's neck
to send an icy run of fear
scampering up the spine—anything,
anything to show them who was near!
. . . Anything, but only to retrieve
some sense that nothing is more
lasting than the love built week by week
for years; I had to believe
again that these were people I'd
give everything, even a life, for.
Then—a second time, and slow—I died.

III.

Now I am a shadow of my
former shadow. Seepage of a kind
sets in. Settled concentrations thin.
Amenably—like the smile become
a pond, the pond a mud-lined
bed, from which stems push, pry
and hoist aloft seed-pods that
crack into a sort of grin—
things come almost but not quite

full circle; within the slow
tide of years, water dilutes to light,
light to a distant, eddying hum . . .
In another time, long ago,

I longed for a time when I'd
still felt near enough to recall
the downy scrape of a peach skin
on my tongue, the smell of the sea,
the pull of something resinous.
By turns, I have grown other-wise.
I move with a drift, a drowse that roams
not toward sleep but a clarity
of broadened linkages; it's in
a state wholly too gratified
and patient to be called eagerness
that I submit to a course which homes
outward, and misses nothing at all.

Between Leaps

Binoculars I'd meant for birds
catch instead, and place an arm's length away,
        a frog
compactly perched on a log that lies
    half in, half out of the river.

He may be preying, tongue wound to strike,
but to judge from his look of grave languor
        he seems
to be sunning merely. His skin gleams with light
    coming, rebuffed, off the water; his back's

tawny-spotted, like an elderly hand,
but flank's the crisp, projecting green
           of new
leafage, as if what ran through his veins
     was chlorophyll and he'd

     tapped that vegetal sorcery
which, making light of physical bounds,
           makes food
of light. Given the amplitude of his
     special greenness, it requires no large hop

     of imagination to see him as
the downed trunk's surviving outlet, from which,
           perhaps,
dragged-out years of collapsing roots
     may prove reversible. With a reflection-

     shattering *plop*, a momentary
outbreak of topical, enlarging rings
           that chase
one another frenziedly, the place's spell
     is lifted: the trunk bare, the frog elsewhere.

Angel

There between the riverbank
and half-submerged tree trunk
it's a kind of alleyway
inviting loiterers—
     in this case, water striders.

Their legs, twice body-length, dent
the surface, but why they don't
sink is a transparent riddle:

the springs of their trampoline
    are nowhere to be seen.

Inches and yet far below, thin
as compass needles, almost, min-
nows flicker through the sun's
tattered netting, circling past
    each other as if lost.

Enter an angel, in
the form of a dragon-
fly, an apparition whose
coloring, were it not real,
    would scarcely be possible:

see him, like a sparkler,
tossing lights upon the water,
surplus greens, reds, milky
blues, and violets blended
    with ebony. Suspended

like a conductor's baton,
he hovers, then goes the one
way no minnow points: straight
up, into that vast solution
    of which he's a concentrate.

A *Quilled Quilt, a Needle Bed*

Under the longleaf pines
The curved, foot-long needles have
Woven a thatchwork quilt—threads,
Not patches, windfall millions
Looped and overlapped to make
The softest of needle beds.

The day's turned hot, the air
Coiling around the always
Cool scent of pine. As if lit
From below, a radiance
Milder yet more clement than
The sun's, the forest-carpet

Glows. It's a kind of pelt:
Thick as a bear's, tawny like
A bobcat's, more wonderful
Than both—a maize labyrinth
Spiraling down through tiny
Chinks to a caked, vegetal

Ferment where the needles
Crumble and blacken. And still
The mazing continues . . . whorls
Within whorls, the downscaling
Yet-perfect intricacies
Of lichens, seeds and crystals.

An Expanded Want Ad

Rent—cttge Pig Riv
3 bdrm stove fridge
20 acr—lovely view

Although it's true
a few screens are torn and various
uninvited types may flutter through,
   some of them to bite you,

and true the floors
buckle and sag like a garden plowed
by moles, which makes the shaky chairs
    seem shakier, and the bedroom doors

    refuse to close
(you'll have three bright bedrooms—and a fine
kitchen, a living room with fireplace,
    and bath with shower hose),

    there's a good view
of the Pigeon, a river that carries
more than its share of sunny jewelry,
    for days here are mostly blue,

    and nights so clear
and deep that in a roadside puddle
you can spot the wobbly flashlight flare
    of even a minuscule star.

    The jolting road,
two muddy ruts, flanks a weedy fan
that slithers against the underside
    of a car, then rises unbowed,

    but better still,
go on foot—though this means mosquitoes—
and stop at the overgrown sawmill,
    with its fragrant wood-chip pile,

    and, stooping, enter
that shack the length of a compact car
where two loggers outbraved the bitter
    sting of a Michigan winter.

    The room is dim,
spider-strung; you'll sense the whittled lives
they led—how plain, pure, and coldly grim
    the long months were to them . . .

Just a short ways
up the road you'll come to a birch clump
which on all overcast mornings glows
   with a cumulus whiteness

   and in the brief
light after sunset holds a comely
allusive blush—a mix that's one half
   modesty, the other mischief.

   While if you hike
to where the road feeds a wider road
you'll find a mailbox above a choke
   of weeds, leaning on its stake;

   it looks disowned,
worthless, but will keep your letters dry
though its broken door trails to the ground
   like the tongue of a panting hound.

   Venture across
this wider road to reach a pasture,
whose three horses confirm that "the grass
   is always greener" applies

   to them as well:
offered shoots from your side of the fence,
they'll joggle forward to inhale
   a verdant airy handful,

   and will emit
low shivering snorts of joy, and will—
while you feed them—show no appetite
   for the grass growing at their feet.

   Now, it may happen
the first nights you'll feel an odd unease,
not lessened by the moths' crazed tapping
   at the glass; and later, sleeping

unsteadily,
as bullfrogs hurl harsh gravelly notes
from slingshot throats, you may wonder why
    you ever left the city.

    Should this occur,
think of the creatures you've not yet glimpsed,
the owl and woodchuck and tense-necked deer
    you'll meet if you remain here;

    remember, too,
morning's flashy gift—for when day breaks
it mends all wrongs by offering you
    drenched fields, nearly drowned in dew.

Rika Lesser

Rika Lesser was born in Brooklyn, New York, in 1953. She received a B.A. from Yale University and an M.F.A. from Columbia University. Her first book of poetry, *Etruscan Things* (1983), was published by George Braziller. Among her many works of translation is *Guide to the Underworld* by Gunnar Ekelöf (1980), which was awarded the Harold Morton Landon Translation Prize for Poetry from the Academy of American Poets. Among her other awards is a fellowship from the Ingram Merrill Foundation.

Canopic Jar

From Sebek's dark waters,
erect in a lotus flower,
the sons of Horus stand
before Osiris' throne.

Human-headed, I am like Imseti,
who held the liver—the seat
of life. Those remains most vital
to the living rot the dead.

I am harder and I hold all of a dead
man in my round body. So light
his ashes would not weigh an ostrich
feather. But they *are* the truth:

The dead cannot be judged.
Thin as the border of life
and death, my lips seal the dead,
keep their secret from you.

La Banditaccia, 1979

A bright, hot day. Late June. The bus from Rome
passed a seaside town—Ladispoli—plagued
by commerce, blessed with a breeze from the sea.
But from Cerveteri the Tyrrhenian
has receded far. Caere it was called
when the Gauls sacked Rome. The Vestal Virgins
took refuge on its high plateau, rising
in steep cliffs above the plain of the coast.
The small, modern village has given up
its ghosts. Peasants follow their ploughs, shepherds
their flocks, unaware of the city trod,
buried underfoot.

From the parched, walled town a road winds ALLE
NECROPOLI. I have come here to walk
the streets of that parallel city, home
of Caere's dead. Dense vegetation masks
the roadside tombs. I find and enter one.
Insects, the color of grass, swarm the dark
entrance. Inside: gray water, ankle-deep;
shallow benches. A sideshow, not the site
I know from Lawrence, Dennis, photographs
and maps. The road seems too long in the heat.
Lost in its ditch, the trickling Manganello
is nowhere in sight.

At the Zone, as in recurrent dreams of
houses, corridors, doors to be opened,
I cross the threshold of a concrete hut,
decipher a sign that says *la grotta*
bella, The Tomb of the Reliefs, is sealed,
closed for repairs. (In my sleep I'd know its
single square chamber with a gabled lid,
its pillowed niches for the important dead,
their household objects stuccoed on the walls.)
A rite of passage, this disappointment;
undeterred, I set foot on the ancient
burial ground.

Just there, outside the first huge cinctured mound,
the tiny markers of women, of men:
stone houses, stone cippi. Like women and
men, opaque, unenterable. The mounds
can be entered. Their doorways, dark mouths, call
me inside. Unasked-for, a guide: "Look at
these marks on the stone couch that runs around
the room. These, shaped like keyholes; men's corpses
covered them." Not keyholes, but phalluses
incised in the stone. "Women lay on plain
benches, safe in sarcophagi or clothes."
Afraid to take my arm, he points out holes
in the floor and the darker alcoves where
the rich rotted in their jewels. I follow
because I need his eyes, his legs that know
when a passageway leads to light.

Into blinding light we come. Seared by sun,
all along the sunken path, jewels are strewn.
Huge stones, bright, hot, cheap, lichen-crusted: red,
gray, amber, green. And the path leads between
mountainous tumuli, shrub-covered, girt
with stones, leveled or high, overgrown with
blooms, grassy, or wearing cypress trees as
feathers in their caps. As once, perhaps, they
wore towers crowned by the creatures that lived
in their makers' dreams.

Here a long range of sepulchres, a block
of flats, stands square in the sun. Out of one,
come to life from a painted wall, a black
bird swiftly flies. Inside these simple tombs,
all not shield or seat or bier carved into
the living rock, all not secured is gone.
Inside: bright yellow stagnant water; wild
green algae swirl through it in those contours
Etruscans traced remembering the waves
of the sea. A flood of memory. Tides
turn, go out.

   A different race left only
a name: La Banditaccia. Unattached.
Abandoned. *Terra bandita*, land set
apart; because the ground is broken though
unfarmed, that ending of ugliness, "accia,"
was tacked on. Into its fissures lives withdrew.
As rain, as flood, the sea seals its wounds.
The place is whole, all of one piece. Broken
ground, uninhabited, pure space.

The News & The Weather

I rush to the newspapers. Seeking
something current. Weeklies, quarterlies
put timeliness in archives, always
smother me with their musts. I require:
the press in motion, the past kept back,
letterpress, linotype, cuts, relief.
On television, I only grasp
the weather: the fronts and whorls, offshore
Agnes, stagnant, menacing the land.

How to love you here, in this *city*—
Garment workers strip me with their eyes.
We live too much inside: In your flat
only the two front rooms have windows.
The sides of the building are blank brick.
The fire escape sags; its iron base
and ladder end eight feet off the ground.
There is no where to walk. Every
crosslight is yellow—hesitation.

At night the sidewalk mica flashes.
Buses make every other stop. Trains
avoid bridges. The Watchtower waits
for someone to heed its words. Your kiss
inspects each plane of my flesh like an
elevator, emptied, jarring at
every flaw. You give me no words to heed.
I rush to the newspaper. On page
twenty-seven, column three, I read:

"On Lake Titicaca's floor, thousands
of giant frogs have grown for years.
The team of French savants who've found them
swear by their savoriness, and though they
fear the hides won't tan, Bolivians
should can the Leviathans." I run
downstairs. Whirlwinds of children pogo
up the street. Disengaged stairways wake
me to the sky. And I fly,
                    I fly.

CAN ZONE, or THE GOOD FOOD GUIDE

What do you mean, you "don't like poetry"?
Did someone force you, as a child, to taste
rancid stanzas, tainted, reeking lines, so poetry
made you sick (not at heart but) to your stomach? Poetry
laid on thick, like peanut butter, may take
its time dissolving on your palate. Poetry
thin as gruel's unpalatable. Still, poetry
made well, like a fine soufflé, will rise and stand.
How can I make a herbivore understand
that words are flesh *and* grass in poetry,
fish and fowl, birdflight, signs we read,
transforming themselves and us because we read?

Twelve years ago in the *Tribune* I happened to read
about GIANT BOLIVIAN FROGS. Of them I made poetry.
Frenchmen canned them, leaving enough to breed,
while chefs the world over steamed, roasted, grilled, and decreed:
No other known creature has such an unusual taste
or transmutable texture. And then the rumors spread:
BIG FROGS RADIOACTIVE! THE DEVIL'S OWN EGGS!
DREDGE LAKE TITICACA! The strangest tales take
shape in poetry. Put down your *Times* and take
less heed of current events. In Ovid you'll read
how the will to change could help a girl withstand
indecent advances. See, by the pond, that stand

of laurels— "Croak!" blurts a frog. "Old myths don't stand
a chance in the—blouagh—modern world! Let's read
of true metamorphoses. Once we had to stand
in for a human prince; but our royal stand-
ard bore a crowned frog salient, King of Poetry!
Marianne Moore, who showed a firm understand-
ing of the natural order, took the witness stand
in behalf of our cousins (she had discerning taste):
In 'imaginary gardens' (not really to our taste)
place 'real toads'; they, warts and all, set stand-

ards for poetry. Subjects, be literal, take
us at our word. Nothing can be worth tak-

ing that serves but once. Amphibians always take
new leases on life; we are its double stand-
ard. Snakes shed their skins, but only we will take
ours off and eat them. Survive! Make no mistake,
on land, in water, you've got to learn to read
between the lines. Don't eat my words, take
them to heart: Leaps, turns, liberties, take
them all; change and be changed or poetry
will die!" Double-talk? Free speech? What else but poetry
encompasses so much? What else can take
bitter experience and camouflage its taste
so we may feed and live and breathe and taste

the next sunrise? What other art can make us taste
what we see: the golden egg whose rising we take
for granted, or set our sights on goose (tast-
ier still) all at once, prodding our taste
buds (smell those cracklings!), forcing our senses to stand
up and take notice? What else awakens taste
for the fruits of knowledge or plants an aftertaste
of first things in apples bitten and apples read?
What but this art can keep our daily bread
from going stale in our mouths?
                                   "To each his taste,"
you say; "I'm hungry and all this talk of poetry
won't fill my gut!"—That only proves poetry

's power of suggestion. "But what if poetry
still gives me indigestion?" —A little taste
will surely settle the question. "What do you take
me for, a guinea pig?" —A hungry child who can't stand
being fed. The world's your oyster. Open wide, now. Read.

Larry Levis

Randall Tosh

Larry Levis was born in 1946. He received a B.A. from California State University at Fresno, an M.A. from Syracuse University, and a Ph.D. from the University of Iowa. He is the author of three books of poetry. *Wrecking Crew* (University of Pittsburgh Press, 1972) won the U.S. Award of the International Poetry Forum. *The Afterlife* (University of Iowa Press, 1977) was the Lamont Selection of the Academy of American Poets. *The Dollmaker's Ghost* (E.P. Dutton, 1981) was selected by Stanley Kunitz as winner of the National Poetry Series Open Competition. His other awards include fellowships from the National Endowment for the Arts and the Guggenheim Foundation. He teaches at the University of Utah.

Picking Grapes in an Abandoned Vineyard

Picking grapes alone in the late autumn sun—
A short, curved knife in my hand,
Its blade silver from so many sharpenings,
Its handle black.
I still have a scar where a friend
Sliced open my right index finger, once,
In a cutting shed—
The same kind of knife.
The grapes drop into the pan,
And the gnats swarm over them, as always.

Fifteen years ago,
I worked this row of vines beside a dozen
Families up from Mexico.
No one spoke English, or wanted to.
One woman, who made an omelet with a sheet of tin
And five, light blue quail eggs,
Had a voice full of dusk, and jail cells,
And bird calls. She spoke,
In Spanish, to no one, as they all did.
Their swearing was specific,
And polite.
I remember two of them clearly:
A man named Tea, six feet, nine inches tall
At the age of sixty-two,
Who wore white spats into downtown Fresno
Each Saturday night,
An alcoholic giant whom the women loved—
One chilled morning, they found him dead outside
The Rose Café . . .
And Angel Domínguez,
Who came to work for my grandfather in 1910,
And who saved for years to buy
Twenty acres of rotting, Thompson Seedless vines.
While the sun flared all one August,
He decided he was dying of a rare disease,
And spent his money and his last years
On specialists,
Who found nothing wrong.
Tea laughed, and, tipping back
A bottle of Muscatel, said: "Nothing's wrong.
You're just dying."
At seventeen, I discovered
Parlier, California, with its sad, topless bar,
And its one main street, and its opium.
I would stand still, and chalk my cue stick
In Johnny Palores' East Front Pool Hall, and watch
The room filling with tobacco smoke, as the sun set
Through one window.
Now all I hear are the vines rustling as I go

From one to the next,
The long canes holding up dry leaves, reddening,
So late in the year.
What the vines want must be this silence spreading
Over each town, over the dance halls and the dying parks,
And the police drowsing in their cruisers
Under the stars.
What the men who worked here wanted was
A drink strong enough
To let out what laughter they had.
I can still see the two of them:
Tea smiles and lets his yellow teeth shine—
While Angel, the serious one, for whom
Death was a rare disease,
Purses his lips, and looks down, as if
He is already mourning himself—
A soft, gray hat between his hands.
Today, in honor of them,
I press my thumb against the flat part of this blade,
And steady a bunch of red, Málaga grapes
With one hand,
The way they showed me, and cut—
And close my eyes to hear them laugh at me again,
And then, hearing nothing, no one,
Carry the grapes up into the solemn house,
Where I was born.

To a Wall of Flame in a Steel Mill, Syracuse, New York, 1969

Except under the cool shadows of pines,
The snow is already thawing
Along this road . . .
Such sun, and wind.

I think my father longed to disappear
While driving through this place once,
In 1957.
Beside him, my mother slept in a gray dress
While his thoughts moved like the shadow
Of a cloud over houses,
And he was seized, suddenly, by his own shyness,
By his desire to be grass,
And simplified.
Was it brought on
By the road, or the snow, or the sky
With nothing in it?
He kept sweating and wiping his face
Until it passed,
And I never knew.
But in the long journey away from my father,
I took only his silences, his indifference
To misfortune, rain, stones, music, and grief.
Now, I can sleep beside this road
If I have to,
Even while the stars pale and go out,
And it is day.
And if I can keep secrets for years,
The way a stone retains a warmth from the sun,
It is because men like us
Own nothing, really.
I remember, once,
In the steel mill where I worked,
Someone opened the door of the furnace
And I glanced in at the simple,
Quick and blank erasures the flames made of iron,
Of everything on earth.
It was reverence I felt then, and did not know why.
I do not know even now why my father
Lived out his one life
Farming two hundred acres of gray Málaga vines
And peach trees twisted
By winter. They lived, I think
Because his hatred of them was entire,

And wordless.
I still think of him staring into this road
Twenty years ago,
While his hands gripped the wheel harder,
And his wish to be no one made his body tremble,
Like the touch
Of a woman he could not see,
Her fingers drifting up his spine in silence
Until his loneliness was perfect,
And she let him go—
Her laughter turning into these sheets of black
And glassy ice that dislodge themselves,
And ride slowly out,
Onto the thawing river.

Sensationalism

In Josef Koudelka's photograph, untitled & with no date
Given to help us with history, a man wearing
Dark clothes is squatting, his right hand raised slightly,
As if in explanation, & because he is talking,
Seriously now, to a horse that would be white except
For its markings—the darkness around its eyes, muzzle,
Legs & tail, by which it is, technically, a gray, or a dapple gray,
With a streak of pure white like heavy cream on its rump.
There is a wall behind them both, which, like most walls, has
No ideas, & nothing to make us feel comfortable . . .
After a while, because I know so little, &
Because the muted sunlight on that wall will not change,
I begin to believe that the man's wife & children
Were shot & thrown into a ditch a week before this picture
Was taken, that this is still Czechoslovakia, & that there is
The beginning of spring in the air. That is why
The man is talking, & as clearly as he can, to a horse.

He is trying to explain these things,
While the horse, gray as those days at the end
Of winter, when days seem lost in thought, is, after all,
Only a horse. No doubt the man knows people he could talk to;
The bars are open by now, but he has chosen
To confide in this gelding, as he once did to his own small
Children, who could not, finally, understand him any better.
This afternoon, in the middle of his life & in the middle
Of this war, a man is trying to stay sane.
To stay sane he must keep talking to a horse, its blinders
On & a rough snaffle bit still in its mouth, wearing
Away the corners of its mouth, with one ear cocked forward to listen,
While the other ear tilts backward slightly, inattentive,
As if suddenly catching a music behind it. Of course,
I have to admit I have made all of this up, & that
It could be wrong to make up anything. Perhaps the man is perfectly
Happy. Perhaps Koudelka arranged all of this
And then took the picture as a way of saying
Goodbye to everyone who saw it, & perhaps Josef Koudelka was
Only two years old when the Nazis invaded Prague.
I do not wish to interfere, Reader, with your solitude—
So different from my own. In fact, I would take back everything
I've said here, if that would make you feel any better,
Unless even that retraction would amount to a milder way
Of interfering; & a way by which you might suspect me
Of some subtlety. Or mistake me for someone else, someone
Not disinterested enough in what you might think
Of this. Of the photograph. Of me.
Once I was in love with a woman, & when I looked at her
My face altered & took on the shape of her face,
Made thin by alcohol, sorrowing, brave. And though
There was a kind of pain in her face, I felt no pain
When this happened to mine, when the bones
Of my own face seemed to change. But even this
Did not do us any good, &, one day,
She went mad, waking in tears she mistook for blood,
And feeling little else except for this concern about bleeding
Without pain. I drove her to the hospital, & then,
After a few days, she told me she had another lover . . . So,

Walking up the street where it had been raining earlier,
Past the darkening glass of each shop window to the hotel,
I felt a sensation of peace flood my body, as if to cleanse it,
And thought it was because I had been told the truth . . . But, you see,
Even that happiness became a lie, & even that was taken
From me, finally, as all lies are . . . Later,
I realized that maybe I felt strong that night only
Because she was sick, for other reasons, & in that place.
And so began my long convalescence, & simple adulthood.
I never felt that way again, when I looked at anyone else.
I never felt my face change into any other face.
It is a difficult thing to do, & so maybe
It is just as well. That man, for instance. He was a *saboteur*.
He ended up talking to a horse, & hearing, on the street
Outside that alley, the Nazis celebrating, singing, even.
If he went mad beside that wall, I think his last question
Was whether they shot his wife & children before they threw them
Into the ditch, or after. For some reason, it mattered once,
If only to him. And before he turned into paper.

Family Romance

"Dressed to die . . ."
        —*Dylan Thomas*

Sister once of weeds & a dark water that held still
In ditches reflecting the odd,
Abstaining clouds that passed, & kept
Their own counsel, we
Were different, we kept our own counsel.
Outside the tool shed in the noon heat, while our father
Ground some piece of metal
That would finally fit, with grease & an hour of pushing,
The needs of the mysterious Ford tractor,
We argued out, in adolescence,

Whole systems of mathematics, ethics,
And finally agreed that *altruism*,
Whose long vowel sounded like the pigeons,
Roosting stupidly & about to be shot
In the barn, was impossible
If one was born a Catholic. The Swedish
Lutherans, whom the nuns called
"Statue smashers," the Japanese on
Neighboring farms, were, we guessed,
A little better off . . .
When I was twelve, I used to stare at weeds
Along the road, at the way they kept trembling
Long after a car had passed;
Or at the gnats in families hovering over
Some rotting peaches, & wonder why it was
I had been born a human.
Why not a weed, or a gnat?
Why not a horse or a spider? And why an American?
I did not think that anything could choose me
To be a Larry Levis before there even *was*
A Larry Levis. It was strange, but not strange enough
To warrant some design.
                                    On the outside,
The barn, with flaking paint, was still off white.
Inside, it was always dark, all the way up
To the rafters where the pigeons moaned,
I later thought, as if in sexual complaint,
Or sexual abandon; I never found out which.
When I walked in with a 12 gauge & started shooting,
They fell, like gray fruit, at my feet—
Fat, thumping things that grew quieter
When their eyelids, a softer gray, closed,
Part of the way, at least,
And their friends or lovers flew out a kind of sky light
Cut for loading hay.
I don't know, exactly, what happened then.
Except my sister moved to Switzerland.
My brother got a job
With Colgate-Palmolive.
He was selling soap in Lodi, California.

Later, in his car, & dressed
To die, or live again, forever,
I drove to my first wedding.
I smelled the stale boutonniere in my lapel,
A deceased young flower.
I wondered how my brother's Buick
Could go so fast, &,
Still questioning, or catching, a last time,
An old chill from childhood,
I thought: why me, why her, & knew it wouldn't last.

The Quilt

"He had stopped believing in the goodness of the
    world."
                                    —Henry James, The Portrait of a Lady

I think it is all light at the end; I think it is air.

Those fields we drove past, turning to mud in April,
Those oaks with snow still roosting in them. Towns so small
Their entire economy suffered if a boy, late at night,
Stole the bar's only cue ball.

In one of them, you bought an old quilt, which, fraying,
Still seemed to hold the sun, especially in one
Bright corner, made from what they had available in yellow
In 1897. It reminded me of laughter, of you. And some woman,
Whose faith in the goodness of the world was
Stubborn, sewed it in. "There now," she might as well
Have said, as if in answer to the snow, which was

Merciless. "There now," she seemed to say, to
Both of us. "Here's this patch of yellow. One field gone
Entirely into light. Goodbye . . ." We had become such artists

At saying goodbye; it made me wince to look at it.
Something at the edge of the mouth, something familiar
That makes the mouth turn down. An adjustment.

It made me wince to have to agree with her there, too,
To say the day itself, the fields, each thread
She had to sew in the poor light of 1897,
Were simply gifts. Because she must be dead by now, &
Anonymous, I think she had a birthmark on her cheek;
I think she disliked Woodrow Wilson & the war;
And if she outlived one dull husband, I think she
Still grew, out of spite & habit, flowers to give away.

If laughter is adult, an adjustment to loss,
I think she could laugh at the worst. When I think of you both,

I think of that one square of light in her quilt,
Of women, stubborn, believing in the goodness of the world.
How next year, driving past this place, which I have seen
For years, & steadily, through the worst weather, when
The black of the Amish buggies makes the snow seem whiter,
I won't even have to look up.
I will wince & agree with you both, &, past the farms
Abandoned to moonlight, past one late fire burning beside
A field, the flame rising up against the night
To take its one solitary breath, even I
will be a believer.

Winter Stars

My father once broke a man's hand
Over the exhaust pipe of a John Deere tractor. The man,
Ruben Vasquez, wanted to kill his own father
With a sharpened fruit knife, & he held
The curved tip of it, lightly, between his first
Two fingers, so it could slash

Horizontally, & with surprising grace,
Across a throat. It was like a glinting beak in a hand,
And for a moment, the light held still
On the vines. When it was over,
My father simply went in & ate lunch, & then, as always,
Lay alone in the dark, listening to music.
He never mentioned it.

I never understood how anyone could risk his life,
Then listen to Vivaldi.

Sometimes, I go out into this yard at night,
And stare through the wet branches of an oak
In winter, & realize I am looking at the stars
Again. A thin haze of them, shining
And persisting.

It used to make me feel lighter, looking up at them.
In California, that light was closer.
In a California no one will ever see again,
My father is beginning to die. Something
Inside him is slowly taking back
Every word it ever gave him.
Now, if we try to talk, I watch my father
Search for a lost syllable as if it might
Solve everything, & though he can't remember, now,
The word for it, he is ashamed . . .
If you can think of the mind as a place continually
Visited, a whole city placed behind
The eyes, & shining, I can imagine, now, its end—
As when the lights go off, one by one,
In a hotel at night, until at last
All of the travelers will be asleep, or until
Even the thin glow from the lobby is a kind
Of sleep; & while the woman behind the desk
Is applying more lacquer to her nails,
You can almost believe that the elevator,
As it ascends, must open upon starlight.

I stand out on the street, & do not go in.
This was our agreement, at my birth.
And for years I believed
That what went unsaid between us became empty,
And pure, like starlight, & it persisted.
I got it all wrong.
I wound up believing in words the way a scientist
Believes in carbon, after death.

Tonight, I'm talking to you, father, although
It is quiet here in the Midwest, where a small wind,
The size of a wrist, wakes the cold again—
Which may be all that's left of you & me.

When I left home at seventeen, I left for good.

That pale haze of stars goes on & on,
Like laughter that has found a final, silent shape
On a black sky. It means everything
It cannot say. Look, it's empty out there, & cold.
Cold enough to reconcile
Even a father, even a son.

Whitman

*"I say we had better look our nation searchingly in
the face, like a physician diagnosing some deep
disease."*
                                        —Democratic Vistas
"Look for me under your bootsoles."

On Long Island, they moved my clapboard house
Across a turnpike, & then felt so guilty they
Named a shopping center after me!

Now that I'm required reading in your high schools,
Teen-agers call me a fool.
Now what I sang stops breathing.

And yet
It was only when everyone stopped believing in me
That I began to live, again—
First in the thin whine of Montana fence wire,
Then in the transparent, cast off garments hung
In the windows of the poorest families,
Then in the glad music of Charlie Parker.
At times now,
I even come back to watch you
From the eyes of a taciturn boy at Malibu.
Across the counter at the beach concession stand,
I sell you hot dogs, Pepsis, cigarettes—
My blond hair long, greasy, & swept back
In a vain old ducktail, deliciously
Out of style.
And no one notices.
Once, I even came back as *me*,
An aging homosexual who ran the Tilt-a-Whirl
At county fairs, the chilled paint on each gondola
Changing color as it picked up speed,
And a Mardi Gras tattoo on my left shoulder.
A few of you must have seen my photographs,
For when you looked back,
I thought you caught the meaning of my stare:
Still water,
Merciless.

A Kosmos. One of the roughs.

Leave me alone.
A father who's outlived his only child.

To find me now will cost you everything.

Irish Music

Now in middle age, my blood like a thief who
Got away, unslain, & the trees hung again in the grim,
Cheap embroidery of leaves, I come back to the white roads,
The intersections in their sleeves of dust,
And vines like woodwinds twisted into shapes
For playing different kinds of silence.
Just when my hearing was getting perfect, singular
As an orphan's shard of mirror, they
Change the music into something I
No longer follow.
But how like them to welcome me home this way:
The house with its doorstep finally rotted away,
And carted off for a stranger's firewood,
And yet, behind the window there,
A woman bent over a map of her childhood, but still
A real map, that shows her people's
Ireland like a bonnet for the mad, on top of
Plenty of ocean.
Hunger kept those poor relations traveling until
They almost touched the sea again,
And settled.
And there have been changes, even here.
In Selma, California,
The band in the park still plays the same song,
But with a fresher strain of hopelessness.
It, too, will pass.
That is the message, always, of its threadbare refrain,
The message, too, of what one chooses to forget
About this place: the Swedish tailgunner who,
After twenty missions, chopped off his own left hand
To get back home. No one thinks of him;
Not even I believe he found another reason, maybe,
For all left hands. So memory sires
Forgetfulness—this settlement of sheds, & weeds,
Where the last exile which the bloodstream always sang
Comes down to a matter of a few sparrows hopping
On & off a broken rain gutter, or down-spout, & behind them,
A barn set up on a hill & meant to stay there,

Ignoring the sky
With the certainty they bolted into the crossbeams—
The whole thing
Towering over the long silent
Farmer & his wife; & that still house
Where their fingers have remembered, for fifty years,
Just where to touch the bannister; & then the steps,
That, one day, led up to me. Come home,
Say the blackened, still standing chimneys, & the missing bell
Above the three room schoolhouse—
You've inherited all there is: the ironic,
Rueful smile of a peasant who's extinct,
Who nods, understanding, too well, the traveler,
And who orders another shot of schnapps
While his wife, pregnant, angry, puts both hands
Under her chin, & waits up.

And always, I pack the car, I answer no . . .
When my own son was next to nothing,
He, too, would wait up with us,
Awake with hands already wholly formed,
And no larger than twin question marks in the book I closed,
One day, in a meadow,
When I reached for her—above the silent town,
Above the gray, decaying smoke of the vineyards.
A stranger who saw us there might have said:
I saw two people fucking on your land.
But afterward, our pulses
Already lulling & growing singular, my eyes
Closed on that hill, I saw
A playground, mothers chatting; water falling because
It was right to *be* falling, over a cliff; & the way
Time & the lights of all home towns grew still
In that tense shape of water just before it fell . . .
I watched it a long time,
And, for no reason I could name, turned away from it,
To take that frail path along the mountainside—
Then passed through alder, spruce, & stunted pine,
Stone & a cold wind,
Up to the empty summit.

William Logan

William Logan was born in Boston, Massachusetts, in 1950. He was educated at Yale University and the University of Iowa. He is the author of three books of poems, *Sad-faced Men* (1982), *Difficulty* (1984), both from David Godine, and *Moorhen* (1984), from Abattoir Editions. Among his awards are fellowships from the Ingram Merrill Foundation and the National Endowment for the Arts. He teaches at the University of Florida.

Jereboda Granger

Sutcliffe and Whitby

The sea, that problem Euclid never solved,
whose black rooks curve
linear demeanors of the shore, burns

under the abbey, a little selfishness
made grace. Neither we, nor the stable-yards,
nor the knacker's tumbled house,

the dead harpooner's cottage, color
the lobster-claw piers pinching
this resort's slummy river from sea,

where the whale's cheesy body wept into wicks,
and jet was ground into tokens
for the living for the dead, a grief of soft coal.

Singers in the sea-wracked graveyard
make early music an English
proposition. Down from the heather

where sheep gather by milestones,
the rude parishioners clatter floors
their fathers' fathers' fathers laid.

We are only the false-coated crew,
the humbled watchers stirring at shipwreck,
while men in open boats oar out and back.

What mastery lies in leaving?
From history fails one landscape, not
the sea exposing its fragile negatives.

Summer Island

We leave the farmland for the formless coast
where broken wreaths of breakers trouble
the luckless gull. Past the driftwood litter,
seals loll and bathers sag toward water.

Our landlocked cottage lifts its eaves
above the brassy bay. To and from
the dumpy port, a shuttling mailship
cheats the tides. The damaged lighthouse winks

and aims its eye over the rolling horizon,
where time shuffles its hour
and land settles seaward.
Odd seasons the locked plates shake

the bearings of the hills and grease
the granite monuments. We cannot wait
for nature's declaration of the breach
that bonds the island to the land. A scarred

seawall carves the current back to shore.
Light swings crazily on the corrugated wake.
Back and forth the peeling buoys twist
like targets. Tomorrow we will separate.

Debora Sleeping

The ferry window frames a pop-art shovel,
jaw drooling gouts of water and harbor mud.
The drawn-in gangplank scrapes against the wood.
A few shy children pelt the boat with gravel,

but the stones fall short. The boat's an oven.
Outside the seagulls circle, lazy and overweight,
crying against decisions of the state
like winged burghers stacked up outside heaven.

The French and Spanish ports decline midway
between bureaucracy and art, but while
waiting for the Fifties to return to style
they condescend to watch our nights and days.

You're asleep again, as on the leaf-lit train,
though here a purple plastic chair's your bed.
The Pre-Raphaelitic curls that wreathe your head
are permanent—at least, immune to rain,

unlike the satin shirt I made you wear
in Paris, that did not outlast the storm.

You spent the evening huddling to keep warm
and whispered phrasebook curses in my ear.

Sleep's our disease, the heart's adagio.
We wallow in its sty, refuse to leave
the rundown precinct of its raveled sleeve,
the only ease bodies so close can know.

Or so I thought. Watching you here
sleep in hard daylight—hulled on that dream beach,
drugged (courtesy Dramamine), silent, out of reach—
I know the first stirring of a distant fear.

The boat wakes toward chalk cliffs closed by fog
where fishermen not out of work still bear
the dying and disputed catch ashore.
Sleep by other means continues dialogue.

Green Island

By runnels and sea-dipped clover, easing
water out of the headlands, the moon in daylight
scars the severed architecture back to grace.
God the competent, god the antique:

the green island arches
above water's shallow back
where brine shrimp scatter and the dark
unmannered boats troll. I measure the evil dates

spent staring the same blind channel
toward lumpish heaven. The water swelled
each evening in its grave surround,
the backlit island glowed and was gone.

And what was there, islanders?
Sand dyeing children's rags,
stolen keels athwart tattooed rocks,
beaches soaked with fisher's slaughter

where gray birds picked the wash for scraps.
What falls away each evening is not
kind authority: the cracked boats adrift,
abandoned swimmers lolling in the crawl,

no green ideal
toward whose curious carvings
one swimmer heads out with broken stroke,
a mote on the horizon, a silent O.

Susan Ludvigson

Paula Feldman

Susan Ludvigson was born in 1942. She is the author of three books of poetry, *Step Carefully in Night Grass* (John Blair, 1974), and *Northern Lights* (1981) and *The Swimmer* (1984), both from the L.S.U. Press. Among her awards are fellowships from the National Endowment for the Arts and the Guggenheim Foundation. She teaches at Winthrop College.

The Child's Dream

If I could start my life again,
I'd keep the notebook
I promised myself at nine—
a record of all the injustice
done by adults: that accusing tone
when they speak, the embarrassments
before relatives, like the time
I had to put on my swimsuit in the car
while Mother chatted with an uncle
who peered in, teasing.
And *wouldn't* they be sorry
later, when they read it,
after I'd been run over by a truck,

their faces darkening
like winter afternoons.
And I, of course (if I survived),
would have a reminder,
in my own hand,
so I'd be the perfect parent,
my children radiant as the northern lights.
It's like poems you hope
will be read by someone who knows
they're for him, and cry
at what he did or didn't do,
wishing to touch your face once more,
to cradle your body.
You can almost hear what he'd tell you
with his voice that sounds
like the sea rolling in
over and over, like a song.

The Widow

A stranger arrives at her door
in a T-shirt, his truck
parked outside like a sign:
This is an honest repairman.
He wants directions, but she
does not know the street.
When he asks to use the phone,
she lets him into the kitchen
where the water has just begun
to boil, steaming the windows
like breath.

She remembers the novel
where a man holds a knife

to a child's small throat,
drawing a thin line of blood,
then takes the young mother
off in his truck to rape her.
She thinks where her knives are,
imagines throwing the water
straight from the stove
in his face.

He murmurs something
into the phone.
She has gone to another room
and can't make out the words,
the tone is too soft,
but she hears the water
boil over, spatter the gleaming
stainless steel of her range
like the hiss of firecrackers
before they explode.
He pulls the pan off the burner,
calls to her,
Lady? Lady?

She hides in the bathroom,
listens, even after she hears
the door open again, and close
like the click of a trigger.
When at last the truck
pulls away, she comes out,
spends the whole afternoon
drifting back and forth
to the window.

Making supper,
she burns her hand,
cries softly
long after the pain is gone.

The next morning, she's amazed
to see she'd forgotten
to lock the back door,
to turn off the lights
that burned all night
in the kitchen.

On Learning That Certain Peat Bogs
Contain Perfectly Preserved Bodies

Under this town's ashes
lies a man, still sweating
the long summer days,
his body
perfect as morning,
even to the bacon and eggs
in his belly.
His skin is damp
in the humid earth,
closed eyes heavier
under rain.
The heart quit pumping early,
but when a rock eases down
and cuts an arm
or grazes his back,
blood still seeps
from the veins,
the clots blooming
like poppies around him.
In the brain
memories lie opened,
one into the other:
the crunch of the ax
as he swings down hard,
his wife calling him in,

a woman singing his name
in the distance.
He does not hear them,
but they are there,
claiming their portions.
By now the wife may be
dead too, the ax passed down
to his son, or rusted
under the woodpile.
The woman cannot recall
her own clear voice
or the features of the man
who should be bones.

Man Arrested in Hacking Death Tells Police He Mistook Mother-in-Law for Raccoon

Every morning she'd smear something brown
over her eyes, already bagged
and dark underneath, as if that would
get her sympathy. She never slept,
she said, but wandered like a phantom
through the yard. I knew it. Knew
how she knelt beneath our bedroom window too,
and listened to Janet and me.

One night when *again* Janet said No
I called her a cow, said she might as well
be dead for all she was good to me.
The old lady had fur in her head
and in her ears,
at breakfast slipped and told us
she didn't think the cows would die.

Today when I caught her
in the garage at dawn, that dyed hair
growing out in stripes, eyes
like any animal surprised from sleep
or prowling where it shouldn't be,
I did think, for a minute,
she was the raider of the garden,
and the ax felt good, coming down
on a life like that.

Mekeel McBride

Mekeel McBride was born in 1950. She was educated at Mills College and Indiana University. She is the author of two collections of poetry, *Ordinary World* (1979) and *This Going Under of the Evening Land* (1983), both from Carnegie-Mellon University Press. Among her awards is a fellowship from the National Endowment for the Arts. She teaches at the University of New Hampshire.

Peter Petrie

A Blessing

"Freely chosen, discipline
is absolute freedom."
> —Ron Serino

1.

The blue shadow of dawn settles
its awkward silks into the enamelled kitchen
and soon you will wake with me into the long
discipline of light and day—the morning sky
startled and starred with returning birds.

You half-whisper, half-sigh, "This will never stop."
And I say, "Look at the constellations
our keys and coins make, there,
on the polished sky of the dresser top."

2.

From what sometimes seems an arbitrary
form or discipline often come two words
that rhyme and in the rhyming fully marry
the world of spoons and sheets and common birds
to another world that we have always known
where the waterfall of dawn does not drown
even the haloed gnat; where we are shown
how to find and hold the pale day moon, round
and blessed in the silver lake of a coffee spoon.

Over the Phone

This is where he finds you. February. Over the phone
his voice has in it: plum tree, pear, a meadow.
Let's say that what he speaks

is an awakening, very early, no alarm.
In each room, you, astonished, find vases, cups and jars
vivid with white heather,

hepatica, great golden daffodils! Wonder
if you have to, who has the extra key,
who walked the house while you lay sleeping, how high

the price will be for this profusion
from the florist's heart; here, every container's filled
to overflowing and you, though unaware, owe

nothing. Simply notice heliotrope
spilling from the open oven—a sweet, blue bread;
the evening scent of honeysuckle

swelling from a yellow kettle—tea, long summer-steeped.
This is still winter, the door
still swollen with cold and difficult to open.

Even so, see how easily that one dizzy tiger lily
lifts from the heart of the keyhole,
shaped like a Tiffany lamp and shining.

Aubade

She wakes long before he does. A fierce shock
of love forces her to look away. Light
the color of gray silk settles among
the dark fronds of a Phoenix palm. Asleep
he laughs, as if in whatever world's
now his own, someone dances drunkenly
with an Alaskan bear, or, on a dare
kisses the mayor's bald head, leaving
a perfect red lip print that will amuse
the sparrows for hours. She watches him sleep
for almost an hour and although he
does not laugh again, nor wake, he talks
a kind of dream-prattle that has in it
parrots and a dove-grey slate still dusty
with the chalk of childhood. She cannot see
his face buried in the pillow but thinks
how in that pillow he must leave some
residue of dream: a name, a scar, parts
of a song in which two people now are
dancing. His red hair flares against

the plain white pillowcase: a benign fire,
rich as any color Rembrandt ever
loved, the first deep whisper of the rising sun.

The Will to Live

On the green lawn of a city park
a sentence of dark insects completes itself:

Believe! Believe!
Above, two Monarchs matter and flash

in this immense summer air.
Small scraps of wing, good weather, a will

to live, they come
from the tenuous country of now

whatever the heart is asking for. Even if I
weren't here

they'd still congratulate the sky
with a fragile disbelief in sorrow. Graceful

as the hands of the deaf
they form a language in air that I understand.

almost not at all. Being human
I might say

they kiss and part and kiss again, but
know they're governed by desire

or law or lack of these
beyond me. They fling themselves

against a sky so big
they do not understand it's there. Clouds

fat and ample, grow
fatter still and if the old June maples

stand weighted and without words
it is not from human grief, or any other.

Heather McHugh

Heather McHugh was born in 1948 in San Diego, California. She received a B.A. from Radcliffe College and an M.A. from Denver University. She is the author of two collections of poetry, *Dangers* (1977) and *A World of Difference* (1981), both from Houghton Mifflin, and the translator of *D'Apres Tout: Poems by Jean Follain* (Princeton University Press, 1981). Among her awards are fellowships from the National Endowment for the Arts and the Rockefeller Foundation. She teaches at the University of Washington, and in the nonresidential writing program at Warren Wilson College, but lives on an island in Maine.

Gregory Biss

Language Lesson, 1976

When Americans say a man
takes liberties, they mean
he's gone too far. In Philadelphia

today a kid on a leash ordered
bicentennial burger,
hold the relish. Hold

is forget, in American.
On the courts of Philadelphia
the rich prepare

to serve, to fault.
The language is a game in which
love means nothing, doubletalk

means lie. I'm saying
doubletalk with me. I'm saying go
so far the customs are untold,

make nothing without words
and let me be
the one you never hold.

Lines

Some are waiting, some can't wait.
The stores are full of necessities.

The sun dies down, the graveyard
grows, the subway is a wind
instrument with so many stops, but
even the underground comes
to an end, and all those flights
of fancy birds settle for one
telephone wire, the one on which

just now, the man in utterly
unheard-of love has caught
the word goodbye. He puts
the receiver back in the cradle

and stands. Outside his window
an old man with a hearing-aid walks
without aim, happy just to be alive.

Impressionist

1.

I wasn't getting anywhere.
What good was the book
of matches, watch
of wheels, defective
mechanisms of my sex?
Where was the most of myself
I meant to make? Mistress
of the minded Q, the pointed I
I knew discretion comes to order
and the million likenesses add up
to one distinction, cells
of color on a riverbank

where the French
girl in the light
blue dress remembers
someone gone.

2.

My mechanic lights a cigarette.
I'm at his desk, revising
the bill. I take a zero out,
I move a dot: this makes all

the difference. He wants
to sell me speed; I need it
like a hole in the head; my head
is overweight. I mean the world

to him. He'll fix my Comet,
I will feed his Milky Way machine,
I mean it matters, mud or moon,
what grounds we have for understanding.

Now I'm getting somewhere,
driving it home. The roadside leaves
are orange, yellow, every kind
of down. A dust of light

is in the drawing room, a dust of flowers
in the living room and in the bedroom, dust
has almost filled
the eyecup of the dead impressionist.

Animal Song

We're flattered they come so close,
amused they seem like us,
amazed they don't.
The animal we named
the sex fiend for
has no known family but ours.
The angels are distinguished by
what random birds in any small backyard
are largely made of. If we do not move

perhaps they may approach us,
in the spirit of

unearthing something.
Everywhere inside the ground
are avenues and townships
of another world, enormously minute.
And when we take upon ourselves
the calm and the largesse
of a blue sky no one knows
where starts or stops

then for a moment
we don't terrify the animals. It's rare
but it happens. So maybe someday, when the something
greater than our lives has come, we'll stop
our businesses of digging
little definitions for a hole. Perhaps we can recall
the language in which we were intimate—before the tower
and before the fall—before we called
the creature names. We'd have to
talk with it, remembering

how animal is soul, and not its opposite.

Capital

For a second the word express appears
in apposition to the word espresso—o
antique, I tell myself, to know
the root of happy—then the bus is gone
from its stop at the coffeehouse door.

I might do something rash if one
more person mentions consciousness.
In every street the bikes
and beggars lie, expertly crippled.

At every corner, stalled about a smoke,
the children of school-boards and clubs look about
as expressive as wood. So what

do a hundred thousand people need
each other for? A public to be private in?
The fifth amendment, that you have to have
a hearing to invoke? A circulation
for the Times? Don't ask, says the cop

on the beat; the street musician
says keep quiet, just in case; and sure enough,
his dark blue velvet box, impressed
with the withdrawn clarinet,
attracts a small downfall of dimes.

A Physics

When you get down to it, earth
has our own great ranges
of feeling—Rocky, Smoky,
Blue—and a heart
that can melt stones.

Miles above, the still pools
fill with sky, as if aloof.
And we have eyes,
for all of this—the earth
and its reminding moon. We too

are ruled by such attractions—
spun and swaddled, rocked
and lent a light. We run
our trains on time, our clocks
on wheels. And all the while

we want to love each other
endlessly. Not only for
a hundred years, not only six feet
up and down. We want the suns and moons
of silver in ourselves, not only

counted coins in a cup. The whole idea
of love was not to fall. And neither was
the whole idea of God. We put him well
above ourselves because we meant,
in time, to measure up.

Sandra McPherson

Sandra McPherson was born in 1943. She holds a B.A. from San Jose State University and has received fellowships from the National Endowment for the Arts, the Ingram Merrill Foundation, and the Guggenheim Foundation. She is the author of four collections of poetry, *Elegies for the Hot Season* (1970), *Radiation* (1973), *The Year of Our Birth* (1978), and *Patron Happiness* (1983), all from the Ecco Press. She teaches at the Oregon Writers' Workshop in Portland.

Andy Hagara

Centerfold Reflected in a Jet Window

There is someone naked flying alongside the airplane.
The man in the seat in front of me is trying to hold her.
But she reflects, she is below zero, would freeze the skin
off his tongue.

Beside me also someone is flying.
And I don't say, "Put on your sweater."
And I don't say, "Come back in this minute,"
though she is my daughter.

And there is an old woman riding inside the earth.
Metal shoulders wear her dresses.
She believed she would be an old woman flying alongside heaven
because she loved, because she had always loved.

To an Alcoholic

I make you sightsee the sheer walls,
The rapids, hanging over them
A ledge of hand-high cactus with a
Bourbon cup.

That's how I keep you sober
As a cony's bed. You get yourself
Drunk. You're in torn hands that wish
To be in good.

There is no blood in the golden flower.
The tuns grow shoved together
Storing up their leap. The country's dry
But snowmelt

Sends the river high. "Up there,"
You say, "a spring's a waitress,
Long legs underground from me"
And "Hardest

Thing on the face of God's earth
To get a glass of whiskey."
I know they're prickly,
Those dry-side

Visions. We need some glory
Always. These know only cache and wait.
Their time is right: to each his own
Piss-golden light.

Urban Ode

I almost caught the bentwood chair
Flung across the soup joint at me.
   But I was hungry.
   The boy with the flying anger

Was quietly dusted out. Who
Knows him? Knows if he's mean
   Or just unwanted? Loneliness
   Used to feed a lot of us.

Bread and cheese, dinner alone;
The company of large empty vessels
   In galleries; one hour with
   A shrink and fifty at a good

Concealed piano that I knew—
That's how my Insufficiency was spent.
   But have we spent up the whole void
   Now we've lost our loneliness,

Plain happy to sidestep elaborate Freud?
After that soup I saw a windowshopping woman
   Walk into a street merchant's shelves
   Of pots until they all

Came down, perfection
In bowling, and lay about her toes
   Like segments of a mud facial
   She laughed over, crying. The potter,

Speechless, sold her the whole
Destruction. Out of loneliness, I've been violent
   To empty containers—
   A baby bottle slung against the wall

Left only a nipple in shag, and safety
Glass. Phoebe was full. Infancy

Needs no romance. A child
Today was chasing around a bush

That was not empty—"Ava, Ava," she cried,
"Come see the jay!" But Ava
    Had seen one before, she said,
    The shrub was vacant for her,

She saw no joy in the blue life.
Still the dress flew round and round
    The little cedar, outside
    At first, then into it.

And the girl who made that möbius
Was never separate from the jay again,
    Never objective, never
    Maunderingly subjective, she

Who had seen many.
In all her running, she'd run out of loneliness.
    What do you think? Can such
    Riches fall into our lives?

What do you think, Patron Happiness?

Pornography, Nebraska

Once, on that highway where a traveler works hard
To remember what he loves intensely in this life,
    Because it is so endlessly bare,
    The highway I mean,

I heard on our CB one trucker tell another
About tattoos around the areolas. About the hurt.

The second man's
Hadn't been as bad, but needling him elsewhere—

To recall a barberpole—
Caused definitive pain. Drunk when he started,
   He couldn't renege until the last prick of ink.
   It was sobering.

On this long journey out of cultivation, sage
At last outspices hay. Bulls twist up dust
   In an hourglass-shaped battle,
   Heads at the center.

A vulture on a fencepost
Like a single staked rose by a farmhouse . . .
   And still the voice of public confession
   Goes through the dotty illustrations on his body,

Forty-some, he says, like milemarkers to the border.
Then I remember losing him,
   If only on the radio.
   It was at last so dark I felt the way I did

When once I was actually leaving someone I dearly loved.
Moonlight traveled
   The bedspring spiral of my notebook
   In which I recorded the distance

From him by the fuel burned.
Wherever the pictured man was, somewhere a spanker
   Like "PJ's" back in Muscatine
   Performed astonished love

As a way of testing out his story, seeing
If she could believe him.
   New voices
   Took over the channel

But they only tattled on a patrol,

Who soon appeared, his outwitted chase-light off.
   Then one last voice—
   A siren at the stateline,

Crying higher, calling out.
It involved catching no one. Lightning
   Had fired the ranges. All the Pine Bluffs,
   Wyoming, Fire Department volunteers

Stopped dreaming. They knew they must cool
Their nakedness; the wail said they must drive,
   As fast as they could,
   Away from their beds.

For Elizabeth Bishop

The child I left your class to have
Later had a habit of sleeping
With her arms around a globe
She's unscrewed, dropped, and dented.
I always felt she *could* possess it,
The pink countries and the mauve
And the ocean which got to keep its blue.
Coming from the Southern Hemisphere to teach,
Which you had never had to do, you took
A bare-walled room, alone, its northern
Windowscapes as gray as walls.
To decorate, you'd only brought a black madonna.
I thought you must have skipped summer that year,
Southern winter, southern spring, then north
For winter over again. Still, it pleased you
To take credit for introducing us,
And later to bring our daughter a small flipbook
Of partners dancing, and a ring

With a secret whistle.—All are
Broken now like her globe, but she remembers
Them as I recall the black madonna
Facing you across the room so that
In a way you had the dark fertile life
You were always giving gifts to.
Your smaller admirer off to school,
I take the globe and roll it away: where
On it now is someone like you?

Lifesaving

For Phoebe

You and I are like an old married couple
Since I pulled you from the swimming pool
(The "blueberry pie" you once described it)

In the evening sunshine of Dunsmuir, California.
My parents, that old married couple, stretched just beyond seeing
On the motel lawn chairs. They were wearing
Fresh clothes and smelled of shower soap.

They watched the rotating colored light play
Through the fountain and over the petunias
(Which must have thought it weird,

In their simple mind). The dust was settling
Out of the air from the highway project.
We had been going south all day and tomorrow
We would go south.

And they never found out. Your father
Never found out. Only in my mind
Do I hear your close call.

We dried off, it was a perfect evening,
The motel owner was playing "The Blue Danube" on his piano.
Mt. Shasta changed in the sunset like the petunias.
You looked over at some teenagers kissing in a shadow;

And you said, "So that's what love is."

Unitarian Easter

Entering here, I hope the confetti
Can jazz up a burden.

The pastor, for instance, calling birds, head back,
Or dancing an old French dance, hopping and kicking.

And now the congregation winds around the chancel,
Carrying damp, strapping forsythia sprigs, slanting them into a vase
Beside the kotoist, her song plucked and bent, a few blossoms raining
      on the strings.

God's weather today—sandals in puddles.
The moment of silence—raindrops on the roof, no comment
On the matter of God.

Alleys

For the man I'd marry I picked a white flower
Out of the dust behind a shed. The alleys
Are bare with such gifts—I'll pick up a penny

Or spots will be a dog approaching. It is
Not even a withered flower anymore,
But the dust of the first kind thing I did for him.

Later I brought in bouquets with creatures on them.
Voiceless, with increasing legs—not
The jays and doves I heard in alleys . . .

How long ago I was morning sick
In that city alley! Frightened
And leaning like a wino against the brick.

Trucks went there, and trash, and there
Was no delivered bird's egg in my path.
Now I am morning glad, all

Is pregnant outside me. I face the rabbit's
Victorious ears, the bumblebee, and mushrooms
On a fallen limb. There's not a house

Whose exit they don't call to,
Whose cries they don't keep
From heading into the street. These widths of sun . . .

A wren fusses inside a hedge; bones have been thrown
To the back of a fence. The dust
Is not all of kindness. I leave a bit

Of blue plate, do not steal the horseshoe
That perhaps I should. Who knows
Where anything is in a cycle? Alleys are behind us,

But sunflowers fall forward into them—
As if to call for rain in the ruts. While in our house
There is the opposite. His unfinished glass of water

Appears to beg me for a flower.

Paul Mariani

George Newton

Paul Mariani was born in 1940. He received a B.A. from Manhattan College, an M.A. from Colgate University, and a Ph.D. from the City University of New York. He has written three collections of poetry, *Timing Devices* (David Godine, 1979), and *Crossing Cocytus* (1982), and *Prime Mover* (1985), from Grove Press. Other books include *William Carlos Williams: A New World Naked* (McGraw-Hill, 1981), *A Usable Past: Essays on Modern & Contemporary Poetry* (University of Massachusetts Press, 1984), and *A Commentary on the Complete Poems of Gerard Manley Hopkins* (Cornell University Press, 1970). He teaches at the University of Massachusetts.

The Lesson

Silent, my jaws working, I knew
as we drove home from Mass he'd learn
his lesson, get it right this time.

I knew it when I pulled him
from the back seat by the scruff
of his neck, squeezing till his shoulders

scrunched, knew it when I half flung him
up the porch steps, through the cold
kitchen and up the stairs. And when I

turned and faltered for a moment to hear
him mutter, I knew that that was that.
I must have taken those goddamned

steps by threes, slamming that bent body,
that cowering shape against the wall. He
set his face hard to meet my shouts—

give him credit—but his eyes
were somewhere else. Glazed, dreamy,
they floated in that round face

of his, they. . . . I can't remember now
just what it was I nailed him for, or
what it was I said or what he said. Let's

call it part of growing up. Once, when I
was ten, an altarboy in that old converted
hangar back in Levittown, I got it

into me to act the clown and fool around
communion time. I slapped my head a dozen times
in wonder at those queuing sheep,

fiddled with my shoes, kept gaping
at my watch. Another Charlie Chaplin.
Except my father saw it different.

He was silent going home, though his jaws
kept working, and that was bad. Once we were
safe inside, though, he rammed me up against

the kitchen wall and held me rigid there,
my neck between his outstretched thumb
and forefinger, to show me how to stand

in church. Some lessons you just can't
forget. So with my own son here in this
ritual re-enactment, this nailing to the wall,

for dark motives one calls "exercise"
of virtue, righteous anger, discipline. Yet
for all that, one thing only keeps playing

back: that slight shaking of the rigid
head, the eyes turning as the
fingers tighten on the scrawny neck.

Coda: Revising History

You know it's all bullshit
the poem you wrote about me
he sd, over the golden oldie
on his tape deck, the butt
stuck between his teeth
as he shifted into overdrive.
You *think* you got me down
on paper but you don't.
It's you you got you solipsistic
bastard. And if you weren't
my dumbass brother and if
I didn't love you I'd slap
a suit so fast on you you
wouldn't know what hit you.
I might do it yet. How much
you got? I know you *think*
you got the classic tragic
stance of the *condition humaine*
but the truth was worse . . .
and better. I know, man, I
was there a long time after *you*
were gone. For two days, two days
we nursed her in her bed,
her poor head rolling

with those sick accusing eyes
until I wanted her or me to die.
And sure Pop had a temper, had
a fist, but remember, numbnuts,
this: at least he didn't skip.
Try to get it straight for once
and see it from where I stand.
Words are whores. They can do *any-*
thing, depending on who's paying.
Drop the highfalutin mannerist
evasions, the this the that.
Keep it simple, stupid. History,
myth and God. Oh yeah? And who told
you? Look, one ounce of this
Hawaiian Gold will help you fly
a lot higher than that silly Mobil
horse of yours. Try to understand:
it's dead history, dead and over.
I'm tired, we're all tired.
Who gives a shit about it anyway?
You got yr. own kids now to think
about. For chrissake give
yr. head a rest. Dig it? Here.
Here! Take a toke of this.

Lines I Told Myself I Wouldn't Write

Nebuchadnezzar, von Hoffman the Great, then
Big Sur and Paterson. Instead: since it was
really my kid's dog, we settled for Sparky.
Better than Killer, I guess, better than

White Fang. An onomastic gesture if ever
there was one, more in line with the Ford

pickups sloped to the sides before the town's
one beerstop. And what with Argentine

conscripts freezing in Darwin and her Majesty's
soldiers leapfrogging the Falklands
out of San Carlo, the *Belgrano* gone
and the *Sheffield* a grave, I promised

myself I wouldn't get soft over one fleabag
arthritic half gone in the head when he didn't
come home. Springtime, we figured, and the old
prunewrinkled groinbag out after women

over in Leverett or up by the lake. But as day
followed day, then a week, then a month,
and his cracked greasy bowl got sacked first
by a tom then by two cranky jays. . . .

There were three nights in there when my wife
kept waking me up, hearing him with each shift
of the wind, and she'd sit up in bed, listening,
the same way she did whenever one of the babies

got stuck in their breathing. I know I said
I wouldn't go weepy when the time came, and I haven't.
At least not that much. And besides, half the neighbors
must be doing the two-step, and the kid who delivers

the papers and used to fling them into the bushes
whenever he heard Sparky can breathe easier now.
And last week a friend put the whole thing
in its proper perspective, reminding me how in Taiwan

and places like that they serve them as delicacies.
So it's over and done with: the backyard service,
the young dogwood planted. Except for the dream,
where an old dog, battered and nettled-flecked, limps

down to the river. Across its wide waters he sniffs
till he sees us. And though at first he shudders,

he knows he must plunge in. When he springs forth
his red coat glistens. His tail whacks

back and forth, back and forth. As in an Aztec
mound painting caught in the flickering gleam
of the torch, the eyes shift, blend into one.
The lips have curled up. The bright eye shines.

Then Sings My Soul

Who can tell a man's real pain
when he learns at last the news
that he must die? Sure we all know
none of us is going anywhere

except in some pineslab box or its fine
expensive equal. But don't we put it off
another day, and then another and another,
as I suppose we must to cope? And so

with Lenny, Leonardo Rodriguez, a man
in the old world mold, a Spaniard
of great dignity and a fine humility,
telling us on this last retreat for men

that he had finally given up praying
because he didn't want to hear
what God might want to tell him now:
that he wanted Lenny soon in spite

of the hard facts that he had his kids,
his still beautiful wife, and an agèd
mother to support. I can tell you now
it hit us hard him telling us because for me

as for the others he'd been the model,
had been a leader, raised in the old Faith
of San Juan de la Cruz and Santa Teresa
de Avila, this toreador waving the red flag

at death itself, horns lowered now
to come hurling down on him. This story
has no ending because there is still life,
and life means hope. But on the third day,

at the last Mass, we were all sitting
in one big circle like something out of Dante—
fifty laymen, a priest, a nun—with Guido
DiPietro playing his guitar and singing

one of those old Baptist hymns in his rich
tenor and all of us joining in at the refrain,
Then sings my soul, my Savior God to Thee,
How Great Thou art, how great thou art,

and there I was on Lenny's left, listening
to him sing, his voice cracked with resignation,
how great thou art, until angry glad tears
began rolling down my face, surprising me. . . .

Lord, listen to the sound of my voice.
Grant Lenny health and long life. Or,
if not that, whatever strength and peace
he needs. His family likewise, and

his friends. Grant me too the courage
to face death when it shall notice me,
when I shall still not understand why
there is so much sorrow in the world.

Teach me to stare down those lowered horns
on the deadend street that will have no alleys
and no open doors. And grant me the courage
then to still sing to thee, *how great thou art.*

Cleopatra Mathis

Vincent McGroary

Cleopatra Mathis was born in 1947 in Ruston, Louisiana. She received her B.A. from Southwest Texas State University and her M.F.A. from Columbia University. She has written two books of poetry, *Aerial View of Louisiana* (1980) and *The Bottom Land* (1983), both published by Sheep Meadow Press. Among her awards is the Robert Frost Award from The Frost Place in Franconia, New Hampshire. She teaches at Dartmouth College.

Getting Out

That year we hardly slept, waking like inmates
who beat the walls. Every night
another refusal, the silent work
of tightening the heart.
Exhausted, we gave up; escaped
to the apartment pool, swimming those laps
until the first light relieved us.

Days were different: FM and full-blast
blues, hours of guitar "you gonna miss me
when I'm gone." Think how you tried
to pack up and go, for weeks stumbling
over piles of clothing, the unstrung tennis rackets.
Finally locked into blame, we paced
that short hall, heaving words like furniture.

I have the last unshredded pictures
of our matching eyes and hair. We've kept
to separate sides of the map,
still I'm startled by men who look like you.
And in the yearly letter, you're sure to say
you're happy now. Yet I think of the lawyer's bewilderment
when we cried, the last day. Taking hands
we walked apart, until our arms stretched
between us. We held on tight, and let go.

Aerial View of Louisiana

The delta lies unchanged, flat
as childhood: a woman gathering pecans
from a yard black with water, purple martins
after mosquitoes, all winter mock lilac.

In the dream of wrought iron
you find them—the grandmother is fierce,
both arms waving you away. Your mother
takes your hand to speak
of fishing from low pine flats
how she loves the nests of water.
She says your pride will be her death.
You wear your grandmother's wild name,
her fan of hair.

You wake to mountains: reflections
off coastal islands, hills of prairie marsh.
Memory is the first claim,
you'll spend your life coming back
to this flatness. By dusk you have forgotten
everything but the bleeding outline
of the river. You watch for New Orleans,
the white cluster of tombs.

For Maria

The hot nights I slept with you,
a leg thrown across your back.
You never complained.
When our stepfather raved, I fought.
You didn't cry with me,
preferring the dog and grassy field.
I thought you lived in your own world.
Now what I know best about you
comes from that night at supper in the hot kitchen.
You clenched your teeth as long as you could
against his slash of belt
on my bare foot. But when the blood came
you screamed in my place, Bastard, bastard!
and stopped us all.

Later in bed we heard the words of our stepfather
through the wall, the breaking of our mother
who couldn't come to us if we called.
Next to the window, you faced the ledge;
the honeysuckle told lies
as you put out your hand, all night
held the small flowers.

Mimosa

After twenty-five years they drag you away.
Nothing left but roots and this wish
To know that you recognized us, the living
Who still come back, the dead who wear the white
Blur of themselves.

The children crying into summer—
We must have seemed hopeless, every unhappiness

Taken to the highest branch,
Our swearing to leave. Remember the dark blue
St. Augustine grass, the roses.

Go back as far as the old man
On his haunches blowing smoke rings. Suspenders,
Long underwear, the handpainted
Delicate cup of thick coffee.
You have been planted an hour.
See the pack of Camels in the grass, the little girl.
She frames the scene
As through glass, which will thicken
And distort, until the man has faded
Into distance. And you and the child
Have moved through years, changed
And disappeared.

William Matthews

Arlene Modica

William Matthews was born in Cincinnati, Ohio, in 1942. His books of poems include *Ruining the New Road* (1970) and *Sleek for the Long Flight* (1972), both from Random House, and *Rising and Falling* (1979), *Flood* (1982), and *A Happy Childhood* (1984), all from Atlantic, Little Brown. He is also co-translator, with Mary Feeney, of *A World Rich in Anniversaries*, prose poems by Jean Follain, published in 1979 by Logbridge Rhodes. He has twice been awarded fellowships from the National Endowment for the Arts, and has received fellowships from the Guggenheim Foundation and the Ingram Merrill Foundation. He has taught throughtout the United States, most recently at the University of Houston, Columbia University, and Brooklyn College.

An Airline Breakfast

An egg won't roll well
nor a chicken fly far:
they're supposed to be local.
Like regional writing or thin
wines, they don't travel well.
I do. I can pack in ten minutes.
I remember what I love when I'm gone
and I do not and do not forget it.
The older I grow, the better
I love what I can't see:

the stars in the daytime,
the idea of an omelet,
the reasons I love what I love.
It's what I can see I have to nudge
myself to love, so wonderful
is the imagination. Even this wretched
and exhausted breakfast is OK:
an omelet folded in thirds
like a letter, a doughy roll
and some "champagne": sluggard
bubbles half the size of peas.
But the butter's unsalted
and from the air the earth
is always beautiful, what little
I can see of its pocked skin.
Somewhere down there a family
farm is dying: long live
the family farm, the thinnning
topsoil, the wheat in full head,
the sow in her ample flesh.
We're better organized than hunger
and almost as profligate.
Across the farmlands a few
of us in a plane are dragging
a shadow-plane, an anchor
that will not grab.

On the Porch at the Frost Place, Franconia, NH

For Stanley Plumly

So here the great man stood,
fermenting malice and poems
we have to be nearly as fierce
against ourselves as he
not to misread by their disguises.
Blue in dawn haze, the tamarack
across the road is new since Frost
and thirty feet tall already.
No doubt he like to scorch off
morning fog by simply staring through it
long enough so that what he saw
grew visible. "Watching the dragon
come out of the Notch," his children
used to call it. And no wonder
he chose a climate whose winter
and house whose isolation could be
stern enough to his wrath and pity
as to make them seem survival skills
he'd learned on the job, farming
fifty acres of pasture and woods.
For cash crops he had sweat and doubt
and moralizing rage, those staples
of the barter system. And these swift
and aching summers, like the blackberries
I've been poaching down the road
from the house where no one's home—
acid at first and each little globe
of the berry too taut and distinct
from the others, then they swell to hold
riot of their juices and briefly
the fat berries are perfected to my taste,
and then they begin to leak and blob
and under their crescendo of sugar
I can taste how they make it through winter. . . .

451 / WILLIAM MATTHEWS

By the time I'm back from a last,
six-berry raid, it's almost dusk,
and more and more mosquitoes
will race around my ear their tiny engines,
the speedboats of the insect world.
I won't be longer on the porch
than it takes to look out once
and see what I've taught myself
in two months here to discern:
night restoring its opacities,
though for an instant as intense
and evanescent as waking from a dream
of eating blackberries and almost
being able to remember it, I think
I see the parts—haze, dusk, light
broken into grains, fatigue,
the mineral dark of the White Mountains,
the wavering shadows steadying themselves—
separate, then joined, then seamless:
the way, in fact, Frost's great poems,
like all great poems, conceal
what they merely know, to be
predicaments. However long
it took to watch what I thought
I saw, it was dark when I was done,
everywhere and on the porch,
and since nothing stopped
my sight, I let it go.

Charming

Because language dreams in metaphors,
charm is always like something else,
like luck, or wealth, or like a tune
to whistle while coaxing soup
from chicken bones and two turnips.

Because ice is like stone, though once
it was water, and because kissed ice
means blue lips, charm needs to know
the names of distress and remedy,
and what words are not spoken, and when.

Because charm is an argument
about politics, that it works best
for the rich, and about magic,
that it works best for those who recant
politics, charm is warily polite.

And because charm is like love,
the way ice is like water, charm
tends its investment and dreams
when it sleeps, and wakes hungry,
as if from exacting work.

And because to fly in a dream is fierce
pleasure, charm wakes with a kind word.
It's important to start in the right place,
like a child possessed of a story.
First the witch, then the snow, and then

the starling-throng like a blizzard
of shameful thoughts, and then winter:
ice to kiss and the right names
in the right order, the sexual secret
of spring's coming back at all.

Though spring is all burgeon and broadcast,
a tosspurse, survival's brash manners,

because charm dwindles and hoards,
because charm repeats, because charm
will save itself before it remembers us.

Loyal

They gave him an overdose
of anesthetic, and its fog
shut down his heart in seconds.
I tried to hold him, but he was
somewhere else. For so much of love
one of the principals is missing,
it's no wonder we confuse love
with longing. Oh I was thick
with both. I wanted my dog
to live forever and while I was
working on impossibilities
I wanted to live forever, too.
I wanted company and to be alone.
I wanted to know how they trash
a stiff ninety-five-pound dog
and I paid them to do it
and not tell me. What else?
I wanted a letter of apology
delivered by decrepit hand,
by someone shattered for each time
I'd had to eat pure pain. I wanted
to weep, not "like a baby,"
in gulps and breath-stretching
howls, but steadily, like an adult,
according to the fiction
that there is work to be done,
and almost inconsolably.

Whiplash

That month he was broke,
so when the brakes to his car
went sloshy, he let them go.
Next month his mother came
to visit, and out they went
to gawk, to shop, to have something
to do while they talked besides
sitting down like a seminar
to talk. One day soon he'd fix
the brakes, or—as he joked
after nearly bashing a cab
and skidding widdershins
through the intersection
of Viewcrest and Edgecliff—
they'd fix him, one of these
oncoming days. We like
to explain our lives to ourselves,
so many of our fictions
are about causality—chess
problems (where the ?! after
White's 16th move marks
the beginning of disaster),
insurance policies, box scores,
psychotherapy ("Were your
needs being met in this
relationship?"), readers' guides
to pity and terror—, and about
the possibility that because
aging is relentless, logic too
runs straight and one way only.

By this hope to know how
our disasters almost shatter us,
it would make sense to say
the accident he drove into
the day after his mother left
began the month he was broke.

Though why was he broke?
Because of decisions he'd made
the month before that,
and so on all the way back
to birth and beyond, for his
mother and father brought
to his life the luck of theirs.

And so when his car one slick day
oversped its dwindling ability
to stop itself and smacked two
parked cars and lightly kissed
another, like a satisfying
billiards shot, and all this action
(so slow in compression and
preparation) exploded so quickly,
it seemed not that his whole life
swam or skidded before him
but that his whole life was behind
him, like a physical force,
the way a dinosaur's body
was behind its brain and the news
surged up and down its vast
and clumsy spine like an early
version of the blues; indeed,
indeed, what might he do
but sing, as if to remind himself
by the power of anthem that the body's
disparate and selfish provinces
are connected. And that's how
the police found him, full-throated,
dried blood on his white suit
as if he'd been caught in a rust-
storm, song running back and forth
along his hurt body like the action
of a wave, which is not water,
strictly speaking, but a force
that water welcomes and displays.

An Elegy for Bob Marley

In an elegy for a musician,
one talks a lot about music,
which is a way to think about time
instead of death or Marley,

and isn't poetry itself about time?
But death is about death and not time.
Surely the real fuel for elegy
is anger to be mortal.

No wonder Marley sang so often
of an ever-arriving future, that verb tense
invented by religion and political rage.
Soon come. Readiness is all,

and not enough. From the urinous
dust and sodden torpor
of Trenchtown, from the fruitpeels
and imprecations, from cunning,

from truculence, from the luck
to be alive, however, cruelly,
Marley made a brave music—
a rebel music, he called it,

though music calls us together,
however briefly—and a fortune.
One is supposed to praise the dead
in elegies for leaving us their songs,

though they had not choice; nor could
the dead bury the dead if we could pay
them to. This is something else we can't
control, another loss, which is, as someone

said in hope of consolation,
only temporary, though the same phrase
could be used of our lives and bodies
and all that we hope survives them.

457 / WILLIAM MATTHEWS

In Memory of the Utah Stars

Each of them must have terrified
his parents by being so big, obsessive
and exact so young, already gone
and leaving, like a big tipper,
that huge changeling's body in his place.
The prince of bone spurs and bad knees.

The year I first saw them play
Malone was a high school freshman
already too big for any bed,
14, a natural resource.
You have to learn not to
apologize, a form of vanity.
You flare up in the lane, exotic
anywhere else. You roll the ball
off fingers twice as long as your
girlfriend's. Great touch for a big man,
says some jerk. Now they're defunct
and Moses Malone, boy wonder at 19,
rises at 20 from the St. Louis bench,
his pet of a body grown sullen
as fast as it grew up.

Something in you remembers every
time the ball left your fingertips
wrong and nothing the ball
can do in the air will change that.
You watch it set, stupid moon,
the way you watch yourself
in a recurring dream.
You never lose your touch
or forget how taxed bodies
go at the same pace they owe,
how brutally well the universe
works to be beautiful,
how we metabolize loss
as fast as we have to.

Twins

One may be a blameless
bachelor, and it is but a
step to Congreve.
     —Marianne Moore

When I was eleven and they
were twenty-two, I fell in love
with twins: that's how I thought
of them, in sum, five run-on
syllables, Connie-and-Bonnie.
They were so resolutely given
as a pair—like father-and-
mother—I never thought to prefer one,
warm in her matching bed
like half an English muffin
in a toaster, though Bonnie
was blonde, lithe, walleyed,
angular, and fey. And Connie
was brunette, shiny-eyed, and
shy, as most true flirts
describe themselves, over and over.

And shouldn't love be an exclusive
passion? To fall in love with twins
made me unfaithful in advance?
It made me paralyzed, or I made
it—my love doubled forever
into mathematical heaven—paralysis.
Frocks rhyme and names confuse
and the world is thicker with sad
futures than lost pasts. And I,
who hoarded names like marbles,
how could I say what I knew?
Indeed, how can I say it now?
I knew the two meanings of *cleave*.
I looked into those eyes I loved,

two brown, two blue, and shut my own
(grey) from any light but mine
and walked straight home and kissed
my parents equally and climbed my growing
body's staircase to the very tip of sleep.

Robert Morgan

Robert Morgan was born in 1944 in
Hendersonville, North Carolina. He
received his B.A. from the University
of North Carolina at Chapel Hill and
his M.F.A. from the University of
North Carolina at Greensboro.
Among his seven collections of poems
are *Red Owl* (W. W. Norton, 1972)
and *Land Diving* (L.S.U. Press,
1976). He has won several prizes for
his poetry, including three fellowships
from the National Endowment for
the Arts. He teaches at Cornell Uni-
versity.

Nancy Morgan

Bricking the Church

At the foot of Meetinghouse Hill
where once the white chapel
pointed among junipers and pulled
a wash of gravestones west,

they've buried the wooden snow that
answered sarvis in bloom
and early morning fogs, in brick,
a crust the same dull red

as clay in nearby gullies.

The little churchhouse now looks more
like a post office or school.
It's hard to find

among the brown winter slopes
or plowed fields of spring.
Brick was prestigious back when
they set their minds and savings to it.

They wanted to assert its form
and presence if not in stone
at least in hardened earth, urban weight,
as the white clapboards replaced

unpainted lumber which replaced
the logs of the original
where men brought their guns to preaching
and wolves answered the preacher.

The structure grows successive rings,
and as its doctrine softens
puts on a hard shell
for weathering this world.

Mountain Bride

They say Revis found a flatrock
on the ridge just
perfect for a natural hearth,
and built his cabin with a stick

and clay chimney right over it.
On their wedding night he lit
the fireplace to dry away the mountain
chill of late spring, and flung on

applewood to dye
the room with molten color while
he and Martha that was a Parrish
warmed the sheets between the tick

stuffed with leaves and its feather
cover. Under that wide hearth
a nest of rattlers,
they'll knot a hundred together,

had wintered and were coming awake.
The warming rock
flushed them out early.
It was she

who wakened to their singing near
the embers and roused him to go look.
Before he reached the fire
more than a dozen struck

and he died yelling her to stay
on the big four-poster.
Her uncle coming up the hollow
with a gift bearham two days later

found her shivering there
marooned above a pool
of hungry snakes,
and the body beginning to swell.

Horace Kephart

Outside the tent on the Little Fork
of the Sugar Fork of Hazel Creek
a man is writing. His table boards

on upended kegs, he drafts meticulously clear
paragraphs and weights the finished pages
with a shotgun shell. Squirrels rippling
in the trees above do not distract him.
The jug by a whitepine is stopped with a cob.

Each sentence he scratches with economy
is payment on a vast unpayable obligation:
to his parents for the years of college, for
the special courses at Cornell, for his tenure
cataloging Petrarch in Florence, for the girl,
his Laura, married in Ithaca and taken
west, for the librarian's post in St. Louis,
for the study of Finnish, for the unwritten
history of western exploration that
excused long camping holidays and nights
away from home and expensive rare editions,
for the weeks of drinking and sulk.

Lean as a mountaineer himself, galluses
swung at his sides, he scribbles to the young
his intensity of woodcraft, weapons, survival,
and of the hillmen his archaic friends and landlords,
makers of spirits. Even now one's loose
hog crashes through the brush into his camp
and knocks a tentline from its stob so
the canvas home sags at one corner on
his narrow cot, and breaks the clothesline.
As he jumps to shout and whack it back
into the undergrowth the unfinished sheet
from an early chapter of *Our Southern Highlanders*
peels off the desk and luffs like a wounded
dove out through scrub and leaves to the creek.

Hay Scuttle

The holes in the floor of the barn loft
were cut for dropping shucks to the stalls.
Pile an armload on the opening
and stuff them through. The cow
is already eating as the rest
splash on her head. The fodder sweet
as tobacco is pushed down for the horse.
Light from below rises with manure
and warm cud-breath.
And bleach from the horse's bed.
Dark up here with the dead grass
and cornsheller, except for the trapdoors.
Only way out to the sun is down
through the exquisite filth.

Secret Pleasures

The sourwood sprouts are long
as flyrods in the field we turned-out
years ago. Its soil had worn
so thin the weeds runted and rocks,
boiled up by frost, began to cobble-over
bare spots and gather in the washes.
Erosion left the ground in swells like graves.
Our granary's now the weathered humps
of clay from which we took
the syrup and left
a fragrant dust. Let it
scab and fur over on its own
and offer no crop bigger than dew
and the beadwork of berrypicking.
My secret pleasure: to come and watch

these shoots work up
their honey from bitter clay.
Lichen gardens improve the scars,
patching over history. I offer
the land my leisure.

Passenger Pigeons

Remembering the descriptions by Wilson
and Bartram, and Audubon and other
early travelers to the interior, of the sky
clouded with the movements of winged pilgrims
wide as the Mississippi, wide as the Gulf
Stream, hundred-mile epics of equidistant wings
horizon to horizon, how their droppings
splashed the lakes and rivers, how
where they roosted whole forests broke down
worse than from ice storms, and the woods floor
was paved with their lime, how the settlers
got them with ax and gun and broom
for hogs, how when a hawk attacked
the endless stream bulged away
and kept the shift long after
the raptor was gone, and having read how
the skies of America became silent, the fletched
oceans forgotten, how can I replace
the hosts of the sky, the warmblooded jetstreams?
To echo the birdstorms of those early
sunsets, what high river of electron, cell and star?

G. E. Murray

Tom Vack

G. E. Murray was born in Buffalo, New York, in 1945. He received his A.B. from Canisius College and his M.A. from Northeastern University. *Repairs* (University of Missouri Press, 1979) was winner of the Devins Award. He has been a Bridgman Scholar at Bread Loaf and is poetry critic for the *Chicago Sun-Times*.

Shopping for Midnight

There you go, it's everywhere
here, waiting for me at ridiculous prices,
    the essential mood—collected
and perfect-bound—hidden, certainly,
    like the best of bargains,
among tampons & pickles & paperwares,
    down these aisles I tour at midnight.

    A browser at heart,
I carry no money. It's safer that way,
    as the average retail clerk

will ply me with replicas, expensive
    imitations of my prize.
And I have been taken for an easy target
  before, buying dreams of blood

    and summer at discount.
Once, guilty of wearing an oversized coat
    to market, a thief, I resisted
the sweet commerce of a career angel,
    boosting her instead
of her temporary goods. But shopping
  for the darkest of bones demands nerve,

    a special setting, instinct.
There are, naturally, no rules of search
  or purchase; no adequate samples.
Not necessary. The time will arrive when
    I round a corner perfectly
and find it, waiting like a mouse, enormous
  as Canada, the perennial top-shelf item.

    It belongs somewhere, and only
there, mine to find alone, marked down
    like contaminated vegetables,
a fish found breathing on the beach, harvest
    of any old night, dampish,
twisted, leaving me to decide whether
  to steal, borrow, or merely adore it.

On the Upside

On Hubbard Street, among factory signs
And the gay bars further west, this winter
In the ditch does not mean enough.
With innocence, a melodrama of duty

Is played by the big Pole city workers,
Flinging rock salt, unplugging sewers
In defense of a surprise freeze.
Their smiles, like habits, break hard.
Their black stocking caps appear
Stark and vulnerable to the young men cruising
Past hand-in-hand, swimming at noon
Toward darkened theaters and bargain hotels,
Requiring sweet ambush, a ration
Of luxury. These filthy buildings don't care,
Can't whistle insults. Soon the Poles,
Immutable as mud, will have picked
These streets clean of ice
And loitering glances, will filter
Home to dinners of wurst and bock beer,
Laying odds against more snow.
And slowly, in its timeliness, a clothesline
Of color will string through the city,
Flapping proudly, ready for collision
With high blue skies, like old lovers
Tossing again in a warehouse loft, straining free.

Northside Chicago, March 1978

Sketch for a Morning
in Muncie, Indiana

Forget the time spent mining the rudiments of praise.
Central Indiana is left to the man who fuels his
morning with soft-boiled eggs and the veins in a fat
waitress's legs.

All his aliases are forgotten; he prefers loneliness
to life among some hairs in his comb. Several inches

beneath his skin there are musicians with arthritic
fingers, hordes of accomplished clarinets, twin pianos
like lobster claws, melodies from a soundless culture.
Only the neat, golden fields of Indiana hear them, and
waltz furiously out of step, like a row of pom-pom
girls drunk on the promise of cherry cokes and the
coach's good looks.

Then the countryside traffic begins to form into
clouds of crows, a symphony of his own that he remembers.
The last gulp of juice goes down like premium gasoline.
He rises, fumbles for spare change with the embarrassment
of a virtuoso searching absentmindedly for a missing
suite. I pick up the tip he leaves, and pocket it.

California Dead

In golden winters one misses them most,
the fabulous dead of California,
baked like bricks
into perpetual tans of the earth's choosing.
I sometimes hear their slight voices,
long gone, rise from the dirt plumbing
in this seaside motel . . .

I think they might come north by mule train,
over some ridge, in the clear of day,
missionaries with tight blue lips,
who would descend like radio signals
to a flock of freeway traffic
roaming in an hour glass. And I think
they would make hay out of flavor straws,
swimmers, set designers, the Sunset Strip,
before drawing close a crucifix of mind.

What antique scabs must line their robes,
what savagery they'd read in junk-car smiles.
It's difficult to watch them naked now,
walking again the plazas of dim instinct,
in search of the one Indian guide
who returned them to this wild territory.

Naomi Shihab Nye

Naomi Shihab Nye was born in 1952 in St. Louis, Missouri, and was educated at Trinity University. She is the author of two books of poetry, *Different Ways to Pray* (Breitenbush Books, 1980) and *Hugging the Jukebox* (E. P. Dutton, 1982) chosen by Josephine Miles for the National Poetry Series. She works in the Poets-in-the-Schools Program in Texas and lectures at the University of Texas at San Antonio.

Michael Nye

Making a Fist

"We forget that we are all dead men conversing with
    dead men."
                    —*Jorge Luis Borges*

For the first time, on the road north of Tampico,
I felt the life sliding out of me,
a drum in the desert, harder and harder to hear.
I was seven, I lay in the car
watching palm trees swirl a sickening pattern past the glass.
My stomach was a melon split wide inside my skin.

"How do you know if you are going to die?"
I begged my mother.
We had been traveling for days.

With strange confidence she answered,
"When you can no longer make a fist."

Years later I smile to think of that journey,
the borders we must cross separately,
stamped with our unanswerable woes.
I who did not die, who am still living,
still lying in the backseat behind all my questions,
clenching and opening one small hand.

Hugging the Jukebox

On an island the soft hue of memory,
moss green, kerosene yellow, drifting, mingling
in the Caribbean Sea,
a six-year-old named Alfred
learns all the words to all the songs
on his grandparents' jukebox, and sings them.
To learn the words is not so hard.
Many barmaids and teenagers have done as well.
But to sing as Alfred sings—
how can a giant whale live in the small pool of his chest?
How can there be breakers this high, notes crashing
at the beach of the throat,
and a reef of coral so enormous only the fishes know its size?

The grandparents watch. They can't sing.
They don't know who this voice is, trapped in their grandson's body.
The boy whose parents sent him back to the island
to chatter mango-talk and scrap with chickens—
at age three he didn't know the word "sad"!
Now he strings a hundred passionate sentences on a single line.
He bangs his fist so they will raise the volume.

What will they do together in their old age?
It is hard enough keeping yourself alive.
And this wild boy, loving nothing but music—
he'll sing all night, hugging the jukebox.
When a record pauses, that live second before dropping down,
Alfred hugs tighter, arms stretched wide,
head pressed on the luminous belly. "Now!" he yells.
A half-smile when the needle breathes again.
They've tried putting him to bed, but he sings in bed.
Even in Spanish—and he doesn't speak Spanish!
Sings and screams, wants to go back to the jukebox.
O mama I was born with a trumpet in my throat
        spent all these years tryin' to cough it up . . .

He can't even read yet. He can't *tell time*.
But he sings, and the chairs in this old dance hall jerk to attention.
The grandparents lean on the counter, shaking their heads.
The customers stop talking and stare, goosey bumps surfacing on their
        arms.
His voice carries out to the water where boats are tied
and sings for all of them, *a wave*.
For the hens, now roosting in trees,
for the mute boy next door, his second-best friend.
And for the hurricane, now brewing near Barbados—
a week forward neighbors will be hammering boards over their windows,
rounding up dogs and fishing lines,
the generators will quit with solemn clicks in every yard.

But Alfred, hugging a sleeping jukebox, the names of the tunes gone
        dark,
will still be singing, doubly loud now, teasing his grandmother,
"Put a coin in my mouth!" and believing what she wants to believe;
this is not the end of the island, or the tablets this life has been
scribbled on, or the song.

                                        Utila, Honduras, 1980

Where Children Live

Homes where children live exude a pleasant rumpledness,
like a bed made by a child, or a yard littered with balloons.

To be a child again one would need to shed details
till the heart found itself dressed in the coat with a hood.
Now the heart has taken on gloves and mufflers,
the heart never goes outside to find something to "do."
And the house takes on a new face, dignified.
No lost shoes blooming under bushes.
No chipped trucks in the drive.
Grown-ups like swings, leafy plants, slow-motion back and forth.
While the yard of a child is strewn with the corpses
of bottle-rockets and whistles,
anything whizzing and spectacular, brilliantly short-lived.

Trees in children's yards speak in clearer tongues.
Ants have more hope. Squirrels dance as well as hide.
The fence has a reason to be there, so children can go in and out.
Even when the children are at school, the yards glow
with the leftovers of their affection,
the roots of the tiniest grasses curl toward one another
like secret smiles.

Catalogue Army

Something has happened to my name.
It now appears on catalogues
for towels and hiking equipment,
dresses spun in India,
hand-colored prints of parrots and eggs.
Fifty tulips are on their way
if I will open the door.

Dishrags from North Carolina
unstack themselves in the Smoky Mountains
and make a beeline for my sink.

I write a postcard to my cousin:
This is what it is like to live in America.
Individual tartlet pans congregate
in the kitchen, chiming my name.
Porcelain fruit boxes float above tables,
sterling silver ice cream cone holders
twirl upside-down on the cat's dozing head.

For years I developed radar against malls.
So what is it that secretly applauds
this army of catalogues marching upon my house?
I could be in the bosom of poverty, still they arrive.
I could be dead, picked apart by vultures,
still they would tell me
what socks to wear in my climbing boots.

Stay true, catalogues, protect me
from the wasteland where whimsy and impulse
never camp.
Be my companion on this journey between dusts,
between vacancy and that smiling stare
that is citizen of every climate
but customer to nothing,
even air.

The Use of Fiction

A boy claims he saw you on a bicycle last week,
touring his neighborhood. "West Cypress Street!" he shouts,
as if your being there and his seeing you
were some sort of benediction.

To be alive, to be standing outside
on a tender February evening . . .
"It was a blue bicycle, ma'am, your braid was flying,
I said hello and you laughed, remember?"

You almost tell him your bicycle seat is thick with dust,
the tires have been flat for months.
But his face, that radiant flower, says you are his friend,
he has told his mother your name!
Maybe this is a clear marble
he will hide in his sock drawer for months.
So who now, in a world of figures,
would deny West Cypress Street,
throwing up clouds into this literal sky?
"Yes, Amigo"—hand on shoulder—
"It was I."

Sharon Olds

Sharon Olds was born in 1942 in San Francisco, California. She was educated at Stanford University and Columbia University. Her first book, *Satan Says* (University of Pittsburgh Press, 1980), received the inaugural San Francisco Poetry Center Award. Her second book, *The Dead and the Living* (Knopf, 1984), was the Lamont Selection of the Academy of American Poets. Her awards include fellowships from the National Endowment for the Arts and the Guggenheim Foundation.

copyright © Thomas Victor

The Death of Marilyn Monroe

The ambulance men touched her cold
body, lifted it, heavy as iron,
onto the stretcher, tried to close the
mouth, closed the eyes, tied the
arms to the sides, moved a caught
strand of hair, as if it mattered,
saw the shape of her breasts, flattened by
gravity, under the sheet,
carried her, as if it were she,
down the steps.

These men were never the same. They went out
afterwards, as they always did,
for a drink or two, but they could not meet
each other's eyes.

Their lives took
a turn—one had nightmares, strange
pains, impotence, depression. One did not
like his work, his wife looked
different, his kids. Even death
seemed different to him—a place where she
would be waiting,

and one found himself standing at night
in the doorway to a room of sleep, listening to a
woman breathing, just an ordinary
woman
breathing.

Sex Without Love

How do they do it, the ones who make love
without love? Beautiful as dancers,
gliding over each other like ice-skaters
over the ice, fingers hooked
inside each other's bodies, faces
red as steak, wine, wet as the
children at birth whose mothers are going to
give them away. How do they come to the
come to the   come to the   God   come to the
still waters, and not love
the one who came there with them, light
rising slowly as steam off their joined
skin? These are the true religious,
the purists, the pros, the ones who will not
accept a false Messiah, love the
priest instead of the God. They do not
mistake the lover for their own pleasure,
they are like great runners: they know they are alone

with the road surface, the cold, the wind,
the fit of their shoes, their over-all cardio-
vascular health—just factors, like the partner
in the bed, and not the truth, which is the
single body alone in the universe
against its own best time.

Race Riot, Tulsa, 1921

The blazing white shirts of the white men
are blanks on the page, looking at them is like
looking at the sun, you could go blind.
Under the snouts of the machine guns,
the dark glowing skin of the women and
men going to jail. You can look at the
gleaming horse-chestnuts of their faces the whole day.
All but one descend from the wood
back of the flat-bed truck. He lies,
shoes pointed North and South,
knuckles curled under on the splintered slats,
head thrown back as if he is in a
field, his face tilted up
toward the sky, to get the sun on it, to
darken it more and more toward the color of the human.

Things That Are Worse Than Death

For Margaret Randall

You are speaking of Chile,
of the woman who was arrested
with her husband and their five-year-old son.
You tell how the guards tortured the woman, the man, the child,
in front of each other,
"as they like to do."
Things that are worse than death.
I can see myself taking my son's ash-blond hair in my fingers,
tilting back his head before he knows what is happening,
slitting his throat, slitting my own throat
to save us that. Things that are worse than death:
this new idea enters my life.
The guard enters my life, the sewage of his body,
"as they like to do." The eyes of the five-year-old boy, Dago,
watching them with his mother. The eyes of his mother
watching them with Dago. And in my living room as a child,
the word, Dago. And nothing I experienced was worse than death,
life was beautiful as our blood on the stone floor
to save us that—my son's eyes on me,
my eyes on my son—the ram-boar on our bodies
making us look at our old enemy and bow in welcome,
gracious and eternal death
who permits departure.

Rite of Passage

As the guests arrive at my son's party
they gather in the living room—
short men, men in first grade
with smooth jaws and chins.

Hands in pockets, they stand around
jostling, jockeying for place, small fights
breaking out and calming. One says to another
How old are you? Six. I'm seven. So?
They eye each other, seeing themselves
tiny in the other's pupils. They clear their
throats a lot, a room of small bankers,
they fold their arms and frown. *I could beat you
up,* a seven says to a six,
the dark cake, round and heavy as a
turret, behind them on the table. My son,
freckles like specks of nutmeg on his cheeks,
chest narrow as the balsa keel of a
model boat, long hands
cool and thin as the day they guided him
out of me, speaks up as a host
for the sake of the group.
We could easily kill a two-year-old,
he says in his clear voice. The other
men agree, they clear their throats
like Generals, they relax and get down to
playing war, celebrating my son's life.

The One Girl at the Boys Party

When I take my girl to the swimming party
I set her down among the boys. They tower and
bristle, she stands there smooth and sleek,
her math scores unfolding in the air around her.
They will strip to their suits, her body hard and
indivisible as a prime number,
they'll plunge in the deep end, she'll subtract
her height from ten feet, divide it into
hundreds of gallons of water, the numbers

bouncing in her mind like molecules of chlorine
in the bright blue pool. When they climb out,
her ponytail will hang its pencil lead
down her back, her narrow silk suit
with hamburgers and french fries printed on it
will glisten in the brilliant air, and they will
see her sweet face, solemn and
sealed, a factor of one, and she will
see their eyes, two each,
their legs, two each, and the curves of their sexes,
one each, and in her head she'll be doing her
wild multiplying, as the drops
sparkle and fall to the power of a thousand from her body.

Stephen Orlen

Stephen Orlen was born in 1942 in Holyoke, Massachusetts. He has published four books of poems, *Sleeping on Doors* (Penumbra Press, 1976), *Separate Creatures* (Ironwood Press, 1977), *Permission to Speak* (Wesleyan University Press, 1978), and *A Place at the Table* (Holt, Rinehart, and Winston, 1981). He teaches at the University of Arizona.

Permission to Speak

For Norman Dubie

Mornings, from my upstairs window, I can see a gray
Stand of birch and further down a hickory grove,
Then the river that powers the mill that grinds flour.
Later, I'll eat the bread. Last night a spring snow
Blurred the countryside, and for a while I lost my way.

I thought I saw a boy in a crimson bathing suit
Whirl downstream on an inner tube; so I closed my eyes
On the old words for *birch* and *hickory* and *snow*
Like a novice in his cell discovering light,

Not the *One*, but another about which he'll remain
Silent all his life. I came to myself at the window.

That boy, already seen in memory, gives me permission to speak.
After a spring snow a father and son took a sleigh ride
Along the riverbank; and what the son couldn't see—
The particular hills and trees lost to whiteness—

Made him cry. The father snapped the reins, and pointed at
What must have been a red fox sliding past a birch:
"Look at that fellow in the bright nightgown!" From which
The son will date his love of the world, traveling swiftly past.

In Praise of Beverly

When you walked downstairs
And touched my root, God knows
What brought you homing there,
Barely fourteen, already known
As the town pump and proud
Of your clear attributes.
With breasts like new clouds,
You were my first, fallen angel.
I don't think we ever kissed,
But lay in a rocky ditch
All one awful summer night,
Alive, in love with heat.
At dawn we toasted marshmallows,
And when the fire caught
The weeds and lit the hillside,
You held me tight and whispered,
"Let's wait and see the fire
Engines come!" You got sent up early
To *The House of Good Shepherd*
Because the mothers were jealous,

Forgive them. When the friendly
Leering cop told me, "I heard
You dipped the wick in Beverly,"
I blushed and stammered, proud.
Then lied, forgive us all,
To save my skin. Beverly,
The night they took you away
I imagined myself in the ditch,
My flesh on fire, curled against
Your careless breathing,
Plotting love. I dreamt
Your face, and your hands
That parted the dark, were mine,
And groaned to share your misery,
But I found mine in good time.

The Madman's Wife

The unleashed dog walks back and forth. The cat
Leaps over the backyard fence. The owl
Shifts. Down this street the madman threads his way
Over curb and cobblestone and does not fall.
At dawn everyone smiles. The butcher has saved
The plumpest hen for him. The barber trims his hair.
The children tease him because he is there,
Less than a child, more than a lump. Later he sits
Across from me at breakfast, talking of suicide.
His plate becomes the tin plate prisoners use
To rattle their complaints. Last night in a bar, he says,
A woman disguised as a wife told him lie after lie.

There's no way to answer, so I put him to sleep.
What does he dream with his eyes open? I might
As well ask what a child dreams before speech
Gives him the power to lie. Out the window

The dog sees the shadow of the cat. The cat looks
After the owl. The owl keeps the moon in place.
To be mad, I know, is to be out of touch with life;
To touch a stranger in a bar and say, *My wife.*
But even the truth would be a betrayal. He wakes.
Read me a story, he begs, *tell me the names.*
I gaze into his white eyes, into the blue gas
Swirling in his heart. *Oh, poor us,* I begin.

The Drunken Man

There's nothing you can say to a man who drinks.
He rises in the gray mist of morning and lights
His cigarette, knowing that soon he'll be elsewhere.
Out in the world the old men sweep their shops
And one barber nods. The full-breasted woman
Airing her pillows, she smiles and squints,
And seeing it is only him, she closes the window.
But it doesn't matter. There's no way of hurting
A man who drinks. His wife floats in his pockets.
His father twists open the cap. His mother whispers
Drink, drink. He moves on down the street.

There are times when I feel obligated to speak.
I take my hands from my pockets.
I slide my glass away from him. In earnest
I'll say something—anything, the weather . . . my son—
And he'll argue at me from some place
I can't know because I'm not a drunk.
Perhaps when I stagger home my wife screams
To shut up, come to bed like a man. My face
Reddens, my shoes drop, I burrow into her flesh.

But a drunk is like a cloud, is like a ship
That sinks but never drowns, is like a feather bed.

Already it is noon. His mother and his father
Are half gone. He's weightless now.
I shouldn't waste pity on a drunken man. At night
In the bar I am his weakness, his hope,
And his family. If I argue back,
If I arm-wrestle him, if the bartender
Is embarrassed by my antics, it's time to go home.
Go home. Go home to my noisy wife.

Life Study

In the Museum Art School at night the men
    And women whose daily work doesn't require
Hand or eye to surrender to such intimacy,
    And the instructor who passes above us,
And everything around the room in shadow
    Manipulates to intensify the light
On the model's body, a woman's, a stranger.

The charcoal starts erratically, almost
    Of its own accord, like a nighthawk
Over the city, caught in the light,
    Lost in darkness, and soon you're hardly aware
Of time anymore, your hand moving to match
    The body's parts to the body's whole,
Nipple, then breast, and then the long waist,

The shadowed haunch like a blue whale
    Slowly, mightily rising out of water
Then back into the feeding dark. We have
    Seen this in the drawings of the Masters.
Clothed in clouds, an angel descends, touches
    Earth, and walks across the yard to water
The hyacinth, lost not in thought but in motion.

When the City Hall bells ring ten, the hands
   Tire, and flexures of the eye,
All the postures of flesh have blurred
   And the merciless overhead lights come on.
The model stretches, puts on her glasses,
   She pads naked and noisily around us—
A silvery carp flapping on a beach,

Or water, as it overflows its banks,
   Seeking its new shape—to see just how
We have seen her, not friends, not lovers,
   Not artists even, but men and women who have come
From our ordinary days toward beauty.
   She bends to pick up her clothes, and with
Her back to us puts them on slowly, bra

And shirt, panties, bluejeans, rubber thongs,
   The way a dreamer waking alone puts on
The morning in order to become a person.
   What burned cooly in shadow, in light,
What lay there in a stillness older than
   Statues of gods made from clay and spit,
Is a teenager in a Rolling Stones t-shirt.

* * *

I remember the men in *Luchini's* Saturday mornings
   Describing the women. The young men swept the air
With the largest motions like liars after
   Hours of no bass at the County Reservoir,
And a wink to the boy who caught the fish
   But didn't know yet that a woman's figure
Mattered enough to tell lies. The hands

Of the old men seemed to stutter. They might
   Have been shaping the map of their youth, Italy,
Stone house, stone wall, the horse nibbling grass,
   The cloud from the long neigh. The hands

489 / STEPHEN ORLEN

That had labored in stone or wood or dirt
   For years, when they were about to fly
From the body, vanished into their pockets.

*   *   *

If she could have watched the lump of charcoal
   Careful to reproduce, she might have thought:
Child playing dead at sunset after supper
   On the front lawn under the privet hedge;
Horizon, hill; hill after hill that someone
   Cares enough about to sit and draw.
We all love to look, and as we can't always

Touch, we walk home to a shape more familiar.
   The curves follow the light from the open
Door, and even as I sit on the bed
   And stare, and wake her, even as my breathing
Begins to echo hers, there is something
   I can't have, the drowsy neck, the hollow
Back of the knees, the ear that goes around,

The feet like a slum at dawn, the blue
   Nipples lanterns that guided me home.
There is also the body as a version of habit,
   Skin deep, the body that goes deeper
Pleasuring itself, pleasuring us,
   The body which is the hotel of the spirit,
Not mine, not hers, belonging to nothing and no one.

Gregory Orr

Elaine Winer

Gregory Orr was born in 1947 in Albany, New York. He received his undergraduate degree from Antioch College and his M.F.A. from Columbia University. He is the author of three collections of poetry, *Burning the Empty Nests* (1973), *Gathering the Bones Together* (1975), and *The Red House* (1980), all published by Harper and Row. His fourth collection of poems, *We Must Make a Kingdom of It*, will be published by Wesleyan University Press in 1986. A book of criticism, *Stanley Kunitz: An Introduction to the Poetry* (1984), was published by Columbia University Press. He has received fellowships from the National Endowment for the Arts and the Guggenheim Foundation. He teaches at the University of Virginia, where he is poetry consultant to *The Virginia Quarterly Review*.

Haitian Suite

1. At the Spring

I am the boy perched in the high
branches of a flamboyant tree,
hidden by its scarlet blossoms
and frondlike leaves. I watch
a Haitian girl squat to fill
her calabash at the gurgling spring

in the gully. She corks the bright
green gourd, hoists it to the cloth
pad on her head. Poised as a queen
under a heavy crown, she passes
beneath me with long, flat strides
and climbs a path that centuries
of naked feet have rubbed
thigh-deep in a limestone cliff.

2. River Ferry Landing

I straddle the mapou branch
above a cove where lotuses
root in muck and send their long
stalks up to flower. The raft
moves out from the far shore.
Ranged along its bow, six gleaming
tins from the slaughterhouse:
blunt teeth in a jaw.
When the raft arrives, I clamber
down the bank with others
from the government farm and climb
aboard. Crouching to grip
the handles, I peer into the thick
reek and mirror of cow's blood
we'll mix with mash for pigs.

3. Hôpital Albert Schweitzer

I pass the old beggar who sits,
sucking on a corncob pipe, in the shade
of a huge gray mapou tree,
its roots stuck with candle stubs,
gifts for the ghosts inside;

down the hill past the stench
of the courtyard where burros are tethered,
across the parched lawn where kin

of the sick squat beside charcoal
fires cooking rice and red beans;

up the steps and through a double set
of screen doors that never yet kept
malaria out. Mother, I'm coming,
down the halls toward the room
where you lie, coughing and soon to die.

And if I had known, as no one
did, that this would be the last visit, what
could I have brought? All I have:
the sweat and sights and smells
of Haiti under my straw hat.

4. The Curtains

She carves a woodblock print
and stamps with purple ink
a border for the linen curtains
she made for my room:
a row of Chinese wind-dragons,
each curled in a box,
biting its own tail.

I bend over my green,
linoleum-topped desk
and struggle by lamplight,
among broken struts and puddles
of spilt glue, to build
a plane that will fly.

                    *   *   *

Hunched over a desk
in another house, I hear
the curtains rustle.
Again she stands behind me,
quiet and tall as a lamp,

while I push clumsy words
around on a page, trying
to make them fit. Closing
my eyes, I feel a summer
breeze warm as breath cross
my face, coming all the way
from a grave in Haiti.

Morning Song

Sun on his face wakes him.
The boy makes his way down
through the spidery dark
of stairs to his breakfast
of cereal in a blue bowl.
He carries to the barn
a pie plate heaped
with vegetable scraps
for the three-legged deer.
As a fawn it stood still
and alone in high hay
while the red tractor
spiraled steadily inward,
mowing its precise swaths.
"I lived" is the song
the boy hears as the deer
hobbles toward him.
In the barn's huge gloom
light falls through cracks
the way swordblades
pierce a magician's box.

An Abandoned, Overgrown Cemetery in the Pasture Near Our House

March; Virginia

All last winter, starved cattle
trampled a muddy flatness
around it, stretched their throats
over the low stone wall
whose top is set with chunks
of quartz like teeth in a jaw.
Inside, vines cover the five
small cherry trees; brambles
everywhere. And the abyss
with its lips of weather
has already kissed away
the names carved on the stones.

*   *   *

I clear it with clippers;
slicing the prickly stalks
and tossing wiry tangles
of briars over the wall
to the cows. It's a warm day.
Working, I sluff off winter's
torpor as a snake sheds skin.
I find a wren's nest, cup
from which ghosts sip.
What's in it? Human tears,
their only food. Always it's empty,
always it's filled to the brim.

The Visitor

Where the spruce wood ends, I step
out on a mottled, sandstone ledge
above the narrow beach I walked as a boy
with my grandfather, searching
the tidewrack for fragments of white-flecked
green, Penobscot flint—arrow tip
or axe head three hundred years before.

And Grandpa's ten years dead
who left a cottage back up the path
where my grandmother sits, reading
her Bible, dying, having outlived
her son and daughters, alone
on this peninsula where the loon's
shrill laughter disturbs the quiet coves.

She believes in a heaven where those
she loves await her; here there is no
talk between us, even as her death draws near.
From a small cliff I watch a man moor
his skiff among black, ebb-tide rocks
and clamber toward me, crablike,
over the slippery, seaweed-covered shore.

End of August

We left our rented farmhouse for three weeks
to escape the heat, returned a day after
our landlord burned down the old barn
at the head of our drive, making room
for his retirement place. A few black
fragments still smoldered as we drove past.

A tractor had pulled the tin roof
flat across the scorched spot
like a handkerchief over the face of a corpse.

The closed-up house was dank and reeked of decay.
We carried chairs and rugs outside to air;
scrubbed walls and floors. Toward dusk I saw
a blue pickup stop where the barn had been—
a young man come to retrieve beams he'd dragged
into nearby weeds. We chatted about a cabin
he hoped to build near the mountains, then I left.
Glancing back I saw him: sweaty, soot-smeared,
a crow moving about the smoking ground.

I grew up among barns. When one caught fire
people gathered from half the county to watch
and talk. I mowed fields in late summer,
hoisted bales into the high lofts.
And played there too: with my brothers
building tunnels and forts, catching
pigeons, walking out on narrow beams to leap
to loose hay. In all that time
I never saw a barn burned on purpose.

A gray sky pressed down as I walked back
to our house. In the front yard two walnut
trees were already loosing yellow leaves.
I thought of T'ang poets writing laments
about their "snow-topped heads" when they
were hardly thirty. All evening I sat
on the porch with a white cloth and my books piled
beside me, wiping blue mold from the spines.

We Must Make a Kingdom of It

So that a colony will breed here,
love rubs together two words:
"I" and "she." How the long bone
of the personal pronoun
warms its cold length against her fur.

*　　*　　*

She plants the word "desire"
that makes the very air
amorous, that causes the light,
from its tall stalk, to bend down
until it almost kisses the ground.

*　　*　　*

It was green, I saw it—tendril
flickering from dry soil
like a grass snake's tongue;
call it "flame"—light
becomes life, what the word
wants, what the earth
in its turning
yearns for: to writhe and rise up,
even to fly briefly
like the shovefull over
the gravedigger's shoulder.

Simon Ortiz

Simon Ortiz was born in Albuquerque, New Mexico, in 1941. His first book, *Going for the Rain* (1976), was published by Harper & Row. Since then he has published four books of poetry, most recently *Fightin'* (1983), from Thunder's Mouth Press. Among his awards are two fellowships from the National Endowment for the Arts.

Marlene Foster-Ortiz

My Father's Song

Wanting to say things,
I miss my father tonight.
His voice, the slight catch,
the depth from his thin chest,
the tremble of emotion
in something he has just said
to his son, his song:

> We planted corn one Spring at Acu—
> we planted several times
> but this one particular time

I remember the soft damp sand
in my hand.

My father had stopped at one point
to show me an overturned furrow;
the plowshare had unearthed
the burrow nest of a mouse
in the soft moist sand.

Very gently, he scooped tiny pink animals
into the palm of his hand
and told me to touch them.
We took them to the edge
of the field and put them in the shade
of a sand moist clod.

I remember the very softness
of cool and warm sand and tiny alive mice
and my father saying things.

Hunger in New York City

Hunger crawls into you
from somewhere out of your muscles
or the concrete or the land
or the wind pushing you.

It comes to you, asking
for food, words, wisdom, young memories
of places you ate at, drank cold spring water,
or held somebody's hand,
or home of the gentle, slow dances,
the songs, the strong gods, the world
you know.

That is, hunger searches you out.
It always asks you,
How are you, son? Where are you?
Have you eaten well?
Have you done what you as a person
of our people is supposed to do?

And the concrete of this city,
the oily wind, the blazing windows,
the shrieks of automation cannot,
truly cannot, answer for that hunger
although I have hungered,
truthfully and honestly, for them
to feed myself with.

So I sang to myself quietly:
I am feeding myself
with the humble presence
of all around me;
I am feeding myself
with your soul, my mother earth;
make me cool and humble.
Bless me.

Juanita, Wife of Manuelito

after seeing a photograph of her in Dine Baa-Hani

I can see by your eyes
the gray in them like by Sonsela Butte,
the long ache
that comes about when I think
about where the road climbs
up onto the Roof Butte.

I can see
the whole sky
when it is ready to rain
over Whiskey Creek,
and a small girl
driving her sheep
and she looks so pretty
her hair tied up
with a length of yarn.

I can see
by the way you stare
out of a photograph
that you are a stern woman
informed by the history
of a long walk
and how it must have felt
to leave the canyons
and the mountains of your own land.

I can see, Navajo woman,
that it is possible for dreams
to occur, the prayers full of the mystery
of children, laughter, the dances,
my own humanity, so it can last unto forever.

That is what I want to teach my son.

A Story of How a Wall Stands

At Acu, there is a wall almost 400 years old which
supports hundreds of tons of dirt and bones—it's a
graveyard built on a steep incline—and it looks like
it's about to fall down the incline but will not for a
long time.

My father, who works with stone,
says, "That's just the part you see,
the stones which seem to be
just packed in on the outside,"
and with his hands put the stone and mud
in place. "Underneath
what looks like loose stone,
there is stone woven together.
He ties one hand over the other,
fitting like the bones of his hands
and fingers. "That's what is
holding it together."

"It is built that carefully,"
he says, "the mud mixed
to a certain texture," patiently
"with the fingers," worked
in the palm of his hand. "So that
placed between the stones, they hold
together for a long, long time."

He tells me those things,
the story of them worked
with his fingers, in the palm
of his hands, working the stone
and the mud until they become
the wall that stands a long, long time.

503 / SIMON ORTIZ

Greg Pape

Gay Chow

Greg Pape was born in Eureka, California, in 1947. He received his M.F.A. from the University of Arizona. He has published two collections of poetry, *Border Crossings* (1978) and *Black Branches* (1984), both from the University of Pittsburgh Press. His awards include the Robert Frost Fellowship in Poetry at Bread Loaf, the "Discovery"/*The Nation* Award, and fellowships from the National Endowment for the Arts. He is Bingham poet-in-residence at the University of Louisville.

My Happiness

That spring day
I stood in the new grass
and watched the man cutting steel
with an arc welder—
the man my mother had just married.
I watched as he leaned in his welder's mask
and held a blue-white star
to a steel rod until it was glowing with heat.
A cloud drifted in front of the sun
and darkened the land
the way sweat darkened his back.
Then with some slip of the body
or misjudgment of a man
given over wholly to his work
a piece of glowing metal
fell like a tiny meteor into his boot.

His hand went down
his fingers seared.
Then the smell of burnt flesh,
a groan of pain, and the crazy hopping.
He fumbled in his pocket for a knife,
slit open the boot and swatted the hot metal
off his ankle. What could I do?
I ran for mother and a bucket of water.
And that spring day I remember my happiness
as I poured the cold water over his wound
and she put her arm around his neck
and the sun came out
and the mysterious healing began
and he was saying oh jeezus
and she was saying oh honey.

In the City of Bogotá

The statue of a rich industrialist
stands in a small plaza
in the city of Bogotá.
People wait in line to whisper
their prayers in his bronze ear.
Pigeons and the leaves shadow them.
A *gamin*, one of the boys
of the streets, is asking for coins,
cigarettes, but receives instead
a small blessing, a hand
on the head and the sign of the cross.
Rain that was falling moments ago
glistens on the slick black hair
of the soldier at the curb
and on the barrel of his rifle.
Water beads are caught in the blue
wool of a woman's sweater, a woman

who looks at her shoes and waits.
A girl stares over the tops
of the buildings and listens still
to the rain moving away
over tin roofs toward the mountains,
a sound like the applause
of a distant multitude.
There must be girls all over
the world listening into the distance
like that. I don't know
what the soldier is thinking.
But I know the fatherless
wild boys of the streets.
And I know there must be
someone who will listen
without judgement to the secrets
and prayers that grow in us each day.
Water drips from the bronze ear
as the woman takes her turn there,
her hands hidden in the sleeves
of her sweater. As she whispers
the pigeons fly, funneling up
into the air above the city of Bogotá
to celebrate the end of rain,
each one a word resisting
everything that conspires to silence.

Sharks, Caloosahatchee River

It is so quiet. It is 1957.
You can place the year
by the fins of the new cars
lined up in the parking lot of The Gulf Motel.
Even in the middle of the day
the rooms are dark, rooms

where lovers thump their beds
against the walls, where someone
goes to sleep forever with the radio playing.
You can't hear the river in those rooms
although the river never stops.
It goes on flowing gray to silver
down through the glades and forests
where the people lived who named it
Caloosahatchee.

A boy opens a door and steps out
into the shock of sunlight, the flashing
chrome of bumpers and grills.
In the shadows between the cars
sparrows peck at the asphalt.
He watches as men line up on the dock
the bloody sharks they caught.
The fins gleam like the waxed fins
of the new cars. Their eyes don't close either.
After the snapshots and jokes
they heave the bodies back into the river
and stroll off to their separate rooms.

They say a dead shark
sinks so slowly its body
is dissolved by saltwater
before it reaches the bottom of the sea.
There in the Caloosahatchee, in the shadows
between the long bodies of sharks
the current pulls toward the Gulf.

Then it is Sunday. The boy's mother
still sleeping, he leaves the darkness
of the room with a quarter in his pocket
and walks a few hundred yards of sunlight
along the river to the Arcade Theater.
It's cool and dark, just a few kids waiting
for the matinee. The screen,
blank silver like the river. Dreaming
and quiet, he could be anyone. He is

the little brother of sharks, a boy
who slips into a car and guns the engine.
Tires burn, blue smoke shoots up, fins
slice the sunlight. Blank eyes and grill
grinning the car speeds across the parking lot
off the dock and into the river.
It sinks so fast, the river so shallow
you can hear the thud of rubber
on the bottom before white water calms
and it's gone.
The doors to the motel open
one by one, light streams in, people walk out
and gather as the boy steps dripping
from the river. No one speaks a word
but stares, as he does, at the water.
The only sound is the murmur of the river
as it moves toward the Gulf. They will listen
until they hear.

Or, more likely, the boy is knocked unconscious
and never steps from the river. The sheriff's
boats drag the bottom with nets and hooks.
Divers search for the body in the gray murk.
But he is gone, drifting with sharks, gone
in the silver glinting on the river.

The Porpoise

Today in the middle of Missouri
the temperature dropped forty
degrees in two hours.

Between St. Louis and Kansas City
the traffic was steady.
A banner of black smoke trailed

south from the power plant stack,
mercury slid down in glass.
By dusk the trees were swimming

in the wind. Rain
muted the sound of engines
and made the tires sing.

Then it was nickels and dimes
falling on the roof of The Blue Note
and The Pow-Wow Lounge.

Night came down wherever
it could, fused with the river,
fastened to the windows,

stood up and stretched
in the stunted fields of corn.
South of this darkness

a woman holds the lost warmth
on her skin. Her steady breathing
adding one more degree

to the quiet air around her
as she sits with a book in her lap
and stares out through the screen door

at some memory swimming
in the trees, a porpoise appearing
and disappearing in the Gulf.

And although the dishes need doing
and there's work in the morning
she's composing an idea of beauty—

the skin of the porpoise shines
with the light of two worlds,
this one and this one.

Jay Parini

Mark Brown

Jay Parini was born in 1948. He received an A.B. from Lafayette College and a Ph.D. from the University of St. Andrews, Scotland. His first book of poems, *Singing in Time* (1972), was published by J.W.B. Laing of Scotland, and a second, *Anthracite Country* (1982), was published by Random House. He is also the author of a critical study of Theodore Roethke (1979) from the University of Massachusetts Press and a novel, *The Love Run* (Atlantic-Little, Brown, 1980). He teaches at Middlebury College.

Amores (after Ovid)

An afternoon in sultry summer.
After swimming, I slept on the long divan,
dreaming of a tall brown girl.

Nearby, a din of waves
blasted in the jaws of rocks.
The green sea wrestled with itself
like a muscular beast in the white sun.

A tinkle of glasses woke me: Corinna!
She entered with fruit and wine.

I remember the motion of her hair
like seaweed across her shoulders.

Her dress: a green garment.
She wore it after swimming.
It pressed to the hollows of her body
and was beautiful as skin.

I tugged at the fringe, politely.
She poured out wine to drink.
"Shy thing," I whispered.

She held the silence with her breath,
her eyes to the floor, pretending,
then smiling: a self-betrayal.

In a moment she was naked.
I pulled her down beside me,
lively, shaking like an eel—
loose-limbed and slippery-skinned.
She wriggled in my arms at play.

When I kissed her closer
she was wet beneath me and wide as the sea.

I could think of nothing but the sun,
how it warmed my spine as
I hugged her, shuddering all white light,
white thighs. Need more be said
but that we slept as if
the world had died together with that day?

These afternoons are rare.

To His Dear Friend, Bones

The arguments against restraint
in love, in retrospect, seem quaint;
I would have thought this obvious
to you, at least, whose serious
pursuit of intellectual grace
is not less equal to your taste
for all things richly formed. No good
will come of what we force. I should
be hesitant to say how long
this shy devotion has gone on,
how days beyond account have turned
to seasons as we've slowly learned
to speak a common tongue, to find
the world's erratic text defined
and stabilized. I should be vexed
to mention time at all, except
that, even as I write, a blear
October dampness feels like fear
externalized; I number days
in lots of thirty—all the ways
we have for counting breaths, so brief,
beside the measures of our grief
and joy. So let me obviate
this cold chronology and state
more simply what I mean: it's sure
enough, the grave will make obscure
whatever fierce, light moments love
affords. I should not have to prove
by metaphysical displays
of wit how numerous are the ways
in which it matters that we touch,
not merely with our hearts; so much
depends upon the skin, dear bones,
with all its various, humid tones,
the only barrier which contrives
to keep us in our separate lives.

The Missionary Visits Our
Church in Scranton

He came to us every other summer
from the jungles of Brazil,
his gabardine suit gone shiny in the knees
from so much praying.

He came on the hottest Sunday, mid-July,
holding up a spear before our eyes,
the very instrument, we were told,
which impaled a brace of his Baptist colleagues.

The congregation wheezed in unison,
waiting for the slides: the savage women
dandling their breasts on tawny knees,
the men with painted buttocks
dancing in a ring.

The congregation loosened their collars,
mopped their brows, all praying
that the Lord would intervene.

Always, at the end, one saw the chapel:
its white-baked walls, the circle of women
in makeshift bras, the men in shirts.

They were said to be singing a song of Zion.
They were said to be wishing us well in Scranton.

Snake Hill

The dirt road rose abruptly through a wood
just west of Scranton, strewn by rusty wire,
abandoned chassis, bottles, bits of food.

We used to go there with our girls, those nights
in summer when the air like cellophane
stuck to your skin, scaling the frenzied heights

of teenage lust. The pebbles broke like sparks
beneath our tires; we raised an oily dust.
The headlights flickered skunk-eyes in the dark.

That way along the hill's illumined crown
was Jacob's ladder into heaven; cars
of lovers, angel-bright, drove up and down.

There was a quarry at the top, one strip
worked out, its cold jaws open, empty-mouthed.
A dozen cars could park here, hip to hip.

There I took Sally Jarvis, though we sat
for six hours talking politics. I was
Republican, and she was Democrat.

We talked our way through passion, holding hands;
the moon, gone egg-yolk yellow in the sky,
tugged firmly at our adolescent glands.

I kissed her once or twice, far too polite
to make a rude suggestion, while the stars
burned separately, hard as anthracite.

The city was a distant, pinkish yawn
behind our backs as we leant head to head.
The dead-end quarry held us there till dawn.

Molly Peacock

Molly Peacock was born in Buffalo, New York, in 1947. She holds an M.A. from Johns Hopkins University, and she is the author of two collections of poetry, *And Live Apart* (University of Missouri Press, 1980), and *Raw Heaven* (Random House, 1984). She has received fellowships from CAPS and the Ingram Merrill Foundation. She teaches at Friends Seminary in New York City.

Raymond Kopcho

Old Roadside Resorts

Summer is a chartreuse hell in the mountains,
green after green after green, the wet smell
of possibility in everything. "Doubt him?"
a memory of a friend's voice asks. Yes! "Well,
why do you love a man who's in a tangle
you yourself would never be in?" So I am,
the hypotenuse of a triangle
watching the other two sides in a jam
of history and pain and veils, like veils
of green washing over the mountain spines
on which perch the broken down summer jails,
pale boxes that housed Chassidim in the pines
years ago. They're richer now, and go elsewhere.
So mice, squirrels, spiders, and raccoons stay there.

The mountains are like the backs of friendly
dinosaurs who, if they heaved in their sleep,

would throw a small car all the way gently
to Syracuse. Moist follicular trees weep
and chatter. I used to be married, goddamn.
Like him, I was in the tangle I'll never be in.
From the third side I had to see the sham,
the last side, the last window to see in.
Inside stolen time and through time's arches
are these places, webby and dusty now,
mosquitoes humming among the old porches,
overgrown, sloping, askew. They are endowed,
the gnaw-footed dreams of passing animals' lairs,
with the vacant stateliness of claw-footed chairs.

So, When I Swim to the Shore

Living alone is like floating on blue
waters, arms out, legs down, in a wide bay
face to the sun on a brilliant white day,
the buildings of the city all around one,
millions of people doing what is done
in yellow buildings ringing a turquoise bay
in which one floats, in a lazy K
arms out, head back, legs spread beneath the brew
the clouds will make later on. One is at
the center of something of which one is
no more a part.

So, when I swim to the shore
and go home and lie down, lips blue, cunt cold, yet
clitoris hard and blue and I am still
alone—never again your finger or lip
or knuckle or two fingers or tongue tip—
what do you think I will do? Send you a bill
for my service as a shill in the carny game

you played with your wife? Hell, let's tame
our own monsters. There's this in being out of love:
I own every blue day I'm not a part of.

The Lull

The possum lay on the tracks fully dead.
I'm the kind of person who stops to look.
It was big and white with flies on its head,
a thick healthy hairless tail, and strong, hooked
nails on its raccoon-like feet. It was a full
grown possum. It was sturdy and adult.
Only its head was smashed. In the lull
that it took to look, you took the time to insult
the corpse, the flies, the world, the fact that we were
traipsing in our dress shoes down the railroad tracks.
"That's disgusting." You said that. Dreams, brains, fur
and guts: what we are. That's my bargain, the Pax
Peacock, with the world. Look hard, life's soft. Life's cache
is flesh, flesh, and flesh.

Now Look What Happened

I'm so sorry I got happy too late
to have children. Finally I met a man
I'd want to have them with, but I had to wait

so long because I lost my father to alcohol
and my sister to alcohol—my God,
what held me back wasn't my own hate wall,

was it? The almost endless waiting
for children who wouldn't grow up to grow up
kept me a child—it was a sort of mother baiting,

like bear baiting only with a child told
you be the mother now. Who cares
that I waited so long because I was *proud*

to *have* to help them? Those who helped me
might care. They might take a true pride,
not like the pride I lost, to know they helped me.

And the arms, hips, groin I trust in the man
I'd bear children for if I could bear them—
he will care, for this will mean he can

by existing restore my waiting. Having held hatred
beyond the time I could have breathed hatred
into a new life allowed me to love

because it was hatred I had to be emptied of,
being empty and deciding to love. My new trust lies
like a harbor a lost ship won't find, however it tries

or questions or waits. I'm sorry to have lost,
as you may be sorry about a chance you lost
or a way or a coin or a limb you lost.

Michael Pettit

Dara Wier

Michael Pettit was born in 1950. He received his B.A. from Princeton University, his M.A. from Hollins College, and his M.F.A. from the University of Alabama. His first book, *American Light* (1984), was published by the University of Georgia Press.

Fire and Ice

From my couch I rise, afire
with Zeno and cosmic conflagration,
to answer. Through the screen door
the mild faces of two Latter Day Saints
smile up at me like seal cubs
from an ice floe. Their shirts
are white, their blue suits creased,
their ponderous shoes tied.
Door to door go their days, face
to frowning face, but I
will not share their message.
Behind me the room floats
with the smoke of cigarettes,
one for each question I have.

Can they answer whether God
is the fiery mind of the world?
Whether chaos or order reigns,
whether it is collapse forever
or just for now? The one who is
the scrubbed blonde they all are
is speaking as I close the door.
His voice weakens like the cries
of a seal puzzled by his blood
splashed across the ice. Go, go.
Your time is up. *Thou art a little
soul bearing about a corpse.*

Herdsman

1.

Here I am whole, I know
at night what I'll find come
morning: skies violet in the west,
a crown of light to the east.
I'll wake, a rainbow:
I don't come out until the storm
is over. Dreams I leave behind.

Here I've learned the cycles last
and how to live within them,
with the brindle dog at my doorstep,
gnawing a bone dragged in from
the woods, dug from the green
circle of earth where I burn
and bury the cattle that winter kills.

And with this: huge red bulls
following their own breath
over the frosted pastures. Gaunt,
sleepless, rutting through the herd
as calves butt their mothers' bags
for more of the blue-white milk.
Here one gold day follows another.

2.

It is Euell Hitt's errant Brangus
cow again and there is one answer.
I unleash my curs at the edge
of the swamp thicket where she hides—
loco, motionless among black leaves
and shadows, waiting. It won't take
long: her scent is fresh, the story
old as those endless prairies of snow
where Arctic winds swirl around
the exhausted caribou, the circling
timber wolves. Winter by winter,
common cells dividing, moving slow
as ice, they've arrived. I hear
snarl and bellow and the brush
gives way: Euell's cow backs out
into the open. Hornless, head lowered,
she stumbles with rage, feigning charges
that the dogs take lightly, grinning,
driving her in flurries toward
the pens, the short ride home.
Black as the deepest wood, in the pens
she stands shivering, bright blood
on her lips, tongue hanging tipped
with blood. With one look she tells me
it is not over, it will never be.

3.

I dream of the night
I'll do it, undress and walk out
into the fields, unearthly,
lit by the crescent moon.
Where there was a hillside,
cows and their calves bedded down,
a herd of steady breathing, breathing,
the wind will travel the hill
to me alone. The grass will move,
thick and tall and untouched
until I lie down, and sleep.
It is in sleep she comes to me,
curious, hesitant, ready
to break at my first motion.
With her rough black tongue
she licks the back of my neck,
my cheek, my eyes. I know, I know—
she has been everywhere, looking
for me. There is no hope unless
I give in and never go back.

Sunday Stroll

Who is this man out walking
his miniature horse on a leash?
It trots by his knee to keep up,
too small for the smallest child.
And who's the woman with him,
pushing a pram down the strict sidewalk?
All along Main Avenue the azaleas
are opening their vivid eyes
to watch, amazed. In the stroller

sits a little black dog too happy
to behave. He chirps like a bird
and birds chirp back. Purple martins
in the air, robins on the lawns.
And why not happy? The sun and wind
are warm; Easter with its resurrection
and parade is only two weeks away.
At any moment the double oak doors
of the First Baptist Church of Northport
will swing open to the bright
mysterious world where my friend,
his wife, his tiny horse and dog
stroll along serene and sanctified.
Where is it they go? I remember
one morning in Mexico, turning
a corner, coming upon a man and woman
wrestling a squealing hog
down the steep cobblestone street.
He had a stout rope to pull;
she had the hog's curly, crappy tail.
They'd heave together, get nowhere
and have to stop. Breathing
heavily, they wiped their sweaty faces
and sat on the hog. All three rested
together. *Vamos al matadero*
the man told me. *We are going
to the butcher* he said, smiling,
scratching the hog's pink ear
as the sun poured down its benediction.

A Day in My Union Suit

Here, at last, is the fever
at sunrise, chills, the head
I can't lift from the pillow.

Each breath burns from
within, the quilts around me
become the whole world.
When I realize I won't die,
I can almost smile: nothing
could make me move.
The windows fill with cold
light, cattle in the fields
are rising. I see myself
loading hay into the truck,
riding over the hard ground,
counting new calves, hoping
that I won't find trouble.
I smile: right now, as
I breathe and let my eyes
close, there is probably trouble.

Robert Pinsky

Robert Pinsky was born in Long Beach, New Jersey, in 1940. He was educated at Rutgers University and Stanford University. His three books of poetry are *Sadness And Happiness* (1975), *An Explanation of America* (1979), both from Princeton University Press, and *History of My Heart* (The Ecco Press, 1984). He is the co-translator (with Robert Hass) of *The Separate Notebooks* by Czeslaw Milosz and the author of *The Situation of Poetry*. He has received awards from the National Institute of Arts and Letters and the Guggenheim Foundation. He teaches at the University of California, Berkeley.

El Bailey

December Blues

At the bad time, nothing betrays outwardly the harsh findings,
The studies and hospital records. Carols play.

Sitting upright in the transit system, the widowlike women
Wait, hands folded in their laps, as monumental as bread.

In the shopping center lots, lights mounted on cold standards
Tower and stir, condensing the blue vapour

Of the stars; between the rows of cars people in coats walk
Bundling packages in their arms or holding the hands of children.

Across the highway, where a town thickens by the tracks
With stores open late and creches in front of the churches,

Even in the bars a businesslike set of the face keeps off
The nostalgic pitfall of the carols, tugging. In bed,

How low and still the people lie, some awake, holding the carols
Consciously at bay, Oh Little Town, enveloped in unease.

Local Politics

A *Section from* An Explanation of America
(a poem to my daughter)

And so the things the country wants to see
Are like a nest made out of circumstance;
And when, as in the great old sermon "The Eagle
Stirreth Her Nest," God like a nesting eagle
Pulls out a little of the plush around us
And lets the thorns of trial, and the bramble,
Stick through and scrape and threaten the fledgling soul,
We see that that construction of thorn and bramble
Is like a cage: the tight and sheltering cage
Of Law and circumstance, scraping through the plush
Like death—whenever the eagle stirreth her nest,
The body with its bony cage of law
And politics, the thorn of death and taxes.

You, rich in rhetoric and indignation,
The jailbird-lawyer of the Hunnewell School,
Come home from some small, wicked parliament
To elaborate a new theme: forceful topics
Touching the sheeplike, piggish ways of that tyrant
And sycophantic lout, the Majority.
The two lame cheers for democracy that I

Borrow and try to pass to you ("It is
The worst of all the forms of government,
Except for all the others"—Winston Churchill)
You brush aside: Political Science bores you,
You prefer the truth, and with a Jesuit firmness
Return to your slogan: "Voting *is not* fair."

I have another saw that I can scrape
For you, out of the hoard of antique hardware,
Cliches and Great Ideas, quaintly-toothed
Black ironwork that we heap about our young:
Voting is one of the *"necessary evils."*
Avoid all groups and institutions, they
Are necessary evils: necessary
Unto the general Happiness and Safety,
And evil because they are deficient in being.
Such is the hardware; and somewhere in between
The avoidance and the evil necessity
We each conclude a contract with the Beast.

America is, as Malcolm X once said,
A prison. And that the world and all its parts
Are also prisons (Chile, the Hunnewell School,
One's own deficient being, each prison after
Its own degree and kind), does not diminish
Anything that he meant about his country:
When the Dan Ryan Expressway in Chicago
Was flooded, "Black youths" who the paper said
Pillaged the stranded motorists like beached whales
Were rioting prisoners . . . a weight of lead
Sealed in their hearts was lighter for some minutes
Amid the riot.
                    Living inside a prison,
Within its many other prisons, what
Should one aspire to be? a kind of chaplain?
But chaplains, I have heard, are often powers,
Political, within their prisons, patrons
And mediators between the frightened groups:
Blue People, Gray People, and their constricting fears,
The mutual circumstance of ward and warder.

527 / ROBERT PINSKY

No kind of chaplain ever will mediate
Among the conquering, crazed immigrants
Of El Camino and the Bergen Mall,
The Jews who dream up the cowboy films, the Blacks
Who dream the music, the people who dream the cars
And ways of voting, the Japanese and Basques
Each claiming a special sense of humor, as do
Armenian photo-engravers, and the people
Who dream the saws: "*You cannot let men live
Like pigs, and make them freemen, it is not safe,*"
The people who dream up the new diseases
For use in warfare, the people who design
New shapes of pants, and sandwiches sumptuous
Beyond the dreams of innocent Europe: crazed
As carpet-bombing or the Berlin Airlift—
Crazed immigrants and prisoners, rioting
Or else, alone as in the secrecy
Of a narrow bunk or cell, whittling or painting
Some desperate weapon or crude work of art:
A spoon honed to a dagger or a bauble,
A pistol molded from a cake of soap,
A fumbling poem or a lurid picture
Urgent and sentimental as a tattoo. . . .
The Dorians, too, were conquering immigrants,
And hemmed in by their own anarchic spirits
And new peninsula, they too resorted
To invented institutions, and the vote,
With a spirit nearly comic, and in fear.

The plural-headed Empire, manifold
Beyond my outrage or my admiration,
Is like a prison which I leave to you
(And like a shelter)—where the people vote,
And where the threats of riot and oppression
Inspire the inmates as they whittle, scribble,
Jockey for places in the choir, or smile
Passing out books on weekdays.
                                On the radio,
The FM station that plays "All Country and Western"

Startled me, when I hit its button one day,
With a voice—inexplicable and earnest—
In Vietnamese or Chinese, lecturing
Or selling, or something someone wanted broadcast,
A paid political announcement, perhaps. . . .
"All politics is local politics"
Said Mayor Daley (in pentameter):
And this then is the locus where we vote,
Prisonyard fulcrum of knowledge, fear and work—
Nest where an Eagle balances and screams,
The wild bird with its hardware in its claws.

The Figured Wheel

The figured wheel rolls through shopping malls and prisons,
Over farms, small and immense, and the rotten little downtowns.
Covered with symbols, it mills everything alive and grinds
The remains of the dead in the cemeteries, in unmarked graves and oceans.

Sluiced by salt water and fresh, by pure and contaminated rivers,
By snow and sand, it separates and recombines all droplets and grains,
Even the infinite sub-atomic particles crushed under the illustrated,
Varying treads of its wide circumferential track.

Spraying flecks of tar and molten rock it rumbles
Through the Antarctic station of American sailors and technicians,
And shakes the floors and windows of whorehouses for diggers and smelters
From Bethany, Pennsylvania to a practically nameless, semi-penal New Town

In the mineral-rich tundra of the Soviet northernmost settlements.
Artists illuminate it with pictures and incised mottoes
Taken from the Ten-Thousand Stories and the Register of True Dramas.
They hang it with colored ribbons and with bells of many pitches.

With paints and chisels and moving lights they record
On its rotating surface the elegant and terrifying doings
Of the inhabitants of the Hundred Pantheons of major Gods
Disposed in iconographic stations at hub, spoke and concentric bands,

And also the grotesque demi-Gods, Hopi gargoyles and Ibo dryads.
They cover it with wind-chimes and electronic instruments
That vibrate as it rolls to make an all-but-unthinkable music,
So that the wheel hums and rings as it turns through the births of stars

And through the dead-world of bomb, fireblast and fallout
Where only a few doomed races of insects fumble in the smoking grasses.
It is Jesus oblivious to hurt turning to give words to the unrighteous,
And is also Gogol's feeding pig that without knowing it eats a baby chick

And goes on feeding. It is the empty armor of My Cid, clattering
Into the arrows of the credulous unbelievers, a metal suit
Like the lost astronaut revolving with his useless umbilicus
Through the cold streams, neither energy nor matter, that agitate

The cold, cyclical dark, turning and returning.
Even in the scorched and frozen world of the dead after the holocaust
The wheel as it turns goes on accreting ornaments.
Scientists and artists festoon it from the grave with brilliant

Toys and messages, jokes and zodiacs, tragedies conceived
From among the dreams of the unemployed and the pampered,
The listless and the tortured. It is hung with devices
By dead masters who have survived by reducing themselves magically

To tiny organisms, to wisps of matter, crumbs of soil,
Bits of dry skin, microscopic flakes, which is why they are called "great,"
In their humility that goes on celebrating the turning
Of the wheel as it rolls unrelentingly over

A cow plodding through car-traffic on a street in Iasi,
And over the haunts of Robert Pinsky's mother and father

And wife and children and his sweet self
Which he hereby unwillingly and inexpertly gives up, because it is
There, figured and pre-figured in the nothing-transfiguring wheel.

Ralegh's Prizes

And Summer turns her head with its dark tangle
All the way toward us; and the trees are heavy,
With little sprays of limp green maple and linden
Adhering after a rainstorm to the sidewalk
Where yellow pollen dries in pools and runnels.

Along the oceanfront, pink neon at dusk:
The long, late dusk, a light wind from the water
Lifting a girl's hair forward against her cheek
And swaying a chain of bulbs.

                  In luminous booths,
The bright, traditional wheel is on its rachet,
And ticking gaily at its little pawl;
And the surf revolves; and passing cars and people,
Their brilliant colors—all strange and hopeful as Ralegh's
Trophies: the balsam, the prizes of untried virtue,
Bananas and armadillos that a Captain
Carries his Monarch from another world.

Faeryland

Thin snow, and the first small pools of dusk
Start to swell from the low places of the park,

The swathe of walks, rises and plantings seeming
As it turns gray to enlarge—as if tidal,

A turbulent inlet or canal that reaches to divide
Slow dual processionals of carlights on the street,

The rare vague beacon of a bar or a store.
Shapes of brick, soiled and wet, yaw in the blur.

Elder, sullen, the small mythical folk
Gather in the scraps of dark like emigrants on a deck,

Immobile in their fur boots and absurd court finery.
They are old, old; though they stand with a straight elegance,

Their hair flutters dead-white, they have withered skin.
Between a high collar and an antic brim

The face is collapsed, or beaked like a baby bird's.
To them, our most ancient decayed hopes

Are a gross, infantile greed. The city itself,
Shoreline muffled in forgotten need and grief,

To us cold as a stone Venus in the snow, for them
Shows the ham-fisted persistence of the new-born,

Hemming them to the crossed shadows of cornice and porch,
Small darknesses of fence-weeds and streetside brush:

We make them feel mean, it has worn them out,
Watching us; they stir only randomly to mete

Some petty stroke of revenge—arbitrary, unjust,
Striking our old, ailing or oppressed

Oftener than not. An old woman in galoshes
Plods from the bus, head bent in the snow, and falls,

Bruising her hip, her bags spilled in the wet.
The Old Ones watch with small grave faces, nearly polite:

As if one of them had willed a dry sour joke, a kind of pun—
A small cruel fall, lost in a greater one.

It means nothing, no more than as if to tease her
They had soured her cow's milk, or the cat spilled a pitcher,

Costing her an hour's pleasure weeding in the heat,
Grunting among the neat furrows and mounds. Tonight,

In the cold, she moans with pursed face, stoops to the street
To collect her things. Less likely, they might

Put the fritz on the complex machines in the tower
Of offices where she works—jam an elevator

Between floors, giving stranded bosses and workers a break,
Panicking some of them, an insignificant leak

Or let in some exquisite operation bobbing
In the vast, childlike play of movement

That sends cars hissing by them in the night:
The dim city whose heedless, clouded heart

Tries them, and apes them, the filmy-looking harbor
Hard in a cold pale storm that falls all over.

Dying

Nothing to be said about it, and everything—
The change of changes, closer or further away:
The Golden Retriever next door, Gussie, is dead,

Like Sandy, the Cocker Spaniel from three doors down
Who died when I was small; and every day
Things that were in my memory fade and die.

Phrases die out: first, everyone forgets
What doornails are; then after certain decades
As a dead metaphor, *"dead as a doornail"* flickers

And fades away. But someone I know is dying—
And though one might say glibly, "everyone is,"
The different pace makes the difference absolute.

The tiny invisible spores in the air we breathe,
That settle harmlessly on our drinking water
And on our skin, happen to come together

With certain conditions on the forest floor,
Or even a shady corner of the lawn—
And overnight the fleshy, pale stalks gather,

The colorless growth without a leaf or flower;
And around the stalks, the summer grass keeps growing
With steady pressure, like the insistent whiskers

That grow between shaves on a face, the nails
Growing and dying from the toes and fingers
At their own humble pace, oblivious

As the nerveless moths, that live their night or two—
Though like a moth a bright soul keeps on beating,
Bored and impatient in the monster's mouth.

The Street

Streaked and fretted with effort, the thick
Vine of the world, red nervelets
Coiled at its tips.

All roads lead from it. All night
Wainwrights and upholsterers work finishing
The wheeled coffin

Of the dead favorite of the Emperor,
The child's corpse propped seated
On brocade, with yellow

Oiled curls, kohl on the stiff lids.
Slaves throw petals on the roadway
For the cortege, white

Languid flowers shooting from dark
Blisters on the vine, ramifying
Into streets. On mine,

Rockwell Avenue, it was embarrassing:
Trouble—fights, the police, sickness—
Seemed never to come

For anyone when they were fully dressed.
It was always underwear or dirty pyjamas,
Unseemly stretches

Of skin showing through a torn housecoat.
Once a stranger drove off in a car
With somebody's wife,

And he ran after them in his undershirt
And threw his shoe at the car. It bounced
Into the street

Harmlessly, and we carried it back to him;
But the man had too much dignity
To put it back on,

So he held it and stood crying in the street:
"He's breaking up my home," he said,
"The son of a bitch

Bastard is breaking up my home." The street
Rose undulant in pavement-breaking coils
And the man rode it,

Still holding his shoe and stiffly upright
Like a trick rider in the circus parade
That came down the street

Each August. As the powerful dragonlike
Hump swelled he rose cursing and ready
To throw his shoe—woven

Angular as a twig into the fabulous
Rug or brocade with crowns and camels,
Leopards and rosettes,

All riding the vegetable wave of the street
From the John Flock Mortuary Home
Down to the river.

It was a small place, and off the center,
But so much a place to itself, I felt
Like a young prince

Or aspirant squire. I knew that *Ivanhoe*
Was about race. The Saxons were Jews,
Or even Coloreds,

With their low-ceilinged, unbelievably
Sour-smelling houses down by the docks.
Everything was written

Or woven, ivory and pink and emerald—
Nothing was too ugly or petty or terrible
To be weighed in the immense

Silver scales of the dead: the looming
Balances set right onto the live, dangerous
Gray bark of the street.

The New Saddhus

Barefoot, in unaccustomed clouts or skirts of raw muslin,
With new tin cup, rattle or scroll held in diffident hands
Stripped of the familiar cuffs, rings, watches, the new holy-men

Avoid looking at their farewelling families, an elaborate
Feigned concentration stretched over their self-consciousness and terror,
Like small boys nervous on the first day of baseball tryouts.

Fearful exalted Coptic tradesman; Swedish trucker; Palestinian doctor;
The Irish works foreman and Lutheran optometrist from St. Paul:
They line up smirking or scowling, feeling silly, determined,

All putting aside the finite piercing restlessness of men
Who in this world have provided for their generation: O they have
Swallowed their wives' girlhoods and their children's dentistry,

Dowries and tuitions. And grown fat with swallowing they line up
Endless as the Ganges or the piles of old newspapers at the dumps,
Which may be blankets for them now; intense and bathetic

As the founders of lodges, they will overcome fatigue, self-pity, desire,
O Lords of mystery, to stare endlessly at the sun till the last
Red retinal ghost of actual sight is burned utterly away,

And still turn eyes that see no more than the forehead can see
Daily and all day toward the first faint heat of the morning.
Ready O Lords to carry one kilo of sand more each month,

More weight and more, so the fabulous thick mortified muscles
Lurch and bulge under an impossible tonnage of stupid,
Particulate inertia, and still O Lords ready, men and not women

And not young men, but the respectable Kurd, Celt, Marxist
And Rotarian, chanting and shuffling in place a little now
Like their own pimply, reformed-addict children, as they put aside

The garb, gear, manners and bottomless desires of their completed
Responsibilities; they are a shambles of a comic drill-team
But holy, holy—holy, becoming their own animate worshipful

Soon all but genderless flesh, a cooked sanctified recklessness—
O the old marks of elastic, leather, metal razors, callousing tools,
Pack straps and belts, fading from their embarrassed bodies!

Katha Pollitt

Deborah Bell

Katha Pollitt was born in New York City in 1949 and was educated at Radcliffe College. Her first book, *Antarctic Traveller* (Knopf, 1982), received the National Book Critics Circle Award for Poetry. She has received fellowships from the Ingram Merrill Foundation, CAPS, and the National Endowment for the Arts. She is literary editor of *The Nation*.

Night Blooming Flowers

In the vacant lot behind the hospital
where rainbeaten trash, smashed bottles, gutted bedsprings
sprawl in a flyblown drowse among cinders and slag

how suddenly
dusk takes on strangeness that is more
than blue air and the blue

transient aspect of things.
Look at the ground now, how it pales and glows
as one by one, night wakers—

catchfly, dame's violet, evening lychnis—
petal by petal unfold their secret hearts
and lift to the moon a whiteness like the moon.

Why does such candor move me
more than these failed acres?
I have cherished my refusals,

I have loved them
as if they were love. I stand,
as in the nineteenth-century photograph

the women of the house, four generations
in formal black, as for a great reception,
stood breathless, hushed in the shadowy conservatory

while under its glass dome
the night blooming cereus
strained its whole being to an inward rhythm

stiffened its thick stalk
and pulsed out its one flower
huge, fleshy, heavy-scented, glowing, green . . .

and later little Alice Emmeline
was carried upstairs by her father, half asleep,
not understanding what it was she'd seen
but trusting it, a mystery that would keep.

Archaeology

You knew the odds on failure from the start,
that morning you first saw, or thought you saw,
beneath the heatstruck plains of a second-rate country
the outline of buried cities. A thousand to one
you'd turn up nothing more than the rubbish heap
of a poor Near Eastern backwater:
a few chipped beads,
splinters of glass and pottery, broken tablets
whose secret lore, laboriously deciphered,
would prove to be only a collection of ancient grocery lists.
Still, the train moved away from the station without you.

How many lives ago
was that? How many choices?
Now that you've got your bushelful of shards
do you say, *give me back my years*
or wrap yourself in the distant
glitter of desert stars,
telling yourself it was foolish after all
to have dreamed of uncovering
some fluent vessel, the bronze head of a god?
Pack up your fragments. Let the simoom
flatten the digging site. Now come
the passionate midnights in the museum basement
when out of that random rubble you'll invent
the dusty market smelling of sheep and spices,
streets, palmy gardens, courtyards set with wells
to which, in the blue of evening, one by one
come strong veiled women, bearing their perfect jars.

A Discussion of the Vicissitudes of
History Under a Pine Tree

The moment is what moves us, after all:
as here, in Taiga's painting,
the smoke-colored sky
swells like a breath, gentle,
already full of evening,
and the mountains, rounded by mist or distance,
rise like the natural
completion of a thought.
The light is a neutral fact of November or February,
a calm between weathers.

Under a pine, two old friends consider
vanished cities, conquests. Think of it,
all those horses: dust. And the men who rode them.
One speaks of last year's leaves,
dry stalks
rattling in the withered field;
the other gestures
to the usual changeless emblems:
pine, sky, mountain . . .

And what is there to say?
The truth is, neither
can really believe this has happened to him,
that he, who recalls the precise
glance of light and each sharp leaf
in a garden glimpsed on a back street fifty years ago,
has become someone else
who sits
in a bare field watching the slow
late glow of afternoon
tinge with faintest rose the monochromatic
landscape of an ambiguous season:

hills neither gray nor green
sky neither blue nor gray.

In Memory

*"But can we not sometimes speak of a darkening
(for example) of our memory-image?"*
                                        —*Wittgenstein*

Over the years, they've darkened, like old paintings
or wainscotting in a damp house in the country,
until now the streets where you roller-skated brim with twilight,
your mother drinks morning coffee from a cup of shadows,
and out in the garden, the hardest August noon
is washed with a tender, retrospective blue—
like woodsmoke, or the shade of an unseen lilac.
Upstairs, you can hardly make yourself out, a child
peering out the window, speechless with happiness,
reciting your future in an endless summer dusk.

At first, this maddened you. You wanted to see
your life as a rope of diamonds: permanent, flashing.
Strange, then, how lately this darkening of memory moves you,
as though what it claimed it also made more true,
the way discoloring varnish on a portrait
little by little engulfs the ornate background—
the overstuffed sofa, the velvet-and-gold festoons
framing an elegant vista—but only deepens
the calm and serious face. The speaking eyes.

Seal Rock

They won't come to you. These nights, you could sit for a year
on the dock behind Arthur's Gift Shop and General Store
before you'd spot with your flashlight
a single silk-backed bather
nosing the trash fish dumped off the lobster boats,
lured to your human light from the night-black water.

Those visits, if they ever took place, ended long ago,
though the fishermen did no harm
to the silver-furred luck-bearing ones
who kept the cold caves we left and the waves no squall
spills the green-glass fullness of—
and even half-believed the old tales:

how they floated this drowner, nudged that skiff off rocks.
We bore them, perhaps. Or simply, their minds are elsewhere.
At any rate no girl
has married their king in centuries,
no sailor learned any secret from them worth shipwreck.

And yet, as the holiday ferry
smacks its smart salt-stiffened flags in the wind
we lean like children over the side: to lee
gleams the craggy castle to which they've withdrawn.
Huge, simple, sleek as Maillol bronzes, they
sprawl in the sun, or powerfully dive
and surface jewelled with spray

then lumber with heavy grace back up to their mates.
They are historyless, at peace. As our boat chuffs by,
the wind floats back fish stench
and a gabble of barks, sharp cries
that remind you of nothing but gulls or the creaking of rope.
They are no Sirens, we only weekend trippers.
Whatever their language, they are not speaking to us.

Thomas Rabbitt

Thomas Rabbitt was born in 1943 in Boston. He received his A.B. from Harvard College, his M.A. from Johns Hopkins University, and his M.F.A. from the University of Alabama. He is the author of two collections of poetry, *Exile* (University of Pittsburgh Press, 1975), winner of the U.S. Award of the International Poetry Forum, and *The Booth Interstate* (Knopf, 1981). He teaches at the University of Alabama.

County Roads

(For Richard Hugo)

1.

You search out Bull Slough Road to slake your thirst
For evidence of how things get a name.
You find instead the preservation plaque:
John Byler built a road not far from here
In 1822, Alabama's first.
First is something, reason enough for fame.

When you find John Byler's road you'll go back,
Northport to the Tennessee, where somewhere
You will have to pay a toll. Settlers did.
When Union soldiers came the road was free
And now so free it isn't even here.
You'd turn for home except your truck has slid
Into the mud and stopped against a tree.
If the cows could, they'd tell you that you're there.

2.

No one drives Bone Camp Road expecting more
Of life, especially yours—one more marker
To tell you why you've turned this far from home
On so remote a road. The Bone Camp Church
Is Methodist, the graveyard full, but poor.
Since 1853 nobody's home
Who counts, except perhaps the Beards. You search
The stones for clues. The afternoon grows darker
Than it should and the road you followed in
Is running out without you. Pavement rots
Under your wheels. The Choctaw camp shows through
The asphalt: this way to an extinction.
One reason for the ribs that look like ruts
Can't be traffic. There's no one here but you.

The Weight Room

The weight room tiled with mirrors is no place
To want to be alone. The modesty
You claim is just another of your lies.
Cosmetic is the word you use for lifting
As if the weights gave strength to lift your face

Out of the grave. The mirror's surgery
Reverses everything except the eyes.
Bodybuilding might be one way of shifting
Your body's guilt back into your own hands.
You might believe the young man opposite
Is you, pumping up with curls—but he smiles,
A thing you could not do. Just where he stands
Is where you want to be—if you could fit
And not bloody your body or the tiles.

Rape

The men chase the boy into the hog shed;
When the pigs panic and the walls collapse,
He runs to the house, to his mother's bed
Where one man finds him underneath. He laughs.
The boy scurries deeper into the dust.
More men arrive. He doesn't understand.
An unrolled condom strikes out like a snake.
A pink fur slipper fills the air with must.
The man's laughter sounds outdoors, like the wind
Over the storm cellar. He smells the smoke
But will not move until his mother comes.
She never does. While the dust ruffle glows
Like a flaming sun on four horizons,
The men turn away and the boy's death grows.

The Dancing Sunshine Lounge

The calendar is ironic. The stripper dances
On my table, her toes awash in beer.
Ash Wednesday drags in once a year. This year
Thursday brings a dust storm from the west.
The day is airborne Oklahoma, a breast
That Lent would like to bare against the east.
The sun comes closer. A silver cast—
Her shield, this target—tarnishes the air.
The stripper's memorial body chances
My hands, my broken glass. She can't care.
We are washing down traildust, we rich dead
Who have blown in, frantic, on the wind,
And she thinks we must be paralyzed with fear.
She can't care. She loves us each like a friend.

Casino Beach

At night the sand wears a corsage of flesh.
She can smell it. The boy is hard, strange,
A summer storm moving in to plague her
With the things he's done. Over the Heights
The wind brings fog. Wind and fog derange
Her new life. Under them, the phosphors flash
And she cries because the season's almost over.
She has waited all her life for these nights.
The boy's thin face disappears. He has tried.
He cannot take her in before she dies.
She tells him she has built a wall
Around herself, an illness, what the papers call
Cancer. She is a fist, a thing everyone pries
Open finger after finger for the small change inside.

Gargoyle

He looks down to watch the river twist
Like a dead vein into the suburbs.
From his height it is all flat, stone-grey
And ugly. He knows he himself is hideous,
Sterile, the artist's pleasantry set up
To scare off devils. He knows nothing.
He is stunning in his pure impossibility.
Enough cherry trees blossom along the river.
Enough paired lovers gaze through the pink air.
Drab birds, disguised as money, sing prettily
And the sun blinds itself in the water.
He hears laughter. He knows nothing.
When the lovers glance up, they take him in.
Their looks are incidental, monumental, sweeping.

Bin Ramke

Bin Ramke was born in 1947 in Port Neches, Texas, and was educated at Louisiana State University, the University of New Orleans, and Ohio University. His first book, *The Difference Between Night and Day* (1978), won the Yale Series of Younger Poets Award for 1977. *White Monkeys* was published by the University of Georgia Press in 1981. He teaches at the University of Denver.

Kenneth Ramke

The Green Horse

Who could be smaller than this child
on the four-horse carousel which plays
the Washington Post March
in front of the discount store?
He cares. His father
counts the time lost more than the quarter.

The child refuses distraction.
He holds tightly and watches
the neck of the yellow horse
while riding the red
in a kind of kept time.

We remember wanting to ride
in front of the supermarkets,
we all look at the child
for an embarrassed moment before
pushing the revolving door. We look
to see if he is there when we come out again.

He cannot be there. No father
will put more than two quarters in,
too much pain. I have never seen
more than two children at one time
on a four-horse carousel. I have never seen

the money removed.
What would it be like to see someone
across the room at a party,
to call out "We met once
twenty years ago,
in front of K-Mart, I was on
the blue horse, you were on the green." To call out.

The Magician

From up my own sleeve I came
and chose my father,
a volunteer from the audience.
I told him to stand
there, in front
of the buzzing saw.
I grabbed him by his long
ears and pulled him
into the hat with me.
There in the silky dark
we slept.

I used to know lots of tricks.
Pick a card, any.
I memorized a card a week
for a year. I turned
rabbits into plowshares.
I escaped from every kind
of closure.

In the hat we slept together
dreaming each our games
of solitaire.
We awoke old;
forgetting everything
we bowed goodbye:
I last saw him walking away
trying to wipe his eyes
with a white handkerchief
that kept becoming a pigeon.

The Obscure Pleasure of the Indistinct

Under light soft as seawater, sounds
brush lightly past: shiver of laughter
from a pale woman's flimsy neck,
the rustle of linen under your own
hand resting on the table. You bite
into the dark meat of the pheasant,
you almost scream—you would,
were it not for your exquisite
parentage. Nestled in the stained
crevice of a molar a piece
of lead, shot, twice brutally painful:

and for a second time the bird flies
in your mind, and the long stiff

feathers brush the long brown leaf
on a cold autumn morning. Then
a sip of Pouilly-Fuisse, cool
on the tongue, soothing. Sounds
from the kitchen again are muffled, vague.

Why I Am Afraid to Have Children

A morning like others, and a father
stood there, black against the light.
The screen of the door buckled softly
in brief wind, the morning heat
already rising.

This ground never made anyone rich,
least of all his father. So his job was in town
and he didn't know how sad he was playing
with his toy farm, paying for it.

I didn't know. I was a child
as small as I would ever be. It is
only a memory, a ragged edge,
and perhaps meaningless. A spindly morning glory
glowed the only spot of color
over his shoulder.

Sadness and Still Life

In a heavy bowl two pears
have room to roll odd paths,
random paths from dents
in their fine gritted skins.

She carries the bowl back
to decorate the table. Dishes
drip on the drainboard. He
might eat pears for dessert.

Here is the story of pears:
like too many women their beauty
condemns them to uselessness;
they go well with cheese;

in Egypt and India they grow
on stunted trees in constant wind,
the horizon slicing the sun,
the earth itself pear shaped;

my grandmother sat
like a pear to wait
for visitors, for us to kiss
her rouge-brushed cheeks.

A woman, as she removed
her blouse, looking away from me,
one breast, like a pear
seemed bruised, blue.

A blue bowl and the overripe
pears sit in sunlight after lunch,
Saturday's light, delicate
membrane still intact.

Paula Rankin

Walter Rankin

Paula Rankin was born in Newport News, Virginia. She received her M.A. from William and Mary College and her Ph.D. from Vanderbilt University. She has published two collections of poetry, *By the Wreckmaster's Cottage* (1979) and *Augers* (1981), both from Carnegie-Mellon University Press.

For My Mother, Feeling Useless

Some people grow chalky dust on their skin
like leaves on a dirt road.
My mother, who would not run to the drugstore
without clean underwear, stockings,
hair pinned, two spots of blusher,
who believed everything mattered,
now sighs, *no need, no need.*

Who am I? she asks
of my father's, my sister's, and my faces
on the wall, under glass.
Her face lies on them
until it cannot bear the likenesses.

If she goes out for supper
no one knows if she comes back
or keeps driving
into the ocean
or down a dirt road spraying dust.

On her last plane ride
she had a vision
of being taken up
beyond the top cloud;
then she heard a voice
telling her she had to go
down, she was needed.

When I was a child,
she owned two dresses,
many aprons. There was great need
for her hands in the sink,
in the threadbox with needles.

There was great need
when my grandfather's brain
turned to mush, when my father lost
his sense of touch.

I leave my house
and go down the clay road
where the trees smother
into ghosts of themselves.
A car spins past, coating my legs
with gravelly powder
and I warn, *Back off, dark space,
I've got connections.*
My husband and children saw me leaving.

Somewhere Else

The waitress
takes our order, but clearly
her mind is
            somewhere else—

It's one of those days,
she says, handing us drinks
for someone else's thirst
which we forgive, though even our forgiveness
interrupts a conversation
                        somewhere else—

Our roast burns
for a man across town,
a thankless child,
bad luck, no money,
customers full of unlikelihoods
here, possibilities
there—

And in our children's eyes
we see the meal we've bought them
go cold, so impatient are they
to be already
where they're going,
spinning rubber down a driveway
where houselights are just beginning to come on,
it's just beginning to be dark.

Middle Age

The groundhog we dumped in the woods
is back in the yard
where he lies with his head in a cloud
of lice, an aura of flies,
a pale apple-green shimmering.

You say the dogs bring him back,
wanting praise, claiming credit.
At first I thought him but one more proof
of Spring, like wasps in vents,
ticks in children. All I know is he's there
when I walk to the mailbox,
when I lie in the sun,
when I look up at the stars
to say we're all nearer
to each other than we are.

He's a message from my father,
refusing to settle with the dead,
warning me I lack the skills
to keep them buried. Something's trying
to keep me from grief, but I'm not fooled:
love doesn't come back
like this, nor second chance.

Children gather to poke the remains,
then go fishing. I'm left
where the dead and the young
would keep me, cleaning up the mess.
What a mess they leave.

Being Refused Local Credit

Too new in town, we're told,
though we give twenty years
of references, debts owed
and paid, companies that begged
us as risks. How long does it take,
I ask; am told, Years.
OK, I shrug to my husband, so we'll pay cash.
But my heart's not in it,
knowing how everything it ever wanted arrived
before the wherewithal,
how without the foolhardy trust
of certain friends and strangers
I'd have had nothing, nothing.

This is the town I'll learn
to be good in, full of counters, aisles
where my credit's no good and my hands
stay in my pockets, counting costs.

On these terms suddenly
we don't need
almost everything. For years
we can think ourselves too new
to be trusted.

We're back in those barracks-turned-apartments
before our first child:
we're reading 1984 in paperback, taking turns
reading aloud the passages that seem most possible,
war and loneliness and rats.

The daughter we can't pay for
takes all this in, with our screams and yelling and rock music;
the tiny clot of heart muscles contracts, perusing . . .

You're working overtime,
not enough. If day shift,

I sweep, huge-bellied, where I can,
visit the woman next door
who seems to me so wise
with grown children.

If third shift, I bolt-lock the doors,
sit up half the night with a book
and butcher knife
as you told me,
asking
Who would want to steal from us? Who?

Alberto Ríos

Alberto Ríos was born in 1952 in Nogales, Arizona. He received his M.F.A. from the University of Arizona. His first book, *Whispering to Fool the Wind* (Sheep Meadow Press, 1982), was chosen by Donald Justice as winner of the 1981 Walt Whitman Award of the Academy of American Poets. *The Iguana Killer: Twelve Stories of the Heart,* winner of the 1984 Western States Book Award, was published by Blue Moon Press. He has received a fellowship from the National Endowment for the Arts and teaches at Arizona State University.

Karla Elling

Morning

He cradled his head in those hands
who might have kept it,
who might have grown into part of his head
but I would come in, and call him, *daddy*,
and they would let go.
Every day I saw a man
who wore one suit
and had a beard hid under his skin.
It was black.

I could see it in the light
see its darkness
as it came out first through his eyes
precisely in their centers
when he looked at me.
Under his suit, under his shirt
and undershirt, it started coming
through his chest too, and on his back.
He thought about his beard
because it was tangled in his head.
It made him unhappy,
his head was heavy
and sometimes he rested it in those hands
letting his beard come out through
their backs, through the backs
of his palms, the backs of his fingers,
through the backs of things lost.

The Purpose of Altar Boys

Tonio told me at catechism
the big part of the eye
admits good, and the little
black part is for seeing
evil—his mother told him
who was a widow and so
an authority on such things.
That's why at night
the black part gets bigger.
That's why kids can't go out
at night, and at night
girls take off their clothes
and walk around their
bedrooms or jump on their

beds or wear only sandals
and stand in their windows.
I was the altar boy
who knew about these things,
whose mission on some Sundays
was to remind people of
the night before as they
knelt for Holy Communion.
To keep Christ from falling
I held the metal plate
under chins, while on the thick
red carpet of the altar
I dragged my feet
and waited for the precise
moment: plate to chin
I delivered without expression
the Holy Electric Shock,
the kind that produces
a really large swallowing
and makes people think.
I thought of it as justice.
But on other Sundays the fire
in my eyes was different,
my mission somehow changed.
I would hold the metal plate
a little too hard
against those certain same
nervous chins, and I
I would look
with authority down
the tops of white dresses.

The Man She Called Honey,
and Married

In her hands she holds
purple blossoms inside
under her sailor-white skin
like a tattoo, like tattoos all over
of the Virgin of Guadalupe and Christ
too old now to have a face
or a body, just pieces of them now
huge on her forearms
and her face,
bigger almost
bursting out larger in some places
than the skin to hold them,
no room in her small eyes
to see more
than these purple flowers and
black and yellow,
bouquets smelling greenhouse hot inside
behind her eyes, in the pit of her head
smelling with her eyes
drawing the breath of pain
through them
into herself, into her small center
for one hard moment like a man,
a sailor, was a sailor, tattooed
and the long second he took
to put his pictures on her
with his hands.

Mi Abuelo

Where my grandfather is is in the ground
where you can hear the future
like an Indian with his ear at the tracks.
A pipe leads down to him so that sometimes
he whispers what will happen to a man
in town or how he will meet the best
dressed woman tomorrow and how the best
man at her wedding will chew the ground
next to her. Mi abuelo is the man
who speaks through all the mouths in my house.
An echo of me hitting the pipe sometimes
to stop him from saying *my hair is a*
sieve is the only other sound. It is a phrase
that among all others is the best,
he says, and *my hair is a sieve* is sometimes
repeated for hours out of the ground
when I let him, which is not often.
An abuelo should be much more than a man
like you! He stops then, and speaks: *I am a man*
who has served ants with the attitude
of a waiter, who has made each smile as only
an ant who is fat can, and they liked me best,
but there is nothing left. Yet I know he ground
green coffee beans as a child, and sometimes
he will talk about his wife, and sometimes
about when he was deaf and a man
cured him by mail and he heard groundhogs
talking, or about how he walked with a cane
he chewed on when he got hungry.
At best, mi abuelo is a liar.
I see an old picture of him at nani's with an
off-white yellow center mustache and sometimes
that's all I know for sure. He talks best
about these hills, *slowest waves*, and where this man
is going, and I'm convinced his hair is a sieve,
that his fever is cooled now underground.
Mi abuelo is an ordinary man.
I look down the pipe, sometimes, and see a
ripple-topped stream in its best suit, in the ground.

565 / ALBERTO RÍOS

Pattiann Rogers

John Rogers

Pattiann Rogers was born in 1940. She received her B.A. from the University of Missouri and her M.A. from the University of Houston. Her first book of poetry, *The Expectations of Light* (1981), was published by Princeton University Press. Among her awards are the Voertman's Poetry Award from the Texas Institute of Letters, a fellowship from the National Endowment for the Arts, and a Guggenheim Fellowship for 1984–85.

For Stephen Drawing Birds

They catch your eye early, those rising black
Out of the water oaks at dusk or those skimming
The grey lakes at dawn. You know you must learn
Them by name, calling the redstart, pointing out
The towhee, the slate-colored junco. You begin
To trace their drummings through the forest, the click
Of their matings in the rocks and grow accustomed
To waiting, sketchbook in hand, for the mottled
Vireo to nurse at the fruit tree, the woodcock to rise
To the spring willow bait. You are patient
With the snow goose appearing at the bottom of the reeds
And the thrasher untangling itself from the hedgerow.
What luck, the day you find a whole cliff of gannets,
Their pale yellow heads as smooth as eggs, their eyelids
And nostrils distinctly blue.

Matching pencil to feather, you begin to take them
One by one—the marbled owl pulling at the skull
Of the lemming, the dusky tanager in the afternoon
Snipping at dragonflies. How well you execute
Their postures, the wings of the overland dove spread
Like a Japanese fan, the jackdaw frozen
At the moment of his descent into the locust.

It grows easier and easier. Soon the cedar shrike stops
On his own and waits for you, gripped to the fence post.
The grosbeak rests all day on the limb by your page,
And when you picture the rare azure-throated swallow,
He suddenly materializes under the eaves, preparing
His mudball. In the evening before the fire,
As you remember the Réunion solitaire, the giant auk,
They appear in the room, roosting on the ginger jars
Above the mantelpiece. You even wake one morning
To discover that the lark bunting has been nesting
Under your knuckles just as you dreamed he was.
There is a definite stir of preening among your papers.

Tonight, a strange chukal hen has flown to the cornice
Above your window. The invisible grey-green thimble bird
Is slowly coming into sight by your glass, and perched
On the bedpost, an unmarked polar hawk is watching
With his stern golden eye over the entire length of your quilt.

The Man Hidden Behind the Drapes

When I entered the room and turned on the lights,
There were his feet bare beneath the edge
Of the draperies, his tendons flexed, the bony
Diamonds of his ankles shadowed. If I'd seen
His face I might have laughed.

Remember the naked feet of Christ seen so often,
Washed, kissed, dried in women's hair,
Or crossed and bleeding, pinioned
Like butterfly wings?

When I opened the door,
There were his feet below the drapes, as quiet
As if they lounged beneath a fine robe. Headlights
Moving slowly up the drive at this point
Would have fully exposed his nude body in the window,
His buttocks tensed, his face turned toward the glare
For that moment, then disappearing again into the darkness.

An artist might have pictured snow on the lawn
And a moon and a child looking out from the house
Across the way, watching the figure behind the glass,
The white panes across his back, his hands reaching
For the parting in the curtains.

When I entered the room the light spread first
In a rectangle straight across the floor to his feet,
His toes squeezing under in a crippled kind of gripping.
Someone watching from the end of the hall behind me
Would have seen my body framed in the light of the doorway
And beyond me the wall of the drapes.

Understand the particular axis at which he stood
In the vision of each different beholder, the multiple
Coordinates of hour and position and place coinciding
With the grids of light and sound and preceding
Interpretations. Consider that indeterminable effect
Of his being on the eye of the one unaware of his existence.

There is a house three blocks away that has no man
Behind the drapes. There is a house on a high sea wall
That has two men and no window. There is a house
That does not speak this language and consequently
Tells us nothing.

Almost laughing, my hand still on the door,
I stood watching his feet, and had there been an old woman
Living in the attic, then looking down through a chink in the ceiling
She would have seen in two dimensions, the knuckles of his toes,
The top of my head.

Achieving Perspective

Straight up away from this road,
Away from the fitted particles of frost
Coating the hull of each chick pea,
And the stiff archer bug making its way
In the morning dark, toe hair by toe hair,
Up the stem of the trillium,
Straight up through the sky above this road right now,
The galaxies of the Cygnus A cluster
Are colliding with each other in a massive swarm
Of interpenetrating and exploding catastrophes.
I try to remember that.

And even in the gold and purple pretense
Of evening, I make myself remember
That it would take 40,000 years full of gathering
Into leaf and dropping, full of pulp splitting
And the hard wrinkling of seed, of the rising up
Of wood fibers and the disintegration of forests,
Of this lake disappearing completely in the bodies
Of toad slush and duckweed rock,
40,000 years and the fastest thing we own,
To reach the one star nearest to us.

And when you speak to me like this,
I try to remember that the wood and cement walls
Of this room are being swept away now

Molecule by molecule, in a slow and steady wind,
And nothing at all separates our bodies
From the vast emptiness expanding, and I know
We are sitting in our chairs
Discoursing in the middle of the blackness of space.
And when you look at me
I try to recall that at this moment
Somewhere millions of miles beyond the dimness
Of the sun, the comet Biela, speeding
In its rocks and ices, is just beginning to enter
The widest arc of its elliptical turn.

Concepts and Their Bodies
(The Boy in the Field Alone)

Staring at the mud turtle's eye
Long enough, he sees *concentricity* there
For the first time, as if it possessed
Pupil and iris and oracular lid,
As if it grew, forcing its own gene of circularity.
The concept is definitely
The cellular arrangement of sight.

The five amber grasses maintaining their seedheads
In the breeze against the sky
Have borne *latitude* from the beginning,
Secure *civility* like leaves in their folds.
He discovers *persistence* in the mouth
Of the caterpillar in the same way
As he discovers clear syrup
On the broken end of the dayflower,
Exactly as he comes accidently upon
The mud crown of the crawfish.

The spotted length of the bullfrog leaping
Lakeward just before the footstep
Is not bullfrog, spread and sailing,
But the body of *initiative* with white glossy belly.
Departure is the wing let loose
By the dandelion, and it does possess
A sparse down and will not be thought of,
Even years later, even in the station
At midnight among the confusing lights,
As separate from that white twist
Of filament drifting.

Nothing is sharp enough to disengage
The butterfly's path from *erraticism*.

And *freedom* is this September field
Covered this far by tree shadows
Through which this child chooses to run
Until he chooses to stop,
And it will be so hereafter.

William Pitt Root

Pamela Uschuk

William Pitt Root was born in 1941 and spent his childhood in rural Florida. He received his B.A. from the University of Washington and his M.F.A. from the University of North Carolina at Greensboro. His six books include, from Atheneum, *The Storm and Other Poems* (1969), *Striking the Dark Air for Music* (1973), and *Reasons for Going It on Foot* (1981). He also publishes short fiction and translations of poetry. His awards include a Wallace Stegner Fellowship at Stanford University and grants from the National Endowment for the Arts and from the Rockefeller and Guggenheim foundations. He currently teaches at the University of Montana.

Wheel Turning on the Hub of the Sun

I was young.
           A hundred yards off at the edge of the reflective mud
tall white birds gathered like spirits for a ceremonial
dance stalked slowly along the bottom
as the surface of the pond gave back the dance.
Each strode in the pool of its own image
and the queer noises they made
made the silence deeper.

The sun was a member of their dance and the trees
lent shadows to the edges of the pond shimmering
like water in a saucer tipped.

What I can remember now
comes as from a dream glowing in the mind until it's
spoken of, and goes away. I know
that they strode in their dance for hours
and drew their long yellow legs up into the commotion of their wings
and rose in a great circle overhead, their wheel
above me turning on the hub of the sun,
—and that when they were gone, standing like one
in a darkness after lightning
in the light that once had seemed sufficient,
I found myself alone.

—*Everglades, Florida*

White Horse of the Father, White Horse of the Son

For Michael Perry

Not the delicate mare who came nosing.
Not the dustdim ironeyed gelding.
This was the one. The bright dancer
who would not approach the fence.

Set in this side of his snowbright face
was the blank blue stare of the sky.
And there in the other, a hazel tunnel.
A swirling of greens and browns that could see.

The hooves were pink as tea-roses,
streaked with the pale of oystershell.
This was the great horse I wanted.
And this was the one for sale!

I wanted to try him alone.
How many moons has the sky?
You insisted my friend ride him too.
And he didn't know how. Didn't know.

My hands crossed the brilliant silk
of his neck as the lips of a prince cross
the princess. Who sleeps in forever.
Who wakes in the world. He woke

to my touch and we raced the proud wind
over grass. Over bushes and ditches.
This was the one, the one my dreams
woke to. Wide-eyed. But my friend,

I could feel him slipping.
Feel him falling back into the grass
as I reached, too late, for his hand.
As my hand reached backward into the blur

of his wide white face and the grass.
He was gone. By the time I could turn
I had heard your voice in my heart.
No Sir. Not this one. No sale.

Father once a son, son become a father,
you riding now the white stallion of your bones!
It is true that I fell from the horse as your son.
That I rode on. Am still riding.

Sometimes Heaven Is a Mean Machine

For Wayne Sloane

It is like riding Death and not dying.

It shudders, snarls and roars like an iron lion.
It shines like the chromed bones of a bull.

At night its single headlight
rakes across the highway like the lowered horn
    of a charging unicorn.

It looks like Death waiting for a taker.

You take it, you ride.

All day, all night for years
while the bright arcs of your breath flex
    into curves repeating earthshapes
    you ride, the road informing you.

You ride
your own death and you do not die.

It shines and you ride its shining.

Answering Dance

Dark abdomen upraised,
pulsing and pulsing,
she signals from
the heart of the web.
He drops everything

to join her,
nimbling through the maze
of stalks and stems
that bramble between him
and the polestar
of his desire.

At web's edge
he pauses, eyes
kaleidoscopic
in the hood of his head.
Alert to any sign
excited in her,
he tenses and waits,
carefully strumming
on one string, importantly
distinguished
from stray fly or bee
by his request.

Her answering dance
invites him on.

Entering her domain
he is entranced
by the spell
all around her of fine lines
and the silkbound husks
staggered at random
among them
and by the global dew
in which worlds
reverse and shine
that will vanish
at the brush
of a leg.

They greet,
an intimate complex
of touches, taps

and nudges as leg
brushes leg after
leg. He mounts her,
shudders, mounts
again and again
the trembling web
scatters its dew.

She grows arch
and still. He
flickers
with exhaustion
beside her, thrums
the single string
and waits, buoyant web
resonant with his appeal.
Allowed to pass,
he vanishes
into the tall grass;
but if he carelessly
alarms her, strikes
one alien note,
stunned by her solution
he is spun into a state
ancient as night
and deep as the hunger
yet to come
of dark sons and daughters.

Exchanging Glances

I stand on the porch
of your second floor apartment, drinking in
the breeze through my loosened shirt and holding
cold beer to my mouth. You are inside bathing

by the window open over the garden, preparing
to be loved. Two weeks gone
is long enough to sweeten our reunion and the bitterness
of beer is sweetened by the chill. At the *slap slap*
of your bare feet approaching from behind
I slip off my sandals, loosen
the sweaty belt in my pants and see, suddenly,
below me peering up through branches,
a small boy, face open as a small bird's mouth.

As we exchange that glance
I see again the huge man guzzling beer and leaning
on the flakey white railing overhead, his shirt sweaty and loose
to the summer heat and his pants half open as he
leans over, looking down
into my startled face: *He's*
going to piss on me I think, freezing
to the spot as he smiles down, salutes me with his beer
and turns to go inside. Raising my empty bottle
to the boy, I smile the promise down to him and turn
back into my own life, your life,
our life as it is now.

Nightswim

For Rachel Goldstein

Perhaps it was because
with all their laughter
and the poolside lights
they disturbed a darkness
in the pruned sullen trees.

Two men, two women,
splashing in a dayblue pool

below stars hidden
in the glare they saw by.
Shooting like otters
down the slide, diving
like seals, each
wellfed and sleek,
regardless in their games.

When one man brushed absently
at a leaf that clung to him,
it bit: a tiny sodden
ghoul-faced bat. Like pins
the teeth and claws.
Tossed from the pool
to the pet cat, it
lay like a wet rag,
hissing among its wings.

For the rest of the night
that man kept glancing
at the dark, waiting
for another scrap of it
to seek him out.

From the Other Shore

For my mother and sisters

Waiting to be served we look from the veranda
down into a river
     whose unpronounceable name
would mean nothing to you. Thick
green trees on the opposite bank ignite
as an elongated sun
     touches their fringes,

and sheep gathered there to drink
slowly retreat into shadows
where their suncharged fleeces
    still glow in the dark.

Much farther downstream,
    beyond where its broad back carries clouds,
some of the black rocks
    gathered at a bend
are in motion, rise and
fall, rising again
    and again as we
see, our eyes now focussed
for the distance,
    the lengths of brightness
each rock flails, causing
the other, dormant stones
    to shine.

Washerwomen. Probably
wives and mothers
    to the shepherds
we sense watching us
from the other shore. Perhaps
the white shirts
    of the waiters brighten
drubbed upon those stones.
By the time the meal
    is served and removed
in a flaring of silver
from these tableclothes
    immaculate in late
sunlight, we can hear
faintly the dull reports
    of wet clothes slung
heavily down upon the stones.

First the flash and only
moments after the slap
    slap these flat stones

have known for centuries
or more, before learning
the roar of cars like ours,
   casually laden
with items worth
more than we had known
   before we saw the
stones of the river rising up
in the forms of women.

Gibbons Ruark

Gibbons Ruark was born in 1941 in Raleigh, North Carolina. He holds degrees from the University of North Carolina and the University of Massachusetts, and is the author of three collections of poetry, A *Program for Survival* (University Press of Virginia, 1971), *Reeds* (Texas Tech Press, 1978), and *Keeping Company* (Johns Hopkins University Press, 1983). He has been the recipient of a fellowship from the National Endowment for the Arts. He teaches at the University of Delaware.

Fritz Zenn

Soaping Down for Saint Francis of Assisi: The Canticle of Sister Soap

*"It took in, that human, that divine
embrace, everything but soap."—Henry James*

Winter sunlight in Assisi, and the birds tilting
    Their small wings over the roof-tiles,
And the mirror lilting from the bedroom wall,
    And the good and lovely and leering Signora
Giving us breakfast and a shower all to ourselves.
    There is soap in Firenze, there is soap in Bologna,
But more than ever there is soap this morning in Assisi.

Henry, if you were here, we would soap your longest sentence down.
As it is we gather into soap whatever sunlight lifts in our direction,
    Shoulders, slippery breasts, long tapering backs,
Eyes clouded after a while against the burning,
    We are soaped all over, we are slithering somewhere,
We are two well-leavened loaves of fresh Italian bread,
    We are the morning hillsides of Assisi.
Great white doves of soapsuds fly from our shoulders,
    Great wings of dazzling soapsuds are waking
And flying and perishing into Assisi sunlight,
    And we are giving the beautiful dirt-loving Francis
More soap than even Henry James could ever think he wanted,
    And the good dead Francis is coming piercingly clean for once
Where we give each other love we never bought or paid for
    In this room of the profane and holy bargain.

Talking Myself to Sleep
in the Mountains

Longing, I have seen you in the water
Flare like a bluefish in your native place.
You are at sea level, dark-headed lover,
Twelve hundred miles of night southeast of here.
I have come up to thirteen hundred feet.
Hammer is with me, fly rod banging
On his shoulder as we clambered uphill
Sweaty with friendship, lying about the South.
We crossed the wind-burned ridgeback wild with berries,
Spooking and being rattled by a doe
In that dry cover, hiking up our packs
And skidding sideways to this run of water,
And the thick trunks smoking up the moon's half-light,
Tall poplar, beech—and saplings for the tent.
Now in the darkness we have pitched our camp.

Clear as it is, the creek will not pool deep
Enough to carry trout, so we fish out
Two cups of stone-cold water, bank the fire,
Bite down on that and whiskey on the tongue.
The fire is smokeless and the talk is good
And sifting into nothing like the fire.
The moon is blurred when I climb down to shiver
In the creek again and watch the light
Through stone-chinks stammer like a dream toward dawn.
Hammer is snoring when I climb back up.
This is a good place, it would be good
To sleep here with you and to bathe downstream
In the pool we are bound to find tomorrow.
It could happen. You could come here with me.
But I am laying on this going fire
The maps of every likely place I've been
For light enough to get back down to you.

Lost Letter to James Wright, with Thanks for a Map of Fano

Breathing his last music, Mozart is supposed
To have said something heartbreaking which escapes me
For the quick moment of your bending to a dime

Blinking up from York Avenue, the last chill evening
I ever saw you, laughter rising with the steam
From your scarred throat, long-remembering laughter,

"Well, the old *eye* is still some good, anyway."
I thought of your silent master Samuel Johnson
Folding the fingers of drowsing vagrant children

Secret as wings over the coppers he left in their palms
Against the London cold and tomorrow's hunger.
You could not eat, I think you could scarcely swallow,

And yet that afternoon of your sleep and waking
To speak with us, you read me a fugitive passage
From a book beside your chair, something I lose all track of

Now, in this dim hour, about the late driftwood letters
Of writers and how little they finally matter.
You wrote to me last from Sirmione (of all things,

Sirmione had turned gray that morning), and it mattered.
We were together when the gray December dusk
Came down on snapshots of the view from Sirmione,

Sunlight ghosting your beard on the beach at Fano.
I had thought to write you a letter from Fano,
A letter which could have taken years to reach you

On the slow river ways of the Italian mails,
And now I write before we even come to leave.
We are going to Fano, where we may unfold this map

At a strange street corner under a window box
Of thyme gone to flower, and catch our breath remembering
Mozart breathing his last music, managing

Somehow to say in time, "And now I must go,
When I have only just learned to live quietly."
Last time I saw you, walking a little westward

From tugboats in the harbor, your voice was already breaking,
You were speaking quietly but the one plume of your breath
Was clouding and drifting west and away from Fano

Toward the river ferry taking sounding after sounding.

Working the Rain Shift at Flanagan's

For Ben Kiely

When Dublin is a mist the quays are lost
To the river, even you could be lost,
A boy from Omagh after forty years
Sounding the Liberties dim as I was
When that grave policeman touching my elbow

Headed me toward this salutary glass.
The town is grim all right, but these premises
Have all the air of a blessed corner
West of the westernmost pub in Galway,
Where whatever the light tries daily to say

The faces argue with, believing rain.
Outside an acceptable rain is falling
Easy as you predicted it would fall,
Though all your Dublin savvy could not gauge
The moment the rain shift would begin to sing.

They are hoisting barrels out of the cellar
And clanging them into an open van,
Gamely ignoring as if no matter
Whatever is falling on their coats and caps,
Though the fat one singing tenor has shrugged

Almost invisibly and hailed his fellow
Underground: "A shower of rain up here,"
He says with the rain, "It'll bring up the grass."
Then, befriending a moan from the darkness,
"Easy there now, lie back down, why won't you,"

As if the man were stirring in his grave
And needed a word to level him again.
His baffled answer rising to the rainfall
Could have been laughter or tears or maybe
Some musical lie he was telling the rain.

This is a far corner from your beat these days,
But why not walk on over anyway
And settle in with me to watch the rain.
You can tell me a story if you feel
Like it, and then you can tell me another.

The rain in the door will fall so softly
It might be rising for all we can know
Where we sit inscribing its vague margin
With words, oddly at ease with our shadows
As if we had died and gone to Dublin.

The Goods She Can Carry:
Canticle of Her Basket Made of Reeds

Beginning I will praise a fine beginning,
    How the cloud of sun came up over the marshland
Where the reeds were green and supple and wind-bent,
    Not yet bent by the veiny hands of the craftsman
Who wove them in her basket while she watched and smiled.
    Even the first time, coming home from the craftsman,
She brought me a round and steaming loaf of bread.
    That loaf broken open on the kitchen table
Left loaves of sunlight piling in the empty basket.
    One morning a week the blouses and the bedsheets,
The schoolgirl smocks and all the delicate underwear
    She carries in the basket to the small Signora
And comes back grinning with an apple in each bare hand.
    On an ordinary evening, maybe an evening
Enough like this one it could happen even now,
    She comes with her basket of reeds overflowing
With basil and fennel, with sweet ham from Parma,
    With fruits of the commune, with flowered zucchini,
With a slender green bottle of Veronese wine.

If I see her through the window I'll just
Whistle softly so she'll look up and right now she
    Looks up and sees me and carries her goods up the stairs,
Calling "Buona sera" to the neighbors as she climbs.
    Beautiful she brings the basket through the doorway
And pray do put it down I hear myself praying
    And let it sit there while the evening sky turns starry.
In the evening, in the late weather of October,
    The wine will cool on its own for a solid hour.
She slips her coat off as she turns to greet me.
    Ending I praise her for putting the basket down.

Michael Ryan

Michael Ryan was born in St. Louis, Missouri, in 1945. He received an A.B. from Notre Dame University, an M.A. from the Claremont Graduate School, and an M.F.A. and Ph.D. from the University of Iowa. His first book, *Threats Instead of Trees* (1974), won the Yale Series of Younger Poets Award. *In Winter* (1981) was published by Holt, Rinehart, and Winston. Among his awards are fellowships from the National Endowment for the Arts and the Guggenheim Foundation. He teaches in the M.F.A. program at Warren Wilson College.

Elaine Miller

When I Was Conceived

It was 1945, and it was May.
White crocus bloomed in St. Louis.
The Germans gave in but the war shoved on,
and my father came home from work that evening
tired and washed his hands
not picturing the black-goggled men
with code names fashioning an atomic bomb.
Maybe he loved his wife that evening.
Maybe after eating she smoothed his jawline
in her palm as he stretched out

on the couch with his head in her lap
while Bob Hope spoofed Hirohito on the radio
and they both laughed. My father sold used cars
at the time, and didn't like it,
so if he complained maybe she held him
an extra moment in her arms,
the heat in the air pressing between them,
so they turned upstairs early that evening,
arm in arm, without saying anything.

Consider a Move

The steady time of being unknown,
in solitude, without friends,
is not a steadiness which sustains.
I hear your voice waver on the phone:

*Haven't talked to anyone for days.
I drive around. I sit in parking lots.*
The voice zeroes through my ear, and waits.
What should I say? There are ways

to meet people you will want to love?
I know of none. You come out stronger
having gone through this? I no longer
believe that, if I once did. Consider a move,

a change, a job, a new place to live,
someplace you'd like to be. *That's not it,*
you say. Now time curves back. We almost touch.
Then what is? I ask. What is?

In Winter

At four o'clock it's dark.
Today, looking out through dusk
at three gray women in stretch slacks
chatting in front of the post office,
their steps left and right and back
like some quick folk dance of kindness,
I remembered the winter we spent
crying in each other's laps.
What could you be thinking at this moment?
How lovely and strange the gangly spines
of trees against a thickening sky
as you drive from the library
humming off-key? Or are you smiling
at an idea met in a book
the way you smiled with your whole body
the first night we talked?
I was so sure my love of you was perfect,
and the light today
reminded me of the winter you drove home
each day in the dark at four o'clock
and would come into my study to kiss me
despite mistake after mistake after mistake.

After

The space we feel inside us
is the space a survivor sees
as he swims endlessly toward a place

where he might put his feet down
and take an easy breath. For now,
the sheer distance means a long time

he must hurt himself enough
to tow his own weight and not give up.
Why, he asks in each stroke,

and in each stroke pain is felt,
muscles do their work, and he thinks
of no one else. Is this what's meant

when we look into ourselves
and feel nothing but the urge to go on?
The sun goes down. He sees nothing.
It's calm.

David St. John

David St. John was born in 1949. He
was educated at California State Uni-
versity at Fresno and the University of
Iowa. He is the author of two books
of poetry, *Hush* (1976) and *The Shore*
(1980), both from Houghton Mifflin.
Among his awards are the James D.
Phelan Prize and fellowships from the
National Endowment for the Arts,
the Ingram-Merrill Foundation, and
the Guggenheim Foundation. He
teaches at Johns Hopkins University.

Bob Durell

The Avenues

Some nights when you're off
Painting in your studio above the laundromat,
I get bored about two or three A.M.
And go out walking down one of the avenues
Until I can see along some desolate sidestreet
The glare of an all-night cafeteria.
I sit at the counter,
In front of those glass racks with the long,
Narrow mirrors tilted above them like every
French bedroom you've ever read
About. I stare at all those lonely pies,

Homely wedges lifted
From their moons. The charred crusts and limp
Meringues reflected so shamelessly—
Their shapely fruits and creams all spilling
From the flat pyramids, the isosceles spokes
Of dough. This late at night,
So few souls left
In the place, even the cheesecake
Looks a little blue. With my sour coffee,
I wander back out, past a sullen boy
In leather beneath the whining neon,
Along those streets we used to walk at night,
Those endless shops of spells: the love philtres
And lotions, 20th century voodoo. Once,
Over your bath, I poured
One called *Mystery of the Spies*,
Orange powders sizzling all around your hips.
Tonight, I'll drink alone as these streets haze
To a pale grey. I know you're out somewhere—
Walking the avenues, shadowboxing the rising
Smoke as the trucks leave their alleys and loading
Chutes—looking for breakfast, or a little peace.

Hotel Sierra

The November air
Has curled the new leaves
Of the spider plant, strung
From an L-bent nail
Driven in the warp of the window
Frame. Maybe the woman down
At the desk has a few more opinions—
On the dying plant, or the high
Bruised clouds of the nearing storm,

Or the best road
Along the coast this time of year
To Oregon. This morning, after
You left to photograph
The tide pools at dawn, the waves
In their black-and-white
Froth, I scavenged in your bag
For books, then picked up one
You'd thrown onto the bed, Cocteau,
Your place marked with a snapshot
Of a whale leaping clear of the spray
Tossed by the migrating
Herd—a totem
Of what you've left to dream. Yet,
It's why we've come—*Hotel Sierra*—
To this place without a past for us,
Where, I admit, a dozen years ago
I stayed a night across
The hall. I never asked why, on this
Ocean, a hotel was named for mountains
Miles inland. I spent that cold
Evening playing pinball in some dank
Arcade. Tonight, I'll take you there,
Down by the marina with no sailboats,
By the cannery's half-dozing, crippled
Piers rocking in the high tides and winds
Where I sat out on the rotted boards,
The fog barely sifting down,
The few lights
Looped over those thin, uneasy poles
Throbbing as the current came and went.
Soon, I could see only two mast lights
Blinking more and more faintly
Towards the horizon. I took
A flask of gin upstairs, just to sit
At the narrow window drinking
Until those low-slung, purposeful
Boats returned. As I
Wait here this morning, for you,

For some fragment of a final scene,
I remember how I made you touch, last
Night in the dark, those
Summer moths embossed upon the faded,
Imperial wallpaper of the room.
Now, as I watch you coming up
The brick-and-stone path to the hotel,
I can hear those loose wood shutters
Of the roof straining in the winds
As the storm closes
Over the shore. I listen as you climb
The stairs, the Nikon buzzing
Like a smoked hive
Each moment as you stop in front of:
A *stair-step; a knob of the banister;*
The worn brass "12" nailed
To our door; the ribbons: knots of paint
Peeling off the hall—
You knock open the door with one boot,
Poised, clicking off shot after
Shot as you slide into the cluttered room,
Pivoting: *me; the dull seascape hung*
Above the bed; the Bible I'd tossed
Into the sink; my hands curled on
The chair's arm; the limp spider plant . . .
Next week, as you step out
Of the darkroom with the glossy proofs,
Those strips of tiny tableaux, the day
And we
Will have become only a few gestures
Placed out of time. But now rain
Slants beyond a black sky, the windows
Tint, opaque with reflected light;
Yet no memory is stilled, held frame
By frame, of this burlesque of you
Undressing. The odd pirouette
As your sweater comes off, at last,
Rain-soaked slacks collapsing on the floor.
Tomorrow, after we leave for good

The long story we've told to each other
So many years not a friend believes it,
After we drive along the shore to Albion
To your cabin set high above the road,
After we drag your suitcases and few boxes
Up to the redwood porch,
After the list of goodbyes and refusals ends,
We'll have nothing to promise. Before I go,
You'll describe for me again those sleek
Whales you love, the way they arc elegantly
Through water or your dreams. How, like
Us, they must travel in their own time,
Drawn simply by the seasons, by their lives.

Guitar

I have always loved the word *guitar*.

I have no memories of my father on the patio
At dusk, strumming a Spanish tune,
Or my mother draped in that fawn wicker chair
Polishing her flute;
I have no memories of your song, distant Sister
Heart, of those steel strings sliding
All night through the speaker of the car radio
Between Tucumcari and Oklahoma City, Oklahoma.
Though I've never believed those stories
Of gypsy cascades, stolen horses, castanets,
And stars, of Airstream trailers and good fortune,
Though I never met Charlie Christian, though
I've danced the floors of cold longshoremen's halls,
Though I've waited with the overcoats at the rear
Of concerts for lute, mandolin, and two guitars—

More than the music I love scaling its woven
Stairways, more than the swirling chocolate of wood

I have always loved the word *guitar*.

Blue Waves

I think sometimes
I am afraid, walking out with you
Into the redwoods by the bay. Over
Cioppino in a fisherman's café, we
Talk about the past, the time
You left me nothing but your rugs;
How I went off to that cabin
High in the Pacific cliffs—overlooking
Coves, a driftwood beach, sea otters.
Some mornings, over coffee, we sit
And watch the sun break between factory
Smokestacks. It is cold,
Only the birds and diesels are starting
To sound. When we are alone
In this equation of pleasure and light,
The day waking, I remember more
Plainly those nights you left a husband,
And I a son. Still, as the clouds
Search their aqua and grey
Skies, I want only to watch you leaning
Back in the cane chair, the Navaho
Blanket slipping, the red falls
Of your hair rocking as you keep time
To the machinery gears, buses
Braking to a slide, a shudder of trains.
If I remember you framed by an
Open window, considering the coleus
You've drawn; or, with your four or five

Beliefs, stubborn and angry, shoving
Me out the door of the Chevy; or, if some
Day or night
You take that suitcase packed under
The bed and leave once again, I will look
Back across this room, as I look now, to you
Holding a thin flame to the furnace,
The gasp of heat rising as you rise;
To these mornings, islands—
The balance of the promise with what lasts.

Hush

For my son

The way a tired Chippewa woman
Who's lost a child gathers up black feathers,
Black quills & leaves
That she wraps & swaddles in a little bale, a shag
Cocoon she carries with her & speaks to always
As if it were the child,
Until she knows the soul has grown fat & clever,
That the child can find its own way at last;
Well, I go everywhere
Picking the dust out of the dust, scraping the breezes
Up off the floor, & gather them into a doll
Of you, to touch at the nape of the neck, to slip
Under my shirt like a rag—the way
Another man's wallet rides above his heart. As you
Cry out, as if calling to a father you conjure
In the paling light, the voice rises, instead, in me.
Nothing stops it, the crying. Not the clove of moon,
Not the woman raking my back with her words. Our letters
Close. Sometimes, you ask

About the world; sometimes, I answer back. Nights
Return you to me for a while, as sleep returns sleep
To a landscape ravaged
& familiar. The dark watermark of your absence, a hush.

The Shore

So the tide forgets, as morning
Grows too far delivered, as the bowls
Of rock and wood run dry.
What is left seems pearled and lit,
As those cases
Of the museum stood lit
With milk jade, rows of opaque vases
Streaked with orange and yellow smoke.
You found a lavender boat, a single
Figure poling upstream, baskets
Of pale fish wedged between his legs.
Today, the debris of winter
Stands stacked against the walls,
The coils of kelp lie scattered
Across the floor. The oil fire
Smokes. You turn down the lantern
Hung on its nail. Outside,
The boats aligned like sentinels.
Here beside the blue depot, walking
The pier, you can see the way
The shore
Approximates the dream, how distances
Repeat their deaths
Above these tables and panes of water—
As climbing the hills above
The harbor, up to the lupine drifting
Among the lichen-masked pines,
The night is pocked with lamps lit

On every boat off shore,
Galleries of floating stars. Below,
On its narrow tracks shelved
Into the cliff's face,
The train begins its slide down
To the warehouses by the harbor. Loaded
With diesel, coal, paychecks, whiskey,
Bedsheets, slabs of ice—for the fish,
For the men. You lean on my arm,
As once
I watched you lean at the window;
The bookstalls below stretched a mile
To the quay, the afternoon crowd
Picking over the novels and histories.
You walked out as you walked out last
Night, onto the stone porch. Dusk
Reddened the walls, the winds sliced
Off the reefs. The vines of the gourds
Shook on their lattice. You talked
About the night you stood
Behind the black pane of the French
Window, watching my father read some long
Passage
Of a famous voyager's book. You hated
That voice filling the room,
Its light. So tonight we make a soft
Parenthesis upon the sand's black bed.
In that dream we share, there is
One shore, where we look out upon nothing
And the sea our whole lives;
Until turning from those waves, we find
One shore, where we look out upon nothing
And the earth our whole lives.
Where what is left between shore and sky
Is traced in the vague wake of
(The stars, the sandpipers whistling)
What we forgive. *If you wake soon, wake me.*

Sherod Santos

Sherod Santos was born in 1949 and was educated at the University of California and the University of Utah, where he received a Ph.D. His first book of poems, *Accidental Weather* (Doubleday, 1982), was chosen by Charles Wright for the National Poetry Series. Among his awards are the "Discovery"/*The Nation* award and fellowships from the Ingram Merrill Foundation and the Guggenheim Foundation. He teaches at the University of Missouri.

Mitchell Hagerstrom

Sirens in Bad Weather

The wet streets are undisturbed by that chronic
high whine—as of a fish hawk over the blue
glaze, over the refracted light which slips in
through the cloud-breaks. A week's rain has
pasted the elm leaves to the sidewalk, and stuck
some against the buildings, and to the tires
of a refrigerator truck which unloads nightly
in the alley below—it's like a brown mildew
spreading through the city. And the constant drip,
drip, in which the passersby in their rainhats
and galoshes seem submerged . . . like the man standing
in the intersection next to his crumpled car:
round-mouthed and motionless, as if underwater,
his scream still rising a block away.

The Breakdown

1.

The sun scanned the river with its lidless
eye; before the heat had choked the saffron
fields, already the fishing-boats spotted
the calms, already our table was laid

for a homecoming. Mother's blue bedroom
window steamed behind the light-chinked blind: there,
awhile, her heart was still quiet enough,
a small boat bobbing on the horizon.

2.

I dug in wet sedge for a woodchuck's hole:
the murky, rank, underwater smell when
I pulled my hands out with a sucking sound,
like a sob, and the imprints filled with mud.

There were puffy white clouds when she stepped out
from the shade. Or was it the heaviness
of the stock-still air that made the shadows
grow increasingly larger around her?

3.

By evening the boats had crossed, without sail,
the glassy waters of the Sound. The gulls
intensified their treble calls—passing
masts were blunted now on the shallow sky.

On the other bank, the pulp-mill had just
shut down: water rats returned to the weeds
by the open sluices; a hip-booted
worker dragged his rake through the sawdust piles.

4.

She stood too long beside the riverbank.
The fronting fishermen's huts had gone blank
in the moonlight; and when the wind lifted
a few leaves fell, and the water's surface

shuddered, as if from emotion . . . Perhaps
she only grew more distant then, staring
downriver as if staring down a road
when there is nothing on it but the night.

5.

The moon floated through the overhanging
willow, as if nosing through shoals; the bed-
spread swam with splotches of light, yellow-white
on pale-blue; and each wind-shift shook the tree

so the air would fill with those silvery
leaves, like scales scraped down the length of an eel.
I pulled the window-blind shut, but the hand
did not loosen, in the darkness, its grip.

The Enormous Aquarium

(After Proust)

All morning long from inside the lobby
Of the Grand Hotel, the empty sea shore
Hung suspended there like a tapestry
Of no particular interest or value,
And it was only at intervals, while cards

Were shuffled and dealt around the tables,
That one of the players, finding nothing
To do, might turn his head to glance outside
At an occasional sail on the horizon.
And so, too, the afternoon hours, immutable
And bland, would pass before the windows
That more and more, as the sun declined,
Came to seem like mirrors in which you look
And find no other face but your own.

But then the evening arrived, the heat
Of the day settled onto the sand,
And suddenly it happened—as though
At the gesture of an imaginary hand—
That a great hidden stream of electricity
Would flood the dining rooms and halls
Until the hotel became, as it were,
An enormous aquarium against whose glass
The fishermen's and the tradesmen's families,
Clustering invisibly in the outer dark,
Would press their faces to watch—how like
Strange fishes or mollusks the occupants
Now seemed as they floated past on those
Golden eddies of unrippling light:

There a Serbian officer whose organdy
Plume was like the blow of spume off some
Great blue whale, and there a young man who
From his earliest years had obviously moved
In the freshest waters of Faubourg Saint-Germain,
Or there, grand and aloof, the dowager Duchess,
Her powdered jaws closing on a morsel of food
Like a primitive shell fish closing
On a spore . . . And the question now lingering
In the air was how the glass could contain
A world so vastly different from the poor,
A world where tea-gowns and sable, grosgrain
And *crepe-de-Chine*, topaz and silver and
The enamelled ring that encircled a wrist

All spoke of a life grown infinitely
Distant and unreal . . . Yet if, from out
Beneath the eaves, the unwearying, gentle
Flight of the sea-martins and swallows
Had not arisen just then—one beyond another,
To shiver the air like a playing fountain,
Like dying fireworks strewn out along
The shore—without the sudden lull
Of that brief interruption, they might
Easily have stayed much later at the glass
Instead of turning, as they did, beneath
A disc of moon as round and white as an eye,
To walk back home down the darkened streets
Like some ancient and magnificent tribe.

Evening Refrain

Small bundles of rotting vines smoke beside
The beanfields, the bells have called the sardine
Boats back into shore, and the fires are lit
That have nearly blackened the tufa walls.

Fish scales glitter on the abandoned stalls,
And everywhere now the smell of limestone
Mixes with peppers and olive oil, smoke
And dung . . . How often I've stood here, bored

With reading in the late afternoon, stood
At the hotel window, watching, as though
From an empty waiting-room, while the sun
Drifted off through the hills. And this evening

I've stood a long time staring out through those
Gradually emptying streets, as though

The streets now held some promise of desire,
Like the blue shadows of the olive groves

Drifting downhill toward the abandoned square,
The leaves combing slowly the mild sea-air.

Goodbye

The great sun has changed itself into a pumpkin moon.
The highways glide out of an ocean of air
Like children's slides out of backyard pools.
And the filtered smokestacks give off fumes
Less visible than those which rise from the floor
Of the heart, though they burn all the same,
So the people outdoors appear all day
To be wiping a sad movie from their eyes—
A movie in which, for days to come, and whenever
Two people are seen parting on the street,
Some closing melody is replayed once more
While the one who is saying goodbye
Lets go the hand of the one left standing.

Philip Schultz

Philip Schultz was born in Rochester, New York, in 1945. His first book of poems, *Like Wings*, was published by Viking in 1978. His second book, *Deep Within the Ravine*, also from Viking, was the 1984 Lamont Selection of the Academy of American Poets. Among his other awards are a fellowship from the National Endowment for the Arts and an award from the American Academy and Institute of Arts and Letters. He teaches at New York University.

Like Wings

Last night I dreamed I was the first man to love a woman
& woke shaking & went outside to watch
the faded rag of the sky burn into dawn.
I am tired of the river before feeling,
the joy we must carve from shadow,
tired of my road-thick tongue.

I cannot hand you my breath or wrap the horizon
round your wrist & be forgiven.

I cannot rub the dry wood of my ribs to fire
& sleep. The edge of sleep isn't sleep.
I go room to room tying my feelings into knots.
The space we filled now fills me.
The light & dark won't mix.

I cannot leave myself like a house frozen in the background.
I am this body & the weather all year round.
I think of the light that opened over you our first morning,
how the glass in my lungs turned to sound
& I saw you woman & child & couldn't breathe, for love.
Fear is the edge that is the risk that is loving.
It stinks of blood, draws sharks.

The nights you waltzed naked round our bed,
myself holding the chair I'd painted blue again,
the cats flowing in the wings of your good yellow hair.
There is much men don't know about women,
how your hands work the air to water, the seed to life,
why the salt at the tips of your breasts glows
& tastes of mollusk.

There are hours when the future gives up all hope
& stops in the middle of busy streets
& doesn't care. But think of the distance we have come,
the hands which have wound us.
There will be others.

I have read of ancient people
who held razors to their doctor's throat
as he operated—as if love could have such balance,
like wings.

One night I followed your tracks through deep snow
& stood in an old schoolhouse watching the new sun
come red & shimmer over the opening fields,
the world white & flat & a light
I'd known all my life burned in my head like a fist of rags,
how I couldn't remember what we feared
we'd taken or left,

my arms opened to your shape, how I couldn't lift
out of my body, my mouth frozen
round the sound of your name.

Balance

Eight years gone & the welfare building is a parking ramp.
The attendant can't recall where it went. Uptown somewhere, he thinks.
But ten thousand people filled those halls & only the ocean
is a carpet big enough to sweep so many under.

I was a clerk who read Chekhov & knew the fate of clerks.
I learned to sway down halls like a dancer & never stop to listen.
Mornings I filed dental reports & wore earplugs against the crying
for crutches, steel hands & mattresses fitted to broken backs.

A Mrs. Montvale perched on my desk & swore she'd kill herself
if her new dentures didn't arrive by Thanksgiving.
A fatalist with rotting gums, she feared dying toothless at a feast.
Near closing time the ghosts lined up around the block, still waiting.

In Central Index I watched the hundred ferris wheels
flip rainbow cards sorting the dead from the quickly dying
& filed the electric buzz of computers into a symphony so grand
it washed the curdled voices from my head.

I'm glad the building's gone. Despair can't be tolerated
in such numbers & Gray's *Anatomy* doesn't explain
how the human body breaks a hundred ways each day & still finds balance.
Lord of Mercy, the dead still need bus fare & salvation!

Mrs. Applebaum's
Sunday Dance Class

Her red pump tapping, ankle-length gown slit at the knee,
Mrs. Applebaum lined us up as her husband tuned his piano,
his bald head shining under the Temple's big bay windows.
I can see it all again, the girls' shy smiles, the boys' faces
scrubbed bright as strawberries, 200 fingers anticipating trouble,
the bowing & curtsying rehearsed to a nervous perfection
by Mrs. Applebaum's high German class—it isn't hard to envision
Sarah Rosen, her bourbon curls tied in a ponytail, stepping forward
like an infant swan to choose that clod Charlie Krieger,
while smiling at me! Call it first intimation of splendor,
or darker knowledge, but can't you see us, twenty dwarfs
colliding Sunday after Sunday, until, miraculously, a flourish here,
a pivot there, suddenly Davie Stern dipping Suzie Fein
to Mrs. Applebaum's shrill, "Und vonce agunn, voys und gurdles!"

Oh Mrs. Applebaum, who could've guessed our wild shoving
would be the start of so much furor? You must've known
there was more to come when our lavish stretching left us dizzy,
clumsy with desire? Weren't you, our first teacher, thinking
of the day when such passion would finally take our teeth & hair?
What really channeled such light into your eyes & swayed
your powerful bosom with such force? What pushed Mr. Applebaum,
never a prize winner, to such heights? Ah Mrs. Applebaum,
didn't you notice how I sighed when Sarah didn't change partners
& stayed in my arms? I'm speaking of that terrible excess,
not the edging back, but the overflowing of all that color
flowering in our cheeks! Please, Mrs. Applebaum, remember
Sarah in pink chiffon foxtrotting, her head back & braced teeth
pressed against all that which was to come—the world of such
profound promise! Yes, remember Sarah, her eyes, for so few moments,
so blue the room everywhere around us filled with light!

My Guardian Angel Stein

In our house every floor was a wailing wall
& each sideward glance a history of insult.
Nightly Grandma bolted the doors believing God

had a personal grievance to settle on our heads.
Not Atreus exactly but we had furies (Uncle Jake
banged the tables demanding respect from fate) & enough

outrage to impress Aristotle with the prophetic unity
of our misfortune. No wonder I hid behind the sofa sketching
demons to identify the faces in my dreams & stayed under

bath water until my lungs split like pomegranate seeds.
Stein arrived one New Year's Eve fresh from a salvation in Budapest.
Nothing in his 6,000 years prepared him for our nightly bacchanal

of immigrant indignity except his stint in the Hundred Years' War
where he lost his eyesight & faith both. This myopic angel knew
everything about calamity (he taught King David the art of hubris

& Moses the price of fame) & quoted Dante to prove others
had it worse. On winter nights we memorized the Dead Sea Scrolls
until I could sleep without a night light & he explained why

the stars appear only at night ("Insomniacs, they study the Torah
all day!"). Once I asked him outright: "Stein, why is our house
so unhappy?" Adjusting his rimless glasses, he said: "Boychick,

life is a comedy salted with despair. All humans are disappointed.
Laugh yourself to sleep each night & with luck, pluck & credit cards
you'll beat them at their own game. Catharsis is necessary in this house!"

Ah, Stein, bless your outsized wings & balding pate & while I'm at it
why not bless the imagination's lonely fray with time, which, yes,
like love & family romance, has neither beginning, middle nor end.

The Hemingway House in Key West

If he wrote it he could get rid of it.
—"Fathers and Sons," Ernest Hemingway

My father left me a book of Hemingway's stories
& I understood he meant this as an explanation
& one year later I drove to Idaho to see Hemingway's grave
& phoned his house as if to beg permission for a grief
that held me like a second spine & I saw the room upstairs
where he killed himself & that night I slept dreamless
in a field until the sun's blank stare singed
the loss into my eyes.

Twenty years later I visit Hemingway's house in Key West.
"You look like you want to hear the real dope on Papa,"
the guide says, pointing to the kitchen table raised
to fit Hemingway's height during late-night eating binges.
Like the good wedding guest buttonholed by obsession,
I listen: insomnia, black dreams, his fear of death
without honor—"His father killed himself too,"
the guide sings by rote as we head toward the back cottage
where Hemingway wrote each morning, "depressed, hung over,
he never missed a morning . . ."

I stare at this cottage as if into the pit
his insomniac hunger only deepened.
This was where his despair was hammered
into an alchemy of language that still echoes
in my own insomniac ears. Yes, the sons of failed fathers
have much to undo, but language doesn't soften the pain
that blackens the heart's Torah & absolution
isn't what I am after.

There is something dark in my nature.

One night I woke to see my father staring
out of my bedroom window. "Papa," I cried
as he turned to show me the fire fading
in his eyes like a pilot light. Our shadows

613 / PHILIP SCHULTZ

locked like clock hands as he whispered,
"I am bankrupt . . . there's something I must tell you . . ."
but he said nothing & the next morning I found his body
in a bed soaked with urine & his eyes staring at the ceiling
as if asking a last question the silence would never answer.

All my life I have wondered what he meant to tell me.

Dave Smith

Lindy Keast

Dave Smith was born in Portsmouth, Virginia, in 1942. He received a B.A. from the University of Virginia, an M.A. from Southern Illinois University, and a Ph.D from Ohio University. He is the author of eight books of poems, most recently *The Round-house Voices: Poems 1970-1985*, from Harper & Row, as well as two books of fiction, *Onliness* (L.S.U. Press, 1981), a novel, and *Southern Delights* (Croissant & Company, 1984), a collection of stories. A book of essays, *Local Assays* (1985), was published by the University of Illinois Press. Among his many awards are fellowships from the National Endowment for the Arts, the Guggenheim Foundation, and an award from the American Academy and Institute of Arts and Letters. He teaches at Virginia Commonwealth University.

Cumberland Station

Gray brick, ash, hand-bent railings, steps so big
it takes hours to mount them, polished oak
pews holding the slim hafts of sun, and one
splash of the *Pittsburgh Post-Gazette*. The man
who left Cumberland gone, come back, no job
anywhere. I come here alone, shaken
the way I came years ago to ride down
mountains in Big Daddy's cab. He was
the first set cold in the black meadow.

Six rows of track gleam, thinned, rippling
like water on walls where famous engines steam, half
submerged in frothing crowds with something
to celebrate and plenty to eat. One engineer takes
children for a free ride, a frolic
like an earthquake. Ash cakes their hair.
I am one of those who walked uphill
through flowers of soot to zing
scared to death into the world.

Now whole families afoot cruise South Cumberland
for something to do, no jobs, no money for bars,
the old stories cracked like wallets.

This time there's no fun in coming back. The second
death. My roundhouse uncle coughed his youth
into a gutter. His son, the third, slid on the ice,
losing his need to drink himself
stupidly dead. In this vaulted hall
I think of all the dirt poured down
from shovels and trains and empty pockets.
I stare into the huge malignant headlamps
circling the gray walls and catch a stuttered
glimpse of faces stunned like deer on a track,
children getting drunk, shiny as Depression apples.

Churning through the inner space of this godforsaken
wayside, I feel the ground try to upchuck and I dig
my fingers in my temples to bury a child
diced on a cowcatcher, a woman smelling
alkaline from washing out the soot.
Where I stood in that hopeless, hateful room
will not leave me. The scarf of smoke I saw
over a man's shoulder runs through me
like the sored Potomac River.

Grandfather, you ask why I don't visit you
now you have escaped the ticket-seller's cage
to fumble hooks and clean the Shakespeare reels.

What could we catch? I've been sitting in the pews
thinking about us a long time, long enough to see
a man can't live in jobless, friendless Cumberland
anymore. The soot owns even the fish.

I keep promising I'll come back, we'll get out,
you and me, like brothers, and I mean it.
A while ago a man with the look of a demented cousin
shuffled across this skittery floor and snatched up
the *Post-Gazette* and stuffed it in his coat
and nobody gave a damn because nobody cares
who comes or goes here or even who steals
what nobody wants: old news, photographs
of dead diesels behind chipped glass
swimming into Cumberland Station.

I'm the man who stole it and I wish you were here
to beat the hell out of me for it because
what you said a long time ago welts my face
and won't go away. I admit
it isn't mine even if it's nobody else's.
Anyway, that's all I catch this trip—bad
news. I can't catch my nephew's life, my uncle's,
Big Daddy's, yours, or the ash-haired kids'
who fell down to sleep here after the war.

Outside new families pick their way along tracks
you and I have walked home on many nights.
Every face on the walls goes on smiling,
and, Grandfather, I wish I had the guts
to tell you this is a place I hope
I never have to go through again.

The Perspective and
Limits of Snapshots

Aubrey Bodine's crosswater shot of Menchville,
Virginia: a little dream composing a little water,
specifically, the Deep Creek flank of the James.
Two-man oyster scows lie shoulder to shoulder,
as if you walk them, one land to another,
no narrow channel hidden in the glossy middle
like a blurred stroke, current grinning at hulls.
It is an entirely eloquent peace, with lolling
ropes and liquid glitter, this vision of traffic
and no oystermen in sight. Clearly, Bodine is not
Matthew Brady catching the trenchant gropes frozen
at Fredericksburg with a small black box. So well
has he excluded the neat Mennonite church, yachts,
country club pool, the spare smell of dignity seeps.
Perhaps it is because of the zoom on the teeth
of the oyster tongs; perhaps it is after all Sunday.

Above the last boat, the flat-faced store squats
at the end of the dirt road as if musing over
accounts receivable. No doubt it has weathered
years of blood spilling. A spotted hound lifts
his nose above what must be yesterday's trash fish,
his white coat luminous against deep foliage. What
Bodine fails to see is the dog turning to lope
uphill under that screen of poplars, behind fat
azaleas that hide the county farm and the drunks
pressed against wire screens, sniffing the James.
One oysterman thumped his noisy wife (the window
was accidental) because she had a knife and mourned
their boy twenty years drowned. If he knew Bodine
stood at the marsh tip where his boy dove, if he
were but told a camera yawned to suck in the years
of his worst sailing shame, he would turn away. He
would whistle up boys in the dust that is dignity
and if he could he would spit in his hand and tell
his nameless black cellmate there are many men
for whom the world is neither oyster nor pearl.

The Roundhouse Voices

In full glare of sunlight I came here, man-tall but thin
as a pinstripe, and stood outside the rusted fence
with its crown of iron thorns while
the soot cut into our lungs with tiny diamonds.
I walked through houses with my grain-lovely slugger
from Louisville that my uncle bought and stood
in the sun that made its glove soft on my hand
until I saw my chance to crawl under and get past
anyone who would demand a badge and a name.

The guard hollered that I could get the hell from there quick
when I popped in his face like a thief. All I ever wanted
to steal was life and you can't get that easy
in the grind of a railyard. *You can't catch me
lardass, I can go left or right good as the Mick,*
I hummed to him, holding my slugger by the neck
for a bunt laid smooth where the coal cars
jerked and let me pass between tracks
until, in a slide on ash, I fell safe and heard
the wheeze of his words: *Who the hell are you, kid?*

I hear them again tonight Uncle, hard as big brakeshoes,
when I lean over your face in the box of silk. The years
you spent hobbling from room to room alone crawl
up my legs and turn this house to another
house, round and black as defeat, where slugging
comes easy when you whip the gray softball over
the glass diesel globe. Footsteps thump on the stairs
like that fat ball against bricks and when I miss
I hear you warn me to watch the timing, to keep
my eyes on your hand and forget the fence,

hearing also that other voice that keeps me out and away
from you on a day worth playing good ball. Hearing
Who the hell . . . I see myself, like a burning speck
of cinder come down the hill and through a tunnel
of porches like stands, running on deep ash,
and I give him the finger, whose face still gleams

clear as a B & O headlight, just to make him get up
and chase me into a dream of scoring at your feet.
At Christmas that guard staggered home sobbing,
the thing in his chest tight as a torque wrench.
In the summer I did not have to run and now

who is the one who dreams of a drink as he leans over
tools you kept bright as a first-girl's promise? I
have no one to run from or to, nobody to give
my finger to as I steal his peace. Uncle, the light
bleeds on your gray face like the high barbed wire
shadows I had to get through and maybe you don't remember
you said to come back, to wait and you'd show me
the right way to take a hard pitch
in the sun that shudders on the ready man. I'm here

though this is a day I did not want to see. In the roundhouse
the rasp and heel-click of compressors is still,
soot lies deep in every greasy fingerprint.
I called you from the pits and you did not come up
and I felt the fear when I stood on the tracks
that are like stars which never lead us
into any kind of light and I don't know who'll
tell me now when the guard sticks his blind snoot
between us: take off and beat the bastard out.
Can you hear him over the yard, grabbing his chest,
cry out *Who the goddamn hell are you, kid?*

I gave him every name in the book, Uncle, but he caught us
and what good did all those hours of coaching do?
You lie on your back, eyeless forever, and I think
how once I climbed to the top of a diesel and stared
into that gray roundhouse glass where, in anger,
you threw up the ball and made a star
to swear at greater than the Mick ever dreamed.
It has been years but now I know what followed there
every morning the sun came up, not light
but the puffing bad-bellied light of words.

All day I have held your hand, trying to say back that life,
to get under that fence with words I lined
and linked up and steamed into a cold room
where the illusion of hope means skin torn in boxes
of tools. The footsteps come pounding into words
and even the finger I give death is words
that won't let us be what we wanted, each one
chasing and being chased by dreams in a dark place.
Words are all we ever were and they did us
no damn good. Do you hear that?

Do you hear the words that, in oiled gravel, you gave me
when you set my feet in the right stance to swing?
They are coal-hard and they come in wings
and loops like despair not even the Mick
could knock out of this room, words softer
than the centers of hearts in guards or uncles,
words skinned and numbered by too many bricks.
I have had enough of them and bring them back here
where the tick and creak of everything dies
in your tiny starlight and I stand down
on my knees to cry, *Who the hell are you, kid?*

Of Oystermen, Workboats

The wide, white, wing-boned washboards of twenty
footers, sloped, ridged to hold
a man's tongs and stride,
                    the good stance
to scrape deep with a motion like big applause,
plunging the teeth true beyond the known
mounds of the dead, the current carried
cloisters of murk,
                    miracles that bloom

luminous and unseen, sweet things to be
brought up, bejeweled, culled from husks,

as oystermen like odd angels glide far off enough
to keep a wake gentle as shirts on a line,
red baseball caps dipping like bloodied
heads upright, the clawed hand slapped
at the air in salute,
                     those washboards that splinter
the sun on tongs downlaid, on tines humming,

those womb-hulls harbored flank to flank at dusk
until the white-robed priest of the moon
stands tall to the sea's spume-pour
in nostrils
          of the men who sway from heel to heel,

the season come again, the socketed gray
of their eyes outward,
forearms naked past longjohns,
the salted breast-beaters at first light

lined up, ready to fly.

Photographic Plate, Partly Spidered, Hampton Roads, Virginia, with Model T Ford Mid-Channel

No one alive has seen such ice but the five-mile floor
of water so clenched itself salt broke down.
Among us even the age-wearied would not dream
you might walk the Chesapeake Bay
and look unafraid on its lucid darkness,

and the fathers of fathers, boatwrights, sailors of all
waters, never guessed this stuttering toy
might take them so far. But someone,
joking maybe, has rolled a small house
on perilous wheels down the banks
of the James, gunned it forward
for skids, runs, circles, a day
of such joyous noise the dead
seemed to have risen, so many
great-booted and black-coated are out there.

We cannot tell what they think, or if they find themselves
dancing on the road where no road ever was,
though there are long skirts, a few
thick-waisted grandmothers, even
a scatter of children cast about.
All of them are facing Norfolk,
where ships doze like unimaginable
beasts the sea has given to the dreams of men.

The Model T is small, black, plain, and appears
cornered like something risen through ice.
Hands reach in the hazed air
but do not touch what must be
chugging in a kind of terror.
The plate is dotted far and near.
Seagulls? Stains? Some mistake of glass?
And do these faces only look averted, cast down?

Among these is the one who will breed us, having crossed
a whiteness he will not speak about even to her
whose skirts he will shake us from.
But now gears spin inside him,
wheels, a future of machines. One day
he will tell my father he walked on water . . .
sick, chugging for breath, shunned as crazy,
who I remember by the habitual odor of gasoline.
When he died my father said he was too frightened to live.

Under the ice where they walk the dark is enormous.
All day I watch the backs turned away for the one face
that is mine, that is going to wheel at me the secrets of many.

In the House of the Judge

All of them asleep, the suspiring everywhere is audible weight
  in the winter-shadowed house where I have dreamed
    night after night and stand now trying
  to believe it is only dust, no more than vent-spew
    risen from the idiotically huffing
grandfather of a furnace in the coal room's heart of darkness.

Haven't I touched the flesh-gray sift on bookshelves, on framed
  dim photographs of ancestors, on the clotted arms
    of the banjo clock that tolls past
  all resemblance to time and clicks like a musket's
    steel hammer? And every day I wipe my glasses but still it comes,
as now, at the top of the whining stairs, I am

come to wait with my hand laid light on the moon-slicked railing.
  I hear the house-heave of sleepers, and go jittery
    with no fear I can name. I feel myself
  shaped by the mica-fine motes that once were one
    body in earth until gouged, cracked,
left tumbled apart and scarcely glowing in a draft-fanned pit.

Pipes clank and gargle like years in the ashen veins of the Judge
  when they came to his house, the dung-heeled, some
    drunk, all with stuttered pleas to free
  their young, who could make it given a chance, just
    one more good chance, so they said. Impassive, in skin-folds thick
as a lizard, he stared at the great one for a sign,

the dog across the room, who kept a wary eye and was a one-man dog.
　Overhead do the same unbearable stars yet wheel
　　in bright, ubiquitous malice, and what
　am I, wiping my glasses, certain this house walks
　　in nail-clicking threat, going to plead?
I look out through warped Civil War glass buffed by men now ash

where the small park he gave in civic pride lies snow-blistered.
　Sub-zero then, as now, sent fire in the opening
　　throat, but they came: tethered horses,
　striding shadows, and women who shrieked nightlong
until even gone they continued in his head. He heard them breathing.
　He painted his house a perfectly sneering white.

I stare at that snow as at a scaffold. Whose lightening footprints
　could soften my fear or say why I sniff like a
　　dog, seem to taste a skim of black air
　upsweeping the maple stairwell, and feel my hair
　　go slowly white? How many hours must
a man watch snow shift the world before he sees it is only a dream

of useless hope stamped and restamped by the ash-steps of those we
　can do no justice to except in loving them? But
　　what could he do before the raw facts
　of men cleaving flesh like boys hacking ice?
I think how he must have thought of his barking teacher of law:
　There is only truth and law! He had learned the law.

But what was the truth to leave him trembling like a child in prayer?
　In late years he kept the monster by his side, two shades
　　walking alone in the ice, the nail-raker, one
　who howled without reason and clawed at the heart
　　of door after door. In the end he was known
inseparable from his beast who, it was said, kept the Judge alive.

Until he was not. Until his house emptied. Until we came who I hear
　breathing, those heads warm as banked ash under my hand
　　laid light as I have laid it on this railing.
　But are we only this upfloating and self-clinging ash

that loops freely through dark houses? Those enigmatic fissures
  I see circling the snow? Are those only the tracks

of the dog I locked out, those black steps no more than a gleaming
  ice, or the face of some brother in the dirt betrayed,
    pleading, accusing? The moon, far off and dim,
  plays tricks with my eyes and the snow path turns dark as
a line of men marched into the earth. Whitely, my breath floats
  back at me, crying *I did not do this,* when the shuddering

Courthouse clock across the square booms me back to myself. Dream's
  aftershock, the heirloom banjo starts to thud and drum
    so I turn and hustle downstairs to halt it.
  Even with my hands laid on its hands it wants to thump
    its malicious heart out, but I can do this
at least: I can hold on to help them sleep through another night.

I can sit for a while with love's ice-flickering darkness where ash
  is heavily filling my house. I can sit with my own
    nailed walker in the snow, one whistled
  under my hand without question or answer. If I sleep
he will pad the floors above the fire-pit. He will claw me awake
  to hear breathing in the still house of the Judge

      where I live.

Leafless Trees, Chickahominy Swamp

Mechanicsville, Virginia

Humorless, hundreds of trunks gray in the blue expanse
where dusk leaves them hacked like a breastwork,
stripped like pikes planted to impale, the knots
of vines at each groin appearing placed by makers

schooled in grotesque campaigns. Mathew Brady's
plates show them as they are, the ageless stumps,
time-sanded solitaries, some clumped in squads
we might imagine veterans, except they're only wood,
and nothing in the world seems more dead than these.

Stopped by the lanes filled with homebound tail-lights,
we haven't seen the rumored Eagle we hoped to watch,
only a clutch of buzzards ferrying sticks for a nest.
Is this history, that we want the unchanged, useless
spines out there to thrust in our faces the human
qualities we covet? We read this place like generals
whose promised recruits don't show, unable to press on:
there is the languor of battle, troops who can't tell
themselves from the enemy, and file-hard fear gone

indifferent in the mortaring sun that will leave them,
night after night, standing in the same cold planes
of water. It never blooms or greens. It merely stinks.
Why can't we admit it's death, blameless, say that
festering, scummy scene is nothing like a blown brainpan?
Why do we sit and sniff the rank hours keeping words
full of ground that only stares off our question: What
happened? Leaf-light in our heads, don't we mean: Why
these grisly emblems, the slime that won't swell to hope?

The rapacious odor of swamps all over the earth bubbles
sometimes to mist, fetid flesh we can't see but know
as cells composing, decomposing, illusions of the heart.
God knows what we'd do in there, we say, easing back
on the blacktop. Once we heard a whistling. Harmonicas?
But who'd listen? Surely all was green once, fragile
as a truce, words braiding sun and water, as on a lake
where families sang. What else would we hope for, do
in the dead miles nothing explains or changes or relieves?

An Antipastoral Memory
of One Summer

It is written that a single hurricane holds the power
to run our whole country for one year. Imagine
lights in Minnesota chicken coops, firebells
ringing every borough of New York, dock pumps
spewing the bilge from Louisiana shrimpers,
the pulse that sends a voice from San Francisco
to Nagasaki where a woman wakes, folds, and refolds
the American edition of news already forgotten.

Yet even in the dark silos of our countrymen who
practice graceful moves at the missile's panel
that is like a piano with the amazing, unplayed
notes not even Beethoven could hear into fusion,
no one dreams how to harness the storm for good.
That is why I think of two people at a bulkhead,
an old woman desperately pushing down the hem
of her flowered dress, holding a boy's small hand
where the waves they have come to see blossom

one after another, sluicing over their driven hair,
the salt sting so strong their eyes begin to swell,
until they fall back across the elegant Boulevard,
and even there the unexpected crescendos boom in
laces and strings of water radiant as new light.
The noise is unforgettable and deafening, the sea
keeps orchestrating, as if it means to address
all our preparations, the boarded windows, the dead

cars with their rain-blistered glass, the sidewalk
clotted now with seaweed like abandoned bodies.
That suddenly, then, the calm eye stalls on them,
a stillness like a lock with no key, a hand
hovering at a switch, waiting for music unheard,
and see—the woman turns, drags the boy brutally
past oaks older than them both, leaves this fall
blinking like lights, trembling, limbs like spears,
two entering a powerless house to huddle, to pray
to the still God, though they call it hurricane.

Cathy Song

Lynette Tom

Cathy Song was born in 1955 in Honolulu, Hawaii. She received a B.A. from Wellesley College and an M.A. from Boston University. Her first book, *Picture Bride* (1983), won the Yale Series of Younger Poets Award and was nominated for a National Book Critics Circle Award. She teaches in Hawaii.

Blue Lantern

The blue lantern light
was like a full moon
swelling above the hush
of the mock orange shrubs
that separated our houses.

It was light
from your grandfather's room.

I remember the music
at night.

I dreamed the music
came in squares,
like birthday chocolate,
through the window
on a blue plate.

From his shakuhachi,
shavings of notes,
floated, and fell;
melted where the stillness
inserted itself back into night.
It was quiet then until dawn,
broken once by a single wailing:
the sound of an animal
whose hind leg is caught in a trap.

It was your grandfather
mourning his dead wife.
He played for her each night;
her absence,
the shape of his grief
funneled through the bamboo flute.
A ritual of remembrance,
keeping her memory alive
with his old breath.
He played unknowingly
to the child next door
who lay stricken by the music
transposed to her body,
waiting for the cry
that always surprised her;
like a glimpse of shadow
darting through the room
before she would drift off into sleep.

I knew you were in the room
just beyond the music.

This was something we shared.
Listening, my eyes closed
as though I were under water
in the blueness of my room;
I felt buoyant and protected.

I imagined you, his grandson,
listening and lying
in your small bed;
your head making a slight
dent in the pillow.

It was as though the weight
of his grief washed over
the two of us
each night like a tide,
leaving our bodies beached
but unbruised,
white and firm like shells.

Beauty and Sadness

For Kitagawa Utamaro

He drew hundreds of women
in studies unfolding
like flowers from a fan.
Teahouse waitresses, actresses,
geishas, courtesans and maids.
They arranged themselves
before this quick, nimble man
whose invisible presence
one feels in these prints
is as delicate
as the skinlike paper

he used to transfer
and retain their fleeting loveliness.

Crouching like cats,
they purred amid the layers of kimono
swirling around them
as though they were bathing
in a mountain pool with irises
growing in the silken sunlit water.
Or poised like porcelain vases,
slender, erect and tall; their heavy
brocaded hair was piled high
with sandalwood combs and blossom sprigs
poking out like antennae.
They resembled beautiful iridescent insects,
creatures from a floating world.

Utamaro absorbed these women of Edo
in their moments of melancholy
as well as of beauty.
He captured the wisp of shadows,
the half-draped body
emerging from a bath; whatever
skin was exposed
was powdered white as snow.
A private space disclosed.
Portraying another girl
catching a glimpse of her own vulnerable
face in the mirror, he transposed
the trembling plum lips
like a drop of blood
soaking up the white expanse of paper.

At times, indifferent to his inconsolable
eye, the women drifted
through the soft gray feathered light,
maintaining stillness, the moments in between.
Like the dusty ash-winged moths
that cling to the screens in summer

and that the Japanese venerate
as ancestors reincarnated;
Utamaro graced these women with immortality
in the thousand sheaves of prints
fluttering into the reverent hands of keepers:
the dwarfed and bespectacled painter
holding up to a square of sunlight
what he had carried home beneath his coat
one afternoon in winter.

Girl Powdering Her Neck

FROM A UKIYO-E PRINT BY UTAMARO

The light is the inside
sheen of an oyster shell,
sponged with talc and vapor,
moisture from a bath.

A pair of slippers
are placed outside
the rice-paper doors.
She kneels at a low table
in the room,
her legs folded beneath her
as she sits on a buckwheat pillow.

Her hair is black
with hints of red,
the color of seaweed
spread over rocks.

Morning begins the ritual
wheel of the body,

the application of translucent skins.
She practices pleasure:
the pressure of three fingertips
applying powder.
Fingerprints of pollen
some other hand will trace.

The peach-dyed kimono
patterned with maple leaves
drifting across the silk,
falls from right to left
in a diagonal, revealing
the nape of her neck
and the curve of a shoulder
like the slope of a hill
set deep in snow in a country
of huge white solemn birds.
Her face appears in the mirror,
a reflection in a winter pond,
rising to meet itself.

She dips a corner of her sleeve
like a brush into water
to wipe the mirror;
she is about to paint herself.
The eyes narrow
in a moment of self-scrutiny.
The mouth parts
as if desiring to disturb
the placid plum face;
break the symmetry of silence.
But the berry-stained lips,
stenciled into the mask of beauty,
do not speak.

Two chrysanthemums
touch in the middle of the lake
and drift apart.

The Youngest Daughter

The sky has been dark
for many years.
My skin has become as damp
and pale as rice paper
and feels the way
mother's used to before the drying sun
parched it out there in the fields.

  Lately, when I touch my eyelids,
my hands react as if
I had just touched something
hot enough to burn.
My skin, aspirin colored,
tingles with migraine. Mother
has been massaging the left side of my face
especially in the evenings
when the pain flares up.

This morning
her breathing was graveled,
her voice gruff with affection
when I wheeled her into the bath.
She was in a good humor,
making jokes about her great breasts,
floating in the milky water
like two walruses,
flaccid and whiskered around the nipples.
I scrubbed them with a sour taste
in my mouth, thinking:
six children and an old man
have sucked from these brown nipples.

I was almost tender
when I came to the blue bruises
that freckle her body,
places where she has been injecting insulin
for thirty years. I soaped her slowly,

she sighed deeply, her eyes closed.
It seems it has always
been like this: the two of us
in this sunless room,
the splashing of the bathwater.

In the afternoons
when she has rested,
she prepares our ritual of tea and rice,
garnished with a shred of gingered fish,
a slice of pickled turnip,
a token for my white body.
We eat in the familiar silence.
She knows I am not to be trusted,
even now planning my escape.
As I toast to her health
with the tea she has poured,
a thousand cranes curtain the window,
fly up in a sudden breeze.

Gary Soto

Gary Soto was born in 1952. He is the author of four books of poetry, *The Elements of San Joaquin* (1977), winner of the U.S. Award of the International Poetry Forum, *The Tale of Sunlight* (1978), *Where Sparrows Work Hard* (1981), and *Black Hair* (1984), all from the University of Pittsburgh Press. Among his other awards are the "Discovery"/*The Nation* award and fellowships from the National Endowment for the Arts and the Guggenheim Foundation. He teaches at the University of California, Berkeley.

The Widow Perez

After a while
She slumped down in the closet
Among a pile of dirty clothes
To become those creases,
Grey with the meaning
Of wind, black
With the crossing of roads.
For hours she stood
In that musk, between
The slouched shoulders of shirts,
Waiting for you to return,
Your eyes the blurred points
Of twilight, your smile blank

Where a tooth was missing
And lodged with a residue
Of years.

But you failed
To come back, old man.
She didn't feel her warmth double
Or tug a sleeve limp
From wear; she didn't touch
Your collar flagged
And grey with distance, your mouth
Sinking into a cup
From which roots lengthen
And push upward
To say what the dead say
In a sad flower . . .
Hours later she came out,
Washed, and set the stove blazing.
One bowl or two? The floor ticked
And she turned to listen.

The Morning They Shot Tony Lopez, Barber and Pusher Who Went Too Far, 1958

When they entered through the back door,
You were too slow in raising an arm
Or thinking of your eyes refusing the light,
Or your new boots moored under the bed,
Or your wallet on the bureau, open
And choking with bills,
Or your pockets turned inside out, hanging breathless as tongues,
Or the vendor clearing his throat in the street,
Or your watch passed on to another's son,

Or the train to Los Banos,
The earth you would slip into like a shirt
And drift through forever.
When they entered, and shot once,
You twisted the face your mother gave
With the three, short grunts that let you slide
In the same blood you closed your eyes to.

At the Cantina

In the cantina
Of six tables
A woman fingers
The ear lobe
Of a bank teller.
It is late,
And this place is empty
As a crushed hat.
A galaxy of flies
Circles the lamp.
Manuel wipes the counter,
Flicking ashes
Onto the floor.
The voices of
That couple
With the faces of oxen
On a hot day
Reach over his shoulder
And vanish
Into the mirror.
Finally they leave
Without nodding good-bye,
His hand on
Her right breast,
Her thumb hooked

In his watch pocket.
Manuel locks up,
Uncorks a bottle
And sits at a table.
All night he drinks
And his hands fold
And unfold,
Against the light,
A kingdom of animal shadows—
The Jackal,
The Hummingbird,
The sleepy-eyed Llama,
An Iguana munching air—
While the rooster stretches
To the day not there yet.

The Point

The moon going orange
Through a cloud
That refuses to move,
Molina in the yard
Talking to a chicken
That blinks with eyes
Blown deep
As targets. It circles
Its droppings
And says nothing
Of the wind that passes
Through a door
Nailed shut
By its own poverty;
Or of the galaxy
Of lint tilting on its axis,

Those unmapped stars
He counted twice
And named for his country.
Why the cloud
That never rained,
The sleep that is something
More than sleep?
Why the crow found
Flat as a glove,
Its beak open on a yawn?
Nothing answered,
He weighs six rocks
Against his hunger
And bursts a streetlight
That won't come to the point:
The sky swallows
Hard on the echo
And Molina's eyes are lost
Between the blue of two stars.

The Map

When the sun's whiteness closes around us
Like a noose,

It is noon, and Molina squats
In the uneven shade of an oleander.

He unfolds a map and, with a pencil,
Blackens Panama

Into a bruise;
He dots rain over Bogotá, the city of spiders,

And x's in a mountain range that climbs
Like a thermometer

Above the stone fence
The old never thought to look over.

The fog presses over Lima.
Brazil is untangled of its rivers.

Where there is a smudge,
Snow has stitched its cold into the field.

Where the river Orinoco cuts east,
A new river rises nameless

From the open grasses,
And Molina calls it his place of birth.

Marcia Southwick

Marcia Southwick was born in 1949. She was educated at Emerson College and the University of Iowa, and is the author of two collections of poetry, *The Night Won't Save Anyone* (University of Georgia Press, 1980), and *Connecticut: Eight Poems* (Pym-Randall Press, 1981). She was a Stanley B. Young Fellow at Bread Loaf and has received a fellowship from the National Endowment for the Arts.

Wayne Southwick

A Burial, Green

It was afternoon, and my brother split
a turtle's head
open in the rain; the tiny skull
glistened, and soon the ants knew
every detail of cracked shell.
For hours he sat in the blue shade
of the elm, planning a burial
for his small dead, until
the shadows knew each curve
of grass around the green and orange
spotted shell, a tiny helmet

filling with air. It was spring
and the bark on the dogwood trees
was slick and wet, the cardinals twittered
on the green feeder.
And my brother thought it was ceremony,
the way the door to our white house opened
and he entered, done with his spade
and boots, the way my mother
hovered in the doorway
and touched his shoulder
without a word
like the rain.

Owning a Dead Man

The geese fly off, but sometimes they don't take
their voices with them. Stretched out like this,
I think my future is simple, like a cornfield
filling with light. I'm happy,
because of the way the geese have left their shadows
drying on the lawn around me, and the way
the long docks lean out into the water,
letting the unpainted boats knock against them.
Once, my mother told me, a woman came to this place
with an urn that held her dead husband's ashes.
The woman's pale hands tossed bits of gray-white
bone and soot onto the marsh, where the quail hid.
My mother was angry that the bones had trespassed
her land. *In a way*, she said, *I own a dead man.*

Now as I lie here, I think of the coming winter,
of his bones, mixed with the bones of the mouse
and the gull, cleansed and shining in the new snow,
but if I try to think too deeply, it's as if a bird

were pulling straws from a dried out nest!
So I wonder if I have ever witnessed the middle
of winter: the birch trees' inability to lose
anything more, or if I have ever seen myself
as more irrelevant than in December—
In that cold and stillness, my blood
and my muscles contracting as I tramp through the snow
couldn't possibly mean anything. And there *are* days
when a landscape feels nothing for its real trees,
only for what lies still in the snow,
or only for what has been.

Dusk

I cannot worry
about what lies beneath the surface,
so I walk into the fragile dusk,
breaking the backs of field mice
still asleep under the snow.
The sunlight that does not reach me
illuminates the distance
between this world and God's,
where winter is simply the white
of perfect concentration.
I would like to believe in God,
just as I would like to believe there is an angel
weeping beneath the Chinese elms,
but He is an abstraction, like forgetfulness
or mathematics. In the mind of God,
winter can be summarized as one dark tree!
And yet, as I walk out over the frozen pond,
the pure white of this winter
enters my mind, and I become more open,
like a clearing in the woods

where light accentuates the dead underbrush
without emphasizing its ugliness.
And so I can live with my faults.
I can be touched
and not feel like a passing shadow.

The Marsh

Each time I return to this place
I expect to find a recurring distance
between myself and the huge trees,
as though I were in a dream
in which I could run toward them forever
and never get there.

Right now the marsh seems unfamiliar
because the crickets have taken me by surprise;
their singing has entered my mind just now,
even though I've been hearing them all along.
So I'm almost afraid,
because there must be other ways
in which I am left out of the landscape—
It's as if the mallards stay hidden in the grass
for a purpose. But I don't think they are there
to make me understand what I don't already know,
only to point out how often I'm surprised.
. And that is why the mallards fly suddenly upward,
leaving the grass empty and essential.

And when I try to summarize the difference
between the tide and the way I remember it,
I find myself unable to explain

all that I have discarded—
The driftwood, fish skeletons
and chipped shells
are remnants of a past life
I can't possibly understand.

Roberta Spear

Roberta Spear was born in 1948 in Hanford, California, and was educated at California State University at Fresno. She is the author of two books of poetry, *Silks* (1980), chosen by Philip Levine for the National Poetry Series, and *Taking to Water* (1985), both from Holt, Rinehart, and Winston. Among her other awards are the James D. Phelan Award, a fellowship from the National Endowment for the Arts, and a Guggenheim Fellowship for 1984. Over the last ten years she has worked both as a social worker and a teacher of creative writing.

The White Dress

I want you to see me in it.

The mirror witches an image
that invents every movement. When I spin
I enter the seven precious stages of flight;
the room is as lively as a dovecote.
Again I turn and stop,
looking into your eyes
where the feathers are drifting down
over my thighs and knees.
The cloth obeys the curves of my body.
It is as simple as this,
a white dress.

Later we will leave the party and walk
the cool sidewalks toward the highway
where junipers nod in the wind.
When my skirt ripples out into darkness
you will move me, like a sail
in its first gentle breaths
toward the open sea. White
is a mixture of many understandings.

The bare arm,
the angle of fiber on skin,
two thin strings at the neck
undoing the world . . .
Now turn away.

Sunlight is living in the storefront window
and the shopkeeper wants her money.
I want your opinion

years from now
when you've forgotten how I look in white.

The Bat

1.

In autumn,
the bats steamed in their fur
like rotten eggs
buried under each shingle.
We looked up—
the ladder shook
as the man pried their fists

loose with a crowbar.
In one burst,
they shot dead-eyed
into the thicket.

2.

Bats never go away;
they settle nearby
on the darkest limbs
where they grow
and get uglier.
In a year's time
they wriggle back
into the beams and nests
of barnstraw, whispering.
The heifers wear out
their heels in the paddock;
people blow softly
into the currents of sleep,
their hands
open at their sides.

3.

Before dawn,
I ease into dreams,
a quilt stretched
over my knees. The little ones
crawl out, fanning
themselves: *pouch-winged*,
graceful *pallid*, I am ready.
Leaf-nosed can't see
me coming and waits
on the last rib
for a slow moth. I steal
his edge on darkness.

4.

Bluejay rams a cherry tree,
hummingbird rests its head
on the bar, asks for another,
the phoebe gives away
her drab color, the wretched crow
gives up and begs for a field mouse
who can't understand.

The answer is the bat
who finds life easy
to swallow. He drops here
like a hankie, but leaves
his song in the other world—
he too is a failure. Try again.

5.

So you took
two clipped steps
toward the window, the curtain
swelled. He was asleep
and with each gust spread
like a burn over the white lace.
You opened a book
and closed it around his body,
tilting the binding
until he fell two floors down
to the bed of dahlias
where the sun began
and the wind, in one word,
offered itself to the earth.

Boundaries

I clipped and the brown petals
piled on the driveway.
Two neighbors marked boundaries
set thirty years ago.
There were certain things
they couldn't say to each other:
One brushed the dirt off
on her washdress and the other
blamed a man who came to the house
when she was a child.

Later, I fought with myself
while trying to plant
a row of seeds on the edge
of this paper. I left the desk
for a pair of socks
and a cigarette. I thought
of my sister's wedding, of days
when we were told that nothing
was too good for us.

My father,
under the arbor of dried concords,
filled his glass over and over;
my grandmother moved her chair
into the sun and settled;
I froze under the bridesmaid's ruffle,
neither fainting nor feeling
the blood in my cheeks.
At dusk, the cyclamen stiffened
on the covered tables.

Yet, if my sister asked,
I would tell her that boundaries
mean nothing. I have a husband
and we come together
in the afternoon. She and I

came together too,
were overheard
and put into separate rooms.

As I clipped, their voices
flew off with robins.
And my eyes followed
a bud in the shadows
kissing its way
into this world.

The Anniversary

It's the first of May—
the last drops of rain are a payment
to the dust and yellow air.
The man beside me preserves dreams
in his dark folds. When the light
settles on the walls, he turns
restlessly as a saint
whose limbs are buried in different cities.
I loosen the fist of sheets,
the clouds move on and return.
After each breath,
he breathes again.

Hours ago, we drove back to town,
the sky contracted on all sides
bolting the branches along the road.
We drank to years of labor,
the ladder of love, to the corn
illumined, growing up into the dead
of night, the vineyards
glowing like spines.
We passed a woman outside a country bar;

under the awning with a cigarette,
she gave quickly to the streams
of alkali, small rivers
filling the furrows.

The possibilities are as endless
as watermarks in the dust.

But in town, it's only rain
and is gone. The first yeses sprout
in a patch of purple outside the window,
an elm bows over the universe
of our bed. Only the two of us,
and you're gone, staggering
into sleep like that senseless jay
through loops of gravel and wet leaves
to his home in the air.
It is as clear as vodka:

I want to wake you now,
saying let's drink up and get back
to the work we did so well last night,
saying as the earth says after rain
this one is on me.

Elizabeth Spires

Madison Bell

Elizabeth Spires was born in 1952 in Lancaster, Ohio. She received a B.A. from Vassar College and an M.A. from Johns Hopkins University. Her first book of poems, *Globe* (1981), was published by Wesleyan University Press. Among her awards are fellowships from the National Endowment for the Arts and the Ingram-Merrill Foundation. She is a visiting assistant professor at Johns Hopkins University.

Tequila

I live in a stone house high in the mountains,
close to the stars . . .
                Last night, a little lonely,
I went to the bar in the valley
where the regulars tell their stories,
one about a man with a runaway dog,
who stood by his door each night calling
Tequila, Tequila. Nobody
knew how long his grief would last
or what he did when his house went dark.
Did he sit all night tipping
a bottle of tequila to his mouth,
legs wrapping the bottle in warmth
the way a shot of tequila

wraps the throat? Or did he sleep
like everyone else, holding his parts
close to himself like a dog? Nobody should
go near a man who wants to be
that lonely. Nobody does.
Bragging, I told them I'd go back
to any year in my life
and live it over. I lied
and said nothing had ever scared me.
They looked at me, all husbands and fathers.
The stars will blind you, they warned,
the ghosts in the alley
will blow smoke in your eyes and steal
your money. I nodded, pretending to know.
But someday I'll leave this place with
only as much as I can carry,
taking the only road
out of the valley, the one that leads
everywhere. And though I'm not friendly,
I'll leave a note on the door,
black writing on a white square, cryptic
and small, so the regulars can make up
my story: *Gone to find Tequila*—

Skins

Above my head the apples on my grandparents' tree
glowed with a pale green light.
I swung on the swing
waiting for them to drop.
Then walked on them, a balancing act,
with unsteady five-year-old feet.
Skins split.
Something sweet floated out and caught to my feet

following me everywhere—past grape arbor
and chicken coop, a trellis of roses and onion patch,
down to an unused outhouse bordering an alley of dust.

I forget what the world meant to me then . . .
people and objects swam past, not bothering
to explain themselves or tell me where they were going.
Like the goldfish cruising in my grandparents' fishpond,
mouths frozen over O-shaped syllables of air
that rose to the surface and popped.
The largest was the size of my hand, its papery skin
an orange bruise that swelled and swelled
as I threw it too much bread.
Was it true a fish would explode if it ate too much?
It was something I'd heard and wanted to see proof of.
The big fish was puffing into a balloon
the week my parents came to take me home.

An early frost froze all the fish into glass floats.
I sat in first grade awkwardly
cutting a fish out of construction paper for a reading race.
My blunt-edged scissors got the tail too long,
the snout pointed and menacing like a shark's.
I printed my name in block letters on the spine, watched
the teacher skewer it with pins to the bulletin board.
What was it like to be stuck in the wrong element
waiting for a thaw? Everything beyond yourself
out of control and no way to move backward or forward?
Dead. The word meant having your eyes sewed shut
and ice water for blood. Above my head a column of fish
swam in blue cellophane, aiming toward a finish line
of yarn. Each day my fish would edge forward,
beating out the others, gold stars stuck to its fin.

Widow's Walk

When he visited Nantucket, Crevecoeur noted, "A
singular custom prevails here among the women. . . .
They have adopted these many years the Asiatic
custom of taking a dose of opium every morning; and
so deeply rooted is it, that they would be at a loss
how to live without this indulgence."
—Walter Teller,
Cape Cod and the Offshore Islands

Captain: the weathervane's rusted.
Iron-red, its coxcomb leans into the easterly wind
as I do every afternoon swinging
a blind eye out to sea. The light
fails, day closes around me, a vast oceanic whirlpool . . .
I can still see your eyes, those monotonic palettes,
smell your whiskeyed kisses!
Still feel the eelgrass of embrace—
the ocean pounds outside the heart's door.
Dearest, the lamps are going on. I'm caught
in the smell of whales burning! Vaporous and drowsy,
I spiral down the staircase in my wrapper,
a shadow among many shadows in Nantucket Town.
Out in the yard, the chinaberry tree
turns amber. A hymn spreads through the deepening air—
the church steeple's praying for the people. Last night
I dreamed you waved farewell.
I stood upon the pier, the buoys tolling
a warning knell. Trussed in my whalebone,
I grew away from you, fluttering in the twilight,
a cutout, a fancy French silhouette.

Courtesan with Fan

Auspicious night.
> The stars balance on poles
as a crescent moon, half-eaten,
rises out of the persimmon tree.

The dragon at the top of the sky
flails the universe

as if I were once more seven,
my mother binding my feet into delicate hooves.
I rocked like a boat, my feet two white moons,
two crescents of pain.

Half-woman, I languished in the sequestered bedchamber
till my body sprouted—
a swollen green shoot tender to strangers.

They handle me, paint
my shoulders with their tongues.

I breathe in the blackness of complete abandon,
as if I were diving for pearls,
> deeper, deeper,
my spiderfine silks changing to seaweed.

Always when it happens, I close my eyes.
My bones bend like watery willows.
The stars, tiny mourners, go out one by one.

Maura Stanton

Richard Cecil

Maura Stanton was born in 1946 in Evanston, Illinois. She received a B.A. from the University of Minnesota and an M.F.A. from the University of Iowa. She is the author of two books of poetry, *Snow on Snow* (1975), winner of the Yale Series of Younger Poets Award, and *Cries of the Swimmers* (University of Utah Press, 1984), as well as a novel, *Molly Companion* (Bobbs-Merrill, 1977). Among her other awards are two fellowships from the National Endowment for the Arts. She teaches at Indiana University.

The Wilderness

Today the trees are only blazed with paint.
The cannon in Hazel Grove cannot fire
Into the maze of forest which we've entered.
I see the next blue mark, drawing us
Along the lines of the Confederate trenches
Now almost invisible in second growth.
I step past you into a huge web
Spun across the trail. You pull me back.
The colorless threads tremble with our breath.
Later, we see other webs, abandoned,
The shiny bits of wing, the hair-fine legs
Scattered over the sticky bars of filament
Like half-erased words on ruled paper—
Like that page in my childhood diary
I tell you, which I remember rubbing out

Horrified at what I'd written down.
What was it? Only the flecks of something
Cross my brain, now dark, now bright,
Changing the aspect of the woods to bleakness
As if what stalked inside me, stalked outside,
Stirring the twigs, stirring nerves in my neck.
I start to rush ahead through chill air.
The jays scream. Your voice calls me back.

Brushing the gnats from hair and lips, we move
Down the sloping trail across the marsh,
Colder now, and silent. This line of trees
Might stretch across the whole continent
In solid waves of pine and oak, all shadow.
I imagine the two armies in the gloom,
Maneuvering for position, and some boy
Awkward with his rifle, who suddenly knew
He was lost forever in his pathless thicket.
Perhaps I was just now near the fourth dimension,
Standing where his heart beat the fastest.
Now I'm further into the autumn woods
Where he paused, near a trickle of cold brook,
To hug his arms together, renouncing hope.
I think he looked up at the sky, like this,
Then bent to memorize the dead shapes
Of maple leaves, of oak, of red sumac—
Trying to interpose God's perfect details
Between history and his own unready eyes.

Palinode

I've saved the milk crystal stone
banged at my door last winter, & the glow-
in-the-dark monster ring from cereal I wear
in bed, so there's always light under the sheet.

On television I see kits that turn
fresh flowers into glass forever, remembering
horseshoe wreaths over a friend's casket
I might have stored behind the armchair.
In a matchbox I've got my cat's grey claws;
when I sprinkle them on linoleum,
she'll bat them idly with her soft, useless paws,
making them click against the stove.
Lately I save everything, even hesitating
over the gnat swimming my beer
or the exploded firecracker from New Year's.
I've tape-recorded my mother's low voice
on the phone, as she describes dahlias,
or the configurations of her latest X-rays,
her intestines shiny with barium
like felled trees we saw once along a road
in Indiana, tented with caterpillar webs;
although I've lost the cocoon I picked up
at that roadside table where we stopped,
my mother, combing her long hair, looking
curiously at the white, shrouded branches.

Biography

Perhaps biography is the flat map
Abstracted from the globe of someone's life:
We are interested in the routes and detours.
So I found myself last summer in a storm
Driving down the Main Street of Red Cloud
Looking for Willa Cather's house, which was closed.
Then I drove to the Geographic Center
Of the United States, where she may have once walked
When the red grasses covered the prairie.
I tried to see for a moment through her eyes.

I looked at cows; I turned my head away
From the abandoned motel and two roadside tables—
But it was those forlorn shapes I remembered
Back in my own life, out on the highway.

Little Ode for X

Sometimes I call X nostalgia.
My mother telephones her fear of snow
caving the roof in; she hired a man
who rakes it off every time, but today
he's sick & so my mother paces room
after room, watching the ceiling . . .
When she hangs up, I imagine
her face resembling the crisp fly wing
stuck on the storm window, or her raisins
heated in pans until they dry out,
although their bitterness ruins cakes.
Last night a child threw a stone
hard against my front door. That's X, too,
for I've no father to chase him away.
Now I find the stone on the step,
milk crystal so strange I wash
my hands over & over in the kitchen sink,
afraid the child soaked it for hours
in poison from his Christmas chemistry set.
X is the fifth time a friend says no
to dinner, preferring to polish heirloom
silverware until the garland handles gleam,
or my brother's letter from Florida
describing a fight with his third wife.
That feeling of ants in my father's chest,
red fighters circling his heart that night
he sat up in bed, sure of death;

that's X, the specific hum of blood
beating against a clot in my mother's leg.
I hold a mirror behind my own knees,
touching the blue tubes running like roots
into my body, finally an equation for X,
as it, too, now grows by subtraction.

Childhood

I used to lie on my back, imagining
A reverse house on the ceiling of my house
Where I could walk around in empty rooms
All by myself. There was no furniture
Up there, only a glass globe in the floor,
And knee-high barriers at every door.
The low silled windows opened on blue air.
Nothing hung in the closet; even the kitchen
Seemed immaculate, a place for thought.
I liked to walk across the swirling plaster
Into the parts of the house I couldn't see.
The hum from the other house, now my ceiling,
Reached me only faintly. I'd look up
To find my brothers watching old cartoons,
Or my mother vacuuming the ugly carpet.
I'd stare amazed at unmade beds, the clutter,
Shoes, half-dressed dolls, the telephone,
Then return dizzily to my perfect floorplan
Where I never spoke or listened to anyone.

I must have turned down the wrong hall,
Or opened a door that locked shut behind me,
For I live on the ceiling now, not the floor.
This is my house, room after empty room.
How do I ever get back to the real house

Where my sisters spill milk, my father calls,
And I am at the table, eating cereal?
I fill my white rooms with furniture,
Hang curtains over the piercing blue outside.
I lie on my back. I strive to look down,
This ceiling is higher than it used to be,
The floor so far away I can't determine
Which room I'm in, which year, which life.

Shoplifters

I'd smoke in the freezer
among the hooked beefsides,
wondering about the shoplifters
who wept when the manager's
nephew tugged them to his office.
He made me search the women.
I found twenty cans of tuna fish
under the skirt of a mother whose son
drowned in a flash flood out west.
Now he haunted her,
begging for mouthfuls of fish.
Candles fell from a nun's sleeves.
She meant to light the route
for tobogganists on the convent hill.
Two old sisters emptied beans
from their big apron pockets,
claiming they cured rheumatism.
Soon I recognized snow
drifting across faces at the door,
watching in the round mirrors
the way hands snatched out
unhesitatingly at onions.
In the mirrors everyone stole,

buttoning coats again, looking
once over their shoulders
while eggs bulged in a mitten
or salt sifted from their hems.
Did they think me an angel
when I glided in my white uniform
down the soap aisle, preventing
some sudden clutch of fingers?
An old man I caught last year
stuffing baloney down his trousers
lived alone in a dim bedroom.
The manager said cupcake papers
blew across his floor—
hundreds, yellow, white & pink.
Now he peers through the window,
watching me bag groceries
for hours until my hands sweat.

Leon Stokesbury

Ed Barham

Leon Stokesbury was born in 1945 in Oklahoma City, Oklahoma. He received his M.A. and M.F.A. from the University of Arkansas and his Ph.D. from Florida State University. His first book, *Often in Different Landscapes* (University of Texas Press, 1976), was a co-winner of the first Associated Writing Programs Poetry Award. He teaches in the graduate creative writing program at McNeese State University.

A *Funny Joke*

A man fell out of grace.
It was my father.

On the north slope of Alaska,
on land belonging to

the Atlantic-Richfield Oil Corporation,
he fell.

He lay there six hours.
Then he was found.

Three hours later,
the Atlantic-Richfield Oil Corporation

flew him to Fairbanks
where doctors were.

They said he was ill.
They said the way

his face, arm, leg, in fact
his whole left side

was drawn up
in a hideous, contorted,

spasm of paralysis
meant he was in ill health.

My brother was there.
My brother said

this was what was in my father's eyes:
fear.

My brother said
his mouth was twisted

into a permanent ghastly grin.
It looked always as if

his was the only smile around,
as if someone had told

the funniest joke finally,
but only he had heard

and we were unaware,
there, that last day

my father was an employee
of the Atlantic-Richfield Oil Corporation.

Unsent Message to
My Brother in His Pain

Please do not die now. Listen.
Yesterday, storm clouds rolled
out of the west like thick muscles.
Lightning bloomed. Such a sideshow
of colors. You should have seen it.
A woman watched with me, then we slept.
Then, when I woke first, I saw
in her face that rest is possible.
The sky, it suddenly seems
important to tell you, the sky
was pink as a shell. Listen
to me. People orbit the moon now.
They must look like flies around
Fatty Arbuckle's head, that new
and that strange. My fellow American,
I bought a French cookbook. In it
are hundreds and hundreds of recipes.
If you come to see me, I shit you not,
we will cook with wine. Listen
to me. Listen to me, my brother,
please don't go. Take a later flight,
a later train. Another look around.

Day Begins at Governor's Square Mall

Here, newness is all. Or almost all. And like
a platterful of pope's noses at a White House dinner,
I exist apart. But these trees now—
how do you suppose they grow this high in here?
They look a little like the trees I sat beneath in 1959
waiting with my cheesecloth net for butterflies.
It was August and it was hot. Late summer,
yes, but already the leaves in trees were
flecked with ochers and the umbers of the dead.
I sweated there for hours, so driven,
so immersed in the forest's shimmering life,
that I could will my anxious self not move
for half a day—just on the imagined chance
of making some slight part of it my own.
Then they came. One perfect pair of just-hatched
black-and-white striped butterflies. The white
lemon-tipped with light, in shade
then out, meandering. Zebra swallowtails,
floating, drunk in the sun, so rare to find
their narrow, fragile, two-inch tails intact.
At that moment I could only drop my net and stare.
The last of August. 1959. But these trees, now,
climb up through air and concrete never hot or cold.
And I suspect the last lepidoptera that found
themselves in here were sprayed then swept away.
Everyone is waiting though, as before a storm—
anticipating something. Do these leaves never fall?

Now, and with a mild surprise, faint
music falls. But no shop breaks open yet.
The people, like myself, range aimlessly;
the air seems thick and still. Then, lights blink on;
the escalators jerk and hum. And in the center, at
the exact center of the mall, a jet of water spurts
twenty feet straight up, then drops and spatters
in a shallow pool where signs announce that none
may ever go. O bright communion! O new cathedral!

where the appetitious, the impure, the old, the young,
the bored, the lost, the dumb, with wide dilated eyes
advance with offerings to be absolved and be made clean.
Now, the lime-lit chainlink fronts from over one hundred
pleasant and convenient stalls and stores are rolled away.
Now, odors of frying won tons come wafting up from
Lucy Ho's Bamboo Garden. And this music, always
everywhere, yet also somehow strangely played as if
not to be heard, pours its soft harangue down now.
The people wander forward now. And the world begins.

To Laura Phelan: 1880–1906

For James Whitehead

Drunk I have been. And drunk I was that night
I lugged your stone across the other graves,
to set you up a hundred yards away.
Flowers I found, then. Drunk I have been.
And am, standing here with no moon to spill
on the letters of your name; my loud fingers
feeling them out. The stone is mossed over.
And why must I bring myself in the dark
to stand here among the sour grasses
that stain my white jeans? Drunk I have been.
See, the thick dew slides on the trees, wet weeds,
wetness smears the air; and a vague surf
of wildflowers pushes my feet, slipping
close to my legs. When the thought comes at last
that people fall apart, that the things we do
will not do. Ends. Then, we come to scenes
like this. This scene of you. You apart:
this is not you; and yet, this is where I stand
and close my eyes, and feel the ragged wind

blow red and maul my hair. In the night somewhere,
dandelions foam. This is not you. Drunk
I have been. Across this graveyard, that
is where you are. Yet I stand here. Would ask
things of your name. Would wish. Would not be told
of the stink in the skull, the eye's collapse.
Would be told something new, something unknown—
A mosquito bites my hand. The only sound
is the rough wind. Drunk I have been,
here, at the loam's maw, before this stone
of yours, which is not you. Which is.

Janet Sylvester

Jane Dennison Myers

Janet Sylvester was born in 1950. She received her M.F.A. from Goddard College and has done postgraduate work at the University of Utah, and S.U.N.Y. at Binghamton. She has been awarded both an Academy of American Poets prize and the Grolier Poetry Prize. Her first book, *That Mulberry Wine*, was published by Wesleyan University Press in September 1985.

The Late Show

"We even had a swing band in our parade.
A firetruck, a jazz band. What a Saturday."
Mickey turns from another customer to me.
Over his shoulder, pennants from local high schools
lift a little as the door behind us tinkles shut.
Mickey, I think, you'll kill yourself with Camels.
"Cigarettes," he says. He knows the label.
Flo, distributing bulk down the store's one aisle,
comes in from the back, smiling. I count.
Four cans of tomato soup, shelved.
Last week there were five. I try not to fasten
on black eyes, Flo's right, Mickey's left.
I imagine how they rise,

turn off the "Sands of Iwo Jima" and haggle
about taxes, the leaking ceiling,
why, behind the firetruck, Mickey kissed
the VFW cashier on her spitcurl.
A siren wails in each of them, cranking up,
poised like two fighter pilots as they bank,
no matter how impossible, eye to eye.
I can see his belly, moon-like on her fat thighs,
and how, in turn, she chooses to make up.
Separate, the two of them billow into the sleep
of Sunday morning. Girlish, Flo walks up to me,
no make-up pastey enough to cover blue.
I know you, I want to tell her
as we chat about the river down the street,
why less lives in it year by year.
I want her to find the place under my eye
where someone once connected.

Hard Strain in a Delicate Place

That day, someone died down the beach,
both legs bitten clean at the knee.
No warning fin separated the wave
that pulled his limbs away.
Later, news would reconstruct the shark,
famous for its blunt approach and execution,
for its hiding game.
And the natives said what they do:
how terrible, but the price you pay
in tropical waters.

That must have been the meaning
of the siren wail that we ignored,
intent on your bad knee, its articulation

as we walked. Something swam into the joint,
and stayed there, cracked and snapped
so only you could hear. "She sang,"
you sang, and spread your arms,
then winced above the pain. I caught you
off-balance in a picture.

We imagined the whole world
was in order, if we could say it then
in someone else's words to the surf.
You stopped mid-stanza. "It hurts,
it hurts. I should see a doctor."
The afternoon gave way as we walked
to the nearest dune and settled, silent,
the tick of my cigarette, newly lit,
audible only to me.
The sky looked faultless, empty.

Arrowhead Christian Center
and No-Smoking Luncheonette

Each Saturday, our father downtown to work,
Eloise tagged along to watch me look
through flaked-gold letters at Arthur Benson, the Baptist.
While I dressed in a magenta sweater
and navy-blue felt skirt with a white poodle
pasted on it, she would roll her eyes,
stick out her tongue and make gagging noises at my choice
of clothes. This Saturday, Arthur wore chino pants
and white bucks and a pullover with no shirt underneath.
First, I lit one of my mother's Old Golds.
Arthur never looked up from his pamphlet.
Then I leaned on the revolving door,
hoping Eloise would go home, where I sent her.

The luncheonette smelled of cooking coffee.
"Arthur," I said, positioning my chest against the counter,
"give me whatever I sign to prove I testify with you
to Jesus." Arthur sauntered over to me
with a sheet of yellow paper that said:
I, blank blank, room for my name, *do renounce fornication,
smoking, dancing, and so on. I will take on the Lord.*
I signed. He asked me out. I had heard that about Arthur.
"Oh Arthur, you're so crazy," I said
as we warmed up his white Chevrolet.
Later, when all the windows were steamy, he kissed me
without opening his lips, and showed my hand
how far it could go inside his pants.
Arthur stretched his arms across the seat back
as I bent, hair falling around my mouth and what it did,
my head wedged against the steering wheel.
"Blackhaired bitch," he whispered, "your hair's like wire."
I had never chugged anything till then
but knew how much, sometimes, you have to swallow in life
to prove a point.

Halfway down the street,
I could see my father waiting on the porch.
Eloise had spied on me and then went home
to tell about that paper.
When he finished hitting me,
Daddy pulled me out into the yard under his fruit trees.
It was only February, but already
there were crocuses uncurling in the flowerbeds.
When he put his arm around me,
all I could think about was Arthur,
how he bucked and crushed my head over and over again
onto his body.
Daddy wasn't saying much so I identified a constellation
that sinks down in the spring, Orion,
and wondered how much loafers stretch from standing
in muddy grass, and saw the moon go in and out
my father's breath. I wedged my head then
into that little cradle below his shoulder, pretending
I would never go near the luncheonette again.

That Mulberry Wine

Cross-legged in my pinafore,
I picked at lacy socks and twisted a curl
around and around my finger.
Such perfect boredom, sitting at her feet
Sunday mornings, the bedroom stuffy,
as she lipsticked and powdered herself,
sweat trickling into her corset. She got up,
let fall a dress over arms stretched above her head.
From the drawer, fragrant with handkerchiefs,
I chose a ring to try on. I wear it now,
the marcasites here and there, missing,
its amethyst scratched.
Why she ever told me then about her beau,
arriving with his derby and borrowed car
for their picnic at the lake: she ninety-eight pounds,
hair straight-braided to her hips, and he,
a printer just in from Kansas,
finding an excuse to take off coat, string tie,
and shirt so she could see him, broad-chested
if a little pale, throw down apples from the tree—
I don't know, I was only eleven—
my white dress reflected in the vanity
as she talked. Mouth gone dry, I heard them
smooth the blanket down
in among orchis and wintergreen. She arranged
two thimbles-full of mulberry wine
and chicken her mother had fixed.
I was hungry. "Wait now," she said,
as I balanced on one leg and he stood over her
then swooped, awkward, to take a kiss.
"Just you wait," she chided as he pushed her down.
I twist the purple stone back and forth on my finger
as she reached a hand with that new ring
and tore a stalk of brownweed out of dirt.
Across his back, the welts rose,
latitudes that haul me crazy to replicate
that day: the tree shaken, and under it
ground rooted with our new name.

James Tate

James Tate was born in Kansas City, Missouri, in 1943. His first book, *The Lost Pilot*, won the Yale Series of Younger Poets Award in 1966. Since then he has published seven books of poetry, most recently *Riven Doggeries* (1979) and *Constant Defender* (1983), both from The Ecco Press. Among his many awards is the National Institute for Arts and Letters Award for Poetry and a fellowship from the Guggenheim Foundation. He teaches at the University of Massachusetts.

Edward Bissell

Who Can Tell When He Is Awake

Is no one awake yet this cold cold winter morn?
I am. I am half awake
floating through a deserted fishing village
with my life like a parachute behind me.

I run in and out of God's eye,
I know that much,
trouble is I don't know when I'm in and when I'm out!

It's the desire to get on my knees
and have a lead bell lowered over me,
or to break out of this dream

and see all things at once
like a blind Peruvian composer,

to jump out of the forest
and swallow a green bird!

O if only it were true!
If only there were a fantastic computer
to tell me all the things I've done backwards . . .

All I want is a cup of tea with no holes in it.
Honestly I don't know why
everybody's looking at me like this.

Riven Doggeries

A miserable day, his dog had leapt
from the window
The dog had leapt
from my seventh-story apartment
into a Police helicopter
that had been hijacked
by some well-meaning murderers.
But it was for dogs
they entertained no mercy.
And that afternoon, late, after
a cold shower I went
for a ride in our elevator,
an immaculate dive, home
of the lost soul and once third base
to late working things.
My animal has sunk
he doesn't exist
he won't come back.

The ideal pet, however,
is unrecognizable when it arrives
in the river awash in the land afar.

Land of Little Sticks, 1945

Where the wife is scouring the frying pan
and the husband is leaning up against the barn.
Where the boychild is pumping water into a bucket
and the girl is chasing a spotted dog.

And the sky churns on the horizon.
A town by the name of Pleasantville has disappeared.
And now the horses begin to shift and whinny,
and the chickens roost, keep looking this way and that.
At this moment something is not quite right.

The boy trundles through the kitchen, spilling water.
His mother removes several pies from the oven, shouts at him.
The girlchild sits down by the fence to stare at the horses.
And the man is just as he was, eyes closed, forehead
against his forearm, leaning up against the barn.

The Motorcyclists

My cuticles are a mess. Oh honey, by the way,
did you like my new negligee? It's a replica
of one Kim Novak wore in some movie or other.
I wish I had a footlong chili dog right now.

Do you like fireworks, I mean not just on the 4th
of July, but fireworks anytime? There are people
like that, you know. They're like people who like
orchestra music, listen to it anytime of day.
Lopsided people, that's what my father calls them.
Me, I'm easy to please. I like pingpong and bobcats,
shatterproof drinking glasses, the smell of kerosene,
the crunch of carrots. I like caterpillars and
whirlpools, too. What I hate most is being the first
one at the scene of a bad accident.

Do I smell like garlic? Are we still in Kansas?
I once had a chiropractor make a pass at me,
did I ever tell you that? He said that your spine
is happiest when you're snuggling. Sounds kind
of sweet now when I tell you, but he was a creep.
Do you know that I have never understood what they meant
by grassy knoll. It sounds so idyllic, a place to go
to dream your life away, not kill somebody. They
should have called it something like the "grudging notch."
But I guess that's life. What is it they always say?
"It's always the sweetest ones that break your heart."
You getting hungry yet, hon? I am. When I was seven
I sat in our field and ate an entire eggplant
right off the vine. Dad loves to tell that story,

but I still can't eat eggplant. He says I'll be the first
woman President, it'd be a waste since I talk so much.
Which do you think the fixtures are in the bathroom
at the White House, gold or brass? It'd be okay with me
if they were just brass. Honey, can we stop soon?
I really hate to say it but I need a lady's room.

Constant Defender

My little finger's stuck in a
Coca-Cola bottle and I've got three
red checkers lodged in my watchpocket.
In a rush to meet my angel, now
I don't even know who my angel was.
I can see seven crimson jeeps lined up
outside Pigboy's Barbecue Shack—
must be a napkin salesmen's convention.
I don't care what cargo as long as
their hats are back on by eleven.
The thing I'm trying to avoid
is talking to my mule about glue futures.
What's a fellow going to do? I must
have a ceiling fan, I can't postpone
twirling blades. And my one stuffed chair
was owned by a hunchback from a hundred years
before I came along. I need some new
knick-knacks to suggest an air of cleanliness
to this sluggish pit of extinct sweet potatoes.
Ah, trickery, you sassy lark, withered black pearl,
unfetter me from these latches, make me
the Director at every meatball's burial,
lacerate this too, too static air
I've been eating my way through.
I lunch on eels and larks in lemonade, Lord,
I'm so happy I woke up in my right mind today.
And those kleptomaniacs, Smitty and Bob,
stole peanuts from a hunchback, snuff from an angel.
My knees click, I won't budge, like a wind-up toy
unwound, my guitar held tightly between my thighs.
Last night a clam fell from the stars:
a festive, if slippery occasion, a vibrating blob
entered our midst—I say "ours" out of some need—
I was alone when it hit me.

Tall Trees by Still Waters

Where the elk stood, stand I, worldly wise.
My maxims crackle like firecrackers
down to a cricket's Waterloo.
The impulse for far-ranging guesswork
attacks, gives dictation like hailstones
the size of hens' eggs. Just kidding.
The elk have gone afishing, they are all
nudists, and I take delight in miming
a few of their ridiculous expressions:
for instance, "cannibalism in the suburbs,"
or this one, "I am ashamed on behalf of my taste
and briskly bid the loathsome Armand farewell."

Where the elk stood, stand I, myself
habitually glittering in the background.
Next to me, on the library shelves
the actual world was pretending again,
no, not pretending, imagining an episode
of unbelievable cruelty, involving invalids.
A grave calm bends toward an outbreak of doubt.
Already one minute has boarded the bus
and left this scene forever. Now's the time.
The quick grey fox is stopped in his tracks,
smells electric fear in the air. A silver leaf.
I lay in bed all day rereading a novel about me:

"A cricket chirps and then dies."

Sloops in the Bay

The sloops in the bay are talking in a little bottle
language, their laughter
is the most difficult number in the book,

a sweeping, a rolling
like the bilious voyage of sleep—

They are starting to burn
like the yellow leaves at the bottom of a dream.

They can't sleep now, it would be quite impossible.
Whispering like a garden of secrets.

If It Would All Please Hurry

I have escaped from the two acre rolled garden
where twenty-five fair Anglo-Irish are
consuming champagne. The gnats, I said,
are quite sending me mad. I hope
you will not think it rude
if I go indoors. In fact,
they are eating me fast.
And those terrible smiles
were eating me too.
They smile but cannot laugh.

I am so sleepy and I do not wish
to share the cliffs with anyone

                    *   *   *

Today I walked up the hill
where they were harvesting the corn,
and right up among the sheep, silly as ever,
to the very top. Underneath
a creeking beech tree I
blew a lot of thistle-down
and admired the different golds

of the cornfield,
and came down again.

There is, for once, so little to say.
I cannot go anywhere, start anything now.
Even the bed seems far away
and I am on it.

*   *   *

In the window which looks out onto the limes
there is an unbalanced construction
of coloured plastic squares,
it quite takes one's mind off
those enormous trees. Of course
they are marvelous trees,
among the finest in the land,

but trees round a house
are really a mistake:
don't they take the oxygen or something?
They get you somehow
The trees, and probably the flowers, get you
long before the water.

Pigeons are flopping about
and the Irish are out on their bicycles.
It is going by so quickly
and the sun is falling behind
that unnecessary bush to the right.

*   *   *

I am sitting here about to get into this bed
and nearly fall out because every night
I feel you are in it too, and in front of me
is the shepherd boy under his glass tree
with his faithful glass dog
and his woolly glass sheep.

I sleep with a Braun electric fan heater
because of being cold I put it in my bed
it just burns bits. So now I am going
to sleep holding you most tight please
tell me where you are.

I do not like not knowing.

*   *   *

Dreamless sleep.
Wake to the usual gloom and forebodings.
If I am some sort of nut who spends life
elaborately avoiding what I like best,
let it be clear.

And I cannot move.
Deep down I feel instinctively I never will.
I cannot *bear* to hurt.
I want to say *don't trust me*,
don't love me, I am hell.

*   *   *

On a foggy morning
outside Golders Green cemetery
a cousin is being committed to the flames.
They slide the box slowly, contrivedly, out of sight.
Then words of dull intonation from a man
who never knew the lady,
the little gilt automatic doors.

Beastly cheap tear jerking movie scene.

I'd like an elaborate service with lots of music
and heaps of prayers just read one after another.

I am hugging you. I am trying
to get into the habit of realizing
you are real.

The telephone warbles and chirps out with someone
I don't know who knows someone who
is writing a book around the corner
and wants a cup of tea so I should go
and put the kettle on for heaven knows
how manyeth time my darling love
are you all right you cannot be alone.

I am feeling very dopey probably not eating
better have an egg or several
I must have drunk twenty cups of tea today
and I feel like a teapot, an old stained one.

What is that incantation I used to mutter as a child,
". . . the terrors and dangers of the night . . ."?
It must be a prayer, and kept me awake hours
waiting to glimpse the terrors and dangers
and watch them being warded off, wondering about
the dreadful life grown-ups must lead
to make up a prayer like that.

Hold tight, squeeze.

Henry Taylor

Sandra Ehrenkranz

Henry Taylor was born in 1942 in Lincoln, Virginia. He received a B.A. from the University of Virginia and an M.A. from Hollins College. He is the author of four books of poetry, *The Horse Show at Midnight* (L.S.U. Press, 1966), *Breakings* (Solo Press, 1971), *An Afternoon of Pocket Billiards* (University of Utah Press, 1975), and *The Flying Change* (L.S.U. Press, 1985). He is also the author of a textbook, *Poetry: Points of Departure* (Winthrop, 1974), and a co-translator of *The Children of Herakles* by Euripides (Oxford University Press, 1981). He has received awards and grants from the National Endowment for the Arts, the National Endowment for the Humanities, and the American Academy and Institute of Arts and Letters. He teaches at The American University.

The Flying Change

1.

The canter has two stride patterns, one on the right lead and one on the left, each a mirror image of the other. The leading foreleg is the last to touch the ground before the moment of suspension in the air. On cantered curves, the horse tends to lead with the inside leg. Turning at liberty, he can change leads without effort during the moment of suspension, but a rider's weight makes this more difficult. The aim of

teaching a horse to move beneath you is to remind him how he moved
when he was free.

2.

A single leaf turns sideways in the wind
in time to save a remnant of the day;
I am lifted like a whipcrack to the moves
I studied on that barbered stretch of ground,
before I schooled myself to drift away

from skills I still possess, but must outlive.
Sometimes when I cup water in my hands
and watch it slip away and disappear,
I see that age will make my hands a sieve;
but for a moment the shifting world suspends

its flight and leans toward the sun once more,
as if to interrupt its mindless plunge
through works and days that will not come again.
I hold myself immobile in bright air,
sustained in time astride the flying change.

To Hear My Head Roar

First, my father taught me to read poetry
aloud; then my teachers in grade school
remembered how he had recited poetry,

how many times he had brought down the school-
house with "Casey at the Bat." Whenever they
could they called me up before the whole school

to be my father's son. I still dream of days they
stood me shaking before my classmates, then
waited while I launched into what they

knew from long experience was coming, then
sat through "Jabberwocky" or "Excelsior"—that was
the full range of my repertory then.

Later I almost liked it, though I was
still forced to it: each week we all recited
at assembly. A terrible, tiring time that was

for my audience, and for me, as I recited
"The Highwayman" and "The Cremation of
Sam McGee." My father coached as I recited

nightly in the living room, and on the day of
my graduation from that place, my sister
and I recited, respectively, "The Ballad of

the Harp-Weaver" and "The Highwayman." My sister
and I fled to our father's side after
it was over, and I can still see my sister

blushing as the old ladies came up after
the performance with tears in their eyes
to tell my father we were wonderful. After

that, it was a long time before my eyes
would follow the tricks of poems, but now I know
dozens of them: they unscroll behind my eyes,

and I own hundreds of books in which I know
I can always find the right thing at the right time,
and I will read to anyone who doesn't know

what he is in for, for hours at a time.
When I try to understand this part of myself,
I think back to that earlier, troublesome time

to find that the explanation of myself
does not lie there entirely; for now I recall being
in high school, just beginning to take myself

seriously, and my father as a human being,
and I think of hours I spent in the attic
rummaging through old file cases, being

surprised to find, in the dark dust of that attic,
the poems my father had written when he
was in college. One afternoon in the attic

yielded an ancient treasure, a recording he
had once made and then forgotten. I
tiptoed out of the attic with it, thinking he

might take it from me, and secretly I
tried it, at first without success, on the machine
downstairs in the living room. At last I

even tried to start the reluctant machine
on the inner end of the groove. It worked.
The thing had been cut on some amateur's machine

and was made to run from the inside out. I worked
with the needle, nudging it over the cracks,
and heard, after what seemed hours of work,

a voice that I recognized, through dusty cracks
and thirty years, as my father's (or my own), say
something I now take to heart as my heart cracks:

"This is Tom Taylor talking; talking," I heard him say,
"to hear his own voice, and reading some poetry
because he wants to have something to say."

Landscape with Tractor

How would it be if you took yourself off
to a house set well back from a dirt road,
with, say, three acres of grass bounded
by road, driveway, and vegetable garden?

Spring and summer you would mow the field,
not down to lawn, but with a bushhog,
every six weeks or so, just often enough
to give grass a chance, and keep weeds down.

And one day—call it August, hot, a storm
recently past, things green and growing a bit,
and you're mowing, with half your mind
on something you'd rather be doing, or did once.

Three rounds, and then on the straight
alongside the road, maybe three swaths in
from where you are now, you glimpse it. People
will toss all kinds of crap from their cars.

It's a clothing-store dummy, for God's sake.
Another two rounds, and you'll have to stop,
contend with it, at least pull it off to one side.
You keep going. Two rounds more, then down

off the tractor, and Christ! Not a dummy, a corpse.
The field tilts, whirls, then steadies as you run.
Telephone. Sirens. Two local doctors use pitchforks
to turn the body, some four days dead, and ripening.

And the cause of death no mystery: two bullet holes
in the breast of a well-dressed black woman
in perhaps her mid-thirties. They wrap her,
take her away. You take the rest of the day off.

Next day, you go back to the field, having
to mow over the damp dent in the tall grass

where bluebottle flies are still swirling,
but the bushhog disperses them, and all traces.

Weeks pass. You hear at the post office
that no one comes forward to say who she was.
Brought out from the city, they guess, and dumped
like a bag of beer cans. She was someone,

and now is no one, buried or burned
or dissected; but gone. And I ask you
again, how would it be? To go on with your life,
putting gas in the tractor, keeping down thistles,

and seeing, each time you pass that spot,
the form in the grass, the bright yellow skirt,
black shoes, the thing not quite like a face
whose gaze blasted past you at nothing

when the doctors heaved her over? To wonder,
from now on, what dope deal, betrayal,
or innocent refusal, brought her here,
and to know she will stay in that field till you die?

Artichoke

*"If poetry did not exist, would you
have had the wit to invent it?"*
   —Howard Nemerov

He had studied in private years ago
the way to eat these things, and was prepared
when she set the clipped green globe before him.
He only wondered (as he always did
when he plucked from the base the first thick leaf,
dipped it into the sauce and caught her eye

as he deftly set the velvet curve against
the inside edges of his lower teeth
and drew the tender pulp toward his tongue
while she made some predictable remark
about the sensuality of this act
then sheared away the spines and ate the heart)
what mind, what hunger, first saw this as food.

Shapes, Vanishings

1.

Down a street in the town where I went
to high school twenty-odd years ago, by doorways
and shadows that change with the times, I walked
past a woman at whose glance I almost stopped cold,
almost to speak, to remind her of who I had been—
but walked on, not being certain it was she,
not knowing what I might find to say.
It wasn't quite the face I remembered, the years
being what they are, and I could have been wrong.

2.

But that feeling of being stopped cold, stopped dead,
will not leave me, and I hark back
to the thing I remember her for, though God knows
how I could remind her of it now.
Well, one afternoon when I was fifteen
I sat in her class. She leaned on her desk,
facing us, the blackboard behind her arrayed
with geometrical figures—triangle, square,

pentagon, hexagon, *et cetera*. She pointed
and named them. "The five-sided figure," she said,
"is a polygon." So far so good, but then when she said
"The six-sided one is a hexagon," I wanted things clear.
Three or more sides is *poly*, I knew, but five only
is *penta*, and said so; she denied it,
and I pressed the issue, I, with no grades
to speak of, a miserable average to stand on
with an Archimedean pole—no world to move,
either, just a fact to get straight, but she
would have none of it, saying at last, "Are you
contradicting me?"

3.

A small thing to remember a teacher for. Since then,
I have thought about justice often enough
to have earned my uncertainty about what it is,
but one hard fact from that day has stayed with me:
If you're going to be a smartass, you have to be right,
and not just some of the time. "Are you
contradicting me?" she had said, and I stopped
breathing a moment, the burden of her words
pressing down through me hard and quick, the huge
weight of knowing I was right, and beaten. She
had me. "No, ma'am," I managed to say, wishing
I had the whole thing down on tape to play back
to the principal, wishing I were ten feet tall
and never mistaken, ever, about anything in this world,
wishing I were older, and long gone from there.

4.

Now I am older, and long gone from there.
What sense in a grudge over something so small?
What use to forgive her for something
she wouldn't remember? Now students

face me as I stand at my desk, and the shoe
may yet find its way to the other foot,
if it hasn't already. I couldn't charge
thirty-five cents for all that I know
of geometry; what little I learned is gone now,
like a face looming up for a second out of years
that dissolve in the mind like a single summer.
Therefore,
if ever she almost stops me again,
I will walk on as I have done once already,
remembering how we failed each other,
knowing better than to blame anyone.

Taking to the Woods

    Clearing brush away
is the mean part of working up firewood from these
  cut-off treetops—a chaotic souvenir
  of the doubtful covenant I made the day
    I marked a dozen white oak trees
    and sold them for veneer.

    There might be more in this
of character or courage if it were need that drove
  my weekly trials in this little wood,
  but this is amateur thrift, a middle-class
    labor as much for solitude
    as for a well-stocked stove.

    For more than safety's sake,
therefore, I take a break to light up and daydream,
  and as the chainsaw ticks and cools, I smoke
  my way back to an hour spent years ago,
    when I knelt above a shallow stream—
    the scanty overflow

from the springhouse at my back.
The ache of holding still dwindled away to less
  than the absent-minded effort that has carved
  these grooves between my eyebrows; on the surface
    oarlocked water-striders swerved
      above the scribbled black

      shadows minnows made
on rippled mud below their bright formations,
  and a dragonfly, the green-eyed snakedoctor
  with wings out of old histories of aviation,
    backed and filled down a stair of nectar-
      scent toward a jewelweed

      and struck a brittle stillness
like the spell the wood boss broke when he touched my hand
  as I stood absorbed in the loggers' technique:
  "Have you ever seen a big tree fall?" "Yes."
    "Good." Not the graceful faint we make
      of tall trees in the mind,

      but swift and shattering.
I counted the growth rings—one hundred sixty-four—
  and found where, fifty years ago, the wood
  drew in against the drought one narrow ring;
    I touched the band that marked the year
      when I was born, then stood

      and let them drop the rest.
This is everyday danger, mundane spectacle,
  spectacular and dangerous all the same.
  I hover between hope that it is practical
    to give young trees more light, and shame
      at laying old trees waste,

      then yank the starting cord
and turn to dropping stovewood from this chest-high limb,
  my touch light, leaving real work to the saw,
  my concentration thorough and ignored

at once, lest the blade take on a whim
of its own; and I think how

our small towns have collected
in legend the curious deaths of ordinary men—
as once, on a siding up the road from here,
Jim Kaylor, if that was his name, directed
the coupling of a single freight car
to the middle of a train—

an intricacy he knew
as most of us know how to shave, say, or shift gears.
That day, he managed to be caught somehow,
and the couplings clicked inside him, just below
the ribcage, and he hung between cars
in odd silence as the crew

swarmed from the depot,
told each other to stand back, give him air, send
for the doctor, and he asked for a cigarette,
received it with steady fingers, smoked, and saw—
well, what could he have seen? The end
of a boxcar, the set

of a face in disbelief,
or something, in smoke shapes before him, that he kept
when he finished the cigarette, flicked it aside,
nodded, and, as the boxcars were slipped
apart, dropped with a sound of relief
to the crossties, and died.

Now I think hard for men
mangled by tractors and bulls, or crushed under trees
that fall to axe or chainsaw in their season,
and for myself, who for no particular reason
so far survive, to watch the woodlot ease
under the dark again,

        withdraw into the mist
of my unfocused eyes, into my waiting stare
    across bare trees that lift toward landscapes
    through which snakedoctors may still wheel to rest,
        then to walk home, behind the shapes
            my breath ghosts in sharp air.

Susan Tichy

Michael O'Hanlon

Susan Tichy was born in 1952 in Washington, D.C., and was educated at Goddard College and the University of Colorado. Her first book, *The Hands in Exile,* chosen by Sandra McPherson for the National Poetry Series, was published by Random House in 1983.

The Hours

The crop plane stalls its engines,
drops an octave and a hundred feet
into a zoom of poison,
plowing through sleep nose first.
That's dawn.

Noon is the whistle,
like a sword blade,
of passing jets.
They go nowhere.

They bomb nothing.
The papers say
no borders are ever crossed.

Dusk we mark by a rumble,
far away, noticed only
when a day's work is done.
The rumble is the animal that guards us.

So, what if I slept on the other side?
Right there, perhaps,
in that small twinkle of lights?
I'd stroke the black, shining hair
of the same animal
and feel safe.

This is peace.
It causes men to grow old. On women
the face of an olive leaf
coarsens
into cracked ground waiting for rain

or darkness.
We each lie down.
Wind lifts soil and branches,
lightening everything
but us.
It even blows the borders
back and forth above our heads:
at twelve we are in Israel,
at two we are not.

At five, when the crop plane
already revs its engines in half light,
we fall asleep and dream,
for half an hour,
that we climb the swaying ladder
to God's house.

Irrigation

Dust on my hair and face,
oil in the dust I can taste
when a truck has passed.
And the sting of grapefruit oil
in the small splinter-holes in my hands.
The smell of the plastic cooler
when I drink, water running down
my chin and throat and shirt,
disappearing in the heat.

A man told me his water truck broke down
in the Sinai, in one of the wars.
As long as convoys passed
he lived like a king
on cigarettes, brandy, chocolate,
and pictures of girls. Their nipples
made his mouth water
in spite of the dust.
The soldiers drank
till they sweated again
and he slept under his truck, dreaming:

The wars were over.
His country was an island
where men worked all day
pouring sand into the ocean.
Some schoolchildren were reciting:
How many people live in heaven?
What color is God?
Where do trees go when they leave the desert?
Why is it cold?

And he heard himself answering:
Don't listen to your own fears.
Pitch your tents in the shadow of running water.
It's cold in heaven.
And there are many gods in this green tree.

Identity Card

For a living I pick apples.
No, that's not true. I could live
perfectly well without them.
I pick grapefruit, but my passion

is for tottering
on the tall, three-wheeled machine
I pilot through the branches.
The whole ocean is visible,
the ocean which is this orchard,
its tossed whitecaps of blossom
gone to fruit. We call it autumn

when the grass around the unpicked trees
is dry. Dew settles on the moon
instead. Its orange face
is the smile I wear in the dark.
Two weeks of that, then rain,
and then the war.

I'm not the only woman
and not the favorite. I work too hard
and drink my tea with sugar.
That makes you sweat, they say.
"In the army, sugar is not allowed."

So I heap more in my cup.
And I work, in the rainy time,
where no one wants to work: on the hills
with the rangy cows, the unswept mines,
and the dazed bull
honking his severed vocal cords.

More sugar! More smell of the diesel
mingling with grapefruit oil!
More nights polishing my old French boots!
Let the enemy reveal himself,

slyly, in the orchard,
or, wearing a clean shirt, at night.
This is all he will learn:

Name? A Polish village.
Rank? Apparently so.
And number? Try the number

on a letter that keeps coming back.
For a living I am insomniac
and drunk—all the time—
like a bee in a wet spring bloom.

In an Arab Town

West Bank

The fat, pale proprietor
stands at his plateglass window
while we drink tea
with sugar, tea with rum
from our pockets—
none of the men refuse.
It makes them
brave, so they reach out,
delicately at first,
for my white skin,
for whose sake also
two Israeli soldiers
loiter in the street. In fact

we don't talk politics
but Persian verse. I learn,
fighting fingers off my knee,

that no poem should be read
in haste, or carried in a pocket
close to the body's heat. The poet
is the tongue of God's voice. His words
should be recorded in script,
and not by a woman
because her hand will shake.

Then one boy, whose manhood
barely shadows his lip,
recites the perfect letters
which he has placed in my lap.
They teach us *mabrook*,
"you are blessed,"
and *fucka*, because all things
are pure to the tongue.

And two girls
who won't come into the teahouse,
who wear so many colors
their men go blind,
pass fruit through the kitchen windows
for us, giggling. Sisters.
We're told they can't read.

But women, we've been warned,
are most dangerous.
Men lose their tempers, their cool,
spread talk, get caught.
Women are perfectly capable
of riding buses,
arms full of chickens and bombs,
giggling all the way
about some fat unmarried neighbor
or some poor man's cock.

Richard Tillinghast

Chase Twichell

Richard Tillinghast was born in Memphis, Tennessee, in 1940. He was educated at the University of the South and Harvard University. He is the author of three collections of poetry, *Sleep Watch* (1969, *The Knife and Other Poems* (1980), and *Our Flag Was Still There* (1984), all from Wesleyan University Press. He was recently Briggs-Copeland lecturer in poetry at Harvard and currently teaches at the University of Michigan.

The Knife

For David Tillinghast

What was it I wonder?
    in my favorite weather   in the driving rain
        that drew me like a living hand
What was it
    like a living hand
that spun me off the freeway
      and stopped me
      on a sidestreet in California
with the rain pelting slick leaves down my windshield

to see the words of my brother's poem
　　afloat on the bright air,
　and the knife I almost lost
　　　falling end over end through twenty years
　　　　to the depths of Spring River—

the knife I had used to cut a fish open,
　　　　caught in time
　the instant where it falls
　　　through a green flame of living water.

My one brother,
　　　who saw more in the river than water
　who understood what the fathers knew,
　　　　　dove from the Old Town canoe
　plunged and found his place
　　　　in the unstoppable live water

seeing with opened eyes
　　　the green glow on the rocks
　　　　　and the willows running underwater—
　like leaves over clear glass in the rain—

While the long-jawed, predatory fish
　the alligator gar
watched out of prehistory
　　schooled in the water like shadows
　　　unmoved in the current,
　watched unwondering.

　　The cold raw-boned, white-skinned boy
　curls off his dive in deep water
　　and sees on the slab-rock
filling more space than the space it fills:

　　　　the lost thing　　*the knife*
　current swift all around it

and fishblood denser than our blood
　still stuck to the pike-jaw knifeblade

which carries a shape like the strife of brothers
—old as blood—
the staghorn handle smooth as time.

Now I call to him
and now I see
David burst into the upper air
gasping as he brings to the surface our grandfather's knife
shaped now, for as long as these words last,
like all things saved from time.

I see in its steel
the worn gold on my father's hand
the light in those trees
the look on my son's face   a moment old

like the river   old like rain
older than anything that dies can be.

Hearing of the End of the War

1.

Clouds dissolve into blueness.
The Rockies float like clouds,
white ridge over blue,
in the shimmery blue heat.

The moon floats there still
like some round marble relic,
its classic face rubbed away by time.

A stranger arrives, all the way from Denver.
        We feed him.
He tells us that the war is over.

For years I have stopped to wonder
    what it would feel like now.
And now I only hear the slight noise
    the moment makes,
        like ice cracking,
as it flows behind me into the past.

2.

I go to the well
    and draw up a bottle of homemade beer.
The coldness from thirty feet down
        beads out wet on the brown bottle.

Breathing dusty pine fragrance,
      I pop open the beer, and drink
till my skull aches from the coldness.

Rubbed white dust is on plum skins
        as they ripen,
           green wild blueberries
    growing from the rocks.

Wind blows in off the peaks,
        high in the dust-flecked sun-shafts
    that light up the dark trees.
Rustlings and murmured syllables from other days
      pass through and linger
      and leave their ponies
to roam among the trees and graze the coarse grass
      off the forest floor.

Treetop breezes, and voices
      returning home
from a fight somebody lost in these mountains
      a hundred and ten years ago—

A horse cries out,
          loose in the woods,
                    running and free.
His unshod hooves thud
          on the hard-packed dirt.

And then each sound drops away
     —like a dream you can't even remember—

     deep behind the leaves of the forest.

3.

From bark-covered rafters
     white sheets hang squarely down,
dividing the still afternoon into rooms
          where we sleep, or read,
          or play a slow game of hearts.

Everyone is unbuttoned and at their ease.

     The baby's clear syllables
               rise into space:
     milky   like the half-moons
          on his tiny fingernails,

     finer than fine paper.

A new life breathes in the world—
          fragile, radiant,
     unused to the ways of men.

From halfway down the valley
     bamboo flute notes rise   float
          flutter
               and shatter
     against the Great Divide.

Return

1.

Sunburst cabbage in grey light
                summer squash bright as lemons
red tomatoes splitting their skins
        five kinds of chilis burning in cool darkness,
       sunflower lion's-heads
                in the blue Chevy pickup.

Hands shaking from the cold
             turn on the headlights; he starts
                down the drive—

A dust you can't see
        settles over the garden and empty cabin

           silent, unnoticed
          like snow after midnight—

Power shut off in the pumphouse
        tools suspended over light-blue silhouettes
       he has painted for each of them.

Dark trees stand
       and watch his old truck
             bump down the hill.

Behind him: star-fall he's not sure he saw,
      bone-chill flute
           certainty of dawn.

He feels the pecans, the wild hazelnuts
        the small but hard and juicy apples
      in the oversized pockets of his coat,
        the cloth worn soft as rabbit-fur.

White dairy-fences border his way,
                    AM radio farm news,
          placidness of black-nosed sheep in ground-fog,
               mist rising over bluegrass.

He drives by Tomales Bay.
          The old fisherman scowls at the low sky and waves,
               squinting to keep out the
          wreathing, first-cigarette smoke.

               Squirrels
                    flash down tree-trunks
when they see him coming—
                    Farmers turn on their lights.

Seeds sprout in the upholstery.
                         Tendrils and runners leap out
          from under his dashboard—

He sails past the whitewashed stumps
                         from the 1906 earthquake,
past the old hotel at Olema,
               stops for a whizz at Tocaloma,
          because of the name.

          Sycamore leaves are falling,
                    I feel them rustling
around his shoulders
               and wreathing his hair.

The shepherd with eyes like his
                    wakes up in a field.
          The farmer goes out to milk,
               his cold hands pink on the pink freckled udders.

The fisherman he could almost be
                    lets down nets into dark water

     and brings up the trout-colored dawn.

2.

For a few miles on the freeway we
                    float in the same skin,
      he and I.
              But the sun rises in my
    rearview mirror.
      I'm myself now.
I cross the bridge and pay my toll.

The city draws me like a magnet—
              first the oil refineries,
the mudflats and racetrack by the Bay,
            the one-story houses,
then a vision of you waking up:
          cheeks reddening, your black hair long,
your eyes that remind me of Russia,
                where I've never been—
        as you look out at
             silvery rain on the fuchsias.

        I find your house by feel.
            How many years are gone?
Your name is gone from the mailbox.
The tropical birds and palm trees and Hawaiian sunset
         you painted with a small brush
are peeling off the beveled glass door.

Forever must be over.
I get into the truck with the good things
        somebody has left here,
             and drive off into the rain—
my left hand asking my right
           a question I could never answer.

Summer Rain

Summer rain, and the voices of children
        from another room.
Old friends from summers past,
we drink old whiskey and talk about ghosts.
The rain ebbs, rattles the summer cottage roof,
   soaks the perished leaves in wooden gutters,
then gusts and
        drowns our fond talk.
It's really coming down, we chatter,
   as though rain sometimes rose.
The power fails.
We sit under darkness, under the heavy storm.
Our children—frightened, laughing—
   run in to be beside us.

The weak lights surge on.
We see each other's children newly.
How they've grown!   we prose
with conventional smiles, acceptingly commonplace,
   as they go back to playing.
Yet growing is what a child does.

And ourselves?
You haven't changed a bit,
   we not exactly lie,
meaning the shock is not so great
      as we'd expected.
It's the tired look around the eyes,
the flesh a little loose on the jaw . . .

Your oldest daughter's a senior at Yale.
We're like our grandparents and our parents now,
      shocked by the present:
A buggy without a horse to pull it?
                  A man on the moon?
       Girls at Yale?
We say goodnight. I can hardly lift

my young son anymore
as I carry him to the car asleep.

The rain comes down, comes down, comes down.
One would think it would wear the earth away.
You told us about a skeleton
      you awoke seeing—
the dawn light on the bone.
It wakes me this morning early.
But I'm sure it wasn't a ghost, you said
         in your sensible way,
It was just my terrible fear of death.

Rain roars on the broad oak leaves
   and wears away the limestone.
I smell the mildewed bindings
   of books I bought as a student.
How shabby, how pathetic they look now
   as they stand there on their shelves unread!
Children are all that matters, you said
   last night, and I agreed.
The children's play-song—repetitive, inane—
   keeps sounding in my head.
I get up—last night's spirits alive
   this morning in my blood—
and write these perishing words down
in the voice of summer rain.

Shooting Ducks in South Louisiana

For David Tillinghast

The cold moon led us coldly
   —three men in a motorboat—
down foggy canals before dawn
      past cut sugarcane in December.

Mud-banks came alive by flashlight.
Black cottonmouth moccasins
   —the length of a man in the bayou—
slid into black water, head high,
   cocky as you might feel
stepping out on Canal Street
   going for coffee at 4 A.M.
            at the *Café du Monde.*

An Indian trapper called to us
   from his motorized pirogue,
            Cajun French on his radio,—
taking muskrat, swamp rat, weasel,
   "anything with fur."

Marsh life waking in the dark:
gurgling, sneaking, murdering, whooping—
   a muskrat breast-stroking through weeds toward food,
      his sleek coat parted smooth by black satin water—
frogs bellowing, bulbous waterlilies adrift
      cypresses digging their roots into water-borne ooze
dark juices collapsing cell-walls,
         oil rigs flaring thinly at daybreak.

Light dawned in our hunting-nerves.
We called to the ducks in their language.
They circled, set wing, glided into range.
      Our eyes saw keener.
Our blood leaped. We stood up and fired—
      And we didn't miss many that day,
            piling the boat between us with mallards.

The whole town of Cutoff ate ducks that Sunday.
      I sat in the boat,
               bloody swamp-juice sloshing my boots,
                  ears dulled by the sound of my gun,—

and looked at a drake I had killed:
    sleek neck hanging limp,
                    green head bloodied,
          raucous energy stopped.
I plucked a purple feather from his dead wing,
and wore the life of that bird in my hat.

Our Flag Was Still There

For Music, "Victory at Sea," or "In the Mood"

"Chessie," the Chesapeake and Ohio's
advertising mascot, snoozes
under sixty-mile-per-hour lamplight.
Two tabby kittens gaze saucer-eyed at their tomcat dad,
who sits alertly on his haunches,
soft fieldcap cocked to one side above neat,
pleasure-pursed lips and regimental whiskers.
One paw bandaged.
A Congressional Medal of Honor
red-white-and-blue-ribboned around his neck.
As convincingly at attention as a military-style,
family-oriented cat can be in a pullman car.
On his well-groomed chest, rows of campaign ribbons.
A dignified, "can do" look
hovers about his muscled smile.

In the luggage rack, a U.S. combat helmet
and a rising-sun flag in tatters.

I had a flag like that.
One of my three red-headed Marine cousins
brought it back from the South Pacific.
I thumbtacked it to the wall of my room.

The Japanese who had fought under it
perished in fierce firestorms.
They and their flag went up in that conflagration.

Our flag was still there.
Against a backdrop of blue sky and innocent clouds,
a line of six blunt-nosed P-47 fighters—
boxy and powerful like the grey Olds
we bought after the War
and drove to the Berkshires for the summer—
flew off on a mission to Corregidor.
The flag, unfurled in the stiff breeze,
was superimposed over the line of airplanes
on the cover of the Sunday magazine
one June morning in 1943.
The wind that made it wave as it does in pictures
blew off long ago toward Japan.

The sun nooned over orange groves and beaches.
Sparks from welding torches
illuminated the sleep of the City of the Angels
and darkened the sleep of other cities,
as women workers beside the men
lowered masks over their faces,
and the children of New Jersey and Mississippi,
Europe and Detroit,
labored to make aluminum fly
and set afloat fleets of destroyers
and submarines radaring to the kill.

Looking ahead, there was a world of blue-grass lawns,
paneled wood enameled white, grandparents' faces
rosy over reassuring, hand-rubbed bannisters,
Yale locks, brass door-knockers, hardwood floors,
the odor of good furniture and wax,
a holiday design of holly leaves and berries on a stiff card,
a little girl holding gift packages as big as she is,
a boy, a real boy, bright as a new penny.

But now, in '43, the men and women pulled apart
like the elders of some stern, taboo-ridden tribe,
putting off till after the War the lives
of those who in twenty-five years
stood baffled on the 4th of July among uncles,
drove good German cars,
floated in tubs of hot, redwood-scented water with friends,
and greeted each other with the word "Peace."

Chase Twichell

Bill Arnold

Chase Twichell was born in 1950. She received her B.A. from Trinity College and her M.F.A. from the University of Iowa. Her first book, *Northern Spy* (1981), was published by the University of Pittsburgh Press. She lives in Florence, Massachusetts, where she works as an editor and typesetter for a small press and does free-lance editorial work.

Watercress & Ice

The grass gave way, and suddenly
you were thigh-deep in water so cold
it made you forget yourself.
You saw two wild blue herons,
and mention these things in your letter.
The brilliant, green-white substance
you walked through was watercress,
watercress and ice. I can see you,
underdressed, wading out
into the breakable, ice-invaded plants.

I cut these lilacs from the wet hedge
half-bloomed, cold to the touch.
Their fragrance has none of the
delicious bitterness you walk through.
The transient herons have gone,

taking their blue lives home.
It's a northerner's story to be cold,
though you know we unfold our maps
with explicit tenderness.
And the lilacs are bitterly beautiful,
opening already in the warm room,
purple and simple,
because I make you see them.
We will not find the wilderness
where we expect it,
nor find, in cold, a home.

Cedar Needles

Vendors croon their welcoming harangues
as we pass pyramids of duck eggs,
cheap dresses, black cheeses,
and the shrunken
mummies of the smoked quail,

but we follow the scent of cedar
up into a valley
of sheep and wind-toughened flowers,
the needles
slippery beneath our feet.

Goats scatter uneasily away,
dung rank in their crusted hides.

The rooftops disappear below us,
hazed by the violet smut of cooking.
Here and there the sun
points out a metal gutter.
The clay tiles shiver in the heat.

At this height,
cow bells and church bells
belong to the wild music of the place.
We are farther from God than ever,
at home among the uncountable,
the yellow denial of their split-eyes.

Blighted with plastic flowers,
the homely little cemeteries
embedded in the hillsides
become another landscape
arrested by the camera,
as one tourist
fixes the other there forever.
Strange to think
we have climbed this far
for only another view of ourselves,
the world being
everywhere equally foreign.

Blurry Cow

Two cows stand transfixed
by a trough of floating leaves,
facing as if into the camera,
black and white. One stamps
at the hot sting of a deerfly.

Seen from the window of a train,
the hoof lifts forever
over hay crosshatched by speed,
and the scales of the haunches
balance. The rest is lost:
the head a sudden slur of light,

the dog loping along the tracks
toward a farm yard
where a woman wavers
in her mirage of laundry.
A blurry cow, of all things,
strays into the mind's eye,
the afterimage
of this day on earth.

Abandoned House in Late Light

A sparrow lights
among the open cones
high in the white pine.
Then slips, a leaf
travelling the green ladders
down to the spiced humus
which feeds on all things
missing, all things lost.
The cloven prints of deer,
a squirrel's immaculate spine,
and somewhere between
the wind and the gray leaves
a far-off waterfall
pours through the cold air,
dismantling a tree,
stripping away the bodies
that the souls may not
linger here among us.
The migrant orioles
disown the paintless birdhouse
vacant in the birch.
Pendulous with grapes, vines
scrawl across the lattice,

scattering raisins
darkened with wine
into the black breakdown of soil.
For years a neighbor swept
the long, cloud colored
boards of his porch,
and the grit suspended,
like the sound of the axe
in the stacked wood.
Now he lives where even
the wind dissolves,
in a house of breathless passages,
the windows open to birds and snow,
a lock full of rust on the door.

Arthur Vogelsang

Arthur Vogelsang was born in Baltimore, Maryland, in 1942. He was educated at the University of Maryland, Johns Hopkins University, and the University of Iowa. His first book of poems, *A Planet* (1983), was published by Holt, Rinehart, and Winston. He lives in Los Angeles, where he is an editor of *The American Poetry Review* and publisher of the Metro Book Company.

Judith Vogelsang

Drive Imagining

I'm speeding west somewhere in the top of Ohio or Indiana,
And to my right is the Arctic Circle, all white and scary.
It is very dark and cold
But my car is very powerful, shut, and too warm.
To my left is super-powerful New Orleans Radio 87,
Beaming girl singers with crooked jaws.
I test you by asking the time but
You trust me to not give you the wheel while you're sleeping.
Your mouth is like the curve of the earth for fifty miles on flat ice.
Out loud, unevenly, I say where the road right goes. No answer.

Your skirt is high and little,
Filling the front of the car with pounds of white.

My nails raise the flesh there;
Electricity from the big dots and standing hair sends the radio signal
Into a trough. Eyes shut, you are awake
Enough to say, I can't breathe, fix the heat.
You sigh and lean back like a snowflake pressing into a marshmallow.
The urge to ask your advice about the possible right turn
To Battle Creek, Canada, and you-know-where
Is a malignant lump in my chest, like facing the dark makes.

And at what point would we drive out onto the nothing but ice?
Cresting she says, Hello truck drivers,
And mentions a more powerful flashlight for them to buy.
That's the trouble with global capabilities,
You can be fighting icebergs and some joker will yodel
In your ear, "You are my sunshine . . ."
I shout that the road right goes you-know-where.
Eyes shut, you are awake enough to say,
All that's stopping us is a lack of gas stations,
My twisted mouth around your fear.

Americans in an Orange Grove

"I become insane with long intervals of horrible sanity."
                                        —Poe

No such luck under the lush, bumpy orange and leaf sky, the owner
A Cuban uncle of your wife's friend, his humble precise English,
The efficient, expansive Land-Rover, three mild, smart women past
Nubility, white folds of their lips, and I swear seemingly pure
Asses hanging out a little in shorts in the healthy, musty grove. Excuse
Me. Far from your home base of drinking and consistent madness you
The man, the poet, muse upon the wonder of civ, the grafting
Of lemons and oranges on the same twig ilization
The long arm of the American police, benign pluck

Of a kind, productive, intelligent uncle from the spite of the
        Communists.
No such luck, you weak bastard, you'll have to bathe in the bath-
Like hot sea and eat the lamb (we're
Having later tonight) with sensible, luxuriant women and get tired, sleep
No prowling corridors alone for promiscuous screams. Sleep. A short nasty
Wind overhead, fierce for sure & w. teeth & a storm
Of oranges before which all run but you, the poet, the man, behold
Yourself, victim of a juicy bombardment, ridiculous loony survivor. Twinges
Of desire in the loins of the enchanted women. In this split-
Second all others but you are utterly happy tho they stare and think
"It won't be all right in the end, it just won't."

Feeling That Way Too

It gets dark and I get scared.
Dogs bark, stop, and bark continuously.
The only sound
As the plunging sun chars orange clouds
In what seems to be Nevada.
You are afraid too and go into the bedroom to sleep
Clothed under blankets in corduroys and wool socks,
Bare chest probably cool.
Our cats blink at me, raise and let limp their heads.
Disturbed too, you heave a little and rustle.
The bed creaks and squeaks seconds after.
I still sit still, monitoring the blood in my ears.
And suppose, though shivering with fright, I *should*
Dance in the pale dark, waving my pants
Over my head, singing I've got bells
That jingle jangle jingle or Pepsi-Cola
Hits the spot? Or switch a light on?
The moon fills up its ugly red cheeks as
Silence comes down like a hunk

Of gooey lead in the ear.
And though a few seconds later you will say
"Oh I feel so good, my bare skin feels so nice, like ice cream,"
Now I hear you walking through the dark hall
Then naked you step quickly through a white beam
In this room then hurry to me in that six-foot wide shaft
Of total blackness between the beam and me and
My eyes tear and I really do reach for the switch.

The Clouds

I am smoking Camels and crying
This activity is helping me think of clouds like white
Cool bathroom porcelain in a rich friend's house
It is 1:08 A.M. in my nice back room in Wichita in late December 1972
And Paul Carroll's book The Poem in Its Skin which sadly enough
I am not in is already be
Come reactionary and a bit bitchy to
Night our President is taking no
Shit one he is tamping about one-third of his power
Into the throats of unfair journalists two he is devoting
Much of his day to the number one bombing
Raid forever in all history since about 1970 we
Have bought a color TV which we can't afford and I will very carefully
Watch football in two days no smoking cig
Arettes I hate, no perusing powerful poetry
Books between plays three the President is right about the TV
Blackouts of the redskins Washingtonians won't
See their game unless they go to Camp David and pick
It up from Pennsylvania he is trying
To do something about all this and I am in unrequited
Love with clouds in Wichita dragging deeply on powerful cigarettes
What a shit I must be they are not even
Clouds no wonder Paul Carroll didn't take any

Of my poems for his truly fabulous but not very powerful on a global scale
Anthology The Young American Poets suppose white clouds
Of the white I described in the second and third lines were
Over the entire earth
"Blanketing" it like a cliché
Now this minute we wouldn't know because of
The fucking dark night so I hate the night quite a bit
But it is my love for the clouds
Which makes me cry and smoke Camels off
And on to 1:35 A.M. the time
Of composition from line 4 to this line it is
Not Frank O'Hara's death or the poking things Paul
Carroll says about him in his book © 1968 it is not the brave
Things on p. 258 and 259 I read Robert Bly
Does I go to the refrigerator and smoke and drip
In it it is very white my wife Judy who I love
Has casually cleaned it after coming home from directing the local lead-ins to
News of President Nixon's activities the door is chillier than cool I stop
Crying and release the faucet's steady bright gray water onto my Camel

But if as I plan to do one can calmly drink a beer to sleep soundly
To wake to write very real clouds in endlessly sunny days
Does one?

Ellen Bryant Voigt

Ellen Bryant Voigt was born in Chatham, Virginia, in 1943. She was educated at Converse College and the University of Iowa. She is the author of *Claiming Kin* (Wesleyan University Press, 1976), and *The Forces of Plenty* (W. W. Norton, 1983). Among her awards are fellowships from the National Endowment for the Arts and the Guggenheim Foundation. She teaches in the M.F.A. Program at Warren Wilson College.

The Victim

Who could remember cause? Both
sought injury, and God knows
they were perfectly matched for pain.
Fenced into their landscape of passion,
each moved to the center and set upon
the other. Always, she would deploy
the tease, the jab, the deft tongue,
until his arm swung out on its hinge,
coming flat-handed against her face,
recoiled, then stiffened to thrust
his fist into her open mouth.

This was not the only violation.
When a child is struck by her father,
she crawls toward him, not away,
bound by habits not yet broken.

Exile

The widow refuses sleep, for sleep pretends
that it can bring him back.
In this way,
the will is set against the appetite.
Even the empty hand moves to the mouth.
Apart from you,
I turn a corner in the city and find,
for a moment, the old climate,
the little blue flower everywhere.

The Bat

Reading in bed, full of sentiment
for the mild evening and the children
asleep in adjacent rooms, hearing them
cry out now and then the brief reports
of sufficient imagination, and listening
at the same time compassionately
to the scrabble of claws, the fast treble
in the chimney—
                     then it was out,
not a trapped bird
beating at the seams of the ceiling,
but a bat lifting toward us, falling away.

Dominion over every living thing,
large brain, a choice of weapons—
Shuddering, in the lit hall
we swung repeatedly against
its rising secular face
until it fell; then
shoveled it into the yard for the cat
who shuttles easily between two worlds.

Jug Brook

Beyond the stone wall,
the deer should be emerging from their yard.
Lank, exhausted, they scrape at the ground
where roots and bulbs will send forth
new definitions. The creek swells in its ditch;
the field puts on a green glove.
Deep in the woods, the dead ripen,
and the lesser creatures turn to their commission.

Why grieve for the lost deer,
for the fish that clutter the brook,
the kingdoms of midge that cloud its surface,
the flocks of birds that come to feed.
The earth does not grieve.
It rushes toward the season of waste—

On the porch the weather shifts,
the cat dispatches
another expendable animal from the field.
Soon she will go inside to cull her litter,

addressing each with a diagnostic tongue.
Have I learned nothing? God,
into whose deep pocket our cries are swept,
it is you I look for
in the slate face of the water.

Blue Ridge

Up there on the mountain road, the fireworks
blistered and subsided, for once at eye level:
spatter of light like water flicked from the fingers;
the brief emergent pattern; and after the afterimage bled
from the night sky, a delayed and muffled thud
that must have seemed enormous down below,
the sound concomitant with the arranged
threat of fire above the bleachers.
I stood as tall and straight as possible,
trying to compensate, trying not to lean in my friend's
direction. Beside me, correcting height, he slouched
his shoulders, knees locked, one leg stuck out
to form a defensive angle with the other.
Thus we were most approximate
and most removed.
                              In the long pauses
between explosions, he'd signal conversation
by nodding vaguely toward the ragged pines.
I said my children would have loved the show.
He said we were watching youth at a great distance,
and I thought how the young
are truly boring, unvaried as they are
by the deep scar of doubt, the constant afterimage
of regret—no major tension in their bodies, no tender
hesitation, they don't yet know
that this is so much work, scraping

from the self its multiple desires; don't yet know
fatigue with self, the hunger for obliteration
that wakes us in the night at the dead hour
and fuels good sex.
                              Of course I didn't say it.
I realized he watched the fireworks
with the cool attention he had turned on women
dancing in the bar, a blunt uninvested gaze
calibrating every moving part, thighs,
breasts, the muscles of abandon.
I had wanted that gaze on me.
And as the evening dwindled to its nub,
its puddle of tallow, appetite without object,
as the men peeled off to seek
the least encumbered consolation
and the women grew expansive with regard—
how have I managed so long to stand among the paired
bodies, the raw pulsing music driving
loneliness into the air like scent,
and not be seized by longing,
not give anything to be summoned
into the larger soul two souls can make?
Watching the fireworks with my friend,
so little ease between us,
I see that I have armed myself;
fire changes everything it touches.

Perhaps he has foreseen this impediment.
Perhaps when he holds himself within himself,
a sheathed angular figure at my shoulder,
he means to be protective less of him
than me, keeping his complicating rage
inside his body. And what would it solve
if he took one hand from his pocket,
risking touch, risking invitation—
if he took my hand it would not alter
this explicit sadness.
                              The evening stalls,
the fireworks grow boring at this remove.

The traffic prowling the highway at our backs,
the couples, the families scuffling on the bank
must think us strangers to each other. Or,
more likely, with the celebrated fireworks thrusting
their brilliant repeating designs above the ridge,
we simply blur into the foreground,
like the fireflies dragging among the trees
their separate, discontinuous lanterns.

Pastoral

Crouched in the yard,
he brings his dirty hands up to his mouth.
No, No, I say. *Yuck. Hurt.*

These are sounds he will recognize.
I say them when he takes an orange
with its hidden seeds and allergenic juice.
No. Yuck. Bad orange. Or reaming
from his mouth a wad of bread,
a lump of odorous cheese.
The fire will hurt.
The stick will break and stab you
in the heart. The reckless wheel,
the cool suggestive music of the pond.

Overhead, summer spreads its blue scarf;
a light wind bends the hollyhocks;
birds, trees—
everything the way I might have dreamed it,
he stands in the grass,
weighing a handful of berries,
a handful of stones.

The Spring

Beneath the fabric of leaves,
sycamore, beech, black oak,
in the slow residual movement
of the pool;
   in the current
braiding over the wedged branch,
and pouring from the ledge,
urgent, lyric,
   the source
marshalls every motion
to the geometric plunder of rock—
arranging a socket of water,
a cold estate
where the muscle wound
in the deep remission of light
waits
  for the white enamel dipper,
the last release, the rush,
the blunt completion

The Lotus Flowers

The surface of the pond was mostly green—
bright green algae reaching out from the banks,
then the mass of water lilies, their broad round leaves
rim to rim, each white flower spreading
from the center of a green saucer.
We teased and argued, choosing the largest,
the sweetest bloom, but when the rowboat
lumbered through and rearranged them
we found the plants were anchored, the separate
muscular stems descending in the dense water—

only the most determined put her hand
into that frog-slimed pond
to wrestle with a flower. Back and forth
we pumped across the water, in twos and threes,
full of brave adventure. On the marshy shore,
the others hollered for their turns,
or at the hem of where we pitched the tents
gathered firewood—
                          this was wilderness,
although the pond was less than half an acre
and we could still see the grand magnolias
in the village cemetery, their waxy,
white conical blossoms gleaming in the foliage.
A dozen girls, the oldest only twelve, two sisters
with their long braids, my shy neighbor,
someone squealing without interruption—
all we didn't know about the world buoyed us
as the frightful water sustained and moved the flowers
tethered at a depth we couldn't see.

In the late afternoon, before they'd folded
into candles on the dark water,
I went to fill the bucket at the spring.
Deep in the pines, exposed tree roots
formed a natural arch, a cave of black loam.
I raked off the skin of leaves and needles,
leaving a pool so clear and shallow
I could count the pebbles
on the studded floor. The sudden cold
splashing up from the bucket to my hands
made me want to plunge my hand in—
and I held it under, feeling the shock that wakes
and deadens, watching first my fingers,
then the ledge beyond me,
the snake submerged and motionless,
the head propped on its coils the way a girl
crosses her arms before her on the sill
and rests her chin there.
                          Lugging the bucket
back to the noisy clearing, I found nothing changed,

the boat still rocked across the pond,
the fire straggled and cracked as we fed it
branches and debris into the night,
leaning back on our pallets—
spokes in a wheel—learning the names of the many
constellations, learning how each fixed
cluster took its name:
not from the strongest light, but from the pattern
made by stars of lesser magnitude,
so like the smaller stars we rowed among.

Marilyn Waniek

John Craig

Marilyn Waniek was born in 1946. Her first book of poems, *For the Body*, was published by the L.S.U. Press in 1978. She is also the translator (with Pamela Espeland) of *Hundreds of Hens and Other Poems for Children* by Halfdan Rasmussen (Black Willow Press, 1983), and the co-author (with Pamela Espeland) of a book of poems for children, *The Cat Walked through the Casserole* (Carolrhoda Books, 1984). Among her awards is a fellowship from the National Endowment for the Arts. A second book of poems, *The Mama Poems*, will be published in 1985 by the L.S.U. Press.

Old Bibles

I throw things away
usually, but there's
this whole shelf
of Bibles in my house.
Old Bibles, with pages missing
or scribbled by children
and black covers chewed by puppies.
I believe in euthanasia,
but I can't get rid of them.
It's a sin,
like stepping on a crack
or not crossing your fingers
or dropping the flag.

I did that once,
and for weeks
a gaunt bearded stranger
in tricolored clothes
came to get me,
moaning,
Give me my flag.
And Bibles are worse,
they maybe have souls
like little birds fluttering
over the dump
when the wind blows their pages.
Bibles are holy, blessed,
they're like
kosher.

So I keep them,
a row of solemn apostles
doomed to life,
and I wait for the great collection
and conflagration,
when they'll all burn together
with a sound like the wings
of a flock of doves:
little ash ascensions
of the Word.

Light Under the Door

I remember hiding in the hall closet,
down with the dust and the extra shoes,
the hems of the big people's coats
brushing my uppermost braids. Daddy was coming.
I could tell from the crunch of wheels,

the thunk of the heavy car door,
the rattle of keys at the lock.
His hard-soled shoes came toward me,
a voice like Othello's
asked my mother where I was.
I was ready to swoon with delight,
but the footsteps dimmed,
the voice asked for dinner.

Three decades later
I remember the smell of wool,
the gritty floor under my palms,
the thin light under the door.
Outside, my mother stirred, chopped,
opened the oven to check on the cornbread.
I heard her answer my sister
while Daddy went into their bedroom
to take off his Air Force uniform.
Outside, a plane like a buzz saw
sliced the distant sky.

That day in kindergarten
a buzzer went off;
Mrs. Liebel jumped up
and made us hide on the polished floor
under our desks.
Not even the naughty boys giggled
as we watched a fly explore
the alphabet over the blackboard
and discovered wads of petrified gum.
I'm sitting in the closet now
waiting for the bomb.

No, that's a lie.
I'm standing here in my kitchen,
a grown-up woman, a mother,
with used breasts. Upstairs,
the man I love and our son
are playing. The baby

touches his father's knee,
steps, stops, then runs away
with his off-balance gait.
His father chases him, hooting,
to the table where they stop for breath,
then the baby squeals and takes off
for the other room.

The sun rises in the window over our breakfast table
as I scramble the eggs. On the radio
a pleasant male voice announces yesterday's
disasters. The jays have carried the larger crumbs off,
now they come back for the rest.

My father opened the closet door. A light like a look
into the heart of fire blinded me for a moment:
I didn't see him there.
I remember the good smell of beans and cornbread
and the clash of plates being put on the table.
I remember Mama's voice humming mezzo
as I walked out into the light.

Women's Locker Room

The splat of bare feet on wet tile
breaks the incredible luck
of my being alone in here.
I snatch a stingy towel
and sidle into the shower; I'm already soaped
by the time a white hand turns the neighboring knob.
I recognize the arm as one that had flashed
for many rapid laps while I dogpaddled at the shallow end.
I dart an appraising glance: She arches down
to wash a lifted heel, and is beautiful.
As she straightens, I look into her startled eyes.

For an instant I remember human sacrifice:
the female explorer led skyward,
her blonde tresses loose on her neck;
the drums of my pulse growing louder;
the heft of the obsidian knife.
Violets grew in the clefts of the stairs.

I could freeze her name in an ice cube,
bottle the dirt from her footsteps
with potent graveyard dust.
I could gather the combings from her hairbrush
to burn with her fingernail clippings,
I could feed her Iago powder.
Childhood taunts, branded ears,
a thousand insults swirl through my memory
like headlines in a city vacant lot.

I jump, grimace, divide like an amoeba
into twin rages that stomp around
with their lips stuck out,
then come suddenly face to face.
They see each other and know that they
are mean mamas.
Then I bust out laughing
and let the woman live.

Dinosaur Spring

A violet wash is streaked across the clouds.
Triceratops, Brachiosaurus, Trachodon
browse the high greenery, heave through
the dissipating mists.
They are as vacant as we are:
They don't see how mountains are growing,

how flowers change spring by spring,
how feathers form.

Last night I walked among the dinosaurs,
hardly taller than a claw.
I touched their feet with my fingertips,
my tongue numb with wonder.

At seven this morning two mallards
and a pair of Canada geese
preened themselves in the light of the pond.
Awake on a morning like this one,
jays screeching from treetop to fencepost,
I have to strain to imagine
how people wake up
in San Salvador, Johannesburg, Beirut.
The background roar grows louder,
a neighbor screams for her child.

Just now I took my baby out of his crib
and teetered on the edge of the vortex.
I saw millions of hands imploring,
mouths open, eyes his.
I fell into a universe of black, starry water,
and through that into monstrous love
that wants to make the world right.

I can comfort my son:
The ghost in the closet, the foot-eating fish
on the floor can be washed away
with a hug and a tumbler of milk.
But the faceless face? The nuclear piñata
over our heads? The bone finger pointing?

Through the window I see the sky
that hung over the dinosaurs.
The flight of a grackle catches my eye
and pulls it down toward the moving water.
I can't see the larger motion, leaves

mouldering into new soil.
If I lay on my back in the yard,
I'd feel how we're hanging on
to this planet, attached even to her
by the sheer luck of gravity.

I have to shake my head, I've grown so solemn.
It's my turn to vacuum the house.
In the din, I go back to my dream:
Holding my son by the hand,
I walk again among the dinosaurs.
In my breast my heart pours and pours
so that it terrifies me, pours and pours out
its fathomless love, like the salt mill
at the bottom of the sea.

Herbs in the Attic

A cat by the fireside, purring.
But I don't stop there; I go
through the living room and up the stairs.
My little brother stirs in his crib.
My sister and I sleep in our tumbled rooms,
and our parents sleep together,
fingers intertwined.

The second stairway's narrow.
It darkens when I close the door
behind me. And I climb up to the attic,
to the bustles and pantaloons
hidden in trunks, the diaries and love-letters,
the photographs, the rings,
the envelopes full of hair.

Here's the old silverware
Great Aunt Irene and Uncle Eric used.
Her fork is curved
from her life-long habit
of scraping the plate.
His knife is broader,
the better for buttering bread.

Here are the bookcases of discarded books:
Tarzan, Zane Grey, a textbook Shakespeare,
piles of *National Geographic, Look* and *Life*:
enough to last me a while.

I sit on the dusty floor
and open a book.
Dream music fills the air
like the scent of dried herbs.

Rosanna Warren

Stephen Scully

Rosanna Warren was born in 1953. She received a B.A. from Yale University and an M.A. from Johns Hopkins University. She is the author of two books, *Snow Day* (Palaemon Press, 1981), and *Each Leaf Shines Separate* (W. W. Norton, 1984). Among her awards are the "Discovery"/*The Nation* award and a fellowship from the Ingram Merrill Foundation. She currently teaches at Boston University.

✓ *Daylights*

So the sky wounded you, jagged at the heart,
glass shard flying from liquor store window smashed.
They had warned you, blue
means danger. The kid runs off
zigzagging the crowd, clutching his prize of Scotch;
the liquor man yells. Those Grecian dreams
endure even New York. You think
you're safe, humdrumming along
the sidewalk's common, readable gray,
calmly digesting your hunk of daily bread,
with flesh enough on your bones to cast some shade,

but puddle flashes, car window glints,
a stranger casts you a glance from a previous life:
the sky! And here you stand
unclouded, un-named, as naked as
the chosen Aztec facing the last shebang—
(*his* last shebang; the globe keeps rolling along
slipslop in its tide of blood)—

So there you stand
holding your sky-sliced heart in your hands
to offer—to whom?—
while the liquor man curses the daylights
out of the cop, and the crowd
clumps dully away.
And you? "What *you* lookin' at?
Move on!" So you
move on, and grateful, by god,
in the grit gray light of day.

✓ Virgin Pictured in Profile

(*Derived from an Egyptian
    Middle Kingdom Tomb Painting*)

A white-gowned woman making offering
rests on one knee, the other raised.
Hands outstretched, palms down,
fingers slightly curved at the tips.
Spine a straight stem. The visible ear
left bare by the black, geometric coiffure.

Where does she gaze with that slant, blank eye?
The amphora before her is empty.
So are the bowl and narrow vase.
She kneels, rigid in ceremony.

No one stands near her,
and the world beyond is milk mist only.

They have gone: maidens, parents, the robed priest,
the people of her town, even the gods.
So rapt she was
in the rite, she did not hear
when they called and trundled away.
Beams crumbled on sand and shards, and wind
curled in from the desert.

She did not hear, nor will she ever.
"Child, child, wake up," they had cried,
but could not break her trance, and so
departed, with all their belongings
wrapped in bright woven cloth, their dogs at their heels.

They died. Somewhere, the river rises still,
fish feed, and fields are tilled,
the newly dead are laid in the living earth.
Of this she will never know.
It is the perfection of emptiness
she offers now, as she offered long ago.

No river rises to her wall,
mud-roiled, flooding with spring.
Her landscape is pure dust.
Nor will it be granted
to her who never soiled her loins with life   *gave birth*
to enter, lotus in hand, and dressed as bride,
the full-thronged kingdom of the truly dead.

Lily

The highway forever draws away
day and night in a whine and purr of trucks,
and your face recedes, as time
accumulates between us,

but I remember a morning when we lay
together on a flat rock
in a brown, unwinding stream
and the sun spread gloss

of gold across the water, and sparrows came
to dabble in the shallows. A stray cloud
shadowed us, vanished,
shadowed us again

and in the fluttered light we were the same
as stone and ripple. Water played out loud
twisting in harness;
one leaf ran

swivelling down the current, green canoe
side-tracked in eddies, released, then lost
for good. In this strange
space we invent

separately day by day between us, you
can't hear me breathing, touch me, taste
the sun's change
on my cheek, can't

hold me, tell me to hush. The wasps crawl
over their paper palace cell by cell
where pupae sleep
and swell toward their brief

flight and the end of summer. Wind riffles tall
pines' sleeves. Beyond, the highway still

trails away, but deep
in its own life

the pond lies motionless. From frog scum
and cloud reflection fractured, the lily blooms,
a white-fleshed star
with dab of sun at heart.

It holds its peace against the tires' hum,
hot miles of fleeing where the asphalt screams,
summer uncoiling in which we are
farther and farther apart.

Alps

The mountains taught us speechlessness.
And held no mercy, either
in ice glint of high noon shatter
or flat light knock-out of white hurled blinding us.

No word measured the fang's rock face
or dolloped height of cloud, or
the whiteness of that particular
snowshoe hare which loped to its place

through powder. We spoke
only below, in the village, and then
of purely human absences, as when
G. departed from our small talk,

or when we had to conclude affairs
that had not been love, or even,
often, affairs—conclude them in
haste, with our hats on, there by the stairs;

for whatever they'd been, they had
at least composed the bleak-
ness; and hard enough it had been to speak
of those un-mountainous matters, in few words, without fraud.

Michael Waters

Gerard Malanga

Michael Waters was born in 1949. He received his B.A. and M.A. degrees from S.U.N.Y. at Brockport, his M.F.A. from the University of Iowa, and his Ph.D. from Ohio University. He is the author of three books of poetry, *Fish Light* (Ithaca House, 1975), *Not Just Any Death* (BOA Editions, 1979), and *Anniversary of the Air* (Carnegie-Mellon, 1985). Among his awards is a fellowship from the National Endowment for the Arts. He teaches at Salisbury State College in Maryland.

The Mystery of the Caves

I don't remember the name of the story,
but the hero, a boy, was lost,
wandering a labyrinth of caverns
filling stratum by stratum with water.

I was wondering what might happen:
would he float upward toward light?
Or would he somersault forever
in an underground black river?

I couldn't stop reading the book
because I had to know the answer,
because my mother was leaving again—
the lid of the trunk thrown open,

blouses torn from their hangers,
the crazy shouting among rooms.
The boy found it impossible to see
which passage led to safety.

One yellow finger of flame
wavered on his last match.
There was a blur of perfume—
mother breaking miniature bottles,

then my father gripping her,
but too tightly, by both arms.
The boy wasn't able to breathe.
I think he wanted me to help,

but I was small, and it was late.
And my mother was sobbing now,
no longer cursing her life,
repeating my father's name

among bright islands of skirts
circling the rim of the bed.
I can't recall the whole story,
what happened at the end . . .

Sometimes I worry that the boy
is still searching below the earth
for a thin pencil of light,
that I can almost hear him

through great volumes of water,
through centuries of stone,
crying my name among blind fish,
wanting so much to come home.

Mythology

Because no one has ever asked,
because the task is incumbent upon me,
I want to reveal the secret
gathering place of heroes:

we scaled the rough, stucco wall
of a row of one-story garages
and loitered on the tar roof,
staring down the weakening sun—

Tommy O'Brien, Glenn Marshall,
everyone's girl, Rosemarie Angelastro,
and the dumb kid, Gregory Galunas,
who let ants walk on his tongue.

We smoked butts and told no one.
Once Billy McAssey jumped
and stove the canvas top
of a cream-and-blue convertible.

At five o'clock the mothers
groaned their chorus from the curb,
each name shouted like a warning
to the worn men leaving work.

But I remained on the roof
till lights blinked on in tenements,
the smell of fish oiled the air,
and radios sent forth tinny polkas . . .

and through a tinted wing of glass
began to read the heavens,
the bright syllables of stars,
as words took shape, lyrical prose,

a whole story
filled with heroes, their great names,

their impending deaths praised
on the darkening pages of the sky.

A smart kid,
when I asked my spiritless father,
"Where do the dead go?"
I already knew the answer.

Singles

I don't know anyone more lonely
than the woman listening
to the late news, memorizing
baseball scores for coffee break.

She must undress so carefully,
folding her beige blouse
as if for the last time,
not wanting to be found unkempt

by detectives in the morning.
Sometimes I hear her talking
as she roams from room to room
watering her plumeria,

the only splash of color.
She sets two places at the table
though no one ever comes,
then turns to the boredom of bed

thinking *Indians 7—Yankees 3,*
Cardinals 11—Mets 2
until she rises before dawn
and drives crosstown to work.

Could anyone be more lonely?
She doesn't acknowledge, again,
the man in the toll-booth
who's spent the whole night there,

not even a magazine before him,
grateful now to be making change
and touching fingers, briefly,
with such a beautiful stranger.

American Bandstand

The boy rehearsing the Continental Stroll
before the mirror in his bedroom—
does he memorize the sweep of hair
tumbling across his eyes
when he spins once, then claps his hands?

Home from school in winter,
he studies the couples on television,
their melancholy largo,
how they glide together, then separate.
Such dancing makes him nervous—
so many hand motions to remember,
where to slide his feet, and
every girl in the gym staring at him.

That boy was familiar, twenty years ago,
saying hello to a loneliness
peculiar to the tender, the high-strung
lanterns suspended above the dance floor,
ousting shadows, leaving him
more alone, trapped in the spotlight.

The Peppermint Twist, The Bristol Stomp,
The Hully Gully are only memory,
but loneliness still dances
among the anxious ghosts of the heart,
preparing to stroll
down a line formed by teenagers
mouthing lyrics, clapping hands,
forever awkward,
each partner dreaming of grace.

Bruce Weigl

Bruce Weigl was born in 1949. He received an A.B. from Oberlin College, an A.M. from the University of New Hampshire, and a Ph.D. from the University of Utah. He is the author of four books of poems, *Executioner* (Ironwood Press, 1976), *Like A Sack Full of Old Quarrels* (Cleveland State University Poetry Center, 1977), *A Romance* (University of Pittsburgh Press, 1979), and *The Monkey Wars* (University of Georgia Press, 1985). He is also the editor of *The Giver of Morning: On Dave Smith* (Thunder City Press, 1982), and the co-editor with T. R. Hummer of *The Imagination As Glory: The Poetry of James Dickey* (University of Illinois Press, 1984). He teaches at Old Dominion University.

Brenda C. Wright

The Harp

When he was my age and I was already a boy
my father made a machine in the garage.
A wired piece of steel
with many small and beautiful welds
ground so smooth they resembled rows of pearls.

He went broke with whatever it was.
He held it so carefully in his arms.
He carried it foundry to foundry.
I think it was his harp.

I think it was what he longed to make
with his hands for the world.

He moved it finally from the locked closet
to the bedroom
to the garage again
where he hung it on the wall
until I climbed and pulled it down
and rubbed it clean
and tried to make it work.

Song of Napalm

For My Wife

After the storm, after the rain stopped pounding,
We stood in the doorway watching horses
Walk off lazily across the pasture's hill.
We stared through the black screen,
Our vision altered by the distance
So I thought I saw a mist
Kicked up around their hooves when they faded
Like cut-out horses
Away from us.
The grass was never more blue in that light, more
Scarlet; beyond the pasture
Trees scraped their voices in the wind, branches
Criss-crossed the sky like barbed-wire
But you said they were only branches.

Okay. The storm stopped pounding.
I am trying to say this straight: for once
I was sane enough to pause and breathe
Outside my wild plans and after the hard rain

I turned my back on the old curses. I believed
They swung finally away from me . . .

But still the branches are wire
And thunder is the pounding mortar,
Still I close my eyes and see the girl
Running from her village, napalm
Stuck to her dress like jelly,
Her hands reaching for the no one
Who waits in waves of heat before her.

So I can keep on living,
So I can stay here beside you,
I try to imagine she runs down the road and wings
Beat inside her until she rises
Above the stinking jungle and her pain
Eases, and your pain, and mine.

But the lie swings back again.
The lie works only as long as it takes to speak
And the girl runs only so far
As the napalm allows
Until her burning tendons and crackling
Muscles draw her up
Into that final position
Burning bodies so perfectly assume. Nothing
Can change that; she is burned behind my eyes
And not your good love and not the rain-swept air
And not the jungle green
Pasture unfolding before us can deny it.

1955

After mass father rinsed the chalice with wine
Again and again.
Drunk before noon
He'd sleep it off in the sacristy
While the other altar boys and I
Rummaged through the sacred things, feeling up
The blessed linen and silk vestments,
Swinging the censer above us so it whistled.
We put our hands on everything we could reach
Then woke the father for mass.

In summer the wool cassock itched
And I sweated through to the white lace surplice.
My head reeled from the incense
So I mumbled through the Latin prayers
And learned to balance the paten
Gracefully under their chins, my face
Turned away from the priest
Who dipped into the cup
As if to pluck a fish
And just like that something took me by the brain
And I saw myself
Torn loose from the congregation,

Floating in the air like an impossible
Balloon of myself and I thought
This must be what my life is
Though I didn't know what it meant
And I couldn't move or swallow and thought I'd panic
Until father scowled and nudged me down the altar
To the next mouth
Open in the O of acceptance
So much like a scream
That can't get out of the lungs . . .
I don't know why my hands should shake,
I'm only remembering something.

Burning Shit at An Khe

Into that pit
    I had to climb down
With a rake and matches; eventually,
    You had to do something
Because it just kept piling up
    And it wasn't our country, it wasn't
Our air sick with the thick smoke
    So another soldier and I
Lifted the shelter off its blocks
    To expose the home-made toilets:
Fifty-five gallon drums cut in half
    With crude wood seats that splintered.
We soaked the piles with fuel oil
    And lit the stuff
And tried to keep the fire burning.
    To take my first turn
I paid some kid
    A care package of booze from home.
I'd walked past the burning once
    And gagged the whole heart of myself—
It smelled like the world
    Was on fire
But when my turn came again
    There was no one
So I stuffed cotton up my nose
    And marched up that hill. We poured
And poured until it burned and black
    Smoke curdled
But the fire went out. . . .
    Heavy artillery
Hammered the evening away in the distance,
    Vietnamese laundry women watched
From a safe place, laughing.
    I'd grunted out eight months
Of jungle and thought I had a grip on things
    But we flipped the coin and I lost
And climbed down into my fellow soldier's

Shit and began to sink and didn't stop
Until I was deep to my knees. Liftships
        Cut the air above me, the hacking
Blast of their blades
        Ripped dust in swirls so every time
    I tried to light a match
        It died
And it all came down on me,
        The stink and the heat and the worthlessness
Until I slipped and climbed
        Out of that hole and ran
Past the olive drab
        Tents and trucks and everything
Green as far from the shit
        As the fading light allowed. . . .
Only now I can't fly.
        I lay down in it
And finger paint the words of who I am
        Across my chest
Until I'm covered and there's only one smell,
        One word.

Homage to Elvis,
Homage to the Fathers

All night the pimp's cars slide past the burning mill
Where I've come back
To breathe the slag stink air of home.
Without words the gray workers trade shifts,
The serious drinkers fill the bar
To dull the steel
Ringing their brains.

As I remember, as I want it to be,
The buick was pastel, pale
In the light burning out of the city's dirty side
Where we lived out our life
Sentences in a company house.
Good people to love and fight, matters
Of the lucky heart that doesn't stop.

Beyond the mill street
Slag heaps loom up like dunes, almost beautiful.
Once we played our war games there
And a boy from the block ran screaming
He's here, it's him at the record store
And we slid down the sooty waste of the mill
And black and grimy we stood outside
Behind the screaming older sisters
And saw him, his hair puffed up and shiny, his gold
Bracelets catching light.

He changed us somehow; we cleaned up.
We spun his 45's in the basement,
Danced on the cool concrete and plastered
Our hair back like his and twisted
Our forbidden hips.
Across the alley our fathers died
Piece by piece among the blast furnace rumble.
They breathed the steel rifted air
As if it were good.

Unwelcome, I stand outside the mill gates
And watch the workers pass like ghosts.
I close my eyes and it all makes sense:
I believe I will live forever.
I believe the world will rip apart
From the inside
Of our next moment alive.

Snowy Egret

My neighbor's boy has lifted his father's shotgun and stolen
Down to the backwaters of the Elizabeth
And in the moon he's blasted a snowy egret
From the shallows it stalked for small fish.

Midnight. My wife wakes me. He's in the backyard
With a shovel so I go down half-drunk with pills
That let me sleep to see what I can see and if it's safe.
The boy doesn't hear me come across the dewy grass.
He says through tears he has to bury it,
He says his father will kill him
And he digs until the hole is deep enough and gathers
The egret carefully into his arms
As if not to harm the blood-splattered wings
Gleaming in the flashlight beam.

His man's muscled shoulders
Shake with the weight of what he can't set right no matter what,
But one last time he tries to stay a child, sobbing
Please don't tell. . . .
He says he only meant to flush it from the shadows,
He only meant to watch it fly
But the shot spread too far
Ripping into the white wings
Spanned awkwardly for a moment
Until it glided into brackish death.

I want to grab his shoulders,
Shake the lies loose from his lips but he hurts enough,
He burns with shame for what he's done,
With fear for his hard father's
Fists I've seen crash down on him for so much less.
I don't know what to do but hold him.
If I let go he'll fly to pieces before me.
What a time we share, that can make a good boy steal away,
Wiping out from the blue face of the pond
What he hadn't even known he loved, blasting
Such beauty into nothing.

Dara Wier

Dara Wier was born in 1949 in New Orleans. She received her M.F.A. from Bowling Green University and is the author of three collections of poetry, *Blood, Hook, & Eye* (University of Texas Press, 1977), *The 8-Step Grapevine* (1980), and *All You Have in Common* (1984), both from Carnegie-Mellon University Press. She has received a fellowship from the National Endowment for the Arts. She teaches at the University of Alabama.

Michael Pettit

Fear

In fall when we went the roads
for the pure reason of pretending
we were still and the world fell
away all around us, the dry fall
kept my tongue circling my lips.
Think how many paths
circles cross. What range
the tongue bringing moisture
to chapped skin laps.
I watched my grandfather rub
petroleum jelly on
his hearing ear. Each of his possessions,
package of black tobacco,
jar of mentholatum,
and, collapsed around a gold coin
he never let me touch,
a leather pouch soft

as damp moss, greygreen,
a lesson. He leaned and touched
his hearing aid battery to my mouth
to burn my lips, a silver spot
of circular burn that comes back,
do you regret knowing
he took your hands around his testicles
when it is easy to believe
those nights taught you
how one thing becomes another.
His back had been a thing burnt
black when he was brought home
from the clinic to recover
from anthrax. I would not touch
a thing he touched. I watched
the black crescents his fingernails
drew as he drew melon seeds
from cotton sacks or wrapped raffia
around the wounds his knife drew
for citrus grafts.

When he squeezed Icthyol salve
on my instep to draw the thick thorn
back, it healed.
The cusp of the deer's hoof
is static in our headlights.
There, a blow we've taken,
movement in shadow near the road;
we've shied, recovered,
and watch for other dangers.
There is the rabbit
whose carelessness could kill us
but she freezes in our headlights
for the next car coming or the random
truck whose driver has no thought
for her or us. Think how many
times it's crossed your mind,
will they kill us, will the deer
rushing across the road for water
batter his neck on the windshield,

will your swerve to miss another skunk
land us in a ditch. What's out there
eager to satisfy need or desire
does not care, knows nothing
about the paths we cross.
My tongue without thinking
drives back another wad of tobacco
to soothe a black jacket's sting.
Think of the traffic a tongue congests,
how the heart crosses and compares
what might not have been
drawn together. Under a perfectly beautiful
moon and on its opening evening
the new highway kills eleven dogs
in its surprising traffic.

Keno

Her mother's old and can't help herself.
Her father's sick, a bitch.
Her fifth ball keno
means big bucks, six,
seven, not bad odds
when even death, desire,
the usual obligations
can't stop her pacing
across the cards she claims
because they've won for her before.
Their numbers knit her nameless
children's names, the anniversary
of her godchild's first communion
or the last three digits
on her Buick's license plate.
Her husband died in a swimming pool,
too heavy and too wet to save.

She's been at it thirty years.
Between rolls she works
the paper's crossword puzzles,
she works whatever pattern
she sees appear. Whatever
she's done she's done
to hurry where numbers,
luck and the caller's voice
are more than she wants
to bear outside.
Her hands sink into circles
of colorful buttons; all around
her gamblers lift their arms
to roll the winning numbers
down. Knock, keno,
knock, knock, split pot.
Every night she knows herself
whether she's lost or won.
Every night it's not like life.

Late Afternoon on a Good Lake

The water gives, it gets us
there, it gives to the footfall
while we catch our balance
to stand up in the boat
to begin to go where
the biggest fish fight
like nobody's business.
Skill and luck come
by different routes we go
by our own lights
and sun's light
leaves the water

to dazzle us so
that skill matters little
and luck is all around us
even when we miss
it moves to overtake us
it takes our gaudy lures
and tangles them in branches
high above our heads
or deep in water
bright because the lucky sun
stays with us a little longer
in the water the black oaks
drill their heights beyond
the other side and when
big fish mistake our lures
for food we bring them in
to the evening's light
which gives up to show off
the fishes' shapes and colors
because what we are
about to lose
puts its polished foot
before us and asks, *will you*
no longer love me, look
what I shape for you to see
two worlds without us
would not meet where we touch
look what we see when it is
evening and the ducks are
at rest we leave the fish
alone and turn to the ducks
who stand up for us and walk
on water while we chase them
look, somewhere luck is
shaking a cup of ice, I want
to drink that water.

This Cold Nothing Else

A housesnake's made her nest in the woodshed.
Your man's gone again to a job.
He says it's south Florida where they build
all winter.

Milk fever makes you sleepy.
If the baby were weaned you'd work.
You've washed each window so they disappear
and it only lets in more weather.

Your one silver goblet shines on the sideboard
like a greedy mouth.
When you wear socks on the wood floor you slip down.
When you cook rice or grits
you hate the way the windows fog
and you feel buried inside.

Today like the wind the child won't quit crying.
When it cries again there's nothing to do
but scald it with milk until it stops.

David Wojahn

Leah Ginusz

David Wojahn was born in St. Paul, Minnesota, in 1953. He was educated at the University of Minnesota and the University of Arizona. His first book, *Icehouse Lights*, was the 1981 winner of the Yale Series of Younger Poets Award and the 1983 winner of the William Carlos Williams Book Award of the Poetry Society of America. Among his other awards is a fellowship from the National Endowment for the Arts. He teaches at the University of Arkansas at Little Rock, where he serves as poetry editor for *Crazy Horse*.

The Man Who Knew Too Much

I've finished with the listlessness
of snow on pine boughs, or the page's invitations,
also snow. That's why this morning
the pines shake it off in gusts,
why I'm tired of the ways we look at ourselves.
From the window I watch you
throwing pinecones for the dogs,
resin on your glove, their breath that rises
like the drastic lights of a winter city
and illustrates nothing. Before,
I thought our lives, these mornings,
could all be ennobling and abstract
but the sky has whitened for days—
there are more than six sides to every question.

Last night you brushed your hair
a hundred strokes in the TV's light
that flickered thirties movies until dawn:
Hitchcock's *The Man Who Knew Too Much,*
who saved himself through irony
and fear. All these mazes of plot—
I can't let them go, as after those nights
we'd argue for hours, finally seeing
we'd come to nothing. We lived in a neighborhood
of Blacks and Chicanos and I'd walk away
to the Mexican movies, though I'd lost
my Spanish years before. This is the way
it always seemed: someone talks and you know
you won't understand. The hombre puts a pheasant
on the kitchen table. The mujer begins to weep.

Abstract movement, where some feeling is trapped
like the hombre frowning at a steamed-up mirror.
He cleans it and forgets what he was thinking.
And I'm leaving my seat, weary
of the dialogue, tired enough for home.

Cold Glow: Icehouses

Because the light this morning is recondite
like figures behind curtains from a long way off,
because the morning is cold and this room is heatless,
I've gone without sleep, I brood.
The protocol of memory: the faucet dripping
into a sponge, then thinking of the way
I saw White Bear Lake freeze over
twenty years ago in Minnesota, the carp oblivious below.

I thought last night of Solomon Petrov,
a Ukrainian rabbi in my college science books
afflicted with total recall, a pathological memory
that made perspective impossible.
Once for doctors he *remembered* running for a train
in Petersburg in winter. They recorded
his quickened pulse, body temperature plunging.
The death by fever of his first wife Tania
was not remembered, but continually relived.

And memory is not accomplishment.
Last night again you described for me
our child pulled dead from your womb. In sleep you talked
to yourself and the child, who passed unnamed
wholly into memory. Now you wanted peace,
some distance. And every memory, said Solomon Petrov,
must proceed unchanged in the mind, going on
like smoke to designate itself again
like a second floor window where I stood as a boy
to watch the fishermen park their cars
on the lake, icehouse lights in the evening below.

Or our child whose name is only ash,
is only a thought too hurtful to free.
Mornings like these, he floats at the window, waiting
and mouthing his name, there through a tangent of ice,
his face and hands ashimmer.

Weldon Kees in Mexico, 1965

Evenings below my window
the sisters of the convent of Saint Teresa
carry brown jugs of water from a well
beyond a dry wash called *Mostrenco*.
Today it was hard to waken,

and I've been dead to the world ten years.
They tread the narrow footbridge
made of vines and planks, sandals clicking:
brown beads and white wooden crosses
between hands that are also brown.
Over the bridge they travel in a white-robed line
like innocent nurses to a field hospital.

Exactly ten. I've marked it on the calendar.
And Maria, who speaks no English,
is soaping her dark breasts by the washstand.
Yesterday she said
she'd like to be a painter and sketched,
on the back of a soiled napkin,
a rendition of a cholla
with her lipstick. She laughed,
then drew below each nipple
a smudged rose. Weldon

would have been repelled
and fascinated, but Weldon is dead.
I watched him fall to the waves
of the Bay, the twelfth suicide that summer.
He would have been fifty-one this year,
my age exactly, an aging man.
Still he would not be a fool
in a poor adobe house, unwinding
a spool of flypaper from a hook
above the head of his child bride.

When she asks my name, I tell her
I am Richard, a good midwestern sound.
She thinks Nebraska is a kingdom
near Peru, and I
the exiled Crown Prince of Omaha.
I've promised to buy her a box of paints
in a shop by my palace in Lincoln.
We'll go back, Maria and I,

with the little sisters of Saint Teresa
who are just now walking across the bridge
for water to be blessed at vespers.

Another Coast

The woman singing in the house
next door draws her bath,
a country-western song—
someone's heart is broken in El Paso—
then she pulls the shades.
We've never spoken, but nights
I watch her set the table for her lover
who visits weekends and outside filets
the bluefish he's just caught.
Later, they'll tip glasses on
the balcony. Animated talk,
then such composure on their faces.

Pointless now to say
how things should have been better with us.
The way I miss you makes the days
portentous, trees not simply barren,
and I walk the tapered
streets of this seaside town,
inns all shuttered, faltering shingles.

Yesterday, a bottle-nosed dolphin
beached herself beyond the pier
and lived for hours. The cafe waiters
checkered her with tablecloths
they'd dipped in seawater
to keep her damp and breathing.
A crowd had gathered
and the next-door couple with their shiny Nikon
argued loudly about who should take the picture.

Years ago, another coast,
we fought all evening in the small apartment,
finally sleeping in separate corners.
Several times we woke, not thinking
there was more to say and later stood
a long time at the window
to watch the taverns' blurry neons—
mugs and dancing glasses—
going out in sequence before the dark,
where a man and woman stood
to batter each other haplessly,
breaking bottles on the street
but not upon themselves.
Maybe some bruises, a little blood.
Finished, they embraced
and parted, the woman shouting *call me,*

call me when you get up.

Baron Wormser

John Suiter

Baron Wormser was born in 1948. He received a B.A. from Johns Hopkins University, an M.A. from the University of California, and an M.L.S. from the University of Maine. He is the author of two books of poetry, *The White Words* (1983) and *Good Trembling* (1985), both from Houghton Mifflin. He works as a librarian.

Piano Lessons

"The Johnsons have her and so must we":
That is how I came to know Miss Lee.
I was to play the piano, if not well
Then enough so that my mother could tell
Another mother I was taking again this year—
It was an expense, but I was a dear.
Miss Lee would coax me and I would cry.
"I can't do any better however I try;
It isn't in me," I'd say and sit down once more.
Miss Lee would motion and start to pace the floor
And we were off again, manacled to one
Another by our common sense of misfortune.
I knew it was harder for her than for me;
She had to watch as I defiled what she esteemed.
At night she played for herself alone;

But even then the music was not wholly her own,
For the neighbor boys would gather on her walk
And at some bravura passage begin to squawk,
Crow, shout, huzzah, yelp, bray,
Until she came out on her porch and they ran away.
Her talent, the town observed, kept her poor,
Once she cursed me, another time she slammed a door
And ran upstairs. I heard her rolling on her bed.
When she came down, she smiled sadly and said,
"That's enough for today." Next week came.
I loitered outside until she called my name
And I shuffled in. "Someday you will be great,"
She said, and I felt she was talking straight
Past me and into another world where
There were no clumsy fingers nor fidgety glares
At the clock on the wall nor hectoring half-notes
Nor folded dollar bills. I took off my coat,
And we walked into the room where the piano stood
For all that we wanted to do yet never would.

Sunday Review Section

Beneath the marmalade, muffins, and tea
Sits this placemat of tendentious summary—
Apollinaire, Babe Ruth, why the Kaiser fought:
Someone is thinking what should be thought
And saying it in just so many paragraphs.
The flag of self-expression is at half-mast—
Cannily reverential, limp, but self-aware.
Like the toaster, history stands in need of repair.

After awhile, you get to know each sort
Of fixer—the genteel sage who holds the fort
While the mob makes ever more awful demands;

The convert who publicly washes his or her hands
Of human error; the Cato of the commonweal;
The mortgaged drone; the cultured actress; the real
Latest academic hotshot; the slob; the memoirist
Who shouldn't tell but can't resist.

The table becomes sticky with received perceptions,
Hedged complaints, and wrong-headed questions.
Sated, the eye considers a sky perplexed
With clouds, a brimming landscape unvexed
By the mysteries of interpretation.
The mind feels something like elation.
A little butter remains on a crust of bread;
The living succeed, and the dead remain dead.

The Mowing Crew

The mourners drive away
And talk about the graves.

Old man Shorey can't
Keep the mowing boys at work.
They take off
Their shirts and lie in the sun
Beside their machines
And go to sleep.

Young as they
Are, the grass doesn't bother them.
Their hair is girl-long,
They smile and spit.

Even when one of their own
Dies with his car on

The state highway, they don't
Seem to exactly believe it.

Standing at the graveside
They look placidly
At the dark riven ground
And nod to each other
As if it were another
Hot day and they felt
Drowsy and wished to lie down.

By-Products

    The legion hall in Atherton contains
Three unclean couches, more than fifty uncomfortable chairs,
    Seven brands of less-than-good whiskey,
A tomcat with one glaucous eye named "Ike,"
Stagnant windowless air, and more often than not

    My legless friend, Stan, who, unlike most
Of the human race in this county and beyond, is content to go
    Unsaved. He drinks ginger-ale, talks about sex
In a voice of awe and disgust, and plays cribbage
For a buck a game. "Here sits," he says sometimes

    Out of the blue and to no one special, "one of
The by-products of Vietnamization" but no one hushes up the way
    They used to because everyone there's a veteran
Of one sort or another, and who, in fact, knows shit
About Korea anymore or, for that matter, Tarawa

    As witnessed by Charley Levesque who, though
Here, never came home? Friday nights it's cards and some
    Mediocre eight-ball and later talk which doesn't

Always wind up back in 'Nam but more often hovers
Between there and here, say in some Pentagon general's

  So-called mind or a television show or a girl's
Smile at a football game fifteen years ago. Neither of us ever had
  Much talent for optimism nor, for that matter,
Rage. Our insignificance lulls us, and we know it
Could all happen again, whatever it was, an obligation

  Split by a moment; or as with me, a lifetime of
Moments, each one praying nothing will happen. Living is the job no
  One's particularly good at, and somedays Stan says
He feels more here than anyone, because he gave something
Up, because there's a difference between being hurt and being afraid.

Poem to the Memory of H. L. Mencken

After I read you, I thought of every mortal
As a mammoth, a stewpot of provocation,
A snuffling barbarian. I liked your antidote—
Our civilization wanted dictionaries and beer.

I see you at your typewriter, bemused and irascible,
Unappalled by yesterday's perishable headlines,
Appalled by the unbridled asininity of some current
Maker of the so-called news. Journalism was the brine
Of celebrity. There were more fools than there was time.

You had a wit's distrust of higher things.
The surest proof of God you could make out
Was the existence of so many God-fearing louts.

As for the republic it was ever-foundering—
That was what made it a republic.

The genius of democracy as you saw it
Was that it gave each simpleton, plutocrat,
Tub-thumper, hack, and two-bit hood
The chance to make as big a spectacle of himself
As he could.

You lived through Niagaras of rhetoric,
Dropped cigar ash on all the reputations of the era,
Blew smoke into America's self-satisfied eyes.

You were a Baltimoron, *adulte terrible*, and crank.
You winked. We understood.
For the great body harried daily by desire and need,
There remained the solace of good prose and good food.

There never was a bad year for crabs in Maryland.
There never was a moment when the word palled—
Until the brain blew up
And you died before your death.

Like a gap-toothed siren, the world called.
Fine, vulgar man, you got your fill.